The BSCI Cram Sheet

This Cram Sheet contains distilled information in key areas of knowledge pertinent to the Cisco BSCI exam. Review this information as the last thing you do before you enter the testing center, paying special attention to those areas in which you feel that you need the most review.

PRINCIPLES OF ROUTING

1. Know that the default administrative distance (AD) values are connected (0), static (1), IGRP (100), OSPF (110), IS-IS (115), and RIP (120). Know the different AD values for internal and external EIGRP and BGP as well.

2. Know and understand the following formula for calculating IGRP metrics:

   Metric=(K1xbandwidth)+[(K2xbandwidth)[dh] (256 load)]+(K3 x delay)

3. Understand the differences between classless and classful protocols, as well as distance vector and link-state protocols (OSPF versus RIPv1).

4. Have a grasp of the convergence process, as well as the components of a routing table.

5. Be able to compare and contrast the general characteristics of RIPv1, RIPv2, IGRP, EIGRP, OSPF, IS-IS, EIGRP, and BGP.

6. Know the fundamental differences between distance vector routing protocols and link-state routing protocols.

ADVANCED IP ADDRESSING SOLUTIONS

7. Understand the characteristics of various methods used for solving IP addressing problems, including:
   - Private IP addresses
   - VLSM
   - Route summarization
   - CIDR (supernetting)
   - IP version 6

8. Know what ip subnet-zero is and the fact that it is enabled by default in configurations of Cisco IOS 12.0 and beyond.

9. Know the advantages of VLSM and the process for calculating VLSM addressing.

10. Know the advantages of route summarization and the methods for summarizing within an octet.

11. Understand how CIDR (supernetting) works and why it is implemented. Know the reasons for using IP unnumbered and IP helper addressing and how to configure them.

OPEN SHORTEST PATH FIRST (OSPF)

12. Understand the advantages of a link-state protocol such as OSPF over a limited distance vector protocol such as RIPv1 in a large internetwork.

13. Be aware of the key terminology related to OSPF operations and the key contents of the Hello packet and OSPF packet header.

14. Be aware of the process that OSPF uses to discover neighbors via the Hello protocol.

15. Understand how OSPF generates a topology database by using the SPF algorithm to select the optimal routes and inject them into the routing table.

16. Be knowledgeable of the OSPF route maintenance process when a change occurs in the topology.

17. Be proficient at configuring a Cisco router in a single-area OSPF network in both a broadcast and non-broadcast scenario. Be cognizant of the command used to verify OSPF operations in a single area as well.

18. Be able to describe the terminology involved with connecting multiple OSPF areas. Be able to explain the contrasts between the different types of OSPF areas, routers, and link-state advertisements.

19. Understand how OSPF provides support for VLSM and route summarization in multiple areas.

44. Be able to verify route redistribution with the proper commands.

45. Know how to configure policy-based routing using route maps.

46. Be aware of the techniques to configure and verify redistribution between different routing domains.

47. Possess the skills to configure and verify policy-based routing operations.

20. Be prepared to describe a multiple-area NBMA environment and various real-world scenarios.

21. Understand the methods for configuring and verifying a multi-area OSPF environment.

INTERMEDIATE SYSTEM-TO-INTERMEDIATE SYSTEM (IS-IS)

22. Know the fundamentals of OSI protocols and the IS-IS and Integrated IS routing protocols. You must know that the connection-oriented protocol is CONP, the connection-oriented service is CMNS, the connectionless protocol is CLNP, and the connectionless service is CLNS.

23. Be aware that ISO-IGRP is a Cisco-proprietary routing protocol for CLNS based on IGRP.

24. Understand the difference between IS-IS and Integrated IS-IS.

25. Know how to define the different areas, levels, and router functions at those levels in IS-IS.

26. Understand the process of OSI addressing and the intricacies of the NSAP address scheme, including the structure of the NSAP address. Remember that a NSAP address with the NSEL set to 00 is known as the NET.

27. Be knowledgeable of the four types of IS-IS packets: LSP, Hello PDUs, PSNPs, and CSNPs.

28. Have a working knowledge of the IP and OSI routing process with Integrated IS-IS, including the OSI forwarding database, routing process, and linking IS-IS domains.

29. Know how to perform basic configuration for Integrated IS-IS and the associated commands:
    - `is-type`
    - `isis circuit-type`
    - `isis metric`
    - `summary-address`
    - `isis priority`

30. Be familiar with the commands used for Integrated IS-IS troubleshooting and verification, such as the following:
    - `show clns protocol`
    - `show clns interface`
    - `show clns neighbors`
    - `show isis database`
    - `isis priority`

ENHANCED INTERIOR GATEWAY ROUTING PROTOCOL (EIGRP)

31. Understand the advantages of Cisco's EIGRP and the definition of the DUAL algorithm.

32. Be able to compare EIGRP to OSPF, especially in regard to the discovery and selection process.

33. Know how EIGRP implements VLSM and route summarization. Know how to disable the EIGRP auto-summarization feature and when this would be necessary.

34. Be able to define how EIGRP can be used to route LAN and WAN traffic, and be able to configure and verify both within the Cisco IOS. You should know these general topics:
    - The proper steps to configure EIGRP
    - How to implement route summarization and why
    - EIGRP load balancing techniques
    - Running EIGRP in a WAN environment
    - Running EIGRP as a scalable verification of the EIGRP operations

BORDER GATEWAY PROTOCOL VERSION 4 (BGP4)

35. Understand the basic features and uses of the BGP protocol as an EGP.

36. Be knowledgeable of the general principles that BGP uses to route between autonomous systems.

37. Be aware that the BGP route selection process considers only synchronized routes without AS loops and a valid next-hop address.

38. You should be familiar with the sequence of characteristics (attributes) that BGP uses for path selection, as follows:
    a. The highest weight that is local on the router
    b. The highest local preference throughout the AS
    c. The route originated by the router
    d. The shortest AS_PATH attribute
    e. The lowest origin code
    f. The lowest MED from another AS
    g. The EBGP path over an IBGP path
    h. The path through the closest IGP peer
    i. The oldest route for EBGP paths
    j. The path with the lowest neighbor BGP router ID
    k. The path with the lowest neighbor IP address

39. Be aware of IBGP scalability issues and how route reflectors and prefix lists provide solutions.

40. Understand the common methods for multihoming links to the Internet through ISPs.

41. Have a grasp of redistribution techniques between BGP and an IGP.

OPTIMIZING ROUTING UPDATES (BGP-4)

42. Know how to control routing update traffic.

43. Understand how to configure route redistribution and be able to resolve path selection problems in redistributed networks.

EXAM CRAM™ 2

BSCI

Michael J. Shannon

que® CERTIFICATION

BSCI Exam Cram 2 (642-801)

Copyright © 2004 by Que Publishing

International Standard Book Number: 0-7897-3017-0

Library of Congress Catalog Card Number: 2003103931

Printed in the United States of America

First Printing: September 2003

06 05 04 03   4 3 2 1

Trademarks

Warning and Disclaimer

Bulk Sales

Que Publishing offers excellent discounts on this book when ordered in quantity for bulk purchases or special sales. For more information, please contact

U.S. Corporate and Government Sales

1-800-382-3419

corpsales@pearsontechgroup.com

For sales outside of the U.S., please contact

International Sales

1-317-428-3341

international@pearsontechgroup.com

Publisher
Paul Boger

Executive Editor
Jeff Riley

Acquisitions Editor
Carol Ackerman

Development Editor
Michael Watson

Managing Editor
Charlotte Clapp

Project Editor
Elizabeth Finney

Copy Editor
Margo Catts

Indexer
Ginny Bess

Proofreader
Juli Cook

Technical Editors
Jacob Beach
John Spangler

Team Coordinator
Pamalee Nelson

Multimedia Developer
Dan Scherf

Interior Designer
Gary Adair

Cover Designer
Anne Jones

Page Layout
Bronkella Publishing

Que
CERTIFICATION

Que Certification • 201 West 103rd Street • Indianapolis, Indiana 46290

A Note from Series Editor Ed Tittel

You know better than to trust your certification preparation to just anybody. That's why you, and more than two million others, have purchased an Exam Cram book. As Series Editor for the new and improved Exam Cram 2 series, I have worked with the staff at Que Certification to ensure you won't be disappointed. That's why we've taken the world's best-selling certification product—a finalist for "Best Study Guide" in a CertCities reader poll in 2002—and made it even better.

As a "Favorite Study Guide Author" finalist in a 2002 poll of CertCities readers, I know the value of good books. You'll be impressed with Que Certification's stringent review process, which ensures the books are high-quality, relevant, and technically accurate. Rest assured that at least a dozen industry experts—including the panel of certification experts at CramSession—have reviewed this material, helping us deliver an excellent solution to your exam preparation needs.

Best Study Guides

We've also added a preview edition of PrepLogic's powerful, full-featured test engine, which is trusted by certification students throughout the world.

As a 20-year-plus veteran of the computing industry and the original creator and editor of the Exam Cram series, I've brought my IT experience to bear on these books. During my tenure at Novell from 1989 to 1994, I worked with and around its excellent education and certification department. This experience helped push my writing and teaching activities heavily in the certification direction. Since then, I've worked on more than 70 certification-related books, and I write about certification topics for numerous Web sites and for *Certification* magazine.

In 1996, while studying for various MCP exams, I became frustrated with the huge, unwieldy study guides that were the only preparation tools available. As an experienced IT professional and former instructor, I wanted "nothing but the facts" necessary to prepare for the exams. From this impetus, Exam Cram emerged in 1997. It quickly became the best-selling computer book series since "...*For Dummies*," and the best-selling certification book series ever. By maintaining an intense focus on subject matter, tracking errata and updates quickly, and following the certification market closely, Exam Cram was able to establish the dominant position in cert prep books.

You will not be disappointed in your decision to purchase this book. If you are, please contact me at etittel@jump.net. All suggestions, ideas, input, or constructive criticism are welcome!

Ed Tittel

I would like to dedicate this book to my loving wife Samie. Thank you for all of your help, patience, and support.

About the Author

Michael J. Shannon is a resident of Fort Worth, Texas. He is married with a 21-year-old daughter and an 18-year-old son. He began configuring hubs and routers in the early '90s while working as a network technician for an Arizona telecommunications company. He has been implementing, consulting, and instructing on internetworking technology for over 12 years.

Mr. Shannon is a full-time author and consultant who has been employed as a senior technician, trainer, consultant, and mentor throughout the U.S. for companies such as ExecuTrain, Mindworks, Mastering Computers, Platinum Technology, and Fujitsu. He holds the CCNP, MCSE 2000, Network+, and iNet+ networking-related certifications. As a security professional, he holds the Certified Information Systems Security Professional (CISSP) and the HIPAA Certified Security Specialist (HCSS) certifications. He also has a Bachelor of Arts degree from Lubbock Christian University.

His hobbies are producing and writing original music, playing guitar, and golfing.

Acknowledgments

I would like to sincerely thank everyone who helped make this book possible including Jack Kriegh, Anthony Scqueira at KnowledgeNet, Jawahara Saidullah at Waterside Productions, Carol Ackerman at Que Certification, and Mary Burmeister and Kim Lindros at LANWrights.

Contents at a Glance

Table of Contents

We Want to Hear from You!

As the reader of this book, *you* are our most important critic and commentator. We value your opinion and want to know what we're doing right, what we could do better, what areas you'd like to see us publish in, and any other words of wisdom you're willing to pass our way.

As an executive editor for Que Publishing, I welcome your comments. You can email or write me directly to let me know what you did or didn't like about this book—as well as what we can do to make our books better.

Please note that I cannot help you with technical problems related to the topic of this book. We do have a User Services group, however, where I will forward specific technical questions related to the book.

When you write, please be sure to include this book's title and author as well as your name, email address, and phone number. I will carefully review your comments and share them with the author and editors who worked on the book.

Email: feedback@quepublishing.com

Mail: Jeff Riley
         Executive Editor
         Que Publishing
         800 East 96th Street
         Indianapolis, IN 46240 USA

For more information about this book or another Que Publishing title, visit our Web site at www.quepublishing.com. Type the ISBN (excluding hyphens) or the title of a book in the Search field to find the page you're looking for.

Introduction

Welcome to the *BSCI Exam Cram 2*. This book is intended to prepare you to take and pass the Cisco BSCI Certification Exam 642-801, as administered by both the Prometric and Pearson VUE testing organizations. This Introduction explains Cisco's BSCI certification program in general and talks about how the *Exam Cram 2* series can help you prepare for that certification exam. You can learn more about Prometric by visiting its Web site at www.prometric.com, and you can learn more about Pearson VUE by visiting its Web site at www.vue.com.

Exam Cram 2 books help you understand and appreciate the subjects and materials you need to pass certification exams. *Exam Cram 2* books are aimed strictly at test preparation and review. They do not teach you everything you need to know about a topic. Instead, the series presents and dissects the questions and problems that you're likely to encounter on a test. In preparing this book, we've worked from preparation guides and tests and from a battery of third-party test-preparation tools. The aim of the *Exam Cram 2* series is to bring together as much information as possible about the certification exams.

Nevertheless, to completely prepare yourself for any test, we recommend that you begin by taking the Self-Assessment immediately following this Introduction. This tool will help you evaluate your knowledge base against the requirements for the Cisco BSCI exam under both ideal and real circumstances.

Based on what you learn from that exercise, you might decide to begin your studies with some classroom training, or to pick up and read one of the many study guides available from third-party vendors, including Cisco Press certification titles. We also strongly recommend that you spend as much time as feasible configuring, optimizing, and monitoring within the Cisco IOS as well as deploying the various BSCI routing protocols in a real-world or test environment on actual Cisco routing devices.

For Whom Is This Book?

This book is for you if

➤ You are an IT professional who already holds a current Cisco Certified Network Associate certification and are preparing for the Cisco BSCI 642-801 examination.

➤ Your job or work involves working in and around the Internet or internetworks, offering you experience and a basic working knowledge of scalable routing technologies.

➤ Your job or work carries some specific networking considerations with it, be it configuration, policy, or network design.

➤ You are interested in pursuing the CCNP, CCIP, and/or CCDP certification from Cisco.

This book is *not* for you if

➤ You are just getting started in networking and have little or no experience with the Cisco IOS, networking concepts, and IP addressing.

➤ You are working in IT but have no systems or network administration experience or explicitly router-related job duties or responsibilities.

➤ You seek a learning tool to teach you all the background, terms, and concepts necessary to understand basic networking.

➤ You are curious about these suddenly popular Cisco certifications and want to explore a potential career change.

If you fall into the category that indicates this book is not for you, you should start your Cisco certification path somewhere else. You should consider preparing for the current Cisco CCNA exam.

Cisco Certifications Requiring the BSCI Exam

Cisco (www.cisco.com) offers a wide range of highly-regarded, broad, and specific network industry certifications that are primarily aimed at intermediate- and advanced-level IT professionals. Here is a list of the three certifications that have the BSCI exam as a requirement:

➤ *CCNP*—The Cisco Certified Network Professional (CCNP) certification confirms advanced or journeyman knowledge of networking. This certification requires you to pass two or four exams. For more information on the CCNP certification, see `http://cisco.com/en/US/learning/le3/le2/le37/le10/learning_certification_type_home.html`.

➤ *CCIP*—The Cisco Certified Internetwork Professional (CCIP) certification demonstrates competency in IP networking pertaining to service provider organizations. This certification requires you to pass four exams. For more information on this certification, go to `http://cisco.com/en/US/learning/le3/le2/le37/le8/learning_certification_type_home.html`.

➤ *CCDP*—The Cisco Certified Design Professional (CCDP) certification certifies advanced or journeyman knowledge of network design. This certification requires you to pass three exams. For more information about this certification, visit `http://cisco.com/en/US/learning/le3/le2/le37/le5/learning_certification_type_home.html`.

Signing Up to Take the Exam

After you have studied this book, have taken the sample tests, and feel ready to tackle the real thing, you can sign up to take the exam either at Prometric or at Pearson VUE. The Cisco BSCI exam costs $125.

Signing Up with Prometric

You can contact Prometric to locate a nearby testing center that administers the test and to make an appointment. The last time we visited the Prometric Web site, a searching system to find the testing center nearest you was located at `www.2ittrain.com`. The sign-up Web page address for the exam itself is `www.2test.com`. You can also use this Web page (click the Contact Us link) to obtain a telephone number for the company if you can't or don't want to sign up for the exam on the Web page.

Signing Up with Pearson VUE

You can contact Pearson VUE to locate a nearby testing center that administers the test and to make an appointment. The sign-up Web page address for the exam itself is `www.vue.com/cisco`.

Scheduling the Cisco BSCI Exam

To schedule an exam, call at least one day in advance, but do not count on getting an early appointment. In some areas of the United States, tests are booked up for weeks in advance. To cancel or reschedule an exam, you must call at least 12 hours before the scheduled test time (or you may be charged). When calling Prometric, be sure to have the following information ready for the representative who handles your call:

➤ Your name, organization, mailing address, and email address.

➤ A unique test ID. For most U.S. citizens, this will be your Social Security number. Citizens of other nations can use their taxpayer IDs or make other arrangements with the order taker.

➤ The name and number of the exam you wish to take. For this book, the exam number is 642-801, and the exam name is BSCI.

➤ If you will be paying by credit card, be sure to have your card handy as well. If you wish to pay by check or other means, you have to obtain the necessary information from the Prometric or Pearson VUE representative with whom you speak.

Taking the Test

When you show up for your appointment, be sure you bring two forms of identification that have your signature on them, including one with a photograph. You won't be allowed to take any printed material into the testing environment, but you can study the Cram Sheet from the front of this book while you are waiting. Try to arrive at least 15 minutes before the scheduled timeslot.

All exams are completely closed book. In fact, you will not be permitted to take anything with you into the testing area, but you will be furnished with a blank sheet of paper and a pen. If allowed by the testing center, we suggest that you immediately write down on that sheet of paper any of the information from the Cram Sheet you've had a hard time remembering, such as variable-length subnet mask (VLSM) techniques.

You will have some time to compose yourself, to record memorized information, and even to take a sample orientation exam before you begin the real thing. We suggest you take the orientation test before taking your first exam, but because they're all more or less identical in layout, behavior, and controls, you probably won't need to do this more than once.

About This Book

Each topical *Exam Cram 2* chapter follows a regular structure, along with graphical cues about important or useful information. Here's the structure of a typical chapter:

➤ *Opening Hotlists*—Each chapter begins with a list of the terms, tools, and techniques you must learn and understand before you can be fully conversant with that chapter's subject matter. Following the hotlists are one or two introductory paragraphs to set the stage for the rest of the chapter.

➤ *Topical coverage*—After the opening hotlists, each chapter covers a series of at least four topics related to the chapter's subject title. Throughout this section, topics or concepts likely to appear on a test are highlighted in a special Exam Alert layout, like this:

This is what an Exam Alert looks like. Normally, an Exam Alert stresses concepts, terms, software, or activities that are likely to relate to one or more certification test questions. For that reason, any information found offset in an Exam Alert format is worthy of unusual attentiveness on your part.

Pay close attention to material flagged as an Exam Alert; although all the information in this book pertains to what you need to know to pass the exam, we flag certain items that are really important. You'll find what appears in the meat of each chapter to be worth knowing, too, when preparing for the test.

Because this book's material is very condensed, we recommend that you use this book along with other resources to achieve the maximum benefit.

➤ *Practice questions*—Although test questions and topics are discussed throughout each chapter, the "Exam Prep Questions" section at the end of each chapter presents a series of mock test questions and explanations of both correct and incorrect answers. We also try to point out especially tricky questions by using a special icon, like this:

Ordinarily, this icon flags the presence of a particularly devious inquiry, if not an outright trick question. Trick questions are calculated to be answered incorrectly if not read more than once—and carefully at that. Although they are not ubiquitous, such questions make occasional appearances on Cisco exams. That is why we say exam questions are as much about reading comprehension as they are about knowing your material inside-out and backwards.

➤ *Details and resources*—Every chapter ends with a section titled "Need to Know More?" that provides direct pointers to Cisco routing resources that offer more details on the chapter's subject. If you find a resource you like in this collection, use it, but don't feel compelled to use all the resources. On the other hand, we recommend only those resources we ourselves use regularly, so none of our recommendations will waste your time or money.

The bulk of the book follows this chapter structure slavishly, but there are a few other elements we'd like to point out. Chapters 11 and 13 each contain an entire sample test that provides a good review of the material presented throughout the book to ensure you're ready for the exam. Chapters 12 and 14 contain the corresponding answer keys to the sample test chapters that precede them. Additionally, you'll find appendixes at the back of the book that include the following information:

➤ A list of Cisco commands (Appendix A)

➤ A list of routing-related products, vendors, and technologies mentioned throughout the book (Appendix B)

➤ An explanation of what's on the CD (Appendix C)

➤ An explanation of how to use the software on the CD (Appendix D)

➤ A glossary that explains terms

➤ An index you can use to track down terms as they appear in the text

Finally, the tear-out Cram Sheet attached next to the inside front cover of this *Exam Cram 2* book represents a condensed and compiled collection of facts, tricks, and tips we think you should memorize before taking the test. You might even want to look at it in the car or in the lobby of the testing center just before you walk in to take the test.

Typographic Conventions

In this book, configuration settings and script fragments are typeset in a monospaced font, as in the following example:

```
RouterA(config)# router ospf 50
RouterA(config-network)# 172.16.4.0 0.0.0.255 area 0
RouterA(config-network)# 172.16.5.0 0.0.0.255 area 2
RouterA(config-network)# area 2 stub
```

This notation will be consistent with the exact syntax and structure of the Cisco IOS on Cisco routers.

Some script fragments include boldface, which indicates commands that should be typed literally. Italic indicates variables, as in the following example:

```
RouterA(config-router)# network address wildcard-mask area area-id
```

How to Use This Book

The order of chapters is what we consider to be a logical progression for someone who wants to review all the topics on the exam. If you feel that you are already up to speed on certain topics, you may elect to skip the chapter or chapters in which those topics are covered. In any case, you should try all the questions in the chapters and the sample tests in Chapters 11 and 13.

If you find errors, sections that could be worded more clearly, or questions that seem deceptive, feel free to let our series editor, Ed Tittel, know by email at etittel@examcram.com.

Self-Assessment

Based on recent statistics, as many as half a million individuals are at some stage of the certification process but have not yet received one of their various certification credentials. Recent polls in *Certification* magazine indicate that two to three times that number might be considering whether to obtain a certification of some kind. That is a huge potential audience!

What we cannot know yet—because the BSCI exam is relatively new as this book goes to press—are precise numbers for the BSCI exam itself. Based on recent salary and job interest surveys, we know enterprise networking is a hot topic for IT professionals and a leading target for upcoming certification studies. One of the main factors that makes the BSCI exam such an excellent career option is that it is a mandatory requirement for the Cisco Certified Network Professional (CCNP), Cisco Certified Internetwork Professional (CCIP), and Cisco Certified Design Professional (CCDP) certifications. BSCI is also an important base of knowledge for other Cisco certifications such as the Cisco Certified Security Professional (CCSP) and, eventually, the Cisco Certified Internetwork Expert (CCIE).

The reason we included a Self-Assessment in this *Exam Cram 2* book is to help you evaluate your readiness to tackle the Cisco 642-801 BSCI exam. But before you tackle this Self-Assessment, let's talk about concerns you might face when pursuing the BSCI exam as well as what an ideal candidate might look like.

Networking Professionals in the Real World

In the next section, we describe an ideal candidate, knowing full well that only a few real candidates will meet this ideal. In fact, our description of that ideal candidate might seem downright scary. But take heart: Although the requirements might seem formidable, they are by no means impossible to meet. However, be keenly aware that it takes time, involves some expense, and requires real effort to get through this process.

Thousands of IT professionals already hold Cisco networking certifications, so it is an eminently attainable goal. You can get all the real-world motivation you need from knowing that many others have gone down similar paths before you, so you should be able to follow in their footsteps. If you are willing to approach the process seriously and do what it takes to obtain the necessary experience and knowledge, you can take—and pass—the BSCI exam. In fact, we have designed our *Exam Cram 2* books to make it as easy on you as possible to prepare for these exams. But prepare you must!

The Ideal BSCI Candidate

The BSCI exam tests you on advanced or journeyman knowledge of local area network (LAN) and wide area network (WAN) technologies. You will be tested for the skills necessary to configure and operate LAN and WAN services for organizations with networks from 100 to more than 500 nodes.

The protocols and technologies you should know by exam time include

➤ Internet Protocol (IP)

➤ Routing Information Protocol (RIP)

➤ Interior Gateway Routing Protocol (IGRP)

➤ Enhanced Interior Gateway Routing Protocol (EIGRP)

➤ Open Shortest Path First (OSPF)

➤ Border Gateway Protocol version 4 (BGP4)

➤ Intermediate System-to-Intermediate System (IS-IS)

➤ Route Redistribution

➤ Route Summarization

➤ Variable Length Subnet Mask (VLSM)

➤ Frame Relay

To ultimately achieve a Cisco Career Certification, you have to read and accept the terms of the Cisco Career Certifications and Confidentiality Agreement. If you fail to complete this step, certification application processing will stop. You can take the BCSI exam on the way to earning the CCNP, CCIP, and CCDP certifications without taking any courses, but you must hold a valid CCNA certificate when you register for the BSCI exam.

The BSCI exam is often the first test taken on the path to CCNP, CCIP, and CCDP certifications. These professional certifications generally endorse an individual's networking skills at the mid-career level. Many BSCI candidates already hold positions such as help-desk engineer, field technician, systems administrator, network administrator, or technical trainer. As a BSCI exam candidate, you should already enjoy knowledge of networking at the small-office, home-office (SOHO) level as well as have the ability to operate in a small business or organization with networks of fewer than 100 nodes. You also should presently be able to install and configure Cisco routers in multi-protocol internetworks using LAN and WAN interfaces. In addition, you should be confident providing Level 1 troubleshooting support as well as optimizing network security and performance.

Fundamentally, this all boils down to about a bachelor's degree in computer science with a strong focus on networking, plus at least two years of experience working in a position involving network design, installation, configuration, maintenance, and/or security. We believe that fewer than half of all certification candidates meet these requirements and that, in fact, most meet less than half of these requirements—at least, when they begin the certification process. But because so many other IT professionals who already have been certified in networking topics have survived this ordeal, you can survive it, too, especially if you heed what our Self-Assessment can tell you about what you already know and what you need to learn.

Put Yourself to the Test

The following series of questions and observations is designed to help you figure out how much work you must do to pursue the BSCI exam and what types of resources you might consult on your quest. Be absolutely honest in your answers; otherwise, you will end up wasting money on an exam you are not yet ready to take (and because the BSCI exam costs around $125, this isn't chump change). There are no right or wrong answers, only steps along the path to certification. Only you can decide where you really belong in the broad spectrum of aspiring candidates.

Two things should be clear from the outset, however:

➤ Even a modest background in computer technologies is helpful.

➤ Hands-on experience with networking and Cisco products and technologies is a key ingredient to certification success.

Before you begin this process, take this simple four-step walkthrough to validate your readiness for the BSCI exam:

1. Do you have a current CCNA certification (requires renewal every 3 years)? [Yes or No]

   If Yes, proceed to step 2; if No, proceed to step 4.

2. Have you taken the Building Scalable Cisco Internetworks (BSCI) v1.2 course from Cisco or a comparable training class? (This should be five days of instructor-led, five days of live e-learning, or 30–35 hours of Web-based training.) [Yes or No]

   If Yes, you should use this *Exam Cram 2* book as a supplement to your acquired knowledge and experience and prepare to take the exam in the near future.

   If No, proceed to step 3.

3. Do you have at least two years of experience in a position such as help-desk engineer, field technician, systems administrator, network administrator, or technical trainer? [Yes or No]

   If Yes, you should use this *Exam Cram 2* book as a supplement to your acquired knowledge and experience and prepare to take the exam in the near future.

   If No, you might want to consider taking the Building Scalable Cisco Internetworks (BSCI) v1.2 course from Cisco or a comparable training class. If you are a disciplined and motivated self-studier, you might want to build a home lab or rent some router time online and purchase the *CCNP Self-Study: Building Scalable Cisco Internetworks (BSCI)* book from Cisco Press (ISBN: 1-5870-5084-6).

4. Because you do not have a current CCNA certification, you must go to www.cisco.com and find out how you can recertify for your CCNA or take the current CCNA exam for the first time to achieve this certification.

Cisco also maintains a list of pointers to training venues on its Web site. Visit http://cisco.com/en/US/learning/le31/learning_learning_resources_home.html.

Hands-on Experience

An important key to success on the BSCI exam lies in obtaining hands-on experience, especially with the Cisco IOS in the LAN and WAN environments. There is simply no substitute for time spent installing, configuring, troubleshooting, securing, and optimizing a Cisco router. If you cannot afford your own equipment or lack the access at work, you can check with companies on the Internet that rent router time. Some even provide written labs specific to the BSCI exam. Even www.ebay.com has many packages at auction that you can bid on.

 You can download objectives, practice exams, and other data about Cisco exams from the official BSCI Exam Web page at **www.cisco.com/warp/public/10/wwtraining/certprog/testing/current_exams/642-801.html**.

Testing Your Exam-Readiness

Whether you attend a formal class on a specific topic to get ready for an exam or use written materials to study on your own, some preparation for the BSCI certification exam is essential. At $125 a pop, pass or fail, you want to do everything you can to pass on your first try. That is where this *Exam Cram 2* comes in.

We have included two practice exams in this book, so if you don't score that well on the first test, you can study more and then tackle the second test. If you still don't hit a score of at least 90% after these tests, you should investigate the practice test resources we mention here (feel free to use your favorite search engine to look for more; this list is by no means exhaustive):

➤ *ExamCram2*. www.examcram2.com

➤ *Boson*. www.boson.com

➤ *MeasureUp*. www.measureup.com

➤ *Transcender*. www.transcender.com

➤ *PrepLogic*. www.preplogic.com

➤ *Self Test Software*. www.selftestsoftware.com

For any given subject, consider taking a class if you have tackled self-study materials, taken the test, and failed anyway. The opportunity to interact with an instructor and fellow students can make all the difference in the world, if you can afford that privilege.

 When it comes to assessing your test readiness, there is no better way than to take a good-quality practice exam and pass with a score of 85% or better. When we are preparing ourselves, we shoot for more than 90%, just to leave room for the "weirdness factor" that sometimes depresses exam scores when taking the real thing. (The passing score on BSCI is 85% or higher; that is why we recommend shooting for 90%, to leave some margin for the impact of stress when taking the real thing.)

In addition to the general exam-readiness information in the previous section, there are several things you can do to prepare for the BSCI exam. As you're getting ready for the BSCI, visit the Web sites at www.examcram2.com and www.cramsession.com. You can sign up for "Question of the Day" services for this exam; join ongoing discussion groups on the exam; and look for pointers to exam resources, study materials, and related tips.

Onward, Through the Fog!

After you have assessed your readiness, undertaken the right background studies, obtained the hands-on experience that will help you understand the products and technologies at work, and reviewed the many sources of information to help you prepare for the test, you will be ready to take a round of practice tests. When your scores come back positive enough to get you through the exam, you are ready to go after the real thing. If you follow our assessment regime, you will know not only what you need to study, but also when you are ready to make a test date at Prometric or VUE. Good luck!

Cisco Certification Exams

Terms you'll need to understand:

✓ Radio button
✓ Check box
✓ Careful reading
✓ Exhibits
✓ Multiple-choice question formats
✓ Simulation questions
✓ Process of elimination

Techniques you'll need to master:

✓ Preparing to take a certification exam
✓ Practicing to take a certification exam
✓ Making the best use of the testing software
✓ Budgeting your time
✓ Guessing (as a last resort)

No matter how well prepared you might be, exam taking is not something most people look forward to. In most cases, familiarity helps relieve test anxiety. You probably won't be as nervous when you take your second or third Cisco certification exam as you will be when you take your first one.

Whether it is your second exam or your tenth, understanding the finer points of exam taking (how much time to spend on questions, the setting you will be in, and so on) and the exam software will help you concentrate on the questions at hand rather than on the surroundings. Likewise, mastering some basic exam-taking skills should help you recognize—and perhaps even outsmart—some of the tricks and traps you are bound to find in several of the exam questions.

This chapter—besides explaining the Cisco BSCI exam environment and software—describes some proven exam-taking strategies you should be able to use to your advantage.

The Exam Situation

When you arrive at the testing center where you scheduled your exam, you will need to sign in with an exam proctor. He will ask you to show two forms of identification, one of which must be a photo ID. After you have signed in, you will be asked to deposit any books, bags, or other items you brought with you. Then you'll be escorted into the closed room that houses the exam seats.

All exams are completely closed book. In fact, you won't be permitted to take anything with you into the testing area. You will be furnished with a pen or pencil and a blank sheet of paper—or, in some cases, an erasable plastic sheet and an erasable felt-tip pen—which you can use to record notes during the test. You will have to turn in the sheet when you leave the room.

Typically, the room will be furnished with anywhere from one to half a dozen computers, and each workstation will be separated from the others by dividers designed to keep you from seeing what is happening on someone else's computer.

Most test rooms feature a wall with a large picture window. This permits the exam proctor to monitor the room, prevent exam takers from talking to one another, and observe anything out of the ordinary that might go on. The exam proctor will have preloaded the appropriate Cisco certification exam—for this book, that's the Cisco BSCI Certification Exam 642-801—and you'll be permitted to start as soon as you are seated in front of the computer. At the beginning of each test is a tutorial you can go through if you are unfamiliar with the testing environment.

All Cisco certification exams allow a predetermined, maximum amount of time in which to complete your work. (This time is indicated on the exam by an onscreen counter/clock in the upper-right corner of the screen, so you can check the time remaining whenever you like.) All exams are computer generated and use primarily a multiple-choice format with 2–5 more simulation questions. These simulation questions test your real-world experience in the actual Cisco interface. You will be required to submit the proper series of commands to accomplish a particular configuration based on the given scenario or diagram. You will also encounter questions that demand a fill-in-the-blank answer that represents the proper Cisco command. The Cisco BSCI exam consists of 55–65 randomly selected questions from a pool of several hundred questions. You can take up to 75 minutes to complete the exam.

Although this might sound quite simple, the questions are formulated to thoroughly check your mastery of the material. Cisco exam questions are also very adept at testing you on more than one area of knowledge with a single question; for example, testing your knowledge of the command syntax as well as the proper command mode. Often, you will be asked to provide more than one answer to a question. Likewise, you might be asked to select the best or most effective solution to a problem from a range of choices, all of which technically are correct. Taking the exam is quite an adventure, and it involves real thinking as well as skill and an ability to manage your time. This book shows you what to expect and how to deal with the potential problems, puzzles, and predicaments you are likely to encounter.

When you complete a Cisco certification exam, the software will tell you whether you have passed or failed. The results are then broken down into several main objectives or domain areas. You will be shown the percentage that you got correct for each individual domain. Even if you fail, you should ask for (and keep) the detailed report the test proctor prints for you. You can use this report to help you prepare for another go-round, if necessary. If you need to retake an exam, you will have to schedule a new test with Prometric or VUE and pay for another exam. Keep in mind that, because the questions come from a pool, you will receive different questions the second time around. Cisco also has a retake policy, which is that you must wait 72 hours between exam attempts.

In the following section, you will learn more about how Cisco test questions look and how they must be answered.

Exam Layout and Design

Some exam questions require you to select a single answer, whereas others ask you to select multiple correct answers. The following multiple-choice question requires you to select a single correct answer. Following the question is a brief summary of each answer selection and why it is either correct or incorrect.

Question 1

Which one of the following statements best represents the EIGRP routing protocol in relation to the route summarization process?

○ A. EIGRP does not provide support for automatic route summarization.

○ B. EIGRP provides support for only automatic route summarization.

○ C. EIGRP automatically summarizes at the classful bit boundary.

○ D. EIGRP automatically summarizes at any available bit boundary.

Answer C is correct. The EIGRP routing protocol automatically summarizes at classful network boundaries. For instance, the 10 contiguous Class B networks of 172.16.1.0 /24 through 172.16.10.0 /24 could be advertised by EIGRP as a single route: 172.16.0.0 /16. Answer A is incorrect because EIGRP does support automatic route summarization. Answer B is incorrect because EIGRP supports manual route summarization as well. Answer D is incorrect because EIGRP summarizes at only the bit boundary.

This sample question format corresponds closely to the Cisco BSCI Certification Exam format—the only difference on the exam is that questions are not followed by answer keys. To select an answer, position the cursor over the radio button next to the answer and then click the mouse button to select the answer. See the practice exam CD that comes with this book for a general idea of what the questions will look like.

Next, we examine a question that requires choosing multiple answers. This type of question provides check boxes rather than radio buttons for marking all appropriate selections. These types of questions can either specify how many answers to choose or instruct you to choose all the appropriate answers.

Question 2

Which of these statements describe the default holdtime for EIGRP? (Choose two.)

- ☐ A. The default EIGRP holdtime is static and cannot be modified.
- ☐ B. The default EIGRP holdtime depends on the amount of RAM in the router.
- ☐ C. The default EIGRP holdtime depends on the hello packet interval.
- ☐ D. The default EIGRP holdtime depends on the network media speed.

Answers C and D are correct. The default EIGRP holdtime is three times the Hello packet interval, and a faster network media speed results in a shorter holdtime interval. Answer A is incorrect because the holdtime can be modified and is a dynamic value. Answer B is incorrect because the router's RAM does not affect the EIGRP default holdtime value.

For this type of question, more than one answer is required. Such questions are scored as wrong unless all the required selections are chosen. In other words, a partially correct answer does not result in partial credit when the test is scored. If you are required to provide multiple answers and do not provide the number of answers the question asks for, the testing software indicates that you did not complete that question. For Question 2, you have to check the boxes next to answers C and D to obtain credit for this question. Realize that choosing the correct answers also means knowing why the other answers are incorrect!

Although these two basic types of questions can appear in many forms, they are the foundation on which most of the BSCI Certification Exam questions are based. Some other complex questions might include exhibits, simple fill-in-the-blank questions, as well as simulation questions. For some of these questions, you will be asked to make a selection by clicking the portion of the exhibit that answers the question or by typing the correct answer(s) in the testing interface. Your knowledge and expertise of router configuration must go well beyond merely memorizing the purpose of various commands. The BSCI exam tests your ability to configure a router in a variety of scenarios and configurations. Do not rely simply on your success at answering traditional multiple-choice questions. Although these represent the core of the exam, your failure to answer the many fill-in-the-blank, simulator, and configuration scenario type questions will lead to an unsuccessful testing session.

Other questions involving exhibits use charts or diagrams to help document a network scenario you'll be asked to configure or troubleshoot. Careful attention to such exhibits is the key to success. In these instances, you might have to toggle between the exhibit and the question to absorb all the information being shown and properly answer the question.

You also might see a question or two where you must enter a simple command into an input box. You will be presented with a long list of available commands as part of the testing interface. You will also encounter from two to five simulation questions. You will be given a simulated scenario you must complete in the Cisco IOS environment. This generally involves performing a series of steps at the command line or possibly dragging and dropping the correct order of a certain procedure. Therefore, actual experience with the Cisco operating system interface and real-world practice are critical to success on the BSCI exam.

Exam-Taking Techniques

A well-known principle when taking certification exams is to first read over the entire exam from start to finish while answering only those questions you feel absolutely sure of. The next time around, you can delve into the more complex questions. Knowing how many such questions you have left helps you spend your exam time wisely. Although this is good overall testing advice, this capability is not available to you on the BSCI exam 642-801. To protect the integrity of the certifications, Cisco does not allow you to mark and go back to review a previously answered question.

It is critical on a Cisco exam that you read each question thoroughly. After you input your answer and move on to the next question, you cannot go back!

As you approach the end of your allotted testing time of 75 minutes, you are better off guessing than leaving a question unanswered.

The most important advice about taking any exam is this: *Read each question carefully.* Some questions are deliberately ambiguous, some use double negatives, and others use terminology in incredibly precise ways. The authors have taken numerous exams—both practice and live—and in nearly every one have missed at least one question because they didn't read it closely or carefully enough.

Here are some suggestions on how to deal with the tendency to jump to an answer too quickly:

➤ Make sure you read every word in the question very carefully, even if it means reading it several times.

➤ As you read, try to reformulate the question in your own words. If you can do this, you should be able to pick the correct answer(s) much more easily.

➤ Sometimes, rereading a question enables you to see something you might have missed the first time you read it.

➤ If you still do not understand the question, ask yourself what you don't understand about the question, why the answers don't appear to make sense, or what appears to be missing. If you think about the subject for a while, your subconscious might provide the details that are lacking or you might notice a "trick" that will point to the correct answer.

Above all, try to deal with each question by thinking through what you know about routing—and the characteristics, behaviors, and facts involved. By reviewing what you know (and what you have written down on your information sheet), you will often recall or understand enough to be able to deduce the answer to the question.

Question-Handling Strategies

Based on exams the authors have taken, some interesting trends have become apparent. For those questions that take only a single answer, usually two or three of the answers will be obviously incorrect, and two of the answers will be possible—of course, only one can be correct. Unless the answer leaps out at you, begin the process of answering by eliminating those answers that are most obviously wrong. A word of caution: If the answer seems too obvious, reread the question to look for a trick. Often those are the ones you are most likely to get wrong. If you have done your homework for an exam, no valid information should be completely new to you. In that case, unfamiliar or bizarre terminology most likely indicates a bogus answer.

As you work your way through the exam, budget your time by making sure you have completed one quarter of the questions one quarter of the way through the exam period and three quarters of them three quarters of the way through the exam. This ensures that you will have time to go through them all. As you know, there will be 55–65 questions to answer in a 75-minute time frame. That gives you an average of a minute to a minute-and-a-half for each question. The simulation questions will probably take longer than the multiple-choice questions, so give yourself ample time.

 Be cautious about changing your answers and second-guessing yourself. Many times the first selection is right and changing your answer might cause you to miss questions that were originally answered correctly.

If you are not finished when 95% of the time has elapsed, use the last few minutes to guess your way through the remaining questions. Remember that guessing is potentially more valuable than not answering because blank answers are always wrong, but a guess might turn out to be right. If you don't have a clue about any of the remaining questions, pick answers at random or choose all As, Bs, and so on. The important thing is to submit an exam for scoring that has an answer for every question.

Mastering the Inner Game

Knowledge breeds confidence, and confidence breeds success. If you study the information in this book carefully and review all the practice questions at the end of each chapter, you should become aware of those areas where you need additional learning and studying.

Follow up by reading some or all of the materials recommended in the "Need to Know More?" section at the end of each chapter. Don't hesitate to look for more resources online. Remember that the idea is to become familiar enough with the concepts and situations you find in the sample questions that you can reason your way through similar scenarios on a real exam. If you know the material, you have every right to be confident that you can pass the exam.

After you have worked your way through the book, take the sample tests in Chapter 11, "Practice Exam 1," and Chapter 13, "Practice Exam 2." This will provide a reality check and help you identify areas you need to study further. Answer keys to these exams can be found in Chapter 12, "Answer Key 1," and Chapter 14, "Answer Key 2."

Make sure you follow up and review materials related to the questions you miss on the practice exam before scheduling a real exam. The key is to know the why and how. If you memorize the answers, you do yourself a great injustice and might not pass the exam. Memorizing answers will not benefit you because you are unlikely to see the identical question on the exam. Only when you have covered all the ground and feel comfortable with the whole scope of the practice exam should you take a real one.

 If you take the practice exam and do not score at least 90% correct, you should practice further. When you practice, remember that it is important to know *why* the answer is correct or incorrect. If you memorize the answers instead, it will trip you up when taking the exam.

With the information in this book and the determination to supplement your knowledge, you should be able to pass the certification exam. However, you need to work at it. Otherwise, you will have to pay for the exam more than once before you finally pass. As long as you get a good night's sleep and prepare thoroughly, you should do just fine. Good luck!

Additional Resources

A good source of information about Cisco certification exams comes from Cisco itself. The best place to go for exam-related information is online. The Cisco CCNP Certification home page, which includes a link to BSCI information, resides at `www.cisco.com/warp/public/10/wwtraining/certprog/lan/programs/ccnp.html`.

Coping with Change on the Web

Sooner or later, all the information we have shared about Web-based resources mentioned throughout this book might go stale or be replaced by newer information. However, there is always a way to find what you want on the Web if you are willing to invest some time and energy. Cisco's site has a site map to help you find your way around, and most large or complex Web sites offer search engines. Finally, feel free to use general search tools to search for related information.

Routing Principles

Terms you'll need to understand:

✓ Administrative distance (AD)
✓ Autonomous system (AS)
✓ Bandwidth
✓ Convergence
✓ Delay
✓ Distance vector
✓ Hop count
✓ Link state
✓ Load
✓ Metric
✓ Path determination
✓ Reliability
✓ Routed protocol
✓ Routing
✓ Routing protocol
✓ Switching

Techniques you'll need to master:

✓ Using the **ip route** command
✓ Using debugging commands to monitor convergence patterns of routing protocols
✓ Analyzing routing tables

In this chapter, you will learn about the major functions of a router as well as various routing protocols that can operate on Cisco routers. In addition, you will find out how to analyze the various fields in a routing table.

Major Functions of a Router

Routing is the process of transferring packets of information from a source to a destination node over an internetwork where at least one intermediary node is traversed along the way. Thirty years ago, internetworks were minimal in their design and monolithic in their architecture. Today, these internetworks are complex matrices of many different physical and logical topologies. Data packets now include information such as email, audio, video, graphics, and text. This complexity of routing has rapidly increased due to greater commercial exposure of large-scale internetworking and distributed-enterprise computing. Routers are regularly compared to bridges or switches, which at first glance seem to perform the same functions. The fundamental difference, however, is that bridging operates at the data-link layer (Layer 2) of the Open Systems Interconnection (OSI) reference model and routing occurs at the network layer (Layer 3). Consequently, routing and bridging use different processes and header information to move data from the source node to the destination node. This book focuses primarily on the goals of building scalable, routed internetworks using routing protocols.

You should have a solid understanding of the International Organization for Standardization's (ISO) seven-layer OSI networking model and the functions of each layer. The following table shows the OSI protocol stack:

Layer Number	OSI Layer
7	Application
6	Presentation
5	Session
4	Transport
3	Network
2	Data-link
1	Physical

A philosophical and technical difference exists between routed protocols and routing protocols that needs to be established from the outset. *Routed* protocols are responsible for the rules and procedures of encapsulating chunks of data. These protocols are actually the ones that are ultimately routed over the internetwork. The most popular routed protocol is Internet Protocol

(IP). Other routed protocols include Novell Internetwork Packet Exchange/Sequenced Packet Exchange (IPX/SPX), AppleTalk, Digital Equipment Corporation Network (DECnet), Banyan VINES, and Xerox Network System (XNS).

A *routing* protocol, on the other hand, is responsible for moving the routed protocol packets across the internetwork from router to router using efficient routing algorithms. Later in this chapter, we will differentiate between static routing and dynamic routing. Common dynamic routing protocols include Routing Information Protocol version 1 and version 2 (RIPv1 and RIPv2), Interior Gateway Routing Protocol (IGRP), Enhanced Interior Gateway Routing Protocol (EIGRP), Open Shortest Path First (OSPF), Border Gateway Protocol version 4 (BGP-4), and Intermediate System-to-Intermediate System (IS-IS). Static routing and default gateway (router) configuration are manually designated protocols that inject routes into a routing table for special circumstances. Generally speaking, routing protocols are leveraged by intermediate systems to construct route tables that are used in the path determination process.

Path Determination

For a router to behave as a network relay device, it needs to have a working knowledge of the logical topology of the network. The basic goals of the routing process involve the determination of optimal routing paths and the transport of packets (known as packet *switching*) through an internetwork. Packet switching is a relatively clear-cut process, whereas path determination can be quite a challenging venture.

Routing protocols use a mechanism called a *metric* to help determine the optimal route a packet will take. A metric is defined as a type of measurement yardstick, such as the number of hops (routing devices) to a destination used by routing algorithms to resolve the best path to a destination network or node (see Figure 2.1). Routing algorithms generate and maintain routing tables to facilitate the path determination process. The type of routing information stored in the table depends on the routing algorithm being used. In addition, different algorithms flood routing tables with an assortment of valuable information. Most routing protocols use auxiliary tables in concert with the routing table to store topology information and calculate optimal paths.

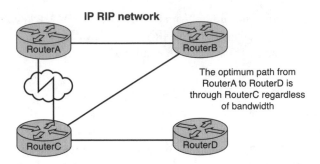

Figure 2.1 RIPv1 routers use hop count as their metric.

Routing tables commonly create mappings to forward the packet to a specific "next hop" router on the way to its final destination. When a router receives an inbound data packet, it references the routing table for the destination address in an attempt to associate this address with a next hop. Routing tables can also store information about the desirability of a path when multiple paths are available to a destination. Depending on the actual routing algorithm being implemented, routers compare different types of metrics to determine optimal and redundant paths.

Routers share this routing table information with other routers in an internetwork using an array of different messages. A common type of communication is the routing *update message*. An update message is typically made up of all, or a subset, of the routing table information. Routers subsequently converge on a complete picture of the network topology by processing routing updates from either a neighbor router or all other routers, depending on the protocol rules. For example, some routing protocols send a link-state advertisement to notify other routers about the status of the sender's network links. This link information can then be used to construct a comprehensive view of the network topology so routers can determine the most favorable routes to the final destination.

Switching

To be an effective routing device, a router must be capable of performing routing functions (such as learning and storing data about the network) as well as switching functions (such as transferring data from an incoming to an outgoing interface). A switching algorithm is comparatively simple and works the same for most routing protocols. The router commonly performs the following basic steps as part of the switching function:

1. After a host decides to send a packet to another host, it gets a router's logical address by some means (such as an ARP broadcast). The host

should have a default gateway configured or the router (gateway) needs to support proxy ARP. With Proxy ARP, a router sends an ARP response on behalf of an end node to the requesting host.

2. The source host then sends a packet addressed specifically to a router's MAC address, including the Layer 3 address of the destination host.

 A MAC address is a data-link layer hardware address that every port or device uses to connect to a LAN segment. MAC addresses are defined by an IEEE standard, have a length of six characters, and use the usual the burned-in address (BIA) of the local LAN interface.

3. Next, the router determines whether it knows how to forward the packet to the next hop according to the entries in its routing table.

4. If the router does not know how to forward the packet, it typically drops the packet and generates an Internet Control Message Protocol (ICMP) error.

5. However, if the router knows how to forward the packet, it changes the destination physical address field in the Layer 2 frame header to that of the next hop and moves the packet along. The next hop might or might not be the last destination. If it is not the ultimate destination, the next hop (usually another router) makes the same switching decisions.

 Remember, as a packet moves through an internetwork, its source physical MAC address changes but its Layer 3 address typically remains the same until it reaches the destination network.

Requirements for Routing

Regardless of the specifics of the routing systems being implemented, all Cisco routers need to have answers to the following three questions to properly route networked packets:

➤ Is a routed protocol module loaded and enabled?

➤ What is the destination network?

➤ What outbound interface represents the best path to the destination network?

A logical Layer 3 address is necessary to properly route packets through an internetwork. The address scheme depends on the individual routed protocol suite loaded into the router's running configuration. After the router determines the addressing method, it needs to look at the current route table for a path to the destination network. If the destination network is not represented in the table, and no default route has been configured, the router should discard the packet and generate an ICMP error notification as mentioned previously. The third step is to determine the outbound interface to use to get the packet to its destination. Because more than one routing process can be in use at a time, the router needs a method for selecting the best path when the same route is learned from several sources. A Cisco router running IP uses a mechanism called the administrative distance (AD) to facilitate the path determination process.

Administrative Distance

Because most routing protocols have metrics and algorithms that are not mutually compatible, the exchange of route information and path determination is essential when running multiple protocols. Administrative distance (AD) is the first decisive tool a router uses for route selection if two protocols provide route information for the same destination. The AD value defines the trustworthiness of a routing protocol by prioritizing protocols in order of the most reliable to the least reliable. Administrative distance has local significance only on the router; it is not advertised to other routers in routing updates.

The lower the administrative distance value, the more dependable the protocol. For instance, if a router receives a route to a destination network from RIP with a default AD of 120 and from IGRP with an AD of 100, the router uses IGRP because it is deemed more reliable based on the smaller administrative distance. The result is that the IGRP route information is injected into the routing table. If the IGRP information is lost—because of a power failure, for example—the RIP-derived information is used until IGRP reemerges. The default administrative distance values of the supported Cisco protocols are shown in Table 2.1.

Table 2.1 Default Administrative Distance Values of the Supported Cisco Protocols	
Source of Route	**Default Administrative Distance**
Connected interface	0
Static route	1
EIGRP summary route	5

Table 2.1 Default Administrative Distance Values of the Supported Cisco Protocols (continued)

Source of Route	Default Administrative Distance
External BGP	20
Internal EIGRP	90
IGRP	100
OSPF	110
IS-IS	115
RIP	120
EGP	140
On Demand Routing	160
External EIGRP	170
Internal BGP	200
Unknown	255

NOTE If the administrative distance value is 255, the router will not trust the source of that route and subsequently will not inject the route into its routing table.

In some complex network environments, the administrative distance of a protocol might need to be tweaked so it takes precedence. Continuing the previous example, if you want your router to select RIP-learned routes instead of the IGRP-learned routes to the same destination, you could increase the AD number for IGRP to a number greater than 120 or decrease the AD number of RIP to a value less than 100. You can modify the administrative distance of a protocol with the distance command in the router configuration. There are no real absolutes for assigning AD numbers because each network has its own requirements. To modify the AD for a static route, you don't use the distance command. Instead, you use the following format:

`ip route network subnet-mask next-hop distance`

Use caution with the distance command, however, because modifying the AD number can cause routing loops and other problems.

The following show ip route command illustrates a router, on an Ethernet network, as shown in Listing 2.1. Notice that in the second show ip route command, after IGRP has been enabled, the IGRP routes are being favored over the RIP routes (AD=120) because the administrative distance of IGRP is lower at 100. This is indicated by the bold text.

Listing 2.1   Two Routers on Which IGRP Routes Are Preferred to RIP

```
RouterA#show ip route
Codes: C - connected, S - static, I - IGRP, R - RIP, M - mobile, B - BGP
       D - EIGRP, EX - EIGRP external, O - OSPF, IA - OSPF inter area
       N1 - OSPF NSSA external type 1, N2 - OSPF NSSA external type 2
       E1 - OSPF external type 1, E2 - OSPF external type 2, E - EGP
       i - IS-IS, L1 - IS-IS level-1, L2 - IS-IS level-2, * - candidate def
       U - per-user static route, o - ODR

Gateway of last resort is not set

          172.16.0.0/24 is subnetted, 5 subnets
R            172.16.5.0 [120/3] via 169.254.1.2, Ethernet0
R            172.16.4.0 [120/2] via 169.254.1.2, Ethernet0
R            172.16.3.0 [120/2] via 169.254.1.2, Ethernet0
R            172.16.2.0 [120/1] via 169.254.1.2, Ethernet0
C            172.16.1.0 is directly connected, Ethernet0
RouterA#


RouterA#show ip route
Codes: C - connected, S - static, I - IGRP, R - RIP, M - mobile, B - BGP
       D - EIGRP, EX - EIGRP external, O - OSPF, IA - OSPF inter area
       N1 - OSPF NSSA external type 1, N2 - OSPF NSSA external type 2
       E1 - OSPF external type 1, E2 - OSPF external type 2, E - EGP
       i - IS-IS, L1 - IS-IS level-1, L2 - IS-IS level-2, * - candidate def
       U - per-user static route, o - ODR

Gateway of last resort is not set

          172.16.0.0/24 is subnetted, 5 subnets
I            172.16.5.0 [100/160240] via 169.254.1.2, Ethernet0
I            172.16.4.0 [100/160140] via 169.254.1.2, Ethernet0
I            172.16.3.0 [100/158240] via 169.254.1.2, Ethernet0
I            172.16.2.0 [100/158140] via 169.254.1.2, Ethernet0
C            172.16.1.0 is directly connected, Ethernet 0
RouterA#
```

If you want to force RouterA to have a preference for RIP routes over IGRP, configure the distance command on RouterA as follows:

```
RouterA(config)# router rip
RouterA(config-router)# distance 90
```

The resulting route table now indicates that RIP routes are preferred, as shown by the "R" entry in RouterA's table in Listing 2.2. Even though the RIP default is 120, the routes are learned with an AD of 90 because of the distance command. The new administrative distance value is relevant only to the routing process on RouterA because RouterB still has IGRP routes in its routing table.

Listing 2.2   RIP Routes Are Preferred Because of the distance Command

```
RouterA#show ip route
Codes: C - connected, S - static, I - IGRP, R - RIP, M - mobile, B - BGP
       D - EIGRP, EX - EIGRP external, O - OSPF, IA - OSPF inter area
       N1 - OSPF NSSA external type 1, N2 - OSPF NSSA external type 2
       E1 - OSPF external type 1, E2 - OSPF external type 2, E - EGP
       i - IS-IS, L1 - IS IS level-1, L2 - IS-IS level-2, * - candidate
➥default
       U - per-user static route, o - ODR

Gateway of last resort is not set

          172.16.0.0/24 is subnetted,  5 subnets
R             172.16.5.0 [90/3] via 169.254.1.2, Ethernet0
R             172.16.4.0 [90/2] via 169.254.1.2, Ethernet0
R             172.16.3.0 [90/2] via 169.254.1.2, Ethernet0
R             172.16.2.0 [90/1] via 169.254.1.2, Ethernet0
C             172.16.1.0 is directly connected, Ethernet0
RouterA#
```

After the administrative distance performs its duty, the routing process must then locate the optimal path to every possible destination network. Again, each protocol algorithm has its own singular definition for what constitutes the best path. The next major function of a router is to advertise these network paths using a configurable value known as the metric.

Routing Metrics

Routing algorithms historically have used different tools for selecting the best route to a destination network. Routing processes choose the path that has the lowest metric value, which can be something as simple as how many routers are passed through to get to the final destination. More advanced routing algorithms, such as EIGRP, can establish a complex route selection process by using multiple metrics to generate a single composite metric. As a Cisco professional, you should be familiar with the following metrics:

➤ Hop count

➤ Reliability

➤ Delay

➤ Bandwidth

➤ Load

We cover each of these in more detail in the following sections.

Hop Count

Hop count is the most common routing metric. It identifies the number (count) of routing devices (hops) a packet must pass through from source to destination. Routing Information Protocol (RIP) is a common protocol used in small IP networks and that uses hop count as a metric.

Reliability

Reliability is a dependability factor typically expressed in terms of the bit-error rate of each network link. Obviously, some links fail more often than others do, and certain links can be repaired more easily or quickly than others. Reliability ratings are arbitrary numeric values that are usually assigned to network links by a network administrator.

Delay

Delay represents the length of time necessary to transfer a data packet from one node to another through the internetwork. Delay depends on factors such as the bandwidth of intermediate network links, the port queues at routers along the path, network congestion on all intermediate network links, and the actual physical distance of the communication. Delay is a commonly used metric because it can represent a collection of several important variables. IGRP and EIGRP are popular routing protocols that use delay as one of the factors to generate their composite metrics.

Bandwidth

IGRP and EIGRP also use the bandwidth value to calculate the composite metric. *Bandwidth* is a number that represents the available capacity for moving traffic on a network link. Simply speaking, a 10Mbps Ethernet link is preferable to a 128Kbps leased line. Just because one link has a greater allowable maximum bandwidth than another link does not guarantee a better route than a slower link. If the faster link is saturated, for instance, the ultimate time to destination could actually be greater. For this reason, bandwidth is usually combined with other values to create a composite metric. Because lower metrics are preferential, the bandwidth is evaluated as a mathematically inverse value; therefore, a higher bandwidth results in a lower metric. Referring to Figure 2.1, the optimal path from RouterA to RouterD in an IGRP or EIGRP network would likely be through the RouterB 10Mbps LAN instead of through the RouterC 128Kbps WAN link because of bandwidth values.

Load

Load is an optional metric used by IGRP and EIGRP; it refers to the degree to which a router's resources are occupied. Load can be calculated as CPU utilization or packets processed per second, but monitoring these parameters on a continual basis can be resource-intensive itself.

Communication cost is another important metric, especially because some companies might not care about performance as much as they care about operating expenditures. Although line delay can be longer, companies can send packets over their own lines rather than through the public lines that have usage time costs.

Neighbor Relationships

After a Cisco router loads a running configuration, it establishes relationships with neighboring (connected) routers or routing devices. The router must open lines of communication to become aware of the network topology. Depending on the routing protocol, this process can include a combination of broadcast Layer-2 frames, hello packets, and ongoing update messages. Ultimately, the topology is learned through the neighbor relationships and the router can then perform its primary task of path determination. As far as EIGRP is concerned, a neighbor is a router within the same autonomous system (AS) running EIGRP. Conversely, in OSPF, a neighboring router is defined as a router that has an interface connected to a common network.

Routing Algorithm Characteristics

Routing protocol algorithms can be classified by type. Key characteristics include the following categories:

➤ Static and dynamic

➤ Single-path and multipath

➤ Flat and hierarchical

➤ Host-intelligent and router-intelligent

➤ Intradomain and interdomain

➤ Distance vector and link-state

➤ Classful and classless

➤ Convergence

We discuss these characteristics in more detail in the following sections.

Static and Dynamic

The static routing process is really not an actual algorithm but rather a set of table mappings established by the network administrator before the beginning of the routing process. These mappings do not change unless the administrator adjusts them. Static routes provide a high degree of administrative simplification, control, and security. They function best in environments in which network traffic is relatively predictable and the network design is relatively simple. The downside to static routing is the administrative overhead and lack of scalability. You use the following global configuration command to add a static route to an IP routing table:

`ip route` prefix mask {address ¦ interface} [distance]

Table 2.2 explains the `ip route` command options.

Table 2.2	Description of the ip route Command
ip route	**Description**
prefix mask	Prefix and mask for the destination added to the IP routing table
address	IP address of the next hop router to the destination
interface	Outbound interface to reach the destination
distance	Administrative distance (optional)

Static routing systems do not react to network changes; therefore, they are generally considered unsuitable for medium to large, constantly changing networks. If only one path exists to the Internet or another autonomous system, it might be appropriate to use a default or static route.

ip route Configuration Options

Some subtle differences exist between the **next-hop address** parameter and the **next-hop interface** parameter. For example, a static route that uses the **next-hop address** has a default AD of **1**, whereas the **interface** parameter sets the AD of the static route to **0**. In other words, the **next-hop address** parameter makes the route appear as a typical static route (AD=1) as opposed to a directly connected link (AD=0). You should use the **next-hop address** option if you are configuring multiaccess media for Ethernet LANs, Frame Relay, ISDN, and so on.

If you want your static route to have an administrative distance that is higher than the default, you can create what is known as a *floating static route*. You can generate a floating static route by setting the administrative distance higher than the default or learned routes. For example, if you wanted to generate a path of last resort, you could statically configure a route to be overridden by routes that are learned via a dynamic routing protocol. If the dynamically learned information became unavailable, you could fail over to the floating static route. You will see some examples of this technique when learning about the BGP protocol in Chapter 8, "Configuring Border Gateway Protocol."

Static routes can complement dynamic routing algorithms when necessary. For example, a router of last resort (the router to which all unroutable packets are sent) can be designated to forward packets if no path to the destination exists in the routing table. If a network has only one outbound WAN connection to an ISP, for example, an administrator can configure a static default route to the provider.

Most of the dominant routing algorithms used today are dynamic routing algorithms, which adjust to changing network circumstances by analyzing incoming routing update messages. If the message indicates that a network change has occurred, the routing software recalculates the routes and sends out new routing update messages. These communications filter through the network and motivate routers to recalculate their algorithms and update their tables accordingly. This book focuses almost exclusively on the operations of dynamic routing algorithms.

Single-Path and Multipath

Some advanced routing protocols support multiple paths to the same destination. Unlike a single-path algorithm, a multipath algorithm allows traffic to be multiplexed over multiple equal-cost or unequal-cost lines. All the covered IP dynamic routing protocols can load balance across multiple equal-cost paths to deliver packets.

Only the Cisco proprietary routing protocols—IGRP and EIGRP—can load balance across multiple, unequal-cost paths.

The advantages of multipath are really seen on the routers that function at the highest hierarchical level (the backbone) of the routing topology. The principle benefit of hierarchical routing is that it can imitate the company's organizational structure and provide support for practical traffic patterns.

Intradomain and Interdomain

The ISO created a hierarchical framework that helps describe the router switching process. Using this framework, network devices that do not have the means of forwarding packets between subnetworks are called *end systems (ESs)*, whereas network devices with these capabilities are called *intermediate systems (ISs)*. ISs are then divided into two subsystems: ISs that can communicate within routing domains are known as *intradomain* ISs, and those that communicate both within and between routing domains are called *interdomain* ISs.

 Some routing algorithms work only within domains or autonomous systems, whereas others work within and between autonomous systems. Intradomain routing protocols are also known as interior gateway protocols (IGPs). These protocols are used to exchange routing information within a domain and are represented by protocols such as RIP and IGRP.

A routing domain (or *area*) is typically defined as a system that is part of an internetwork and under a common administrative authority controlled by a specific set of rules. Routing domains are also commonly known as autonomous systems. In addition, routing domains can be further divided into routing areas with certain routing protocols even though intradomain routing protocols are still used for switching both within and between areas.

Interdomain protocols are sometimes generically referred to as *Exterior Gateway Protocols (EGPs)*. This is a broad term that represents protocols used to exchange routing information between autonomous systems. Border Gateway Protocol (BGP) is a commonly used interdomain EGP. Because the very nature of these two algorithm types is different, it stands to reason that the best choice for an intradomain routing algorithm would not necessarily be an optimal interdomain routing algorithm.

Classful and Classless

Routing protocols can also be categorized as classful or classless protocols. RIPv1 and IGRP are considered *classful* protocols because they do not send subnet mask information with the network address in the routing update message. Classful addresses use a scheme in which the major network number is either Class A, B, C, D, or E. In a classful protocol environment, all the subnets of the major network address class must use the same subnet mask. For instance, if a router receives an update that has the same major network number (for example, 172.16.0.0) that is configured on the inbound interface, the router applies the subnet mask configured for the interface. However, if the routing update is for a major network different from the inbound interface, the default Class A, B, or C subnet mask is used and applied to the routing table.

 You must know how to determine the class of an IP address by looking at the decimal value of the first octet. This is discussed in more detail in Chapter 3, "Extending IP Addresses."

If routing information is swapped between networks using different major network numbers, the receiving routers will not know the subnet mask being implemented because the subnet information is not stored in the routing update packets. As a result, subnetwork information from all the major networks must be summarized to a classful network number using the default subnet mask before the update is added to the table. Only routers configured for the major networks to which the subnets belong can trade subnetted route information; the routers that belong to different major networks trade the classful summary routes. Classful routing protocols automatically generate a classful summary route at major network boundaries, as shown in Figure 2.2.

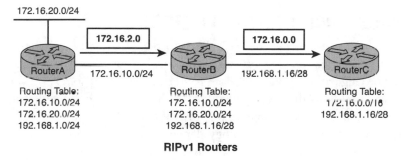

RIPv1 Routers

Figure 2.2 RIPv1 routers do not deliver subnet mask information.

As you can see, only routing devices within the same major network share subnetworked route information. Classful summary routes are automatically generated at Class A, B, and C network boundaries by routers using classful routing protocols such as RIPv1 and IGRP.

 Be sure that you allocate the same subnet mask to all interfaces on all of the routing devices in the major network in the classful routing area. This is crucial to ensure the proper advertisement of all subnetwork routes.

Classless routing protocols were originally developed to overcome the limitations inherent to classful protocols such as RIPv1. The classless routing protocols commonly used by Cisco router devices are OSPF, EIGRP, RIPv2, IS-IS, and BGP-4. *Classless* protocols have the advantage of including the subnet mask for each route to perform a more advanced lookup in the routing table. Classless routing protocols also implement a manual summarizing technique that allows summarization at any bit position in the network. Route summarization is the process of consolidating advertised addresses in a routing table. This technique leads to smaller routing tables, reduced update traffic, and lower processing and memory overhead. This really comes in handy because the routing tables of the Internet routers seem to expand almost exponentially with the growth of the Web. Route summarization is also referred to as route aggregation.

Classless routing protocols have the benefit of understanding the concept that different routes can have different masks in a major network. This technique of using different subnet masks is called *variable-length subnet masking (VLSM)*. VLSM enables network engineers to optimize the available address space and construct a hierarchical addressing scheme that fits the environment. This concept is explored in depth in Chapter 3.

Distance Vector and Link-state

The notion of a *vector* in networking relates to both the distance and the direction to a destination. *Distance vector* protocols, such as RIP, use the Bellman-Ford algorithm and call for each router to send all or some portion of the routing table to their directly connected neighbors. Distance vector routers know about, and send updates to, only these neighbors. Therefore, a router's picture of the network topology depends on the perspective of its neighbors. This process is also affectionately known as *routing by rumor*. The Cisco IOS supports several distance vector protocols, including RIPv1, RIPv2, and IGRP. As far as the OSI model is concerned, IGRP functions at the network layer with a protocol number of 9 in the IP header. RIP also functions primarily at the network layer, uses UDP port 520, and finds the best path to a remote network using hop count as a metric. IP RIP has a maximum hop count of 15, and IGRP has a maximum of 255. Tables 2.3 and 2.4 show the characteristics and comparisons of distance vector routing protocols, respectively.

Table 2.3 Attributes of Distance Vector Protocols

Attribute	Description
Protocols	RIPv1, RIPv2, IGRP, and EIGRP (hybrid).
Periodic updates	Updates sent at a set interval—for example, 30 seconds with RIPv1.
Full table updates	Pure distance vector sends the entire routing table.
Broadcast updates	Devices running distance vector routing protocols listen for broadcast updates to 255.255.255.255.
Triggered updates	Flash update is sent when change occurs apart from default update.
Split horizon	Prevents routing loops and preserves bandwidth by preventing a network from being forwarded on the same interface on which it was learned.
Count to infinity	Maximum hop count value varies with protocol.
Algorithm	Bellman-Ford and Diffusing Update Algorithm (DUAL). DUAL is a hybrid convergence algorithm used in Enhanced IGRP.

Table 2.4 Contrasting IP Distance Vector Routing Protocols

Attribute	RIPv1	RIPv2	IGRP	EIGRP
Count to infinity	X	X	X	
Split horizon	X	X	X	X
Hold-down timers	X	X	X	
Triggered updates with route poisoning	X	X	X	X
Equal path load balancing	X	X	X	X
Unequal path load balancing			X	X
Metric	Hops	Hops	Composite	Composite
Algorithm	Bellman-Ford	Bellman-Ford	Bellman-Ford	DUAL
Maximum hop count (default)	15	15	100	100
Support for VLSM		X		X

Link-state algorithms, such as OSPF, are also referred to as *shortest path first* algorithms. Link-state protocols generate routing updates only when a change occurs and flood the resulting routing information to all nodes in the internetwork in the form of a link-state advertisement (LSA). Each router sends only a portion of the routing table that describes the state of its own links. Link-state routers build a picture of the entire network in a topology table and typically require a hierarchical design (except EIGRP). Because they can converge more quickly, link-state algorithms are somewhat less prone to routing loops than distance vector algorithms. On the other hand, link-state algorithms typically require more CPU power and memory than distance vector protocols. Although link-state protocols are generally more scalable than distance vector protocols, they can also be more expensive to implement and support. EIGRP is actually a hybrid routing protocol that has some attributes of link-state operation. Other link-state protocols covered in this book are OSPF and IS-IS. Tables 2.5 and 2.6 show the characteristics and comparisons of link-state routing protocols, respectively.

Table 2.5   Attributes of Link-state Protocols

Attribute	Description
Protocols	OSPF, IS-IS
Periodic updates	Only when a change occurs. OSPF also sends a summary every 30 minutes
Broadcast updates	Devices running link-state routing protocols listen for broadcast updates to a multicast address
Database	IP routing table that holds all topological information
Convergence	Faster than distance vector
Resources	Higher CPU and memory resource usage
Algorithm	Dijkstra

Find out more about Dijkstra in Chapter 4, "Implementing OSPF in a Single Area" and Chapter 5, "Interconnecting OSPF Areas."

Table 2.6   Contrasting IP Link-state Routing Protocols

Attribute	EIGRP	IS-IS	OSPF
Requires hierarchy		X	X
Retains information of all possible routes	X	X	X
Manual route summarization	X	X	X
Automatic route summarization	X		
Announcements triggered by changes	X	X	X
Equal path load balancing	X	X	X

Table 2.6   Contrasting IP Link-state Routing Protocols *(continued)*

Attribute	EIGRP	IS-IS	OSPF
Unequal path load balancing	X		
Metric	Composite	Cost	Cost
Algorithm	DUAL	IS-IS	Dijkstra
Maximum hop count (default)	100	1024	Unlimited
Support for VLSM	X	X	X

Convergence

Routing algorithms must provide at least one single, loop-free route to every possible destination network. All the routing tables in the routing domain or area must eventually be synchronized and in agreement with a useable route to each destination network. This course of action is known simply as convergence. *Convergence* is defined as the rate and capability of a collection of router devices running a common routing protocol to agree on optimal routes. When a network event causes routes to either go down or become recently available, routers dispense routing update messages to permeate the network and stimulate the recalculation of optimal routes. The goal is to eventually cause all routers to agree on these optimal routes. Routing algorithms that suffer from slow convergence can create routing loops or even network outages. As with the other characteristics of routing protocols previously mentioned, convergence time varies depending on the efficiency of the routing algorithm being used, the size of the network, and several configurable timers.

A route that is going up and down in a short period of time is referred to as a *flapping* route. The cause of this phenomenon is typically the intermittent failure of network device interfaces and network media.

Convergence is affected by changes in the status of network links, and several ways are available to detect them. For example, if a device functioning at OSI Layer 1 or 2 (an Ethernet network interface) fails to receive a certain number of consecutive keepalive messages, the link is marked as down. In addition, if the Layer 3 protocol fails to receive a number of consecutive hello packets or regular update messages, the link is marked as down. Most routing algorithms use different sets of timers for loop prevention and network topology stabilization during times of recalculation of routing tables.

Understanding how individual protocols converge is critical to effective network engineering as well as success on the Cisco exam.

RIPv1 and RIPv2 Convergence Basics

The RIP version 1 routing protocol is one of the first interior gateway protocols used and has a long history in several routed network environments, including Unix and Microsoft. Besides the lack of scalability (it has a maximum hop count of 15), the other downside to RIPv1 is its rather high time to converge after a network event. Regardless, this routing protocol is the first example to help demonstrate the basic convergence process. Figure 2.3 shows how various routing protocols accomplish convergence.

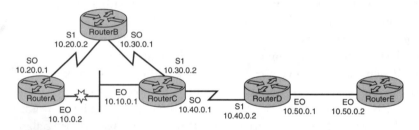

Figure 2.3 Sample network to demonstrate various methods of convergence.

In Figure 2.3, RouterC notices a failure on network 10.10.0.0 between itself and RouterA. RouterC generates an update, called a *flash update*, when an event occurs. This special update consists of the full routing table as well as a RIP poisoned route with a metric of 16 (unreachable). The flash update is sent to the neighbors of RouterC: RouterB and RouterD. Subsequently, RouterD generates a flash update and sends it to RouterE. Next, RouterC removes the entry for network 10.10.0.0 and all associated routes from its route table. Because this network is running RIPv2, RouterC sends a query to multicast address 224.0.0.9 to locate another path to network 10.10.0.0 (RIPv1 would use broadcast address 255.255.255.255). RouterD overrides the split horizon rule by sending a poison reverse to network 10.10.0.0. RouterB responds to RouterC with a higher hop count to RouterA, and RouterC adds it to the routing table because it purged it early in the process. Responses to queries are also complete routing tables.

During the state of hold-down, advertised routes that have the same or a poorer metric value than the one the router originally held for a network are summarily ignored.

Next, RouterD goes into a state of hold-down, and it eventually gets an advertisement from RouterC with the weaker metric it learned from RouterB. According to the rules of hold-down, RouterD ignores the weaker metric. Eventually, RouterD and RouterE come out of hold-down (180 seconds) and update their routing tables with the path to network 10.10.0.0 through RouterB. The time for RouterE to converge fully could be as much as 3 1/2 minutes.

You should run the **debug ip rip** and **debug Ip routing** commands in your test environment to thoroughly monitor and understand the process of RIPv1 and RIPv2 convergence.

IGRP Convergence Basics

Using Figure 2.3 as the prototypical design, IGRP offers greater scalability and flexibility but typically a longer convergence time than RIP. After RouterC notices the failed Ethernet 10.10.0.0 it shares with RouterA, it poisons the route with a flash update to RouterB and RouterD.

Distance vector networks, such as RIP and IGRP, have a maximum network diameter (or hop count) in that they were not designed to operate in environments with hundreds of links and routers. The maximum network diameter designates the distance that a datagram can travel (the maximum number of hops) before the destination is considered unreachable, forcing the datagram to be discarded. IP RIPv1 and RIPv2 both have a maximum hop count of 15, which means anything beyond 15 hops is unreachable. IGRP's default maximum hop count is 100, although it is technically configurable up to 255 hops.

Next, RouterD generates and sends its own flash update to RouterE as RouterC flushes the directly connected downed link from its routing table. Just as with RIP, an IGRP-loaded RouterC also eradicates all the routes related to that link from its routing table. Next, RouterC broadcasts all its interfaces, using logical network address 255.255.255.255, to its neighbors in search of another path to 10.10.0.0. RouterD generates a poison reverse, and RouterC then issues a flash update omitting the failed link that was purged.

Remember that the poison reverse update message is an override exception to the split horizon rule.

Next, RouterB responds to RouterC with a poorer metric value to network 10.10.0.0 than the one originally held by RouterC. RouterC adds it to its routing table and floods the network with a flash update containing the new information. RouterD ignores this update from RouterC because it is in hold-down and the metric is poorer than the one originally known for network 10.10.0.0. It continues to send poisoned updates to RouterC, however. After RouterD and RouterE reach the hold-down timer interval (the default is 280 seconds), they update their tables with the new route from RouterC. The time for RouterE to converge fully could be almost 7 minutes taking into consideration all the IGRP timers.

 You should run the **debug ip routing** and **debug ip igrp transactions** commands in your test environment to thoroughly monitor and understand the process of IGRP convergence.

EIGRP Convergence Basics

Continuing with the network infrastructure shown in Figure 2.3, EIGRP can provide very rapid convergence in contrast to RIP and IGRP. Although this process is covered in greater detail in later chapters, it is necessary to address some terminology before exploring the EIGRP convergence process. Table 2.7 introduces some key EIGRP concepts.

Table 2.7 Survey of EIGRP Terminology Relating to Convergence	
Concept	Description
Advertised distance	The cost between the next-hop router and destination
Feasible distance (FD)	The lowest-cost route to a destination
Feasible successor (FS)	A downstream neighbor with respect to the destination but not the least-cost path for forwarding decisions
Successor	A neighboring router used for forwarding packets along a least-cost path
Topology table	Structure that holds all destinations advertised by neighbor routers

In this routing convergence scenario, the EIGRP-loaded RouterC observes a link failure between itself and RouterA on network 10.10.0.0. RouterC then looks in its topology table to find a feasible successor but does not find a suitable alternative route and begins to look for a new route (the Active state) by sending a query to neighbor routers on EIGRP multicast address 224.0.0.10. RouterD replies that there is no other path to network 10.10.0.0, and RouterB replies with an alternative route containing an entry with a higher feasible distance.

NOTE

EIGRP uses a bidirectional update scheme in which all routers acknowledge each other's updates to ensure that the neighbor is aware of any changes to the topology.

Next, RouterC sends a new message out all interfaces with this updated information from its topology and routing tables. All of RouterC's neighbors acknowledge the update and send their updates back to RouterC to synchronize and converge the EIGRP network topology. The time for RouterE to converge fully is very rapid and efficient, occurring in as few as 2–3 seconds.

TIP

You should run the **debug ip routing, debug ip eigrp neighbors, debug ip eigrp summary**, and **debug ip eigrp notification** tools in your testing to observe and comprehend EIGRP convergence.

OSPF Convergence Basics

Although the OSPF routing protocol is covered extensively in later chapters, we should look at how OSPF converges compare to the previous distance vector protocol types. OSPF also has its own set of terms that set it apart from other algorithms, as shown in Table 2.8.

Table 2.8 Survey of OSPF Terminology Relating to Convergence	
Concept	Description
Dead interval	Amount of time an OSPF router will wait before announcing that its neighbor is down
Designated router (DR)	Router chosen to generate LSAs on the OSPF network
Hello packets	Sent periodically to ensure that the router interfaces are still alive
Link-state advertisement	Broadcast packets used to maintain path cost and neighbor information in OSPF routing tables

Referring back to Figure 2.3, the moment that OSPF RouterC notices the failed link to RouterA, it attempts to carry out an election for a designated router (DR) on interface E0. When it fails to reach the neighbor, it deletes the route to network 10.10.0.0 from the routing table. Next, RouterC floods an LSA to RouterB and RouterD. These routers, in turn, flood a copy of this LSA packet out every interface other than the one on which it was received. By default, OSPF routers wait 5 seconds after they receive an LSA before recalculating the shortest path first algorithm. Next, RouterC adds the new route through 10.20.0.0 to its routing table, and RouterB, RouterD, and RouterE update the metric in their routing tables as well.

After a 40-second dead interval, RouterA sends an LSA because it has not received a hello packet from RouterC. The DR on the network up to this point was RouterC, so RouterA becomes the DR and floods another advertisement on the network. The other routers wait 5 seconds and run the shortest path first algorithm so that, eventually, network 10.10.0.0 is reached via RouterB. RouterE eventually becomes converged based on the total detection time and the total LSA flooding time plus 5 seconds. The time for the entire network to converge, however, could take from 45 seconds to 1 minute based on the network design.

 You should run the **debug ip routing**, **debug ip ospf adj**, **debug ip ospf events**, and **debug ospf packet** commands so you can better understand the OSPF convergence process.

Anatomy of a Routing Table

To summarize the process of propagating routing tables, standard distance vector protocols broadcast the entire routing table to directly connected routing devices in regular update intervals as well as in flash updates. This makes the bandwidth overhead higher with traditional distance vector algorithms. Link-state protocols, on the other hand, use triggered multicast advertisement packets to notify other routers about changes in the topology. Only the specific topology changes are sent, not the entire routing table.

OSPF is a little different from the rest in that it also sends a required announcement every 30 minutes to maintain the synchronization of the topology database among all the routers in the area. The IP routing table, similar to Listing 2.3, can be displayed by simply typing show ip route at the Cisco IOS EXEC prompt.

 Remember that if the information in the routing table seems outdated, you can refresh the table by issuing the **clear ip route** command from the Cisco IOS **EXEC** prompt.

Listing 2.3   A Sample IP Routing Table Using RIPv2

```
RouterA#show ip route
Codes: C - connected, S - static, I - IGRP, R - RIP, M - mobile, B - BGP
       D - EIGRP, EX - EIGRP external, O - OSPF, IA - OSPF inter area
       N1 - OSPF NSSA external type 1, N2 - OSPF external type 2
       E1 - OSPF external type 1, E2 - OSPF external type 2, E - EGP
       I - IS-IS, L1 - IS-IS level-1, L2 - IS-IS level-2, * - candidate def
       U - per-user static route, o - ODR
       T - traffic engineered route

Gateway of last resort is not set

     172.16.0.0/16 is variably subnetted, 9 subnets, 2 masks
R       172.16.9.0/24 [120/1] via 172.16.3.2, 00:00:23, Serial0/1
R       172.16.8.0/24 [120/1] via 172.16.3.2, 00:00:23, Serial0/1
R       172.16.7.0/24 [120/1] via 172.16.3.2, 00:00:23, Serial0/1
C       172.16.6.0/24 is directly connected, Loopback2
C       172.16.5.0/24 is directly connected, Loopback1
C       172.16.4.0/24 is directly connected, Loopback0
C       172.16.3.0/30 is directly connected, Serial0/1
R       172.16.2.0/24 [120/1] via 172.16.3.2, 00:00:00, Serial0/1
C       172.16.1.0/24 is directly connected, Ethernet0/0
```

The routing table in Listing 2.3 stores all the information needed to properly perform the routing functions. It also contains a number of pieces of information, including the following:

➤ The manner in which the route was learned as indicated by one of the provided codes

➤ The destination network or subnet (and a host address on rare occasion)

➤ The AD number

➤ The metric as a hop count or aggregate cost

➤ The logical address of the next hop device

➤ The amount of time the information has been in the routing table since last updated

➤ The interface used to reach the destination network

In Listing 2.4, you can see that the manner in which the route was learned is through the RIP routing protocol (the letter R beginning the entry) and the destination network or subnet is 172.16.9.0/24. The administrative distance for RIP is 120 with a metric (hop count) of 1. The logical address of the next hop device is via 172.16.3.2, and the age of the entry since the last update is 23 seconds. Finally, the interface used to reach the destination is Serial0/0.

Listing 2.4   A Snippet from Listing 2.3

```
RouterA#show ip route
Codes: C_- connected, S - static, I - IGRP, R - RIP, M - mobile, B - BGP
       D - EIGRP, EX - EIGRP external, O - OSPF, IA - OSPF inter area
       N1 - OSPF  NSSA  external  type 1, N2 - OSPF  external  type 2
       E1 - OSPF external type 1, E2 - OSPF external type 2, E - EGP
       I - IS-IS, L1 - IS-IS level-1, L2 - IS-IS level-2, * - candidate def
       U - per-user static route, o - ODR
       T - traffic engineered route

Gateway of last resort is not set

       172.16.0.0/16 is variably subnetted,  9 subnets,  2 masks
R         172.16.9.0/24 [120/1] via 172.16.3.2,  00:00:23,  Serial0/1
```

The routing table always displays the optimal path to all network destinations. As mentioned, however, some routing algorithms support multiple equal-cost paths to a destination. Listing 2.5 shows the result of the show ip route command on an OSPF router.

Listing 2.5   A Sample IP Routing Table Using the OSPF Protocol

```
RouterB#show ip route
Codes:   C_- connected, S - static, I - IGRP, R - RIP, M - mobile, B - BGP
     D - EIGRP, EX - EIGRP external, O - OSPF, IA - OSPF inter area
     N1 - OSPF  NSSA  external  type 1, N2 - OSPF  external  type 2
     E1 - OSPF external type 1, E2 - OSPF external type 2, E - EGP
     I - IS-IS, L1 - IS-IS level-1, L2 - IS-IS level-2, * - candidate def
     U - per-user static route, o - ODR
     T - traffic engineered route
Gateway of last resort is 10.50.5.5 to network 0.0.0.0
     172.16.0.0/24 is subnetted,  2 subnets
C        172.16.10.0 is directly connected, Loopback100
C        172.16.11.0 is directly connected, Loopback101
O   E2       172.22.0.0/16 [110/20] via 10.30.3.3,  01:01:13,  Serial1/2
                           [110/20] via 10.40.4.4,  01:01:13,  Serial1/3
                           [110/20] via 10.50.5.5,  01:01:13,  Serial1/4
O   E2    192.168.4.0/24 [110/20] via 10.40.4.4, 01:01:13, Serial1/3
C   E2    192.168.5.0/24 [110/20] via 10.50.5.5, 01:01:13, Serial1/4
     10.0.0.0/24 is subnetted, 4 subnets
C        10.50.5.0 is directly connected,  Serial1/4
C        10.40.4.0 is directly connected,  Serial1/3
C        10.30.3.0 is directly connected,  Serial1/2
C        10.10.1.0 is directly connected,  Serial1/0
O   E2    192.168.3.0/24_[110/20] via 10.30.3.3, 01:01:15, Serial1/2
S*        0.0.0.0/0_[1/0] via 10.50.5.5
```

The previous sample routing table shows multiple equal-cost paths to network 172.22.0.0 via three separate serial interfaces in bold. Look at the following snippet:

```
O   E2       172.22.0.0/16 [110/20] via 10.30.3.3,  01:01:13,  Serial1/2
[110/20] via 10.40.4.4,  01:01:13,  Serial1/3
[110/20] via 10.50.5.5,  01:01:13,  Serial1/4
```

Although the order of entries displayed in the routing table seems arbitrary, the Cisco router actually has a purpose behind the order. The router calculates the order of entries in the routing table to optimize the lookups using the subnet mask length value.

Additional information about a particular route in the routing table can be extracted by specifying an individual network number using the **show ip route [*network*]** command.

Exam Prep Questions

Question 1

Which attribute of a Cisco-supported routing protocol makes it capable of rapidly learning about modifications to the network topology?

- ○ A. Hold-downs
- ○ B. Flash updates
- ○ C. Administrative distances
- ○ D. Classful routing

Answer B is correct. Flash updates send asynchronous responses to changes in the network topology. Answer A is incorrect because hold-downs are a state into which routers are placed to purge the network of bad information. Answer C is incorrect because AD numbers simply rate the trustworthiness of the source of routing data. Answer D is incorrect because classful routing pertains to the lack of prefix length information in the routing protocol header.

Question 2

Which of the following statements best describes the reason a distance vector protocol takes longer to converge than other routing protocols?

- ○ A. While in a state of hold-down, distance vector protocols do not accept updated route information concerning a particular route unless the update has a better metric value.
- ○ B. Distance vector protocols actually converge more quickly than most other routing protocols.
- ○ C. Distance vector protocols take longer to converge because they use only classful addressing schemes.
- ○ D. Convergence time is a router hardware issue and has little to do with the routing protocol algorithm being implemented.

Answer A is correct. Hold-down timers help prevent bad information from propagating through a distance vector area to prevent loops. This can add to the total convergence time because distance vector protocols do not route updates unless the update has a better metric value than the one previously stored. Answer B is incorrect because the opposite is true. Answer C is incorrect because some distance vector protocols, such as RIPv2 and IGRP, can use classless addressing. Answer D is incorrect because, although router hardware is a factor, the routing algorithm and other mechanisms are the key contributors to convergence.

Question 3

What is the default maximum hop count metric for the IGRP routing protocol?

○ A. 255

○ B. 150

○ C. 100

○ D. 15

Answer C is correct. Although the maximum hop count for IGRP is configurable to 255, the default maximum hop count is 100. Therefore, answer A is incorrect yet tricky. Answer B is incorrect, and answer D is the maximum hop count for the RIP routing protocol.

Question 4

Which of the following routing protocols implements broadcast packets to disseminate topology update information throughout an internetwork? (Choose two.)

❏ A. EIGRP

❏ B. IGRP

❏ C. OSPF

❏ D. RIPv1

Answers B and D are correct. IGRP and RIPv1 are distance vector protocols that use a Bellman-Ford algorithm and broadcast update packets to their neighbors. Answer A is incorrect because EIGRP implements a hybrid link-state method for more rapid convergence. Answer C is incorrect because it is a link-state routing protocol that typically uses multicasting to designated routers as opposed to broadcasting.

Question 5

Which of the following routing protocols support variable-length subnet masking for Layer 3 addressing schemes? (Choose two.)

❑ A. EIGRP

❑ B. IGRP

❑ C. RIPv1

❑ D. RIPv2

Answers A and D are correct. EIGRP and RIPv2 are both capable of specifying a different subnet mask for the same network number on different subnets. Answers B and C are incorrect because IGRP and RIPv1 are classful routing protocols and do not carry information about the prefix length.

Question 6

Which of the following are valid metrics used by routing protocols? (Choose all that apply.)

❑ A. Reliability

❑ B. Delay

❑ C. Bandwidth

❑ D. Trustworthiness

Answers A, B, and C are correct. The valid routing metrics that were covered in this chapter include path length, reliability, delay, bandwidth, load, and cost. Answer D is incorrect because, trustworthiness is the measurement designated by the administrative distance (AD), not a routing metric.

Question 7

Which one of the following statements best describes the difference between static and dynamic routing?

- ○ A. The dominant routing algorithms used today are static as opposed to dynamic because they better adapt to changing network conditions by analyzing incoming routing updates.

- ○ B. Dynamic routing is always preferred over static routing, especially in environments in which network traffic is relatively predictable and network design is fairly simple.

- ○ C. Dynamic routing is configured by a network administrator and cannot self-adjust to topology changes, whereas static routing adjusts to topology changes by analyzing incoming routing updates without human intervention.

- ○ D. Static routing is configured by a network administrator and cannot self-adjust to topology changes, whereas dynamic routing adjusts to topology changes by analyzing incoming routing updates without human intervention.

Answer D is correct. One of the advantages of static routing is the level of security and control that comes from manual administrative configuration. Answer A is incorrect because the dominant routing protocols in use are dynamic and because static protocols do not analyze incoming routing updates. Answer B is incorrect because this is actually a scenario in which static routes are often used rather than dynamic routing. Answer C is incorrect because it is the opposite of the correct answer.

Question 8

Which of the following protocols are classified as link-state because they exhibit link-state characteristics? (Choose all that apply.)

- ❑ A. IGRP
- ❑ B. OSPF
- ❑ C. IS-IS
- ❑ D. EIGRP

Answers B, C, and D are correct. OSPF, IS-IS, and EIGRP are all technically link-state routing protocols. OSPF uses the Dijkstra algorithm, IS-IS uses the IS-IS algorithm, and EIGRP uses the DUAL algorithm. Answer A is incorrect because IGRP uses a distance vector algorithm.

Question 9

To avert routing loops and preserve bandwidth when sending routing updates, which mechanism prevents a network entry from being forwarded out on the same interface on which it was learned?

- ○ A. Split horizon
- ○ B. Broadcast update
- ○ C. Triggered update
- ○ D. Count to infinity

Answer A is correct. Split horizon is a mechanism that keeps information from exiting a router interface that was learned on that same interface. It is helpful for preventing loops and conserving precious bandwidth. Answer B is incorrect because a broadcast update is a data packet advertised to all nodes on a network. Answer C is incorrect because a triggered update is a special packet generated when a network event occurs. Although a loop prevention mechanism, answer D is incorrect because count to infinity relates to maximum hop count.

Question 10

While observing the entries in the routing table, you notice that some of the entries seem a little suspect. Which command can you run to refresh the routing table?

- ○ A. **Router>clear ip route**
- ○ B. **Router#clear ip route**
- ○ C. **Router>clean ip route**
- ○ D. **Router#clean ip route**

Answer B is correct. This is a tricky question that is actually common to Cisco-type exams because it tests two elements of knowledge: the correct syntax and the proper command-mode prompt. If the information in the routing table seems outdated, you can refresh the table by issuing the `clear ip route` command from the Cisco IOS privileged EXEC prompt. Answer A is incorrect because it is the USER mode prompt. Answer C is the incorrect prompt and command. The `clean` command is not a valid Cisco IOS command. Answer D is incorrect because it is the correct prompt but the wrong command.

Need to Know More?

 Colton, Andrew. *Cisco IOS for IP Routing*. Tempe, AZ: Rocket Science Press, 2002.

 Halabi, Sam, et al. *Internet Routing Architectures, Second Edition.* Indianapolis, IN: Cisco Press, 2000.

 Visit the Cisco Systems IP Routing Web site at www.cisco.com/en/US/ tech/tk648/tk365/tech_protocol_family_home.html.

 Complete list of Requests for Comments at www.cis.ohio-state.edu/ htbin/rfc/rfc-index.html.

Extending IP Addresses

Terms you'll need to understand:

✓ CIDR

✓ IETF

✓ **ip helper**

✓ **ip subnet-zero**

✓ IPv6

✓ Prefix length

✓ Route summarization

✓ Supernetting

✓ Variable-length subnet masking (VLSM)

Techniques you'll need to master:

✓ Reviewing the IP subnetting process

✓ Understanding the formulas for calculating subnets and hosts

✓ Implementing CIDR addressing or supernetting

✓ Expressing various networks and subnets with their CIDR representations

✓ Using VLSM to extend an IP address scheme

✓ Deploying route summarization techniques

✓ Configuring the **ip helper** command for controlled broadcasts

The Internet Engineering Task Force (IETF) is a governing body that consists of more than 80 groups working together to develop Internet standards. The Internet Protocol (IP) is the primary Layer 3 protocol used to encapsulate data in the Internet suite. In addition to being routable, IP provides error coverage, fragmentation, and reassembly of datagrams for transmission over networks with different maximum data unit sizes. The IETF first defined a globally unique, 32-bit number for IP addressing in 1981. These globally unique logical addresses enable IP networks to communicate with each other from anywhere in the world.

Due to the global and somewhat random allocation of this finite pool of addresses (2^{32}), the Network Information Center (InterNIC) has run out of address space. In addition, approximately 5,000 routes were using the Internet in 1990. By the end of the millennium, more than 72,000 routes existed on the Internet, and today there are easily more than 100,000. The sizes of routing tables have been growing seemingly exponentially. This chapter focuses on some of the solutions and mechanisms the Cisco professional is expected to know to help decrease the routing table size as well as create a more hierarchical addressing scheme.

Review of TCP/IP Subnetting

Because the Cisco Certified Network Associate (CCNA) should already have in-depth knowledge of IP addressing, this section is merely a brief refresher course. An IP address is divided into three sections. The first part represents the network address, the second part represents the subnet address (if applicable), and the third part is the actual host address on the major network or subnetwork. Five IP address classes are defined by the IETF. You can determine which class any IP address is in by examining the first four bits of the IP address, or you can simply memorize the values in Table 3.1. Most of the public Class A, B, and C addresses have been assigned, although some ranges are still available for a price. Class D addresses are used by many vendors and organizations, including Cisco, for multicasting. Class E addresses are reserved for future use, so these should not be used for host addresses.

Table 3.1 The Decimal Equivalents of the First Octet of Each Address Class			
Address Class	**Starting Bit**	**First Octet Address As Decimal**	**Default Subnet Mask**
A	0	1–126	255.0.0.0
B	10	128–191	255.255.0.0
C	110	192–223	255.255.255.0

Table 3.1 The Decimal Equivalents of the First Octet of Each Address Class (continued)

Address Class	Starting Bit	First Octet Address As Decimal	Default Subnet Mask
D	1110	224–239	255.255.255.240
E	1111	240–255	Reserved

Notice that the number 127 is missing from this table. Addresses beginning with 01111111 (or decimal 127) in the first octet are reserved for loopback and internal testing on a local computer, as in the following command:

```
RouterA#ping 127.0.0.1
```

In addition, three IP network addresses are reserved for private internal networking as defined in RFC 1918. These addresses are 10.0.0.0–10.255. 255.255, 172.16.0.0–172.16.255.255, and 192.168.0.0–192.168.255.255. They are commonly used for internal IP networks, such as labs, classrooms, or home networks.

Private addresses are also used behind a network address translation service or a proxy server/router. You can safely use these addresses because routers on the Internet are configured to route these packets to the bit bucket (interface null0) and will never forward packets coming from these addresses. The main purpose of the private addressing scheme is to preserve the globally unique Internet address space by using it only where it is necessary. The immediate benefit of network address translation (NAT) is the temporary resolution of the IP address depletion problem for networks that need access to the Internet. Cisco IOS NAT eliminates issues and bureaucratic delays related to acquiring NIC-registered IP addresses by dynamically translating (mapping) hidden internal addresses to a range of Class C addresses, which are plentiful as compared to Class B addresses. A second benefit is that if a site already has registered IP addresses for its internal LAN clients, it can to hide them for security purposes. Thirdly, Cisco IOS NAT gives you total control over your internal addressing scheme, which is derived from the IANA-reserved address pool. In addition, you can use a non-routable solution on your internal LAN and hide it from the outside routable protocol solutions. A final advantage is that this mapping can take place within your organization without it being affected by address changes at the interface between your LAN and the Internet.

The NAT service functions on a router that links two networks together. One network is specified as *inside* and utilizes private (or obsolete) addresses that are translated into legal addresses before the packets are sent onto another network, which is designated as *outside*. The outside network is generally an Internet service provider (ISP) or other vendor. This translation works in parallel with the usual routing process, and NAT services can simply be enabled on the ISP customer's Internet access router as necessary. NAT can transport any TCP/UDP traffic that does not carry source and/or destination IP addresses in the application data stream. Individual interfaces are configured and tagged as to whether they are on the inside or the outside. Only the packets that arrive on the NAT tagged interface are subject to translation services. The following syntax shows the basic configuration of an interface:

```
Router(config-if)# ip nat { inside ¦ outside }
```

For more information on NAT, refer to the "Need to Know More?" section at the end of this chapter.

Another structural addressing mechanism is the process of dividing major networks into smaller components called *subnetworks*, or *subnets*, by "borrowing" from the remaining host bits to create a subnet field. As an administrator, you can segment a network into subnetworks for the purpose of developing a multi-level, hierarchical routing design.

For example, if a network is assigned a Class B address of 172.16.0.0, the administrator can subdivide this one Class B network into smaller subnets by borrowing from the 16 remaining bits of the host portion to create a subnet field. If the network administrator decides to borrow 8 bits for subnetting, the entire third octet of a Class B IP address provides the subnet number. In our example, an address of 172.16.1.1 refers to major network 172.16, subnet 1 (of a possible 256), and a host address 1 (of a possible 254). Remember that the first available host number (0) is the actual network and the last possible host address (255) is the mandatory broadcast address for the network.

Formula for Available Subnets

For years, textbooks and courses have taught the subnetting formula of $2^n - 2$ available subnets and $2^n - 2$ available hosts. After you subnet a network address, the first obtained subnet is called subnet zero and the last subnet obtained is called the all-ones subnet. Historically, it was recommended that subnet zero and the all-ones subnet be avoided for addressing. According to RFC 950, "It is useful to preserve and extend the interpretation of these special (network and broadcast) addresses in subnetted networks. This means the values of all zeros and all ones in the subnet field should not be assigned to actual (physical) subnets." Technically speaking, the all-ones subnet has always been legal according to RFC 1918, and subnet zero is enabled by default on all Cisco routers and specifically declared in the configuration in a Cisco IOS release of 12.0 and later. For example, the following is an example of a configuration on the Cisco 2620XM router:

```
Building configuration
Current configuration : 566 bytes
!
version 12.0
no service pad
service timestamps debug uptime
service timestamps log uptime
no service password-encryption
!
hostname RouterXM
!
!
ip subnet-zero
```

The number of bits that can be borrowed for the subnet address varies. For instance, the subnet mask that specifies 8 additional bits of subnetting for a Class B address is 255.255.255.0 instead of the default 255.255.0.0. In similar fashion, the subnet mask that specifies 16 bits of subnetting for a Class A address is 255.255.255.0.

NOTE   To determine the total number of hosts available for your network class and subnet mask, simply multiply the number of subnets by the number of available host nodes. Also, note that, although allowed, subnet masks with noncontiguous mask bits are not recommended.

Many complete subnet tables are available for Class A, Class B, and Class C networks on the Internet. These tables show all the possible subnet masks for each class and calculations of the number of networks, nodes, and total hosts for each subnet.

Classless Interdomain Routing

Classless Interdomain Routing (CIDR) is referenced in RFCs 1518, 1519, and 2050, which were developed for Internet service providers (ISPs) so they could aggregate contiguous blocks for efficient addressing schemes. With the classful system of allocating IP addresses, anyone who needed more than 254 host addresses was often forced into a public Class B address, providing more than 65,500 host addresses. Many companies and organizations wasted even more addresses by using only a fraction of their 16 million host Class A addresses. As a matter of fact, only a small percentage of the allocated Class A and Class B address space has been actually assigned to host computers on the Internet.

It became clear that by circumventing the class system, you could actually allocate just the amount of address space needed. In a large network, you want to avoid the situation where routers are maintaining a large number of routes in the routing tables and the IP address pool is used up. The process of route summarization, also known as *aggregation* or *supernetting*, allows you to represent a string of network numbers is a single summary address. By implementing CIDR, an ISP can embody a block of addresses with a single summarized route or supernet.

For example, if you needed around 1,000 addresses, four Class C networks of 250+ hosts each could be supernetted to represent 1000 hosts with a single summarized address. Figure 3.1 shows four Class C routers with a 24-bit mask summarized at the ISP router with a 22-bit mask:

```
RouterA: 192.168.128.0 (11000000.10101000.10000000.00000000)
Subnet mask: 255.255.255.0 (11111111.11111111.11111111.00000000)
RouterB: 192.168.129.0 (11000000.10101000.10000001.00000000)
Subnet mask: 255.255.255.0 (11111111.11111111.11111111.00000000)
RouterC: 192.168.130.0 (11000000.10101000.10000010.00000000)
Subnet mask: 255.255.255.0 (11111111.11111111.11111111.00000000)
RouterD: 192.168.131.0 (11000000.10101000.10000011.00000000)
Subnet mask: 255.255.255.0 (11111111.11111111.11111111.00000000)
```

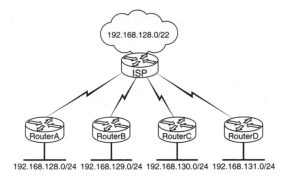

192.168.128.0/24 192.168.129.0/24 192.168.130.0/24 192.168.131.0/24

Figure 3.1 Major ISPs use CIDR addressing schemes to summarize multiple Class C addresses.

In this example, the subnet 192.168.128.0 includes all the addresses from 192.168.128.0 to 192.168.131.255; therefore, by supernetting the subnet address to be 22 bits instead of 24 bits, it will look like this:

```
Supernet: 192.168.128.0 (11000000.10101000.10000000.00000000)
Subnet mask: 255.255.252.0 (11111111.11111111.11111100.00000000)
Broadcast: 192.168.131.255 (11000000.10101000.10000011.11111111)
```

As seen in the binary version of the subnet mask, the network is represented by 22 bits and the host portion is made up of 10 bits, resulting in $2^{10} - 2 = 1022$. This offers the "around 1000" hosts that are needed in this scenario.

With the CIDR system, the subnet mask notation is expressed with a simplified shorthand. In the previous example, instead of writing the address and subnet mask as

```
192.168.128.0, subnet mask 255.255.252.0
```

the CIDR network address is simply written as

```
192.168.128.0/22
```

CIDR notation is also used with classful addresses and can be written as /8 for Class A, /16 for Class B, and /24 for Class C. With CIDR, the largest ISPs are given large portions of address space, typically with a subnet mask of /19 or smaller. The ISP's customers are then provided networks from the resulting large pool of addresses. As a conversion guide, Table 3.2 displays the CIDR conversions for standard Class B network and the various subnets masks. The table also includes the number of subnet bits, the subnet mask and CIDR mapping, the number of subnets, and the number of hosts per subnet.

Table 3.2 Class B-to-CIDR Conversion Table				
Number of Bits	Subnet Mask	CIDR	Number of Subnets	Number of Hosts per Subnet
2	255.255.192.0	/18	2	16,382
3	255.255.224.0	/19	6	8,190
4	255.255.240.0	/20	14	4,094
5	255.255.248.0	/21	30	2,046
6	255.255.252.0	/22	62	1,022
7	255.255.254.0	/23	126	510
8	255.255.255.0	/24	254	254
9	255.255.255.128	/25	510	126
10	255.255.255.192	/26	1,022	62
11	255.255.255.224	/27	2,046	30
12	255.255.255.240	/28	4,094	14
13	255.255.255.248	/29	8,190	6
14	255.255.255.252	/30	16,382	2

It is imperative that you know how to express the various networks and subnets with their CIDR implementations.

IP Version 6

CIDR will most likely serve the Internet well for the next few years. However, waiting in the wings for its moment in the sun is the Internet Protocol version 6 (IPv6) with a 128-bit address. With IPv6, every person could receive one billion unique IP addresses.

The goals of IPv6 are to enhance the existing IPv4 protocol by providing much more address space, easier configuration, and more security for the next-generation Internet. ISPs, corporate enterprises, and government organizations are looking to IPv6 for help in supporting cutting-edge applications, such as IP telephony, and new networking services, as well as emerging IP-aware devices. The demands for increased address space and plug-and-play networking capabilities are answered by the implementation of IPv6. According to Cisco, the threefold benefits of IPv6 are the expansion of network addressing to service future growth in IP devices and users, the auto-configuration capability of IP addressing, and integrated support for IP Security (IPSec) and mobile IP.

The extended IPv6 address goes from a 32-bit to a 128-bit addressing scheme with the colon (:) being used as a delimiter instead of the dot (.). IPv6 also introduces newer unicast and broadcasting methods, including *anycast*. Anycast is a communication link between a single sender and the single closest interface (in terms of routing distance) that is identified by the anycast address. An anycast address is assigned to multiple interfaces. To facilitate delivery, the routing system must know about the interfaces that have anycast addresses assigned to them and their distance as measured by routing metrics. A multicast address is implemented for one-to-many communications with transport to multiple interfaces. An anycast address, on the other hand, is used for one-to-one-of-many communication, with delivery to a single interface that represents a list of interfaces.

The IPv6 address is a hexadecimal-formatted, eight-part address, separated by colons. Because each part can equal a 16-bit number and is 8 parts long, the address length is 128 bits ($16 \times 8 = 128$). IPv6 addresses are n:n:n:n:n:n:n:n, which equals a 4-digit hexadecimal integer. Here is an example IPv6 address:

```
FE80:0000:0000:0001:0200:F6FF:Fe75:50CE
```

IPv6 addresses can also be further simplified by suppressing the leading zeros within each 16-bit part. Realize that each block must have at least a single digit. Look at how the previous address can be further simplified in the following example:

```
FE80:0:0:1:200:F6FF:Fe75:50CE
```

Because some IPv6 addresses end up having long sets of zeros, you can further simplify the depiction of an IPv6 address by compressing the address to "::" (also known as a double colon). For example, the IPv6 address FE80:0:0:0:3BB:FF:ED9A:4CB3 could be compressed to FE80::3BB:FF:ED9A:4CB3. The multicast address FF0A:0:0:0:0:0:0:4 could be further compressed to FF0A::4. To determine how many 0 bits are expressed by the double colon, simply count the number of parts in the compressed address, subtract this number from 8, and then multiply the result by 16. For example, in the address FF0A::4, there are two parts (FF0A and 4.) The number of bits expressed by the double colon is then $(8-2)\times16=96$. You can use zero compression only one time in a particular IPv6 address.

An IP version 4 interface normally has only one IPv4 address assigned to it (excluding subinterface configuration). IPv6 nodes, on the other hand, typically have multiple assigned IPv6 addresses (multihomed). These include the link-local address, additional unicast addresses, and the loopback address (::1). In addition, every IPv6 interface is listening for traffic on several standard multicast addresses as well. A link-local address enables a node to communicate with other nodes on the link and can be used to configure the node even further.

The link-local address is typically autoconfigured from a combination of the interface identifier and the link-local prefix FE80::0. The autoconfiguration feature enables nodes to connect to a network and automatically generate IPv6 addresses without needing manual configuration or a DHCP server. IPv6-enabled routers can advertise prefixes in router advertisement messages, as well as function as default routers for the link. Router advertisements are transmitted occasionally and in response to router solicitations sent by hosts at system startup. A node automatically configures an IPv6 address by simply appending its 64-bit interface ID to the 64-bit prefixes (see next paragraph) included in the router advertisements. These subsequent 128-bit IPv6 addresses generated by the node are then tested for duplicates to make sure that they are unique on the network. Hosts send router solicitation packets at system startup so that they can immediately autoconfigure without having to wait for the next scheduled router advertisement.

IPv6 prefixes for identifying subnets and routes are expressed in the same way as CIDR notation for IPv4. An IPv6 prefix is expressed in the address/prefix-length notation. For example, 24EB:D3::/48 is a route prefix and 24EB:D3:0:2F3B::/64 is a subnet prefix. The 64-bit prefix is used for discrete subnets and all subnets have a 64-bit prefix. Any prefix that is less than 64 bits is a summarized route or address range portion of the IPv6 address.

Using static routes in IPv6 is similar to configuring static routes for IPv4, with a few differences. The ipv6 route command is used to configure IPv6 static routes. Some of the IPv4 keywords, such as `tag` and `permanent`, are not yet supported. The syntax for a static Ipv6 command is

```
Router(config)# ipv6 route ipv6-prefix/prefix-length {ipv6-address |
interface-type interface-number [ipv6-address]} [administrative-distance]
```

For example, the following is a sample static route that is being configured to a specified next hop address, with no interface:

```
Router(config)# ipv6 route 2001:0BD6::/422022:808B:F0FE::1
```

For detailed information on Cisco's efforts with IPv6, go to `www.cisco.com/ipv6`. The specifications for IPv6 can be found in RFC 1519 (`www.faqs.org/rfcs/rfc1519.html`). For the current list of permanently assigned IPv6 multicast addresses, visit `www.iana.org/assignments/ipv6-multicast-addresses`.

Using VLSM to Extend the IP Addresses Scheme

As IP subnets have grown, administrators have looked for ways to use their address space more efficiently and flexibly. One of the resulting techniques is called *variable-length subnet masking (VLSM)*. VLSM is a method of designating a different subnet mask for the same network number on different subnets. Thus, a network administrator can use a long mask on networks with few hosts and a shorter mask on subnets with many hosts. If VLSM is not supported on your routers, your organization is stuck with the prospect of using a single subnet mask for an entire growing Class A, B, or C network. VLSM facilitates a hierarchical design that is more representative of an organization's logical network topology. Cisco supports VLSM with RIP version2, Open Shortest Path First (OSPF), Integrated Intermediate System-to-Intermediate System (IS-IS), Enhanced Interior Gateway Routing Protocol (EIGRP), and Border Gateway Protocol version 4 (BGP4), as well as with static routing. RIP version 1 and IGRP do not allow for VLSM because they are classful protocols, which do not transport subnet mask information in their updates. In Figure 3.2, RouterA has three subnets with two masks (/24 and /30).

Obviously, you want to use the available IP address space as efficiently as possible. A VLSM scheme is a much better method of allocating existing address space. In other words, you want to use the fewest number of subnet bits as necessary and the fewest number of host bits as necessary. A simple example of VLSM can be demonstrated through a connection between two Cisco routers over a wide area network (WAN) serial link. If you used a network address such as 172.16.2.0 with an 8-bit subnetting mask (the entire third octet), you would be wasting 252 addresses for a WAN point-to-point link that needs only two addresses. Because you need only two host addresses, you could use the following formula:

```
2ⁿ - 2 = 2 evaluates to:
2ⁿ = 4 which results in
n = 2
```

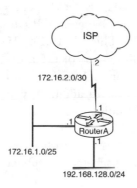

Figure 3.2 A router with three subnets using different masks.

You need only 2 bits to represent two host addresses. Therefore, the subnet mask used for only two hosts is 255.255.255.252, or /30. If your network was originally using subnet 172.16.2.0 /24, you could reassign the following to your first two WAN interfaces using VLSM, as shown in Table 3.3 and Figure 3.3.

Table 3.3 Using VLSM to Apply a 30-bit Mask to Subnet 172.16.2.0 for More Efficient WAN Link Addressing		
Description	**Decimal**	**Subnetwork Binary**
Subnetwork address	172.16.2.0 /30	.00000010.00000000
First WAN interface	172.16.2.1 /30	.00000010.00000001
Second WAN interface	172.16.2.2 /30	.00000010.00000010
Broadcast address	172.16.2.3 /30	.00000010.00000011

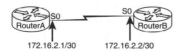

Figure 3.3   Using VLSM for WAN point-to-point serial links for more efficient address allocation.

You could then use the remaining subnetwork addresses for additional WAN point-to-point serial links as necessary. Here's an example:

```
172.16.2.4 /30
172.16.2.8 /30
172.16.2.12 /30
...
172.16.2.252 /30
```

Addresses need to be planned and assigned carefully because VLSM can add a higher level of complexity to your network administration. To really understand this process of subnetting a previously subnetted address, let's look at a practical scenario. Assume that you have been tasked by your CIO to redesign your existing Class B subnet of 172.16.1.0 /25. This 172.16.1.0 /25 scheme already gives your organization more than 500 subnets of 126 hosts each. However, you have been mandated to divide this one subnetwork into three departmental broadcast domains of 30 hosts each. In addition, you need to use this same address space for several WAN point-to-point serial links. Currently, your Class B subnet address of 172.16.1.0 with a subnet mask of 255.255.255.128 leaves you 7 bits for host addresses, or 126 hosts ($2^7 - 2 = 126$). Table 3.4 shows your present addressing scheme for subnet 172.16.1.0 /25.

Table 3.4 The Addressing Scheme for Subnet 172.16.1.0 /25		
Description	**Decimal**	**Subnetwork Binary**
Subnetwork address	172.16.1.0	.00000001.00000000
First available host	172.16.1.1	.00000001.00000001
Second available host	172.16.1.2	.00000001.00000010
Last available host	172.16.1.126	.00000001.01111110
Broadcast address	172.16.1.127	.00000001.01111111

To subnet 172.16.1.0 /25 down to a VLSM to gain four subnets, you need to first write down the original subnetwork in its binary representation, like so:

```
10101100.00010000.00000001.00000000
```

Next, identify the bits that make up the original subnet mask with italics:

```
10101100.00010000.00000001.00000000
```

Because you need to borrow some bits from the remaining 7 bits for a VLSM mask, calculate the number you need:

```
2ⁿ = 4 results in
n = 2
```

So, you need two more bits for your VLSM mask, like so:

```
1 0 1 0 1 1 0 0.0 0 0 1 0 0 0 0.0 0 0 0 0 0 0 1.0 0 0 0 0 0 0 0
_____network_____|_____subnet_____|VSM|__hosts  |
```

Now that you have 5 bits remaining for the hosts, you can determine the number of available host addresses:

```
n is the remaining subnet bits, therefore:
n = 5
2n - 2 = 30 hosts per subnetwork
```

Therefore, you need the last 5 of the 7 original host bits to generate these 30 hosts per subnet. This combination works well for your needs.

Your new VLSM mask is 255.255.255.224, or /27. This is now the subnet mask for all the hosts in your three departments. As shown in Table 3.5, of the original 7 hosts bits, the first 2 bits are used to give you four new subnetworks and the remaining 5 bits are used for the 30 hosts on each subnet.

Table 3.5 The Binary Representation of Your Four New VLSM Subnets				
	Network	**Subnet**	**VLSM**	**Host**
First subnet 172.16.1.0/27	10101100.00010000	.00000001.0	**00**	00000
Second subnet 172.16.1.32/27	10101100.00010000	.00000001.0	**01**	00000
Third subnet 172.16.1.64/27	10101100.00010000	.00000001.0	**10**	00000
Fourth subnet 172.16.1.96/27	10101100.00010000	.00000001.0	**11**	00000

To reiterate, your four new VLSM subnets are

➤ 172.16.1.0 /27 (the all-zeros subnet)

➤ 172.16.1.32 /27

➤ 172.16.1.64 /27

➤ 172.16.1.96 /27 (this subnet can be used for WAN links)

Table 3.6 shows your new addressing scheme for the first subnet (subnet zero) of 172.16.1.0 /27.

Table 3.6 The Addressing Scheme for the First of Your Four New VLSM Subnets (Subnet Zero)

Description	Decimal	Subnetwork Binary
Subnetwork address	172.16.1.0	.00000001.00000000
First available host	172.16.1.1	.00000001.00000001
Second available host	172.16.1.2	.00000001.00000010
Last available host	172.16.1.30	.00000001.00011110
Broadcast address	172.16.1.31	.00000001.00011111

Table 3.7 shows the second subnet of 172.16.1.32 /27.

Table 3.7 The Addressing Scheme for the Second of Your Four New VLSM Subnets

Description	Decimal	Subnetwork Binary
Subnetwork address	172.16.1.32	.00000001.00100000
First available host	172.16.1.33	.00000001.00100001
Second available host	172.16.1.34	.00000001.00100010
Last available host	172.16.1.62	.00000001.00111110
Broadcast address	172.16.1.63	.00000001.00111111

Table 3.8 shows the third subnet of 172.16.1.64 /27.

Table 3.8 The Addressing Scheme for the Third of Your Four New VLSM Subnets

Description	Decimal	Subnetwork Binary
Subnetwork address	172.16.1.64	.00000001.01000000
First available host	172.16.1.65	.00000001.01000001
Second available host	172.16.1.66	.00000001.01000010
Last available host	172.16.1.94	.00000001.01011110
Broadcast address	172.16.1.95	.00000001.01011111

Table 3.9 shows the fourth subnet (all ones) of 172.16.1.96 /27, which is used for further VLSM subnetting WAN serial links.

Table 3.9 The Addressing Scheme for the Last of Your Four New VLSM Subnets

Description	Decimal	Subnetwork Binary
Subnetwork address	172.16.1.96	.00000001.01100000
First available host	172.16.1.97	.00000001.01100001
Second available host	172.16.1.98	.00000001.01100010

Table 3.9   The Addressing Scheme for the Last of Your Four New VLSM Subnets (continued)

Description	Decimal	Subnetwork Binary
Last available host	172.16.1.126	.00000001.**01**111110
Broadcast address	172.16.1.127	.00000001.**01**111111

With that task accomplished, you now need to accommodate for your WAN serial links. However, it is critical that you understand that you can only further subnet a subnetwork that is presently unused. Therefore, you must use the fourth VLSM subnet, 172.16.1.96 /27, to create your WAN addressing scheme. As mentioned, these subnetworks need only two hosts each. Let's use the formula with two hosts:

```
2ⁿ -2 = 2 evaluates to:
2ⁿ = 4 which results in:
n = 2
```

Table 3.10 shows the efficient WAN link address assignments you can use now because of the flexibility of variable-length subnet masking.

Table 3.10   An Addressing Scheme for the WAN Serial Connections Using VLSM Subnets

Description	Decimal	Subnetwork Binary
WAN subnet 1	172.16.1.96 /30	.00000001.011*000*00
First WAN link on subnet 1	172.16.1.97 /30	.00000001.011*000*01
Second WAN link on subnet 1	172.16.1.98 /30	.00000001.011*000*10
Broadcast address on subnet 1	172.16.1.99 /30	.00000001.011*000*11
WAN subnet 2	172.16.1.100 /30	.00000001.011*001*00
First WAN link on subnet 2	172.16.1.101 /30	.00000001.011*001*01
Second WAN link on subnet 2	172.16.1.102 /30	.00000001.011*001*10
Broadcast address on subnet 2	172.16.1.103 /30	.00000001.011*001*11

Because you needed only 2 bits to represent two host addresses, the subnet mask for your WAN links is 255.255.255.252, or /30. Your network was originally using subnet 172.16.1.0 /25 for a single subnetwork of 126 hosts. You have now used VLSM to more efficiently reallocate your address pool with several contiguous ($2^3 = 8$) IP addresses left over for WAN connections. The flexibility of VLSM should be obvious by now, and you will be leveraging these techniques throughout the remaining chapters of this book. You can now start reassigning the new IP addresses and masks to your router interfaces, as shown in Listing 3.1. Remember that you must be running a routing protocol that supports VLSM and classless addresses, such as EIGRP or OSPF to name a few.

Listing 3.1   A Sample Router Configuration Using VLSM

```
RouterA(config)# interface ethernet 0/0
RouterA(config-if)# ip address 172.16.1.1 255.255.255.224
RouterA(config)# interface ethernet 0/1
RouterA(config-if)# ip address 172.16.1.33 255.255.255.224
RouterA(config)# interface ethernet 0/2
RouterA(config-if)# ip address 172.16.1.65 255.255.255.224
RouterA(config)# interface serial 0/0
RouterA(config-if)# ip address 172.16.1.97 255.255.255.252
RouterA(config)# interface serial 0/1
RouterA(config-if)# ip address 172.16.1.101 255.255.255.252
```

Route Summarization

IP *route summarization* is a mechanism used to design networks that are more flexible and perform better. Although some routing protocols summarize only at the boundaries of major network numbers, others support route summarization (aggregation) at any bit boundary. Variable-length subnet masks enable routing protocols to summarize on bit boundaries. This aggregation process can work hand-in-hand with VLSM to build hierarchically structured networked environments. The following are some of the many advantages to summarizing addresses into a hierarchy:

➤ Reduces the amount of information stored in routing tables

➤ Allocates an existing pool of addresses more economically

➤ Makes the routing process more efficient

➤ Lessens the load on router processor and memory resources

➤ Lowers the network convergence time

➤ Isolates topology changes

➤ Facilitates monitoring, reporting, and troubleshooting

If no method existed for route summarization, every router would need to have a route to every subnet in the network environment. With summarization, routers can condense some groups of routes down to a single link advertisement, resulting in a reduction in both the resource load on the router and the overall network complexity. As the size of the network gets bigger, the more important the function of route summarization becomes.

The reduction in route propagation and routing information overhead can be significant. Take our previous sample network of 172.16.1.0 /25. Without summarization, each router in a large enterprise network of 500 subnets ($2^9 = 512$ subnets with $2^7 - 2 = 126$ hosts each) would need to know about 500 routes. With route summarization, you can quickly reduce the size of the routing tables by almost 75%. If the 172.16.0.0 Class B network used 7 bits of subnet address space (/23) instead of 9 bits (/25), the original 500 subnets could be broken up into four major subnetworks of 125. Each router would still need to know all the routes for each subnet in its network number. However, that number would be reduced to 125 routers plus one additional route for each of the other three major networks, for a total of only 128 routes. This process of collapsing many subnet routes into a single network route is a fundamental goal of route summarization. This can be seen using the 172.16.0.0 /25 subnet in Figure 3.4.

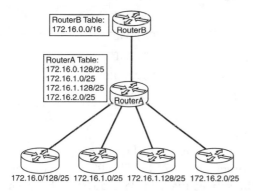

Figure 3.4   Routers share the first 16 high-order bits and summarize on network 172.16.0.0 /16.

In Figure 3.4, RouterA advertises that it can route from the 172.16.0.0 /25 subnets to the 172.16.0.0 /16 network via RouterB. Instead of sending four routing update entries, RouterA can summarize these addresses into just one network number. Another advantage is that if one of the interfaces on a downstream router is flapping, the summarized route 172.16.0.0 /16 does not change and RouterB is unaffected.

Here is one more common summarization scenario with EIGRP or OSPF as a routing protocol. Suppose an organization is using the familiar 172.16.0.0 /24 addressing scheme with 8 bits for subnetting. You must first determine whether a range of addresses can even be summarized. Table 3.11 shows a portion of the third octet of subnet addresses that can be summarized.

Table 3.11 IP Subnet Address Range of the Third Octet for Summarizing 172.16.0.0 /24		
Subnet	**Mask**	**Subnetwork Binary**
172.16.1.0	255.255.255.0 (/24)	.0000**0001**
172.16.2.0	255.255.255.0 (/24)	.0000**0010**

Table 3.11 IP Subnet Address Range of the Third Octet for Summarizing 172.16.0.0 /24 (continued)

Subnet	Mask	Subnetwork Binary
172.16.3.0	255.255.255.0 (/24)	.00000**011**
172.16.4.0	255.255.255.0 (/24)	.00000**100**
172.16.5.0	255.255.255.0 (/24)	.00000**101**
172.16.6.0	255.255.255.0 (/24)	.00000**110**
172.16.7.0	255.255.255.0 (/24)	.00000**111**
172.16.8.0	255.255.255.0 (/24)	.00001**000**
172.16.9.0	255.255.255.0 (/24)	.00001**001**
172.16.10.0	255.255.255.0 (/24)	.00001**010**
172.16.11.0	255.255.255.0 (/24)	.00001**011**
172.16.12.0	255.255.255.0 (/24)	.00001**100**
172.16.13.0	255.255.255.0 (/24)	.00001**101**
172.16.14.0	255.255.255.0 (/24)	.00001**110**
172.16.15.0	255.255.255.0 (/24)	.00001111

Look at the binary representation of the subnets 1–16. A common thread appears: The first four high-order bits are the same. The binary representation of those four common high-order bits is 240 (11110000), so you can summarize all these subnets to the subnet mask of 255.255.255.240 in an OSPF or EIGRP network. An EIGRP-loaded router, for example, would need to send only 1 update for the range of 172.16.0.0–172.16.15.0 as opposed to 16 separate updates, as shown in Listing 3.2.

Listing 3.2 A Sample EIGRP Summarization Configuration

```
RouterA(config)# router eigrp 10
RouterA(config-router)# no auto-summary
RouterA(config)# interface serial 0/1
RouterA(config-if)# ip summary-address eigrp 10 172.16.1.0 255.255.255.240
```

When a router is choosing an optimal route, the longest prefix is used to route the packet. A prefix is the slash symbol followed by a number that represents the total number of bits used for the network and subnet portion of the IP address, for example, /25.

With EIGRP, you need to include a **no auto-summary** entry because EIGRP automatically summarizes IP subnetworks. OSPF does not need this command because it does not auto-summarize.

To properly implement summarization in a network, the multiple addresses must share similar high-order bits. In Figure 3.4, the routers all share the first 16 high-order bits and summarize on 172.16.0.0 /16, and in Table 3.11, the routers all share the first 28 high-order bits and summarize on 172.16.1.0 /28. In addition, the routing protocol being used must transport the subnet mask information (called the *prefix length*) as well as a 32-bit address.

Configuring IP Helper to Manage Broadcasts

The `ip helper` mechanism is an excellent way to forward certain broadcast traffic for manageability and inter-WAN communication. The interface configuration command ip helper-address is utilized to set up an interface to expect and receive broadcasts. By default, Cisco routers do not forward broadcasts to prevent broadcast storms that can easily disrupt a network. This is especially common in large, flat network designs indicative of legacy network environments. One of the most common situations is when a Dynamic Host Configuration Protocol (DHCP) client attempts to get configuration information from a DHCP server on the other side of a router in another broadcast domain. Unless a DHCP service or relay agent is available on the client's network segment, the client does not receive its configuration because broadcast packets are dropped at the router interface, as shown in Figure 3.5.

The `ip helper-address` command can be used on RouterA and parameterized with either the IP address of the DHCP (BOOTP) server or a direct broadcast address for the segment on which the server resides. The `ip helper` command works by changing a broadcast message to a unicast message. It is common to have multiple DHCP servers on your network, as in Figure 3.5, for fault tolerance. You can configure multiple entries of the command with different IP addresses as shown in Listing 3.3.

Listing 3.3 The ip helper Settings on RouterA

```
RouterA(config)# int e0/0
RouterA(config-if)# ip helper-address 172.16.1.200
RouterA(config-if)# ip helper-address 172.16.1.201
```

DHCP (BOOTP) is not the only service upon which the `ip helper` command operates. After you enable the `ip helper` command on RouterA, it automatically forwards on eight UDP ports by default. Table 3.12 displays the services and standard port settings.

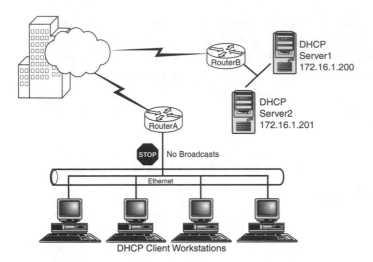

Figure 3.5 The default behavior of Cisco routers is not to forward broadcasts.

Table 3.12 The Default Services and Ports Automatically Enabled by ip helper	
IP Service	**UDP Port**
Time	37
TACACS	49
DNS	53
BOOTP server	67
BOOTP client	68
TFTP	69
NetBIOS name service	137
NetBIOS datagram service	138

If you want to designate a particular broadcast packet to forward on your router globally, you can use the `ip forward-protocol` command. For example, to forward only the time service, use the following command:

```
ip forward-protocol udp 37
```

To shut down an automatically forwarded service, such as Trivial File Transfer Protocol (TFTP), use the following command:

```
no ip forward-protocol udp 69
```

Remember that the BOOTP and DHCP services both use port 68 even though it is always called the BOOTP port.

Exam Prep Questions

Question 1

One of the advantages of variable-length subnet masking is the capability to structure your network in hierarchical fashion. Which of the following represents the benefits of hierarchical addressing? (Choose two.)

- ❑ A. Reducing the amount of information stored in routing tables
- ❑ B. Enabling the use of addressing with discontiguous networks
- ❑ C. Allocating IP addresses more efficiently
- ❑ D. Allowing for classful routing algorithms

Answers A and C are correct. Hierarchical addressing schemes make routing tables smaller and allocate addresses more efficiently. Answer B is incorrect because discontiguous networks are problematic and not an advantage of a hierarchical structure. Answer D is incorrect because, although related, classful algorithms are not a direct benefit of hierarchical addressing schemes.

Question 2

Which mechanism would you use to reduce the number of routing table updates generated from implementing a large number of Class C addresses?

- ○ A. VLSM
- ○ B. The **ip helper** command
- ○ C. CIDR
- ○ D. OSPF

Answer C is correct. CIDR reduces the number of updates by allocating a contiguous block of addresses. Answer A is incorrect because VLSM enables you to further subnet a subnetwork. Answer B is incorrect because the `ip helper` command allows you to break the router rule that prevents the forwarding of broadcast packets. Answer D is incorrect because OSPF is a link state routing protocol and not necessarily a mechanism for classless IP addressing.

Question 3

CIDR is predominantly used in which of the following scenarios?

○ A. OSPF only

○ B. EIGRP only

○ C. Route summarization

○ D. Classless routing

Answer D is correct. CIDR stands for Classless Interdomain Routing and is predominately used in classless routing scenarios. Answers A and B are incorrect because CIDR can be used with OSPF and EIGRP, among others. Answer C is incorrect because classful protocols also summarize at major network boundaries by default.

Question 4

You are presented with an IP address with a prefix of /22. How many more subnets can you add to your design if you further subnet with a VLSM mask of /27?

○ A. 256

○ B. 64

○ C. 32

○ D. 16

Answer C is correct. 27 bits – 22 bits = 5 bits. 2^5 = 32 subnetworks gained. Answer A is incorrect because there would need to be 8 bits separating the original subnet bit and the VLSM bit to generate 256 subnets. Answer B is incorrect because there would need to be 6 bits separating the original subnet bit and the VLSM bit to generate 64 subnets. Answer D is incorrect because there would need to be 4 bits separating the original subnet bit and the VLSM bit to generate 16 subnets as opposed to the 5 bits that generate 32 subnets.

Question 5

Which one of the following is not an address reserved for private networking according to RFC 1918?

- ○ A. 10.10.255.255
- ○ B. 172.16.100.0
- ○ C. 192.168.16.100
- ○ D. 196.128.10.254

Answer D is correct. 196.128.10.254 is not within a reserved private address range. Answer A is incorrect because it is within the private Class A range of 10.0.0.0–10.255.255.255. Answer B is incorrect because it is within the private Class B range of 172.16.0.0–172.31.255.255. Answer C is incorrect because it is within the private Class C range of 192.168.0.0–192.168.255.255.

Question 6

Which formula should be used to determine the number of subnets needed on a Cisco router running Cisco IOS release 12.0 or higher?

- ○ A. $n-2$
- ○ B. 2^n-2
- ○ C. 2^n
- ○ D. $2^n/2$

Answer C is correct. The standard formula for subnets now is 2^n subnets available. The all-ones subnet has always been legal according to the RFC, and subnet zero is enabled by default on all Cisco routers with a Cisco IOS release of 12.0 and higher. Answer A is incorrect because the math is simply wrong. Answer B is incorrect because that is the formula for calculating the available hosts. Answer D is incorrect because the math is wrong.

Question 7

> Which of the following are valid terms relating to the general concept of grouping contiguous classless addresses? (Choose all that apply.)
>
> ❑ A. Supernetting
> ❑ B. Subnetting
> ❑ C. Aggregation
> ❑ D. Summarization

Answers A, C, and D are correct. These are all terms related to CIDR and the grouping of classless addresses. Answer B is incorrect because subnetting is the specific process of arbitrarily dividing up networks to provide a more hierarchical routing design.

Question 8

> Which one of the following prefixes is most often implemented on WAN point-to-point serial links with VLSM?
>
> ◯ A. /16
> ◯ B. /24
> ◯ C. /28
> ◯ D. /30

Answer D is correct. This particular VLSM mask provides for only two hosts, which is perfect for WAN connections. Answer A is incorrect because it is a standard Class B mask of 16 bits of CIDR subnetting. Answer B is incorrect because it is a standard Class C mask of 24 bits of CIDR subnetting. Answer C is incorrect because, although it provides a good subnet for breaking up larger subnets, /30 is the most efficient choice for WAN links.

Question 9

> Which of the following protocols supports VLSM in a Cisco routing environment? (Choose all that apply.)
>
> ❑ A. Static routing
> ❑ B. OSPF
> ❑ C. IS-IS
> ❑ D. EIGRP
> ❑ E. RIPv2

Answers A, B, C, D, and E are correct. Static routing, OSPF, IS-IS, EIGRP, and RIP version 2 all support VLSM. BGP4 also supports VLSM. RIPv1 and IGRP do not support VLSM.

Question 10

Which of the following statements relating to VLSM and route summarization are true? (Choose all that apply.)

❑ A. OSPF must have the **no auto-summary** entry configured because OSPF automatically summarizes IP networks.

❑ B. You can only further subnet a subnetwork that is currently unused.

❑ C. The routing protocol being used must transport the prefix length as well as use a 32-bit address.

❑ D. To properly implement summarization in a network, the multiple addresses must share similar low-order bits.

Answers B and C are correct. You cannot further subnet a network using VLSM if the address space is already in use. Also, VLSM and route summarization demand a 32-bit addressing routing protocol that carries the prefix length (subnet mask information). Answer A is incorrect because EIGRP, not OSPF, must have the no auto-summary entry configured. Answer D is incorrect because the multiple addresses must share similar high-order bits.

Need to Know More?

Comer, Douglas E. *Internetworking with TCP/IP Vol. I: Principles, Protocols, and Architecture, Third Edition.* Indianapolis, IN: Prentice Hall PTR, 1995. ISBN 0132169878.

Doyle, Jeff. *Routing TCP/IP Volume I (CCIE Professional Development).* Indianapolis, IN: Cisco Press, 1998. ISBN 1578700418.

Doyle, Jeff. *Routing TCP/IP, Volume II (CCIE Professional Development).* Indianapolis, IN: Cisco Press, 2001. ISBN 1578700892.

Cisco article on basic NAT services: www.cisco.com/warp/public/cc/pd/iosw/ioft/ionetn/prodlit/1195_pp.htm.

RFC 950, RFC 1918. For a complete list of Requests for Comments: www.cis.ohio-state.edu/htbin/rfc/rfc-index.html.

Implementing OSPF in a Single Area

Terms you'll need to understand:

✓ Shortest Path First algorithm
✓ Autonomous system (AS)
✓ Interior Gateway Protocol (IGP)
✓ Area
✓ Router ID
✓ Topology Table
✓ Link-state advertisement (LSA)
✓ Link-state update (LSU)

✓ Link-state acknowledgement (LSAck)
✓ Cost
✓ Neighbor
✓ Hello
✓ Adjacency
✓ Designated router (DR)
✓ Backup designated router (BDR)

Techniques you'll need to master:

✓ Understanding the differences between OSPF and RIP
✓ Knowing how the Hello protocol works
✓ Comprehending the eight possible states that an OSPF router can go through during the initialization process

✓ Using IP unnumbered and loopback addressing
✓ Configuring and verifying different OSPF operations for a single area

The Internet Engineering Task Force (IETF) first developed the Open Shortest Path First (OSPF) routing protocol in 1988. The most recent version of this link-state protocol is OSPF version 2 and is defined by RFC 2328. The RFC that describes the modifications to OSPF that support IPv6 is RFC 2740. OSPF employs the *Shortest Path First algorithm* to fill its routing table with information and share it with other routers in the network. OSPF distributes routing information primarily between internal routers in a single *autonomous system* (AS). Therefore, OSPF is categorized as an *Interior Gateway Protocol* (IGP). An AS is simply a collection of universally administered OSPF networks that share a common routing strategy. These systems are often broken down into areas. An *area* is a logical grouping of network segments that consists of a single AS. An area is also a subset of an AS and is often deployed to decrease the number of routing updates as well as improve convergence time. All the routers in an OSPF area share common administration and link-state databases. An area provides an added level of routing protection and minimized network traffic. This chapter focuses on implementing the OSPF routing protocol in a single area.

The first OSPF area that you configure will be Area 0. The area ID 0 is used to represent this area. A *backbone router* (BBR) is a router that has at least one interface linked to Area 0. Therefore, Area 0 is commonly referred to as the backbone area. A *backbone* is simply the portion of a network that functions as the primary path for source traffic to flow to other networks. This area will serve as the core or backbone through which all other areas in the autonomous system will transit.

The most important criteria for the backbone area are stability and redundancy. Stability is achieved through maintaining a reasonable backbone size. Every router in the backbone has to recompute its routes after every change in the link-state topology. You can minimize the probability of a change as well as reduce the CPU cycles required to recompute routes by keeping the backbone as small as is feasible. The average number of routers in each area (including the backbone) of newer, large enterprise environments is about 150. Redundancy is critical in the backbone; therefore, backbones should be designed so that no single link failure can cause link-state database problems. All routers in the backbone should be connected directly to other backbone routers. You should avoid placing hosts such as workstations, file servers, or other shared resources in the backbone area to enable smoother internetwork scalability and provide greater stability. Stability can also be maintained by ensuring that your routers have enough CPU and memory to handle the potential load.

Each OSPF router has a database that depicts the AS topology. Each participating router has an identical copy of this link-state database. OSPF routers use a flooding process to distribute their local state throughout the AS. Whenever a change to the topology occurs, OSPF's link-state algorithm quickly recalculates the routes, using as little traffic as possible. OSPF also offers support for equal-cost multipath routing and authenticated packet exchanges.

OSPF is a widely used routing protocol that is known for its rapid convergence speed, support for variable-length subnet masking (VLSM), scalability, efficient use of bandwidth, and improved path determination techniques. Here are the general objectives that will be covered in this chapter:

➤ OSPF versus RIP in a large internetwork

➤ OSPF discovery, selection, and route maintenance

➤ OSPF operation in a single area non-broadcast multi-access (NBMA) setting

➤ OSPF configuration and verification for operation in a single area

OSPF Versus RIP in a Large Internetwork

The best way to understand the intricacies of the OSPF protocol is to compare it with a more familiar interior routing protocol: the Routing Information Protocol version 1 (RIPv1). OSPF implements a Dijkstra Shortest Path First algorithm to populate a routing table, whereas RIPv1 uses the Bellman-Ford distance vector algorithm. Here is a list of the fundamental differences between and features of the RIP and OSPF interior routing protocols:

➤ OSPF converges a lot faster than RIPv1 because it propagates changes immediately. This results in more timely and accurate routes as well as fewer packets being lost while the network topology is converging.

➤ RIPv2 and OSPF both support Variable Length Subnet Mask (VLSM), whereas RIPv1 does not.

➤ RIP networks cannot grow larger than 15 hops; OSPF networks are technically unlimited in size.

➤ RIP uses much more bandwidth because of its distance-vector behavior. RIP broadcasts the entire routing table every 30 seconds by default. OSPF sends a multicast update only when a change to the topology occurs.

➤ RIP does not understand factors such as delay and bandwidth cost. RIP bases the routing decision completely on hop count as a metric, which can result in pinhole congestion.

➤ OSPF can utilize VLSM masks for route summarization, which can reduce the number of routing table entries, as well as the amount of update traffic and router overhead.

➤ OSPF enables you to tag external routes coming from other autonomous systems to help identify and manage routing between OSPF and other non-OSPF systems for administrative purposes.

➤ Both OSPF and RIP can load balance packets across equal cost paths (four by default).

➤ The Cisco IOS offers a richer set of tools for configuring, monitoring, and troubleshooting with OSPF. On the other hand, RIP is less difficult to configure, monitor, and troubleshoot than the more complex and configurable OSPF routing protocol.

➤ Although OSPF is run on a wide variety of routing devices, it can consume a considerable amount of CPU and memory resources, especially on high-end routers where many shortest path first (SPF) calculations are performed for multiple OSPF processes.

➤ OSPF and RIPv2—but not RIPv1—offer authentication in the packet.

It is highly recommended that you download the entire RFC 2328 and read this 100+-page document at least one time through. Although it is not leisure reading, the benefits are substantial for additional exam preparation. For instance, it is an excellent source for a complete terminology and definition of the OSPF protocol version 2.

Now that you have a general idea of the many advantages of OSPF in scalable networks, it is imperative to master the many terms and concepts used with OSPF. Refer to the following list throughout this chapter and the rest of the book:

➤ *Link*—The interface between an OSPF router and a connected network.

➤ *Link-state*—Condition of the link between two routers sharing link-state advertisements. Information is used by OSFP routers to build SPF topology. Depending on the implementation, the link can be in the down, init, two-, exstart, exchange, loading, or full state.

➤ *Link-state advertisement (LSA)*—OSPF broadcast packets that contain updates used to maintain routing tables that contain data about neighbors and path costs.

➤ *Area*—Grouping of routers and networks with the same area ID number and link-state information. All OSPF routers must be in an area.

➤ *Autonomous System (AS)*—Collection of routers that share OSPF routing information and are under the same network administration. For example, an entire company could be an AS administered by a single IT group. On the other hand, a large corporation or organization might divide administration into ASs across geographical, political, departmental, or logical boundaries for the sake of managing costs, migration, and other corporate operations.

➤ *Cost*—The metric OSPF uses. Represented by a numerical value assigned to a link based on the speed of the connection output. A lower cost is preferable to a higher cost.

➤ *Router ID*—Unique number on a Cisco router that is typically represented by the highest configured IP address, the highest configured IP address loopback address, or manual assignment.

➤ *Neighbor*—Two routers that have links on a common network.

➤ *Hello*—A type of packet used by OSPF to establish and manage neighbor relationships.

➤ *Topology table*—A table that holds every link in the entire network. Also known as the link-state database.

➤ *Adjacency*—Condition that occurs when two OSPF routers have traded information to the point where they have identical topology tables.

➤ *Routing table*—Table created when the SPF algorithm is run on the link-state database. Also called the *forwarding database*.

➤ *Designated router (DR)*—OSPF router with many duties in a multi-access network, including generating LSAs. Having a DR lowers the number of adjacencies necessary in a multi-access topology and reduces traffic and topology database size.

➤ *Backup designated router (BDR)*—Receives the same data as the DR but functions as a standby DR in the case of a DR failure.

➤ *Backbone*—The primary path for traffic on a network; the part of the network that is most often sourced from as well as transmitted to other networks.

➤ *Area border router (ABR)*—A router that sits on the border of more than one OSPF area and connects those routers to the backbone.

➤ *Autonomous system boundary router (ASBR)*—An area Border Router (ABR) that sits between an OSPF AS and a non-OSPF network (such as

RIP) and runs multiple routing protocols. An ASBR can also link two OSPF networks from different autonomous systems.

➤ *Router priority*—An 8-bit number (1–255) that designates the priority of a router in the DR/BDR election process and can be manually reconfigured as necessary.

OSPF Discovery, Selection, and Route Maintenance

The best way to understand OSPF discovery, selection, and continuance is to look at OSPF operations in a single-area, broadcast, multi-access scenario. Before anything can happen, OSPF routers must discover one another so they can exchange basic information.

The Hello Protocol

A Hello packet is essentially a multicast packet used by OSPF routers to facilitate neighbor discovery, selection, and maintenance. Neighboring routers can be dynamically discovered with this protocol because Hello leverages the existing broadcast capability of a network. The OSPF designated router (DR), mentioned in the previous bulleted list, is also elected with the Hello protocol. Hello is actually a separate protocol used by several routing protocols to accomplish similar tasks. Hello packets use multicast 224.0.0.5, the AllSPFRouter address, out each OSPF link on the router.

NOTE Multicasting is the process in which a host system sends a packet to a collection of hosts that form a multicast group. Each member of the multicast group uses the same multicast address to receive a copy of the packet. Multicast routers copy and deliver packets to those hosts. Membership in a multicast group is dynamic, and a host can join or exit a group at any time. A host can also transmit packets to a multicast group without being a member of that group. Every multicast group has a unique multicast (Class D) address, such as 224.0.0.5 and 224.0.0.6 for OSPF routers.

As you will discover later in this chapter, OSPF can operate over non-broadcast networks in one of two different modes: non-broadcast multi-access (NBMA) such as Frame Relay or point-to-multipoint like in a multipoint serial-link implementation. The option you choose establishes the behavior of the Hello protocol and the flooding process. The choice between NBMA and point-to-multipoint also affects the way that the network is represented in the link-state database. Table 4.1 shows the different fields in the OSPF Hello packet and provides a brief description of each.

Table 4.1 OSPF Hello Protocol Packet Information

Hello Packet Field	Description
Router ID	32-bit number identifying the router in an autonomous system used for establishing neighbor relationships and organizing SPF messages. Router ID is also used in DR/BDR election process.
Hello/dead intervals	The Hello interval is how often the router sends Hello messages. The default on multi-access networks is 10 seconds. Dead interval is the amount of time a router waits to hear from a neighbor before tagging it as down. The default is four times the Hello interval.
Neighbors	Neighbors who have launched a two-way communication channel. This is confirmed when the router sees itself in a neighbor's Hello packet.
Area ID	Numerical area identifier. Routers must be in the same area to communicate. The first area in an OSPF network is backbone Area 0; all other areas extend from there.
Router priority	An 8-bit number that specifies the router priority for electing a DR/BDR.
Designated router IP address	The IP address of the DR if known.
Backup designated router IP address	The IP address of the BDR if known.
Authentication password	Optional authentication password shared by peer routers.
Stub area flag	Designates this as a Hello packet in an area that does not carry external routes, only default, intra-area, and inter-area routes.

The Hello intervals, dead intervals, area-ID, authentication password, and stub area flag entries must match on all neighboring routers if applicable

OSPF Point-to-Point Operation

We begin tackling the intricacies of the OSFP exchange process by looking at a simple point-to-point network. When two OSPF routers come up at the same time, an exchange process takes place with the Hello protocol. There are several different states that a router transitions through during this process. These states relate to the progression that occurs to establish communications with neighbor routers and create adjacency relationships. Hello packets are exchanged so that the router can populate its adjacency table with the router IDs from neighboring routers. Eventually, the router will enter the full state and begin the data routing activities. Here is a list of the eight possible states that an OSPF router can go through during the initialization process:

➤ Down

➤ Attempt

➤ Init

➤ Two-way

➤ Exstart

➤ Exchange

➤ Loading

➤ Full

When an OSPF router is rebooted, it proceeds sequentially through several operational states, culminating with the full state. The full state indicates that the router has successfully exchanged and installed all database updates and has established adjacencies with neighboring routers. The process of reaching the full state begins with the down state, as shown in Figure 4.1. In this state, the routers have received no Hello packets because no information has been exchanged.

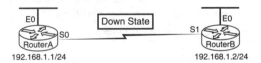

Figure 4.1 RouterA is in the down state.

Of the eight OSPF states, only the attempt state is confined to NBMA network implementations. During this state, neighbors on serial links are manually configured to establish communications and create adjacencies. Therefore, the attempt state is not applicable to this simple point-to-point scenario.

After Hello packets have been received, the router enters the init state. During the init state, RouterA sends Hello packets out via multicast address

224.0.0.5 (AllSPFRouters). On physical point-to-point networks, the IP destination is always set to the address AllSPFRouters. RouterB receives the Hello packet from RouterA and adds RouterA to its adjacency table, as shown in Figure 4.2.

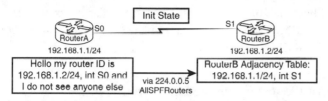

Figure 4.2 The init state.

RouterB sends a Hello reply back to RouterA with all of its accumulated information in the neighbor field of the Hello packet. This next stage, the two-way stage, indicates that the routers have established two-way communications and their router IDs have been entered into their adjacency tables, as shown in Figure 4.3.

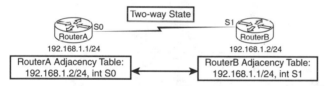

Figure 4.3 The two-way state.

The **ip unnumbered** command is applied to serial lines in point-to-point connections. The **ip unnumbered** command allows you to enable IP processing on a serial interface without actually assigning it in an IP address. The **type** and **number** keywords are used to map to any of the other IP addresses belonging to the router. For this reason, at least one IP address must be assigned to the router. Here is an example of what you could do on RouterA in Figure 4.1. You could assign IP address 192.168.1.1 /24 to Ethernet0 and use **ip unnumbered** to map address 192.168.1.1 /24 to Serial0, instead of assigning it directly to the physical interface like so:

Router(config)# interface Ethernet0
Router(config-if)# ip address 192.168.1.1 255.255.255.0
!
Router(config)# interface Serial0
Router(config-if)# ip unnumbered Ethernet0

In addition, a loopback address is often used to map to an unnumbered interface. A loopback address is a virtual interface that always remains active and does not go down as a physical interface is known to do.

From this point on, the exchange and subsequent discovery operations depend upon the topology being implemented. On physical point-to-point networks and point-to-multipoint networks, neighboring routers become adjacent whenever they can communicate directly. The previous figures show a point-to-point network joining a pair of routers over a serial interface such as a T1 link. These neighboring routers become adjacent by direct communication and no DR or BDR election takes place. As a matter of fact, the concept of DR and BDR is nonexistent in point-to-point mode.

The next phase is the exstart state, in which database description (DD) packets are swapped so that the router with the highest router ID becomes the master in the neighbor relationship. Next, DD and link-state request (LSR) packets are exchanged during the next exchange state. New LSAs, if applicable, trigger the loading state. During the loading state, LSRs are sent to neighbors requesting the new advertisements. After all LSA information is reclaimed, the router finally enters the full state. The OSPF router state of full characterizes a router that has exchanged all the necessary information to establish adjacencies with neighbors. The full state is shown in Figure 4.4.

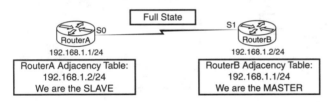

Figure 4.4 The full state.

OSPF Broadcast Multi-Access Operation

In a broadcast multi-access environment such as Ethernet, the OSPF router must elect a DR and a BDR on the network for OSPF operations. OSPF DRs and BDRs consolidate the process of forwarding and synchronizing updates to reduce the traffic on multi-access network segments. To establish adjacencies among every OSPF router in the multi-access network, it would require $n \times (n-1)$ adjacency relationships. For example, in Figure 4.5, it would take 20 adjacency relationships to service OSPF Area 0 ($5 \times 4 = 20$). As you scale this network up to dozens of routers, the relationships also scale proportionately.

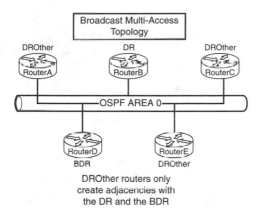

Figure 4.5 OSPF broadcast multi-access mode.

Therefore, OSPF uses a single DR to function as the information clearinghouse for the entire network. As link-state information changes, it is forwarded to the DR, which in turn propagates the changes to all other OSPF routers on the Ethernet segment. This effectively reduces the number of relationships needed between OSPF routers, lessens update traffic overhead on the network, and cuts down on the number of potential routing errors.

The BDR passively accepts all the updates received by the DR without actively forwarding or synchronizing the update traffic. However, if the DR fails to transmit LSAs before the holdtime interval expires (40 seconds on multi-access networks), because of being offline or a malfunction, the BDR takes over the process of forwarding and synchronizing updates.

Referring back to the exchange states, after the routers get to the two-way state and have each other in their tables, the routers must determine who the DR and BDR will be. This must take place before link-state information can be exchanged in a multi-access environment. The multi-access exstart state is where the DR and BDR are elected and master-slave relationships are established between every router and its adjacent DR and BDR. (Refer back to Figure 4.5.)

To choose the DR and BDR, the routers view each other's priority values during the original exchange of Hello packets. The following steps are used to determine the election:

1. The router with highest priority value is DR.

2. The router with the next highest priority value is BDR.

3. In case of a tie (which is likely because the default priority on all OSPF routers is 1), the router ID value is used instead to elect the DR and BDR. The highest IP address on an active router interface (often a loopback address) is typically used.

4. Any router with a manually configured priority of 0 is disqualified from the election.

5. Any router that is not elected DR or BDR is known as a DROther router.

6. If a router is added to the network and it has a higher priority value, the DR and BDR routers do not change unless one goes down. Refer to the following note.

If you add another router to an Ethernet segment that has a higher router priority value than the current DR, no election occurs, and the current DR continues to act as the DR for the Ethernet segment as long as the current DR remains online. For example, you may have purchased a newer, more powerful router that you want to force into being the DR no matter what the other assigned addresses are. If the DR goes down, however, the BDR takes over and a new DR is chosen. If the BDR fails, a new BDR is chosen.

The **ip ospf priority 0** command can be used to modify the default OSFP interface priority to prohibit participation in DR/BDR elections. For example, you may want to explicitly prevent this router from ever becoming the DR or BDR because it is an older, lower-end model with fewer resources.

Continuing with the exstart state, the DR and BDR have now been elected according to the previous steps and you are ready to discover the link-state data concerning the network. Again, the goal is to get to the full state of operations.

First, in the exstart phase, the DR and BDR routers establish adjacency relationships with all the other routers on the network. These relationships remain intact until a change occurs in the full state. A master-slave relationship is formed between each DROther router and its adjacent DR and BDR. As shown in Figure 4.6, the router with the highest router ID is the master, assuming that all routers have the default priority of 1.

In the exchange state, OSPF master and slave routers exchange database description (DBD) packets, which have LSA summary information from the master's link-state database. The different LSA types are covered in Chapter 5, "Interconnecting OSPF Areas." When the slave, RouterA in Figure 4.7, gets the DBD packets from the master, RouterB, it sends an acknowledgement echo message (LSAck). This process is shown in Figure 4.7.

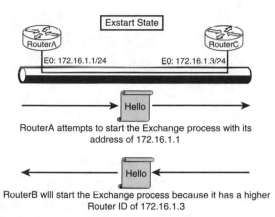

RouterA attempts to start the Exchange process with its
address of 172.16.1.1

RouterB will start the Exchange process because it has a higher
Router ID of 172.16.1.3

Figure 4.6   OSPF broadcast multi-access mode exstart state.

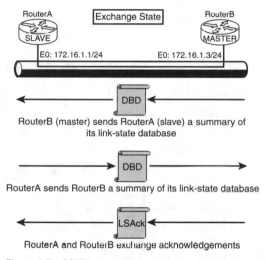

RouterB (master) sends RouterA (slave) a summary of
its link-state database

RouterA sends RouterB a summary of its link-state database

RouterA and RouterB exchange acknowledgements

Figure 4.7   OSPF broadcast multi-access mode exchange state.

Next, in the loading state, RouterA compares the update to its own table. If
the slave has a more recent entry in its link-state table, it sends an LSR to the
master, RouterB. RouterB answers with a link-state update (LSU) containing
complete information, and RouterA acknowledges this update. All the
routers propagate their link-state databases with the new link-state information during the loading state as shown in Figure 4.8.

After all the link-state requests have been addressed, the adjacent routers are
in the synchronized full state. Now that the routers have complete link-state
databases, they can choose the best routes and inject them into their routing
tables to generate route traffic. The OSPF packet header contains a lot of
information used for complex routing processes. Table 4.2 explains the contents of the 24-byte OSPF packet header.

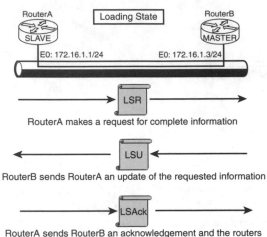

RouterA makes a request for complete information

RouterB sends RouterA an update of the requested information

RouterA sends RouterB an acknowledgement and the routers
are now ready to enter the Full state

Figure 4.8 OSPF broadcast multi-access mode loading state.

Table 4.2 The OSPF Routing Protocol 24-byte Packet Header		
OSPF Header Data Entry	**Length (bytes)**	**Description**
Version Number	1	The OSPF version type
Type	1	Type of OSPF packet, that is, Hello, DD, LSR, LSU, or LSAck
Packet Length	2	The length of the OSPF packet, including the header, in bytes
Router ID	4	Identifies the source of the packet
Area ID	4	The area to which the packet belongs
Checksum	2	Checks for corruption to packet while in transit
Authentication Type	2	Type0: no authentication, Type1: clear-text, or Type2: MD5
Authentication	8	Authentication data
Data	variable	Encapsulated upper-layer routing information

The OSPF Routing Process Revisited

RIP protocols select the optimum path based on hop count, and link-state
protocols use a cost metric based on the Dijkstra algorithm. Generally speaking, cost is an arbitrary value used by the routing protocol to compare paths
through an internetwork. In Cisco OSPF implementations, however, the

default cost metric is a value assigned to a connection based on the media speed (bandwidth). The OSPF cost is a metric assigned to the interface represented by a number between 1 and 65535 (16-bit).

Cisco routers use the following formula to calculate the path cost:

```
10' : bandwidth (in bps)
```

For example, the default cost for Ethernet would be 10 and the default cost for a 1.544Mbps T1 link would be 64. In other words a 10Mbps Ethernet link has a lower cost than a T1 line because it is faster. Using the link-state database as the data source, Cisco routers then run the algorithm to construct a routing table. The Dijkstra algorithm simply adds up the total costs between the local (root) router and each destination network. This is known as the *path cost*. If multiple paths to a destination exist, then the lowest-cost path is preferred.

For load balancing purposes, OSPF stores up to four equi-cost routes to the same destination in the routing by default. You can use the **maximum-paths** command in router configuration mode to utilize up to six equal routes to the same target.

In the case of link-state changes or flapping interfaces, a number of LSUs might be spawned. Changes to the link-state database can occur when routing devices are added or removed from the network or when bandwidths change. Flapping can occur when there are intermittent interface failures. This forces OSPF routers into a relentless state of routing table computations. Flapping can become so severe that convergence will never happen. OSPF routers wait for a default interval of five seconds every time an LSU is received before recalculating to curtail this problem. You can set these timers in the router configuration mode of the Cisco IOS by using the following syntax:

```
RouterA(config-router)# timers spf spf-delay spf-holdtime
```

OSPF Operation in a Single Area NBMA Setting

A non-broadcast multi-access environment is one where there are more than two routers without a native broadcast capability. Frame Relay is a popular technology that commonly uses a NBMA implementation. Other examples of NBMA technologies are X.25 and Asynchronous Transfer Mode (ATM).

The most popular NBMA topology is frame relay, where a core router at a central site uses a single interface to connect several virtual circuits to several other sites over a frame cloud. A representation of this and other NBMA topologies is shown in Figure 4.9.

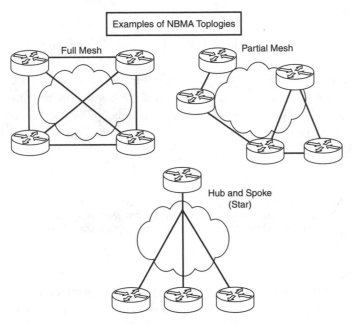

Figure 4.9 NBMA topologies.

OSPF approaches an NBMA environment just like any other broadcast network such as Ethernet. Full- and partial-mesh topologies can become costly, however, because of the formula mentioned earlier in the "OSPF Broadcast Multi-Access Operation" section. To emulate broadcast behavior with a full mesh of 15 sites, for example, would entail 15×(15–1)=210 permanent virtual circuits (PVCs). Although a partial mesh is often used to alleviate some of these costs, the star topology is the most common and economically feasible logical configuration for frame relay.

NBMA Mode

There are two formal modes of running OSPF over a NBMA topology according to RFC 2328: NBMA and point-to-multipoint. With NBMA mode, routers are usually configured in a full-mesh topology to establish the proper adjacencies and emulate broadcasting. In a full-mesh design, all the routers have virtual circuits established with all the other possible destinations in the network. Although this solution provides redundancy, it may be cost-prohibitive for some organizations. OSPF then imitates a broadcast environment by electing a DR and BDR for the NBMA topology, using the OSPF techniques discussed earlier. LSA updates and link-state acknowledgement (LSAck) packets are then flooded to all neighbors listed in the neighbor tables. This is actually a very efficient way to configure OSPF over NBMA when you have a limited number of neighbors. It offers more manageable link-state database sizes and generally decreased levels of traffic. It can be CPU and bandwidth intensive, however, in larger environments.

Please note that in some resources, you'll see both link-state advertisement and link-state acknowledgement represented as LSA. To clarify, we represent link-state advertisement as LSA and link-state acknowledgement as LSAck.

With OSPF running in NBMA mode, all routers are in a single subnet and neighbors must be statically defined at the outset to get the DR election process started. After the DR router is chosen, it generates an initial LSA for the network to get the ball rolling. There is one DR and one BDR per network segment so that when a change occurs it can be processed and flooded throughout the single OSPF area. The OSPF flooding process on a multi-access link happens according to the following four-step process:

1. If a change occurs in the link state, the router that detects the change multicasts an LSU to the multicast address of all OSPF DRs and BDRs at 224.0.0.6.

2. The DR acknowledges the modification and floods an LSU to other routers via 224.0.0.5. Because each LSA must be acknowledged, each router responds with an LSAck packet back to the DR.

3. A router connected to another subnetwork also floods the update to the link-state to the DR of the other subnetwork (or an adjacent router in point-to-point mode).

4. The routers update their link-state databases when the updates are received. It uses the new data to calculate a new routing table from the shortest path first algorithm. Don't forget that OSPF routers wait for a default interval of five seconds every time an LSU is received before recalculating, as previously mentioned.

If your NBMA-mode routers are not configured in a full-mesh topology, you must manually select the DR and BDR and have full connectivity to every other router.

Subinterfaces

It is also possible to break an NBMA network into additional logical subnets by using subinterfaces, particularly when a full mesh is not feasible because of campus design limitations, bandwidth constraints, or IP addressing issues. Using subinterfaces tends to be administratively complex and error-prone, so you might be better off running your OSPF over NBMA in point-to-multipoint mode. This scenario is addressed later in this chapter in the "Point-to-Point Mode" section.

Subinterfaces are often employed to partition a physical interface into several logical interfaces in NBMA environments. This allows each subinterface to operate as its own point-to-point or point-to-multipoint interface. On non-broadcast networks where a direct link does not exist between all the routers, you can use subinterfaces to create logical subnetting schemes and group router interfaces accordingly. With subinterfaces, each subnet could be in its own NBMA or point-to-point subnetwork because each virtual circuit is defined in a separate logical subnet. Another advantage to subinterfaces is network stability. If you were simply using a single, physical interface for a permanent virtual circuit and the interface went down, the router would indicate that the link had failed. With subinterfaces, however, you get the benefit of the physical interface remaining up, even if the subinterface has a problem.

Point-to-Multipoint Mode

In a nutshell, point-to-multipoint is really a collection of point-to-point links where routers identify their neighbor routers but do not elect DRs or BDRs. This provides an additional advantage of no added election traffic or LSAs being propagated for the network. In large networks, you get the added benefit of a reduction in the number of virtual circuits that need to be established as well. Point-to-multipoint is commonly used in partial mesh and sometimes star topologies (refer to Figure 4.9). Subinterfaces also come in handy with point-to-multipoint links. For example, assume that you are the network engineer for an organization. You have allocated a single subnet for your frame relay network and you would also like to avoid DR and BDR elections, subinterfaces, or manual neighbor configurations. Your internetwork is made up of four sites that are linked in a partial-mesh Frame Relay topology, as shown in Figure 4.10.

Point-to-multipoint mode has the following benefits and characteristics:

➤ No DR or BDR is elected.

➤ There are no LSAs for the network, but rather additional LSUs to describe neighboring routers.

➤ Non-adjacent neighbors can route through a common router configured for point-to-multipoint mode.

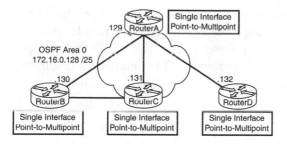

Figure 4.10 Four sites connected in a hub-and-spoke, partial mesh frame relay topology using a single IP subnet.

➤ Multicast Hello packets discover neighbors dynamically so that static neighbor configuration is not necessary.

➤ All the routers are on a single subnet.

➤ LSA and LSAck packets are duplicated and sent to each interface's neighbor.

In Figure 4.10, we use point-to-multipoint mode on all four routers on single interfaces (no subinterfaces) in a single subnet. This enables us to avoid having to manually configure neighbors as well as prevent DR and BDR elections. This mode can also be configured with the `ip ospf network point-to-multipoint` interface configuration command. Broadcast mode would require a DR/BDR election. Point-to-point mode with subinterfaces would not demand a DR/BDR election; however, it would need a separate subnet for each configured virtual circuit (VC).

NBMA (frame relay) clouds can be fully meshed or arranged in many variations of hub-and-spoke and/or partially meshed topologies. OSPF, however, sees the NBMA cloud as a broadcast medium, so you must correctly configure OSPF to operate within the frame relay cloud. Cisco has defined additional NBMA modes to explain OSPF neighbor relationships that go beyond the standards. Cisco also defines a point-to-multipoint broadcast mode, broadcast mode, and point-to-point mode.

Point-to-Multipoint Non-Broadcast Mode

Point-to-multipoint non-broadcast mode is a Cisco-defined mode that extends the RFS 2328-compliant point-to-multipoint mode covered in the previous section. Some point-to-multipoint networks use non-broadcast media such as IP over ATM and frame relay switched virtual circuit (SVC) routers that do not perform dynamic neighbor discovery. Although you must define your neighbors with static configurations, you have the added flexibility of modifying the costs of the links to represent different bandwidths. The partial-mesh or star topologies are used in these environments and neighbors must have the same subnet number. The interface is configured with the `ip ospf network` *point-to-multipoint nonbroadcast* command.

Broadcast Mode

Broadcast mode is another Cisco-defined method for getting around having to list all the neighbors with a static configuration. The interface is configured with an `ip ospf network` *broadcast* command so it acts just as it does on a LAN; therefore the neighbors must belong to the same subnet. You should use a full-mesh topology here or else rig the DR election with an interface priority configuration. This is the default setting for a broadcast multi-access network such as Ethernet.

Point-to-Point Mode

The point-to-point mode is typically implemented when you have only two nodes on your NBMA (frame relay) network. However, you can also implement it by using subinterfaces on NBMA networks with more than two nodes. Subinterfaces are configured with the `ip ospf network` *point-to-point* command and each point-to-point connection is one IP subnet. Table 4.3 reviews the key details for each mode.

Table 4.3 OSPF over NBMA Modes (RFC- and Cisco-defined)		
OSPF over NBMA	**IP Subnets Needed**	**Description**
NBMA	1 (same subnet number)	Fully meshed; manually configured adjacencies; DR/BDR elected; RFC2328-defined
Point-to-Multipoint	1 (same subnet number)	Partial mesh or star; automatic adjacency; no DR/BDR elected; RFC2328-defined
Point-to-Multipoint non-broadcast	1 (same subnet number)	Partial mesh or star; manually configured adjacencies; no DR/BDR elected; RFC2328-defined
Broadcast	1 (same subnet number)	Fully meshed; automatic adjacency; DR/BDR are elected; Cisco-defined
Point-to-Point	Separate subnet for each subinterface	Partial mesh or star; subinterfaces; automatic adjacency; no DR/BDR elected; Cisco-defined

To help ensure your success on the BSCI exam, memorize the preceding table until you have it down cold.

OSPF Configuration and Verification for Operation in a Single Area

To enable the OSPF process on a Cisco router, type the following command while in global configuration mode:

```
RouterA(config)# router ospf process-id
```

The OSPF process ID is an integer value between 1 and 65,535 that is used to assign an identifier to the OSFP process operating on the router. A router uses the OSPF router ID number for internal purposes only and may run more than one OSPF process at a time. You must use the router ospf process-id command to get to the OSPF process in which you want the interfaces to be configured. If you have existing processes running, simply type this command first to take you to that process. This is comparable to entering interface configuration mode. The prompt reflects this change (config-router) to indicate that you are in a router configuration mode.

Next, you should designate the IP networks on the router that are part of the OSPF network with this command in router configuration mode:

```
RouterA(config-router)# network address wildcard-mask area area-id
```

The address keyword represents the network address, subnet, or interface address of the link. The wildcard-mask keyword is an inverse mask where the 0 bit value is a match and a 1 bit value represents a wildcard. Finally, the area area-id portion of the command designates the OSPF area associated with the IP address expressed as a decimal or A.B.C.D format. This value is mandatory because every OSPF interface must be assigned to an area. The following is a sample OSPF configuration snippet:

```
RouterA(config)# router ospf 100
RouterA(config-router)# network 172.16.0.0 0.0.255.255 area 0
```

If you want to run OSPF on every interface on your Cisco router, use the following command:

RouterA(config-router)# network 0.0.0.0 255.255.255.255 area 0

You can also use some optional commands to change an OSPF router's default behavior. For example, you may want to assign a loopback address to important routers and configure the IP address to the highest number so that it becomes the router ID value. You can "publish" a loopback address as you would advertise any network with the `network area` command. Remember that an unpublished loopback address cannot be pinged, so there is a caveat. Here is the syntax to configure a loopback interface:

```
RouterA(config)# interface loopback number
RouterA(config-if)# ip address address mask
```

To rig the DR and BDR election process, you can use the interface configuration command `show ip ospf priority number` command to manually configure interface priority value. Here is a sample of the command:

```
RouterA(config-if)# ip ospf priority number
```

The `number` keyword is an integer between 1 and 255 used to manually configure priority. The higher the number, the higher the router's priority. Again, configuring the priority to 0 removes the selected interface from all future DR and BDR elections.

You can override a connection's default link cost value if necessary. The Cisco OSPF link cost is based on the link's bandwidth. You may have to modify the value for interoperability with other vendors or for better control. Cisco routers use the formula of 10^8 divided by bandwidth (bps) to generate the cost. The greater the bandwidth, the lower the cost. For example, a 56Kbps serial link has a default cost of 1785, whereas Ethernet has a default cost of 10. The syntax to change the cost in interface configuration mode is

```
RouterA(config-if)# ip ospf cost cost
```

As previously mentioned, you configure OSPF over NBMA by using the RFC-defined NBMA and point-to-multipoint modes or the Cisco-defined point-to-multipoint non-broadcast mode, broadcast mode, or point-to-point mode. The interface command `ip ospf network` is used to configure the network type when OSPF is configured over NBMA networks such as frame relay. The command syntax to configure the interface is as follows:

```
RouterA(config-if)# ip ospf network {broadcast | non-broadcast |
➥point-to-point | point-to-multipoint | point-to-multipoint
➥non-broadcast}
```

OSPF in NBMA-Mode Configuration

Because NBMA mode is the default in Cisco, you do not need to use the `ip ospf network non-broadcast` command. Because the non-broadcast environment precludes IP multicasting, which OSPF requires for DR/BDR election and adjacency formation, an administrator must use the `neighbor` command to manually identify all OSPF neighbors in the cloud.

 Although the **neighbor** command is a little dated because of newer Cisco-compliant modes, it is still applicable for some situations and may be mentioned on the exam.

Here is the syntax of the `neighbor` command:

```
RouterA(config-router)# neighbor ip-address [priority number]
➥[poll-interval sec] [cost number]
```

The `ip-address` keyword is the IP address of the neighbor and the rest of the keywords are optional. Refer to RFC 2328 for explicit details. Here is a sample configuration:

```
RouterA(config)# router ospf 100
RouterA(config-router)# network 172.16.1.0 0.0.0.255 area 0
RouterA(config-router)# neighbor 172.16.1.1
RouterA(config-router)# neighbor 172.16.1.2
RouterA(config-router)# neighbor 172.16.1.3
```

OSPF in Point-to-Multipoint–Mode Configuration

OSPF point-to-multipoint interfaces are actually one or more point-to-point interfaces in a single subnet as far as the Cisco router is concerned. Here is a sample configuration:

```
RouterA(config)# int S1
RouterA(config-if)# ip address 172.16.1.1 255.255.255.0
RouterA(config-if)# encap frame-relay
RouterA(config-if)# ip ospf network point-to-multipoint
RouterA(config-router)# neighbor 172.16.1.1
RouterA(config)# router ospf 100
RouterA(config-router)# network 172.16.1.0 0.0.0.255 area 0
```

OSPF in Point-to-Multipoint Non-broadcast–Mode Configuration

When you use the non-broadcast parameter, the point-to-multipoint network is considered a nonbroadcast Cisco network. You need to use the `neighbor` command with this mode. Because this is a relatively new feature, you may need to do some further investigation at www.cisco.com.

OSPF in Broadcast-Mode Configuration

As mentioned, OSPF in broadcast-mode configuration is a way to circumvent the `neighbor` keyword in a fully meshed network (preferably). Here is a sample configuration of OSPF in broadcast mode:

```
RouterB(config)# int S1
RouterB(config-if)# ip address 172.16.1.1 255.255.255.0
RouterB(config-if)# encap frame-relay
RouterB(config-if)# ip ospf network broadcast
RouterB(config)# router ospf 100
RouterB(config-router)# network 172.16.1.0 0.0.0.255 area 0
```

OSPF in Point-to-Point–Mode Configuration

Because each subinterface in point-to-point mode is regarded as a physical point-to-point network, the adjacencies are automatically formed. You need to go into the interface configuration and strip away any IP addressing assigned to the physical interface. Next, assign the IP address to the subinterface and encapsulate the subinterface as Frame Relay. Configure the subinterfaces, IP addresses, and data-link connection identifier (DLCI) numbers. Because point-to-point mode is the default, your job is done. Here is a sample configuration of OSPF in point-to-point mode:

```
RouterA(config)# int S0
RouterA(config-if)# no ip address
RouterA(config-if)# encap frame-relay
RouterA(config)# interface S0.1 point-to-point
RouterA(config-subif)# ip address 172.16.1.1 255.255.255.0
RouterA(config-subif)# frame-relay interface-dlci 61
RouterA(config)# interface S0.2 point-to-point
RouterA(config-subif)# ip address 172.16.2.1 255.255.255.0
RouterA(config-subif)# frame-relay interface-dlci 62
RouterA(config)# router ospf 100
RouterA(config-router)# network 172.16.0.0 0.0.255.255 area 0
```

OSPF Verification

The primary command used to see information about router statistics such as timers and filters is `show ip protocols`. This command outputs data such as the running IP routing processes, update, invalid, holddown and flush timers, and outgoing and incoming update filters. Here is sample syntax:

```
RouterA# show ip protocols
```

If you want to show all the routes that the router is aware of and how it learned them, use the `show ip route` command. If you only want to see the OSFP routes, use the `show ip route ospf` command. You will be looking at the contents of your router's routing table with this popular command. This is one of the primary methods for verifying connectivity between your router and the entire network, as shown in the following snippet:

```
RouterA# show ip route
_____172.16.0.0/16 is variably subnetted, 7 subnets, 4 masks
C           172.16.4.128/25 is directly connected, Loopback1
O           172.16.5.32/27 [110/1010] via 172.16.1.2, 00:01:27,
➡Ethernet0/0
O           172.16.6.1/32 [110/11] via 172.16.1.2, 00:01:27, Ethernet0/0
C           172.16.5.0/27 is directly connected, Loopback2
O           172.16.6.2/32 [110/11] via 172.16.1.2, 00:01:27, Ethernet0/0
C           172.16.4.0/25 is directly connected, Loopback0
C           172.16.1.2/24 is directly connected, Ethernet0/0
```

The OSPF-related EXEC-MODE command show ip ospf interface [*type number*] shows the priority of the local OSPF router as well as confirms that interfaces are in the proper OSPF areas. Other information provided by this command includes OSPF timers and neighbor details. The type-number parameter is used to designate a particular interface for verification.

To find out how many times the shortest path first algorithm has been run on your router, use the show ip ospf command as shown in the following truncated output:

```
RouterB# show ip ospf
    Routing Process "ospf 100" with ID 172.16.1.129
<output omitted>
    Number of areas in this router is 1. 0 normal 1 stub 0 nssa
        Area 1
            Number of interfaces in this area is 2
            It is a stub area
            Area has no authentication
            SPF algorithm executed 4 times
<output omitted>
```

The show ip ospf neighbor syntax conveys OSPF neighbor information on an interface-by-interface basis. There are several optional keywords to use for additional functionality and data gathering. The command is as follows:

```
RouterA# show ip ospf neighbor [type number] [neighbor-id] [detail]
```

The optional *type* keyword is used to designate the interface type that you want to output, and the *number* keyword is for the interface number. The neighbor-id keyword is another optional parameter to extract a particular neighbor. If you want to see all the neighbors in detail, you can list all the neighbors with the *details* keyword. Here is an example of using the *detail* parameter:

```
RouterB# show ip ospf neighbor detail
Neighbor 172.16.96.54, interface address 172.16.96.54
    In the area 0.0.0.1 via interface Ethernet0
    Neighbor priority is 1, State is FULL
    Options 2
    Dead timer due in 0:00:17
```

The EXEC-MODE command show ip ospf database is used to show the contents of the OSPF topological database (topology table). You can also use this to view the router ID and OSPF process ID numbers. Use this command to ensure that your router sees all network segments.

The primary troubleshooting and monitoring command for OSPF is the debug ip ospf syntax. You can use this to monitor a wide range of OSPF events. If you issue the debug ip ospf ? command, you will see several options. The most common option to run is debug ip ospf adj to monitor the DR and BDR election process.

Exam Prep Questions

Question 1

Which one of the following pairs of documents defines the Open Shortest Path
First version 2 (OSPF v2) routing protocol and OSPF for Internet Protocol version 6 (IPv6), respectively?

○ A. 2178 and 2740

○ B. 1058 and 2178

○ C. 2328 and 2740

○ D. 2328 and 1878

Answer C is correct. RFC 2328 defines OSPF version 2 and 2740 defines
OSPF for IPv6. Answer A is incorrect because RFC 2178 is an obsolete RFC
for OSPF that was replaced by 2328. Answer B is incorrect because 1058
defines RIP and 2178 is obsolete. Answer D is incorrect because 1878 defines
VLSM for IPv4.

Question 2

Which of the following phrases best describes the OSPF exchange state?

○ A. The phase in which routers have not shared information with other
routers' networks

○ B. The phase in which all the routers see each other in their own
neighbor lists

○ C. The phase in which master and slave routers can discover link-state
information packets

○ D. The phase in which all adjacent routers are synchronized and ready to
route traffic

Answer C is correct. In the exchange state, OSPF master and slave routers
exchange database description (DBD) packets that have LSA summary information from the master's link-state database. Answer A is incorrect because
this describes the down state. Answer B is incorrect because this is the two-
way state. Answer D is incorrect because this represents the full state.

Question 3

Which of the following OSPF over nonbroadcast multi-access modes are Cisco-defined? (Choose all that apply.)

- ❑ A. NBMA
- ❑ B. Point-to-point
- ❑ C. Broadcast
- ❑ D. Point-to-multipoint non-broadcast
- ❑ E. Point-to-multipoint

Answers B, C, and D are correct. Point-to-point, broadcast, and point-to-multipoint non-broadcast are all three Cisco-defined extensions of the RFC 2328 definition. NBMA and point-to-multipoint are both the RFC 2328-compliant modes; therefore, answers A and E are incorrect.

Question 4

You want to implement OSPF in an NBMA nonbroadcast multi-access mode environment for four sites. How many subnets will you use for this topology?

- ○ A. 4
- ○ B. 3
- ○ C. 2
- ○ D. 1

Answer D is correct. With OSPF running in NBMA mode, all routers are in one subnet and neighbors are statically defined at the outset to get the DR election process initiated. Answers A, B, and C are incorrect because all NBMA routers use the same subnet number.

Question 5

Which of the following best describes an advantage of using OSPF instead of RIPv2? (Choose two.)

- ○ A. OSPF supports VLSM and RIPv2 cannot.
- ○ B. OSPF can tag external routes from another AS and RIPv2 cannot.
- ○ C. An OSPF network can grow well beyond 15 hops and RIPv2 cannot.
- ○ D. OSPF can load balance packets across equal cost paths and RIPv2 cannot.

Answers B and C are correct. Answer A is incorrect because RIPv2 and OSPF both support VLSM, whereas RIPv1 does not. Answer D is incorrect because OSPF and RIP can both load balance packets across equal cost paths (four by default). In addition, OSPF is not limited by network diameter, or hop count, like RIP.

Question 6

Which of the following is the proper command to execute on your Cisco router to run OSPF on all router interfaces after you have entered the router OSPF **process-id** command?

- O A. R1(config-router)# network 255.255.255.255 0.0.0.0 area 0
- O B. R1(config-router)# network 0.0.0.0 255.255.255.255 area 0
- O C. R1(config-if)# network 0.0.0.0 255.255.255.255 area 0
- O D. R1(config-if)# network 255.255.255.255 0.0.0.0 area 0

Answer B is correct. At the router configuration prompt, enter the network command where 0.0.0.0 is all networks and 255.255.255.255 is a 24-bit wildcard mask for Area 0. Answer A is incorrect because the network and mask parameters are in the wrong order. Answer C is incorrect because you are in interface configuration mode and not router configuration mode. Answer D is incorrect because the mode is wrong and the parameters are juxtaposed.

Question 7

Which one of the following commands would an administrator of a Cisco router input at the IOS to facilitate full connectivity through the selection of a DR and BDR while configuring OSPF in NBMA mode?

- O A. Router(config-router) neighbor 172.16.1.1
- O B. Router(config) neighbor 172.16.1.1
- O C. Router(config-router) network 172.16.1.1
- O D. Router(config) network 172.16.1.1

Answer A is correct. The neighbor command can be used with an ip-address parameter to configure OSPF routers linking to nonbroadcast networks. Answer B is incorrect because it is the wrong IOS mode prompt. Answer C is incorrect because the network command is used rather than the neighbor command. Answer D is incorrect because it uses the command mode prompt and the wrong command.

Question 8

Which of the following **EXEC-MODE** commands is used to show the contents of the OSPF topology table?

- ○ A. **debug ip ospf adj**
- ○ B. **show ip ospf neighbor detail**
- ○ C. **show ip route ospf**
- ○ D. **show ip ospf database**

Answer D is correct. The `show ip ospf database` command displays the contents of the OSPF topological database. You can also use this command to see the router ID and OSPF process ID numbers. Answer A is incorrect because `debug ip ospf adj` is commonly used to monitor the DR and BDR election process. Answer B is incorrect because `show ip neighbor detail` is used if you need to list all the routers' neighbors. Answer C is incorrect because this displays the OSPF routing table, not the topology table.

Question 9

Which of the following types of OSPF packets are valid messages used for discovering routes? (Choose two.)

- ❏ A. Hello
- ❏ B. LSP
- ❏ C. DBD
- ❏ D. ICMP

Answers A and C are correct. Hello packets and DBD packets are both used in the route discovery and exchange process. Answer B is incorrect because it is an acronym for link-state messages. Answer D is incorrect because it is the Internet Control Message Protocol, which functions independently of the particular routing protocol and is not used specifically for OSPF route discovery.

Question 10

Which of the following IP multicast addresses is also known as the ALLSPFRouter address?

○ A. 224.0.0.6

○ B. 225.0.0.4

○ C. 224.0.0.5

○ D. 226.0.0.6

Answer C is correct. 224.0.0.5 is also referred to as the AllSPFRouter address. Answer A is incorrect because multicast address 224.0.0.6 goes to OSPF DRs and BDRs. Answer B is incorrect because the multicast addresses 225.0.0.0 through 231.255.255.255 are reserved according to the IANA IPv4 Multicast Guidelines set forth in RFC 3171. Answer D is incorrect because multicast network 226.0.0.0 is also reserved by the IANA.

Need to Know More?

 Parkhurst, William R. *Cisco OSPF Command and Configuration Handbook*. Indianapolis, IN: Cisco Press, 2002. ISBN 1587050714.

 Thomas, Tom. *OSPF Network Design Solutions, Second Edition*. Indianapolis, IN: Cisco Press, 2003. ISBN 1587050323.

 Complete list of Requests for Comments: `www.cis.ohio-state.edu/htbin/rfc/rfc-index.html`.

Interconnecting OSPF Areas

Terms you'll need to understand:

✓ Area

✓ Backbone

✓ Backbone router (BBR)

✓ Internal router (IR)

✓ Area border router (ABR)

✓ Autonomous system boundary router (ASBR)

✓ Virtual link

✓ Router ID

✓ Loopback interface

✓ Stub area

✓ Totally stubby area

✓ Not-so-stubby area (NSSA)

Techniques you'll need to master:

✓ Design your area network properly

✓ Configure virtual links and loopback interfaces

✓ Master the various link-state advertisement (LSA) types

✓ Understand how multicasting works for internal routers

✓ Deploy route summarization in OSPF NBMA environments

✓ Configure and verify multi-area OSPF operations

Now that you are familiar with the concepts and techniques for operating OSPF in a single-area implementation, it is time to move on to more scalable solutions involving multi-area network designs. Autonomous systems that comprise a single area are often divided into smaller multiple areas for the following reasons:

➤ A growing network is creating too much overhead on your routers because of the increasing number of SPF recalculations that occur every time a change is made to the topology.

➤ The link-state topology table is getting too large and unmanageable.

➤ The routing tables are getting overwhelmed with entries from a large single-area deployment.

➤ Your network is affected by departmental, geographical, or political changes.

In this chapter, we continue our discussion of OSPF and look at linking multiple areas and OSPF addressing in multiple areas, as well as the different types of areas, routers, and link-state advertisements. Also, you continue configuring and verifying your Cisco router for OSPF multi-area operations.

OSPF Areas, Routers, and LSAs

The process of breaking up a single area into multiple smaller areas is also known as hierarchical design. OSPF can operate well in larger environments with a hierarchical routing design in which multiple areas span or link to the core backbone Area 0. In addition to the benefits mentioned in the introduction, network problems such as flapping can be isolated to smaller areas without an adverse effect on the backbone area due to excessive SPF recalculations. When designing an OSPF network, you need to establish which routers and links are to be included in the backbone and which ones are to be placed in each area.

As you know, an *area* is a logical grouping of network segments that consists of a single autonomous system (AS). An area can also be viewed as a subset of an AS that is defined to reduce the number of routing updates and SPF calculations. In addition, confining link-state updates to defined areas of the internetwork can reduce convergence time. There are several different types of areas that are used to manage link-state information propagation. We will explore these in greater detail after you have learned about the varying network and link-state data types.

OSPF Router Types

The area ID 0 must be used to represent the backbone area. A *backbone router* (BBR) is characterized as a router that has at least one interface connected to Area 0 (or OSPF transit area). Therefore, Area 0 is commonly referred to as the *backbone area*. A *backbone* is simply the portion of a network that functions as the primary path for source traffic to flow to other networks. The backbone can also be a collection of OSPF routers acting as a conduit for information moving between different OSPF autonomous systems.

Internal routers (IRs) have all their interfaces connected to a single OSPF area. Therefore, internal routers in a single area share the same link-state databases. Internal routers can exist in a backbone, a standard area, or a stub area. Standard and stub areas are defined later in this chapter.

By definition, routers that have interfaces linked to multiple areas and that contain separate link-state databases for each area are called *area border routers* (ABRs). Practically speaking, ABRs are the routers that connect an area to the backbone. An area can have one or more ABRs. Area border routers serve as the gateways of last resort for internal routers that are sending information to external routes. They are the principal exit points for the area, so routing data meant for another area must travel through the local ABR to get there. Areas should have a contiguous set of network (and/or subnet) addresses so that they can deploy route summarization techniques for smaller routing tables. It is preferable to have more than one ABR per area for fault tolerance and performance reasons. Internal routers have identical link-state databases, whereas ABRs maintain a separate link-state database for each area in the router's autonomous system.

Real-world implementations typically have a minimum of 20 routers (not necessarily ABRs) per single area, up to a maximum of approximately 350 routers per area.

An *autonomous system boundary router* (ASBR) is an OSPF router with at least one interface connected to an external non-OSPF EGP network, another IGP, or between different OSPF autonomous systems. These routers facilitate the transport of information between the IGP (OSPF is the IGP used in this scenario) and the border gateway protocols (BGPs). The ASBR bridges the gap between the OSPF interface and the BGP-bound link by exchanging routing table data with the BGP.

A router can be categorized as more than one type. For instance, a router that has interfaces linked to Area 0, Area 10, and another non-OSPF system could be described as a backbone router, an ABR, and an ASBR.

Table 5.1 displays the four main types of OSPF routers that can participate in an autonomous system, and Figure 5.1 illustrates all the router types.

Table 5.1 Types of Routers	
Router Type	**Description**
Backbone router (BBR)	An internal router or ABR that is a member of the internetwork backbone area
Internal router (IR)	A router that has all its interfaces in the same area
Area border router (ABR)	A router that has interfaces in more than one area
Autonomous system boundary router (ASBR)	An OSPF router with at least one interface connected to an external non-OSPF EGP network, another IGP, or between different OSPF autonomous systems

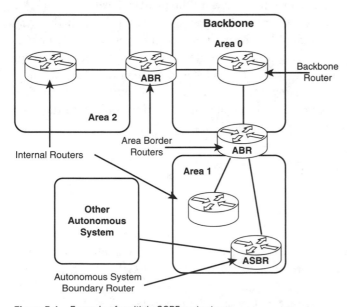

Figure 5.1 Example of multiple OSPF router types.

In Figure 5.1, the ABRs connecting Area 0 to Areas 1 and 2 can both be categorized as backbone routers as well as ABRs. If the backbone router inside Area 0 were connected to another external AS, it would be defined as an

ASBR and backbone router. In a multi-area OSPF network, Area 0 (the backbone) collects link-state advertisements from all areas of the internetwork.

Every area must either be physically or logically connected to Area 0. For areas that are not physically connected to the backbone area, OSPF includes the concept of virtual (logical) links. A *virtual link* generates a logical path that transits between two ABRs, a backbone ABR, and another area that has no physical link to Area 0. Although this mechanism is provided, it is not recommended that you design an OSPF network to require virtual links. The use of virtual links is a stopgap measure for the short term until a better solution is implemented. Because the stability of a virtual link is dependent upon the stability of the underlying area, this can make troubleshooting more difficult. In addition, virtual links cannot run across stub areas.

You can use the area virtual-link router configuration command on the ABRs that reside on either side of the area that is being traversed (this can also be referred to as a transit area). Here is the official syntax for the command:

```
RouterA(config-router)# area area-id virtual-link router-id
```

The *area-id* parameter is the area identifier for the transit area. The *router-id* parameter is the router for the virtual link neighbor. To remove a virtual link, use the following router configuration command:

```
RouterA(config-router)# no area area-id virtual-link
```

In Figure 5.2, the area virtual-link router configuration command is used to create a logical connection between Area 2 and the backbone Area 0. Although the backbone area is usually configured as the transit area, Area 1 would be considered the transit in this example.

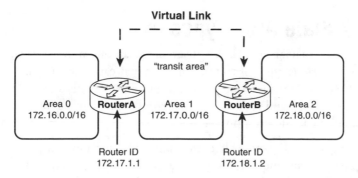

Figure 5.2 Creating a virtual link.

Here is the correct configuration for RouterA and RouterB to establish a virtual link between Area 0 and Area 2:

```
RouterA(config)# router ospf 50
RouterA(config-router)# network 172.16.0.0 0.0.255.255 area 0
RouterA(config-router)# network 172.17.0.0 0.0.255.255 area 1
RouterA(config-router)# area 1 virtual-link 172.18.1.2


RouterA(config)# router ospf 70
RouterA(config-router)# network 172.17.0.0 0.0.255.255 area 1
RouterA(config-router)# network 172.18.0.0 0.0.255.255 area 2
RouterA(config-router)# area 1 virtual-link 172.17.1.1
```

The *router ID* value is derived from the highest IP address value that is configured for the router's active interfaces. Administrators often configure an IP address as a loopback address, so that the higher loopback address becomes the router ID. A loopback address is a virtual interface that always remains active and will not fail as a physical interface is known to do. To configure a loopback address on a router, use the following syntax:

```
RouterA(config)# interface loopback 1
RouterA(config-if) ip address 192.168.200.254 255.255.255.0
```

You can then publish a loopback address as you would advertise any network with the `network area` command, as follows:

```
RouterA(config)# router ospf 10
RouterA(config-router)# network 192.168.200.254 0.0.0.0 area 0
```

Remember, an unpublished loopback address cannot be pinged.

You have now established a static router ID that is not dependent on the status of a particular active interface using a loopback address. Layer 3 addressing remains active for OSPF router operations even if an individual physical interface goes down.

OSPF Link-State Area Types

We have determined that an area is a subset of an autonomous system. However, there are various types of routing updates that can be propagated depending on the environment. To control the number of SPF activities, diminish the size of tables, and reduce LSU overhead, areas can be defined according to the following descriptions:

➤ *Standard (normal) area*—Functions like the single area environment covered in Chapter 4, "Implementing OSPF in a Single Area." A standard area can receive link updates, route summaries, and external route information. Routers in standard—or normal—areas do not typically generate default routes.

➤ *Backbone area*—Is commonly the transit area and is the central connection conduit for other areas. All the other areas must connect to it either physically or logically (virtual links) for purposes of sharing information. The backbone area always has the area ID of 0.

➤ *Stub area*—Carries default route information, intra-area routes (link updates), and inter-area routes (route summaries), but not external routes (outside the AS or OSPF internetwork). A stub area that accepts summary route information from another area is the AS.

➤ *Totally stubby area*—Is a Cisco proprietary area type that does not accept external AS routes or summaries from other areas in the AS. If a totally stubby router has to send data to a network outside the area, it uses a default route (0.0.0.0).

➤ *Not-so-stubby area (NSSA)*—Is a type of hybrid stub area that can receive some AS external route information known as Type 7 LSAs. Refer to RFC 1587 for more information.

OSPF Link-State Advertisement Types

By default, OSPF floods link-state updates (LSUs) to every adjacent neighbor every 30 minutes to make certain that each router in the OSPF routing domain has a current link-state database. These neighbors then update their own link-state databases and continue flooding the link-state change to their adjacent neighbors.

This 30-minute periodic OSPF process is also referred to as a *paranoid update*.

When an OSPF router senses a change in the topology, it sends the change information via an LSA combined with an LSU packet to the multicast address 224.0.0.6. OSPF uses only multicast—not broadcast—addresses when flooding link-state modifications throughout a network. This action tells the DR and BDR that a topology change has occurred. After acknowledging receipt of the packet to the sourcing router, the DR uses the multicast address 224.0.0.5 to flood the LSU through all its active interfaces. Any OSPF router listening to this address will be notified of the change, acknowledge receiving the LSU, and continue flooding the LSU until convergence occurs. OSPF routers send a complete copy of their topology database only when initially establishing adjacency with a neighbor router.

Table 5.2 explains the six different types of link-state advertisements supported by Cisco routers and a detailed description of how they are generated, as well as which area types they are associated with. This is an important table to memorize for a testing scenario. Compare the following table with Figure 5.3 to visualize how the different LSA types are implemented.

Table 5.2	Types of Link-State Advertisements (LSAs) Supported by Cisco Routers	
LSA Type	**Designation**	**Description**
1	O—router link entry	Initiated by each router for its own area to describe state of router links. Flooded within specific single area only.
2	O—network link entry	Initiated by DRs in multi-access OSPF networks and describes group of routers attached to specific network. Flooded within the single area containing the network.
3	IA—summary link entry	Initiated by ABRs and defines links between ABR and internal routers. Flooded throughout single backbone area to other ABRs. Describes routes to networks within the local area sent to the backbone area. Not flooded through totally stubby areas. May or may not be summarized.
4	IA—summary link entry	Initiated by ABRs and defines links between ABR and internal routers. Flooded throughout single backbone area to other ABRs. Describes reachability to ASBRs. Not flooded through totally stubby areas. May or may not be summarized.
5	E1 and E2—AS external link entry	Initiated by ASBRs and defines routes to external (AS) destinations. Distributed throughout entire OSPF AS with exception of stub, totally stubby, and NSSA areas.
7	N1 and N2—NSSA AS external link entries	Initiated by ASBR in a NSSA and flooded only within the single NSSA. At ABR, certain Type 7 LSAs are converted into Type 5 LSAs and flooded into backbone. See RFC 1578.

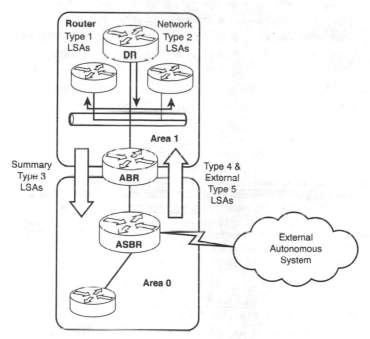

Figure 5.3 Different OSPF LSA types are used intra-area and Inter-area.

OSPF Support for Variable-Length Subnet Masking (VLSM) and Route Summarization in Multiple Areas

When you start to design your OSPF internetwork, it is important to realize that address assignment and route summarization are fundamentally connected. To build a scalable OSPF internetwork, you simply must implement route summarization. To review, route summarization is the process of aggregating routes to contiguous subnets into a single summary address. Route summarization is performed only on the area border routers because network routes are summarized for the purpose of injecting them into the OSPF backbone area. The result of this aggregation will be smaller routing tables on the ABRs, faster table lookups, and an overall decrease in the size of the link-state advertisements. Instead of advertising many specific routes from an area, the ABR needs to advertise only one or more summary routes. Route summarization will actually diminish the size of the routing tables on all routers in an AS while maintaining route availability.

Deploying an efficient hierarchical addressing scheme will have a huge impact on the performance and scalability of your OSPF internetwork. Variable-length subnet masking provides economical allocation of IP addresses and can be implemented in either single-area or multi-area OSPF routing domains. OSPF is a classless protocol for which route summarization is configured manually at either major or arbitrary bit boundaries.

Despite the flexibility that comes from VLSM and route summarization, you should shoot for making your addressing scheme as straightforward as possible, without oversimplifying the design. Although simple addressing can save some maintenance and troubleshooting time, shortcuts may have certain harsh long-term consequences. You need to design a scalable and structured addressing environment that starts with a large block at the edge, breaks into smaller networks inside, retains contiguous address space along the way, and plans for growth at each layer. This should provide the proper combination of present applicability, flexibility, and room to grow without requiring you to redo your entire scheme. Make sure that route summarization can be accomplished effectively at all your area border routers.

OSPF summary routes are configured on a router in router configuration mode so summary routes are not associated with any specific interface. OSPF summarization is enabled by default. You tell the ABR to perform route summarization for a specific area before injecting the routes (designated as IA routes in the routing table) into a different area with the `area range` command. You use this command to summarize routes between OSPF areas (summarizing the IA routes). Here is the syntax of the `area range` command. Notice that you will be in router configuration mode:

```
RouterA(config-network)# area area-id range address mask
```

The `area-id` parameter identifies the area for which routes will be summarized. The `address` keyword is the summary address specified for a particular range of addresses. The `mask` keyword is the subnet mask of the summary route. Figure 5.4 and Listing 5.1 show ABR RouterA summarizing the subnet range 169.254.96.0 through 169.254.127.0 into a single range of 169.254.96.0 with a mask of 255.255.224.0. In addition, Area 2 is summarizing the range 169.254.32.0 with a mask of 255.255.225.0 into Area 0.

Listing 5.1   Configuring Route Summarization on OSPF ABR Routers

```
RouterA>en
RouterA#config t
Enter configuration commands, one per line.  End with CNTL/Z.
RouterA(config)#router ospf 10
RouterA(config-router)#network 169.254.32.1 0.0.0.0 area 2
RouterA(config-router)#network 169.254.96.1 0.0.0.0 area 0
RouterA(config-router)#area 0 range 169.254.96.0 255.255.224.0
RouterA(config-router)#area 2 range 169.254.32.0 255.255.224.0
```

Listing 5.1   Configuring Route Summarization on OSPF ABR Routers *(continued)*

```
RouterA(config-router)#exit
RouterA(config)#


RouterB>en
RouterB#config t
Enter configuration commands, one per line.  End with CNTL/Z.
RouterB(config)#router ospf 10
RouterB(config-router)#network 169.254.64.1 0.0.0.0 area 1
RouterB(config-router)#network 169.254.127.1 0.0.0.0 area 0
RouterB(config-router)#area 0 range 169.254.96.0 255.255.224.0
RouterB(config-router)#area 0 range 169.254.64.0 255.255.224.0
RouterB(config-router)#exit
RouterB(config)#
```

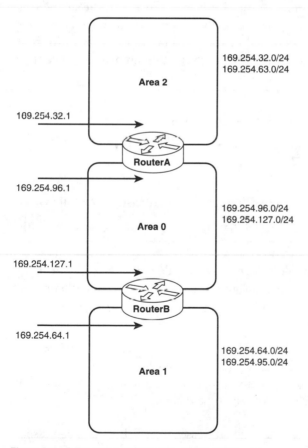

Figure 5.4   Route summarization into multiple OSPF areas.

Although the area range command is used on ABRs to summarize internal
routes, the summary-address router configuration command is typically used

on an ASBR to summarize external routes that will be injected into the OSPF routing domain. This is not a hard and fast rule as this command can also be used on an ABR. You can configure the ASBR to summarize external routes prior to injecting the routes into the OSPF domain. Here is the syntax of the command. Notice that you will be in router configuration mode:

```
RouterA(config-network)#summary-address address mask [prefix mask]
➥[not-advertise] [tag tag]
```

This command is typically used on the ASBR that is injecting external routes into the OSPF domain (refer to Figure 5.3), but it may also be configured on an ABR. The address and mask keywords are the summary address specified and subnet mask for the summary route, respectively. The prefix keyword represents the IP route prefix for the destination, and mask is the subnet mask for the summary route. Not-advertise is an optional parameter that is implemented for route suppression, and the optional tag value is used with route maps. For example, the following snippet shows the summarization configuration of an external route on RouterA:

```
RouterA>en
RouterA#config t
Enter configuration commands, one per line.  End with CNTL/Z.
RouterA(config)#router ospf 10
RouterA(config-router)#summary-address 172.18.0.0 255.255.0.0
RouterA(config-router)#exit
RouterA(config)#
```

When you are planning your OSPF internetwork, consider the following:

➤ Plan your addressing scheme so that the range of subnets assigned within an area is contiguous.

➤ Your address space should enable you to divide areas easily as your network scales up. For instance, assign subnets according to simple octet boundaries. If you understand your entire address scheme, you can better implement future changes.

➤ Always allow for the addition of new routers to your OSPF environment and ensure that they are properly placed as internal, backbone, ABR, and/or ASBR routers. This action will generate a new topology and a recomputing of subsequent tables, so be deliberate.

One of the simplest ways to allocate addresses in OSPF is to assign a separate network number for each area, thereby creating a backbone area and multiple connected areas. Then you simply assign a separate IP network number to each area. Figure 5.5 illustrates this sort of design.

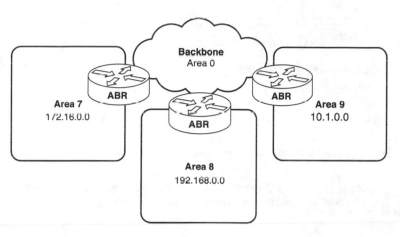

Figure 5.5 Separate network numbers for each area connected to a backbone area.

In the network illustrated in Figure 5.5, each area has its own unique NIC-assigned address. These can be Class A (Area 9), Class B (Area 7), or Class C (Area 8). The payback for this kind of design is a relatively easy scheme to configure and troubleshoot. Also, the internetwork operations are streamlined because each area has a unique major network number. In this example, the route summarization configuration at the ABRs is greatly simplified. Routes from Area 7 injecting into the backbone can be summarized as follows: "All routes starting with 172.16 are found in Area 7."

The chief disadvantage of this approach, however, is the tremendous waste of address space. With this simpler approach, you must make certain that ABRs are explicitly configured to do route summarization (enabled by default in OSPF). We look at more elaborate summarization techniques in the next section, which covers operation in a multiple-area NBMA environment.

OSPF Operation in a Multiple-Area NBMA Environment

OSPF activities across multiple areas include operations such as creating link information, flooding techniques, and routing table construction. If a packet is heading for an intra-area network, it will be forwarded from an internal router to the destination router within the single area. Refer to the Type 1 and Type 2 LSAs for Area 1, as shown in Figure 5.3. However, as a packet needs to exit the area to another area, it follows these three steps:

1. The packet is routed from the originating network to an area border router.

2. The area border router transmits the packet through the transit area (backbone) to the ABR servicing the target network.

3. The target area border router forwards the packet on through its area until it arrives at the destination network.

It is the responsibility of the ABR to produce routing information concerning each area to which it is connected. The ABR then assumes the task of flooding the data into the backbone area and onward to other connected areas.

 The entire area must be converged and synchronized before an area border router can commence the process of flooding summary link-state advertisements.

An ABR sends out summary LSAs for each network that it knows about, by default. As mentioned, you can reduce the volume of LSAs by implementing solid route summarization techniques on the ABRs. Summary link-state updates are Type 3 and Type 4. These summary updates are put into an LSU packet and sent through all interfaces of the ABR. There are a few exceptions, however. For example, if an interface on the ABR is connected to a totally stubby area, or if the summary includes Type 5 external route information and is linked to a stub or totally stubby area, the packet will not be sent. After the destination ABR or ASBR obtains the LSU, it inserts it into the link-state database (topology table) and subsequently floods it into the local area. The internal area routers also add the entry to their local databases, so if you want to prevent this operation, make the area a stub area.

After all the various router types get their updates, they will inject the data into their topology tables and recalculate their routing tables. According to RFC 2328, there is an order of preference. Paths to intra-area routes (flagged as o in the route table) get added first. Again, these are Type 1 and Type 2 LSAs. Next, all the routers will then compute the optimal paths to the other areas inside the internetwork and generate the resulting Type 3 and Type 4 entries (o IA in the route table), as shown in Listing 5.2. An intra-area route to a destination will take precedence over an inter-area route to that same destination and is consequently injected into the routing table. Finally, all routers, except for stub area routers, compute the autonomous system external Type 5 destinations, if applicable, and distribute them. These external routes are marked as o E1 and o E2 in the route table. Listing 5.2 shows all the OSPF codes highlighted in the top section. After these operations are complete, the routers are prepared to reach any network inside or outside the AS.

Listing 5.2   Routers Compute Paths to Other Areas and Generate Type 3 and Type 4 Entries

```
ABR1#show ip route
Codes:  C - connected, S - static, I - IGRP, R - RIP, M - mobile, B - BGP
        D - EIGRP, EX - EIGRP external, O - OSPF, IA - OSPF inter area
        N1 - OSPF NSSA external type 1, N2 - OSPF external type 2
        E1 - OSPF external type 1, E2 - OSPF external type 2, E - EGP
        I - IS-IS, L1 - IS-IS level-1, L2 - IS-IS level-2, * - candidate
default
        U - per-user static route, o - ODR
        T - traffic engineered route

Gateway of last resort is 10.14.0.1 to network 0.0.0.0

        10.0.0.0/8 is variably subnetted,  9 subnets,  2 masks
O  IA   10.20.0.0/16 [110/128] via 10.14.0.1,  00:09:13,  Ethernet0
C       10.10.3.0/24 is directly connected, Serial0
O  IA   10.30.0.0/16 [110/148] via 10.14.0.1,  00:07:47,  Ethernet0
C       10.10.2.0/24 is directly connected, Serial1
<Output Omitted>
```

Configuring and Verifying a Multi-Area OSPF Network

A router becomes an ABR or ASBR according to the types of areas to which it is connected. The first step to configure OSPF on the router is to enable the OSPF routing protocol process and then designate the IP networks on the router that are members of the OSPF network, like so:

```
RouterA(config)# router ospf process-id
RouterA(config-router)# network address wildcard mask area area-id
```

If your router is connected to another non-OSPF network, you need to configure it as an ASBR and properly place it on the routing protocol network to which you are distributing routes. We will explore route distribution in greater detail in Chapters 9, "Scaling BGP Networks," and 10, "Optimizing Routing Updates."

One of the first planning decisions you need to make is which areas should be configured as stub or totally stubby to optimize network performance. A stub area prevents the flooding of Type 4 and Type 5 LSAs into the area. Routers in a stub area can access both intra-area and inter-area routes by using a default route (0.0.0.0) to access networks located outside the local AS. A default route is an entry in the routing table that is added for the purpose of directing packets when an explicit entry does not appear for them in the routing table. The technique that OSPF uses to produce a default route depends on the type of area into which you are injecting the route. For stub areas and totally stubby areas, the ASB to the stub area sends a summary LSA with link-state ID 0.0.0.0 (default). For a standard (or normal) area, you can simply advertise the default route into the area with the network command or, if the router does not have the default route set, you could use the following router configuration command to have an OSPF router generate a default route:

```
RouterA(config-router)# default-information originate always
```

This command generates a type 2 link with a link-state ID of 0.0.0.0 and network mask of 0.0.0.0, in essence, making this router an ASBR.

Stub areas cannot contain an ASBR, and the area cannot be configured as the backbone Area 0. You will usually see stub areas in hub (headquarters) and spoke (branch office) topologies, where a spoke is configured as a stub with a single exit point from the area.

A totally stubby area is a Cisco-proprietary type that does not accept flooding of Type 3, Type 4, or Type 5 packets into the area. Therefore, a totally stubby area can access only intra-area routes (advertised with Type 1 and Type 2 LSAs). The key difference is that a stub area accepts Type 3 LSAs, so that routers inside the stub areas can access both intra-area and inter-area routes. Both stub areas and totally stubby areas use a default route to get out of the local area.

Because totally stubby areas do more to reduce update information than stub areas, it is usually a better option to use them to improve scalability and stability in a Cisco OSPF environment.

To configure your area as a stub area or totally stubby area, first configure basic OSPF processing. The command router ospf [process-id] invokes an OSPF process on the router with a process ID number. The network area command then associates the router's configured IP networks with a specific OSPF area ID. Next, define the area as stub or totally stubby. You are basically setting the stub flag in the Hello packet (refer to Chapter 4). This configuration is performed by running the area stub command in router configuration mode on the ABR, as follows:

```
RouterA(config-router)# area area-id stub [no-summary]
```

This area stub command needs to be placed on all the stub area routers if they are to become neighbors and exchange routing information. The area-id parameter is a designator for the stub area and is represented by either a decimal or IP address value. The no-summary command is the process that actually creates the totally stubby area. It should be configured on only an ABR that is linked to a totally stubby area so that it will not send summary LSAs (Type 3) into the stub area.

Another option that you have on ABRs is to configure the cost of the default route that is being infused into your stubby area. The cost value is a 24-bit number and has a default value of 1. This is configured with the default-cost command, as shown in the following snippet:

```
RouterA(config-router)# area area-id default-cost cost
```

Here is a sample code snippet for configuring a stub area:

```
RouterA(config)# router ospf 50
RouterA(config-network)# 172.16.4.0 0.0.0.255 area 0
RouterA(config-network)# 172.16.5.0 0.0.0.255 area 2
RouterA(config-network)# area 2 stub
```

Here is a snippet that displays a totally stubby configuration sample:

```
RouterA(config)# router ospf 50
RouterA(config-network)# 172.16.4.0 0.0.0.255 area 0
RouterA(config-network)# 172.16.5.0 0.0.0.255 area 2
RouterA(config-network)# area 2 stub no-summary
```

The only difference between the configuration for a stub area and a totally stubby area is the no-summary command.

Figure 5.6 represents a hub-and-spoke, multi-area OSPF over NBMA network in which RouterA is configured in the backbone Area 0 and the spoke routers, RouterB and RouterC, are configured as Area 1. One benefit of this configuration is the reduction of network traffic to the NBMA (Frame Relay) cloud because the stub area will not receive Type 5 external LSA messages. In addition, changes to the topology of Area 1 remain in the backbone area.

If we configure Area 1 in Figure 5.6 as a stub area, the only routes that will appear on the RouterB and RouterC routing tables will be the following:

➤ Intra-area routes specified as o entries

➤ The default route to the ABR RouterA, specified with an *

➤ Inter-area routes denoted with an IA entry

If you want to configure Area 1 as a totally stubby area, configure the no-summary command on the ABR RouterA in Figure 5.6 to prevent summary LSAs from being sent into Area 1 and further reducing the number of link-state advertisements. This forces RouterB and RouterC to have only intra-area routes.

OSPF over NBMA

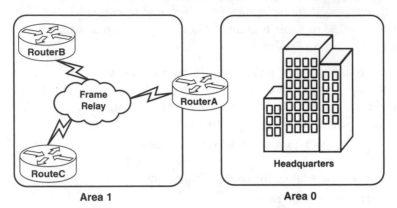

Figure 5.6 A simple OSPF-over-NBMA scenario.

You need to understand the benefits of configuring a totally stubby area. Primarily, the routing tables are smaller because external and summary routes are not inserted into totally stubby areas. Totally stubby areas also result in lower amounts of routing information circulation, and you can get greater scalability and stability on your OSPF internetwork.

Summary Route Costs

The cost of a summary route will be the lowest cost for a particular inter-area route that displays in the summary, added to the cost of the ABR connection to the backbone Area 0. These calculations are automatically computed for each summary route. The cost of an external route, however, is dependent upon the external type configured on the ASBR. There are two types of external origin codes: E1 and E2.

E1 routes are also called OSPF external Type 1 routes, and they take into consideration the internal cost of the path to the ASBR, added to the external cost, when determining the overall metric value of the route. External Type 2 routes, on the other hand, are distributed inside the local autonomous system by AS external link entries (Type 5 LSAs). As indicated in Table 5.2, Type 5 LSAs are originated only by ASBRs and define routes to external ASs. E2 routes use only the external cost to the next hop router outside the local AS for their routing metric. E2 is the default route type for OSPF Type 2 external routes, and a router will always prefer an E2 route over an E1 route, unless both routes share identical cost values.

Listing 5.3   Route Entry with an Origin Code of E2

```
Border# show ip route

Codes:  C_- connected, S - static, I - IGRP, R - RIP, M - mobile, B - BGP
        D - EIGRP, EX - EIGRP external, O - OSPF, IA - OSPF inter area
        N1 - OSPF  NSSA  external  type 1, N2 - OSPF  external  type 2
        E1 - OSPF external type 1, E2 - OSPF external type 2, E - EGP
        I - IS-IS, L1 - IS-IS level-1, L2 - IS-IS level-2, * - candidate
default
        U - per-user static route, o - ODR
        T - traffic engineered route

Gateway of last resort is not set

   *    172.16.0.0/24 is subnetted,  3 subnets
C            172.16.1.0 is directly connected,  Serial 0
O  E2      172.16.2.0 [110/10] via 10.0.1.1,  00:21:29
C            172.16.3.0 is directly connected,  Ethernet 0
```

You can see from Listing 5.3 that the selected entry will be flooded throughout the entire autonomous system and it has a cost metric that considers only the external cost of the route. Whenever you see a route entry with an origin code of E2, it indicates that an OSPF external Type 2 route was used. The technique called "redistribution" is used whenever different routing protocols need to exchange routing information. For example, you need to exchange OSPF routing information with RIP, EIGRP, or IS-IS protocols. This distribution process is covered in greater detail in Chapter 10.

A Type 7 LSA is a special form of external route announcement that is implemented with OSPF not-so-stubby areas (NSSAs). This creates a sort of hybrid stub area for some AS external routes. These special Type 7 LSAs are originated by ASBRs inside the NSSA and are flooded only within the local NSSA. An ABR, however, can convert the Type 7 LSAs to Type 5 LSAs and flood these into the backbone area. Internet service providers (ISPs) or network engineers that need to connect OSPF to remote sites using another protocol, such as RIP or EIGRP, primarily use these. For more information, refer to RFC 1587, "The OSPF NSSA Option."

Default Routes

As previously mentioned, a default route is the route to which all unknown traffic is sent. By creating a default static route to your ISP or headquarters, you have configured your ABR or ASBR to forward any traffic that it cannot resolve through its routing table. If your area or internetwork has only one point of exit, it makes sense to propagate this default route to all internal routers and ABRs in the local AS, if applicable. To create a default static route, use the global configuration command:

```
RouterA(config)# ip route 0.0.0.0 0.0.0.0 exit-interface
```

The `exit-interface` parameter is the name of the interface to which unknown traffic is sent.

The `default-information originate` command is an optional command used to propagate a Type 7 default route into the NSSA, as shown in the following sample:

```
RouterA(config-router)#default-information originate
```

The `default-information originate [always]` command can be used to distribute the default route to all routers inside the routing domain. The `always` keyword signifies that the route should be propagated regardless of the presence of the default route. To disable default route propagation, issue this command from the router configuration mode:

```
RouterA(config-router)# no default-information originate
```

show ip ospf *[process-id area-id]* database *[keyword]*

Several powerful command tools are available for verification, monitoring, and troubleshooting your multi-area OSPF environment. You learned about several fundamental commands in Chapter 4. The `show ip ospf process-id` command exhibits information about every area to which the router is connected for a particular process. It also designates whether the router is an ABR, ASBR, or both. Listing 5.4 is a sample of the `show ip ospf` command without added parameters because there is only one OSPF process running on this router.

Listing 5.4   A Sample of the show ip ospf Command

```
Router# sh ip ospf
 Routing Process "ospf 10" with ID 192.168.1.1
 Supports only single TOS(TOS0) routes
 SPF schedule delay 5 secs, Hold time between two SPFs 10 secs
 Minimum LSA interval 5 secs. Minimum LSA arrival 1 secs
 Number of external LSA 0. Checksum Sum 0x0
 Number of DCbitless external LSA 0
 Number of DoNotAge external LSA 0
 Number of areas in this router is 1. 0 normal 1 stub 0 nssa
    Area 1
         Number of interfaces in this area is 2
         It is a stub area
         Area has no authentication
         SPF algorithm executed 5 times
         Area ranges are
         Number of LSA 5. Checksum Sum 0x25804
         Number of DCbitless LSA 0
         Number of indication LSA 0
         Number of DoNotAge LSA 0
```

The following commands offer a more granular approach to maintaining your OSPF routers. This command set is invoked to display the contents of the topology database of the router. You can use a rich set of optional keywords to generate more granular information. Table 5.3 shows the keywords and associated descriptions.

Table 5.3 show ip ospf database Keywords	
Keyword	Description
network	Shows the network link-state information.
summary	Shows the router link-state summary information.
asbr-summary	Shows the ASBR link-state information.
external	Shows the AS external link-states.
database summary	Shows the database summary data and totals.

show ip ospf border-routers

The privileged EXEC-mode command show ip ospf border-routers reveals all the OSPF router's internal routes to all ABRs and ASBRs in an autonomous system. Here is a sample of this command:

```
Router#show ip ospf border-routers

Codes: i - Intra-area route, I-Inter-area route

Type  Dest Address  Cost  NextHop      Interface  ABR  ASBR  Area  SPF
i     10.10.1.1     10    192.168.1.1  Ethernet 2 TRUE FALSE 0     3
i     10.20.1.2     10    192.168.1.2  Ethernet 2 TRUE FALSE 0     3
```

The output consists of the ABR or ASBR IP addresses, next-hop address to the ABR, route cost, router type, route type, area number, and the SPF calculation number.

show ip ospf virtual links

The show ip ospf virtual-links command features information concerning the status of any configured virtual link on a router. As you know, a virtual link is a logical connection between the backbone area and a non-backbone area that is not directly connected to Area 0. The following snippet shows a sample of this command output:

```
Router#show ip ospf virtual-links

Interface address: 10.10.1.136 (POS 1/1/1) cost: 1, state: P To P, transit
area:
 1.2.3.4 hello: 10, dead: 40, retrans: 5 nbr id: 10.10.1.103, nbr address:
 10.10.1.103 nbr state: Full, nbr mode: Master, last hello: 38
```

Exam Prep Questions

Question 1

What designator must the OSPF backbone always use when being configured?

- ○ A. IA
- ○ B. Area 0
- ○ C. Standard
- ○ D. Area51

Answer B is correct. Area ID 0 is used to represent the backbone area. A backbone router is characterized as a router that has at least one interface connected to Area 0 (or OSPF transit area). Therefore, Area 0 is commonly referred to as the backbone area. Answer A is incorrect because IA is a designator in the routing table for an inter-area entry. Answer C is incorrect because the word "standard" is not a designator. The term is used to describe a single area environment that receives link updates, route summaries, and external route information. Answer D is incorrect because Area51 is a common theme of science fiction movies.

Question 2

Which one of the following is *not* a valid type of OSPF router?

- ○ A. Autonomous system boundary router
- ○ B. Area border router
- ○ C. Backbone router
- ○ D. Area system backbone router
- ○ E. Internal router

Answer D is correct. An internal router is an amalgam of various valid router types. Answer A is incorrect because an ASBR is an OSPF router that has interfaces in more than one AS. Answer B is incorrect because an ABR is an OSPF router that has interfaces in more than one area. Answer C is incorrect because a backbone router is an OSPF internal router or ABR that is a member of the internetwork backbone area. Answer E is incorrect because an internal router is an OSPF router that has all its interfaces in the same area.

Question 3

Which of the following statements represent valid advantages specific to implementing a totally stubby area in your internetwork? (Choose two.)

- ❑ A. Routing table sizes can be reduced because external and summary routes are not inserted into totally stubby areas.
- ❑ B. A router always prefers an E2 route on top of an E1 route.
- ❑ C. Network traffic is reduced because the totally stubby area does not process Type 2 network link entries.
- ❑ D. Totally stubby areas typically result in lower amounts of routing information being propagated.

Answers A and D are correct. First of all, the routing tables will be smaller because external and summary routes are not inserted into totally stubby areas. In addition, implementing a totally stubby area results in lower amounts of routing information propagation as well as greater scalability and stability on your OSPF internetwork. Answer B is incorrect because this statement relates to the cost of an external route configured on an ASBR and is not a function of totally stubby areas. Answer C is incorrect because (although it is not necessarily an advantage) a totally stubby area DR can indeed process Type 2 network link entries.

Question 4

You want to summarize routes for a certain area on an ABR in your OSPF multi-area environment. Which one of the following commands would you use?

- ○ A. **area area-id default-cost cost**
- ○ B. **area area-id stub [no-summary]**
- ○ C. **network address wildcard-mask area area-id**
- ○ D. **area area-id range address mask**

The correct answer is D. You instruct the ABR to perform route summarization for a specific area before injecting the routes into a different area with the `area range` command. Answer A is incorrect because the `area area-id default-cost cost` command is used to configure the cost of the default route that is being infused into a stubby area. Answer B is incorrect because the `no-summary` command is the process that actually creates the totally stubby area. Answer C is incorrect because this is the syntax used to designate the IP networks on the router that are a part of the OSPF network.

Question 5

Which one of the following LSA types is generated by designated routers in multi-access OSPF networks to describe a collection of routers attached to a specific network?

- ○ A. Type 1
- ○ B. Type 2
- ○ C. Type 3
- ○ D. Type 5

Answer B is correct. Type 2 LSAs are initiated by DRs in multi-access OSPF networks and describe a group of routers attached to a specific network. They are flooded within the single area containing the network. Answer A is incorrect because Type 1 LSAs are generated by each router for its own area to describe the state of router links. Answer C is incorrect because Type 3 LSAs are initiated by ABRs and define links between ABRs and internal routers. Answer D is incorrect because Type 5 LSAs are generated by ASBRs and define routes to external (AS) destinations.

Question 6

The **summary-address** router configuration command is used on which OSPF router types to summarize external routes to be injected into the OSPF routing domain?

- ○ A. Area system backbone router
- ○ B. Area border routers only
- ○ C. Autonomous system boundary routers
- ○ D. Internal routers

Answer C is correct. Although the `area range` command is used on ABRs to summarize internal routes, the `summary-address` router configuration command is implemented on an ASBR to summarize external routes that will be injected into the OSPF routing domain. You configure the ASBR to summarize external routes prior to injecting the routes into the OSPF domain. Answer A is incorrect because there is no such thing as an area system backbone router. Answer B is incorrect because the `summary-address` router configuration command is not used on routers that are only ABRs and are not ASBRs. Answer D is incorrect because the command is not run on internal routers.

Question 7

Which one of the following is a true statement concerning area border routers?

- ○ A. You cannot implement route summarization on an ABR, only on ASBRs.
- ○ B. Packets are transmitted from the ABR only if an interface on the ABR is connected to a totally stubby area.
- ○ C. Type 5 external route information will be transmitted from the ABR only if the summary is being sent to a stub area.
- ○ D. The entire area must be synchronized before an ABR can commence the process of flooding summary link-state advertisements.

Answer D is correct. The entire area must be converged and synchronized before an area border router can start the process of flooding summary LSAs. Answer A is incorrect because you can indeed implement route summarization on ABRs and ASBRs. Answer B is incorrect because packets will *not* be transmitted from an ABR if an interface on the ABR is connected to a totally stubby area. Answer C is incorrect because Type 5 external route information will *not* be transmitted from the ABR interface if the summary is being sent to a stub area.

Question 8

A Type 7 LSA is a special form of external route announcement that is implemented according to RFC 1587. Into what type of area is this special LSA flooded?

- ○ A. Stub
- ○ B. Not so stubby
- ○ C. Totally stubby
- ○ D. Partially stubby

Answer B is correct. A Type 7 LSA is a special form of external route announcement that is implemented with OSPF not-so-stubby areas. Answer A is a stub area and does not accept Type 7 LSAs. Answer C is incorrect because a totally stubby area does not accept Type 7 LSAs. Answer D is incorrect because there is no such thing as an OSPF partially stubby area.

Question 9

Which of the following commands are used specifically in conjunction with configuring default routes? (Choose two.)

- ❑ A. **ip route 0.0.0.0 0.0.0.0 exit-interface**
- ❑ B. **router ospf process-id**
- ❑ C. **default-information originate**
- ❑ D. **network address wildcard-mask area area-id**

The correct answers are A and C. To create a default static route, you use the global configuration command `ip route 0.0.0.0 0.0.0.0 exit-interface`. The `default-information originate` command is an optional command used to propagate a Type 7 default route into the NSSA. Answer B is incorrect because the `router ospf process-id` command is used specifically to enable the OSPF routing process on a router. Answer D is incorrect because the command is used to designate the networks that are part of the OSPF environment.

Question 10

Which one of the following commands is used exclusively to display information about a logical connection between the backbone area and a non-backbone area that is not directly connected to Area 0?

- ○ A. **show ip ospf process-id**
- ○ B. **show ip ospf virtual-links**
- ○ C. **show ip ospf border-routers**
- ○ D. **show ip ospf database summary**

The correct answer is B. The `show ip ospf virtual-links` command displays information regarding the status of any configured virtual link on a router. Answer A is incorrect because the `show ip ospf process-id` command exhibits information about every area to which the router is connected, as well as designates whether the router is an ABR, ASBR, or both. Answer C is incorrect because the `show ip ospf border-routers` command shows all of the OSPF router's internal routes to all ABRs and ASBRs in an autonomous system. Answer D is incorrect because the `show ip ospf database summary` command shows the router link-state summary information in the topology database.

Need to Know More?

 Parkhurst, William R. *Cisco OSPF Command and Configuration Handbook*. Indianapolis, IN: Cisco Press, 2002. ISBN 1587050714.

 Thomas, Tom. *OSPF Network Design Solutions, Second Edition*. Indianapolis, IN: Cisco Press, 2003. ISBN 1587050323.

 Complete list of Requests for Comments: http://www.cis.ohio-state.edu/htbin/rfc/rfc-index.html.

Applying Integrated IS-IS

Terms you'll need to understand:

✓ Intermediate system (IS)

✓ End system (ES)

✓ Connectionless Network Protocol (CLNP)

✓ End system–to–intermediate System (ES-IS)

✓ Level 1

✓ Level 2

✓ L1L2

✓ International Organization for Standardization-Interior Gateway Routing Protocol (ISO-IGRP)

✓ Circuit

✓ PDU

✓ DIS

✓ NSAP

Techniques you'll need to master:

✓ Understanding OSI models and protocols

✓ Identifying IS-IS networks, routers, and interface types

✓ Developing an IS-IS addressing scheme

✓ Configuring and verifying Level 1 and Level 2 ISs

The Intermediate System–to–Intermediate System (IS-IS) routing protocol is a flexible and robust routing protocol suitable for both ISO *Connectionless Network Protocol (CLNP)* and IP applications. In the IP world, it has emerged as the sole realistic alternative to OSPF for Interior Gateway Protocol (IGP) applications in ISP internetworks. IS-IS was originally designed to be used as a dynamic routing protocol for the ISO CLNP and was later adapted for routing IP in addition to CLNP as integrated IS-IS or dual IS-IS. IS-IS is the IGP of choice in most tier 1 ISP environments and telecommunications companies, which explains why Cisco has included it in the BSCI exam knowledge base requirements. IS-IS is a link-state protocol comparable to OSPF. OSPF has enjoyed a more formal evolution, whereas IS-IS has developed as needs have arisen. It was originally called DECnet Phase V Routing and renamed to IS-IS when it was adopted by the ISO in 1988.

IS-IS Networks and Interfaces

As a CCNA, you are well aware of the ISO OSI networking structure. However, a fundamental distinction must be made at the outset of this chapter. The ISO developed an Open Systems Interconnection (OSI) networking suite that consists of two major components. The first piece is the familiar and often-memorized OSI reference model, which is an abstract network construct represented by a seven-layered model. The second component is the OSI protocol suite, which is a collection of standard networking protocols that includes CLNP and ES-IS, among others, which are covered in this chapter. We are concerned with the OSI Network and Transport layers and their relationship to OSI protocols and services that function at these layers.

OSI Routed Network Protocols and Services

OSI connectionless network services are made possible through the Connectionless Network Protocol (CLNP) and Connectionless Network Service (CLNS), as described in the ISO 8473 standard. CLNP is an OSI Network layer protocol that carries upper-layer data and error messages over connectionless exchanges. CLNP offers the interface between the CLNS and the upper layers. CLNS provides Network layer services to the Transport layer through CLNP. CLNS does not conduct connection setup, maintenance, or termination because the paths are resolved independently for each packet transmitted through a network. Although CLNS does its best to deliver the packet, there is no built-in certainty that data will not be lost, damaged, duplicated, or delivered out of order. CLNS depends on Transport layer protocols to conduct error detection and correction services. This is altogether different from the Connection-Mode Network Service (CMNS).

The Connection-Oriented Network Protocol (CONP) and CMNS provide OSI connection-oriented network services. CONP is an OSI Network layer protocol that transports upper-layer data and error messages over connection-oriented links. CONP is built on the existing X.25 Packet-Layer Protocol (PLP), as defined in ISO 8208. CONP is an OSI protocol that operates at the Network layer and acts as an interface for the upper-layer data and error information of the CMNS. The duties of CMNS are related to the definite formation of communication paths between Transport layer units. These tasks include the setup, maintenance, and termination of connections, as well as individual quality of service (QoS) requests. In a nutshell, for OSI connection-oriented data transfer, CONP is the protocol and CMNS is the service. For OSI connectionless data transfer, CLNP is the protocol and CLNS is the service. End stations do not communicate via the CLNP protocol.

OSI Routing Protocols

OSI breaks up its routing into a multilevel hierarchy to make router design and functionality simpler. Level 0 routing is comparable to the ARP protocol function in IP. The *end system–to–intermediate system (ES-IS)* discovery protocol performs routing between hosts and routers to enable the end-to-end exchange of data in the internetwork. *Level 1* routing occurs between intermediate systems (ISs), or routers, in the same area. (Every end system exists in a particular area.) A Level 1 IS is concerned only with the path to the nearest Level 2 IS. Level 2 routing happens when Level 1 ISs exchange information between Level 1 areas to create an intradomain core or backbone. In other words, Level 2 routing occurs between different areas within the same routing domain. Level 3 routing is the process of routing between separate domains. Table 6.1 lists Cisco-supported CLNS/CLNP routing protocols.

Table 6.1	OSI CLNS/CLNP Routing Protocols Supported by Cisco
Protocol	**Description**
ISO-IGRP	A Cisco-proprietary protocol for CLNS based on IGRP that uses distance-vector techniques to exchange routing information.
IS-IS	A link-state protocol utilized in ISO CLNS for dynamic routing of CLNP. The protocol allows routers running as ISs to exchange routing information with other ISs. A Cisco router is a Level 1, Level 2, or Level 1–2 IS (as an exit point from the area). Integrated IS can propagate IP or CLNS, or both in dual mode.
Static routes (CLNS)	Although not technically a routing protocol, static CLNS routes can be implemented when routing in an OSI CLNS/CLNP environment.

When an *end system (ES)* needs to send data to another end system, routing can commence as soon as the ES discovers its neighbor through the exchange of hello packets. This process is similar to the way ARP works in IP and is the very nature of Level 0 routing. If the destination end system address is on another network (or subnetwork) in the same area, then the *intermediate system (IS)* knows about the route and sends it along accordingly. This is Level 1 routing. If the destination end system is in a different area, then the Level 1 end system sends the packet to the closest Level 2 IS to be forwarded along until the destination area is reached. This is Level 2 routing. If the packet has to be forwarded to another routing domain, then Level 3 routing takes over. Three primary protocols are used.

Integrated IS-IS Networks

The most current IS-IS specification is ISO 10589, which documents the IS-IS intradomain route exchange functionality. IS-IS was designed to offer Interior Gateway Protocol functionality, whereas the Border Gateway Protocol (BGP) is a widely deployed routing protocol with broad capabilities for interdomain routing. BGP is covered in detail in upcoming Chapters 8, "Configuring Border Gateway Protocol," and 9, "Scaling BGP Networks." Normally, routing protocols support only one OSI Layer 3 protocol. For example, OSPF and IP RIPv2 support the IP-routed protocol. So if you are using routers to concurrently link multiple network layer protocols, they are typically configured with separate routing protocols for each Layer 3 protocol supported (IP RIPv2 and IPX RIP, for example). Integrated IS-IS, however, supports both the ISO CLNP and IP Network layer protocols. The Cisco proprietary Enhanced Interior Gateway Routing Protocol (EIGRP) protocol also simultaneously supports multiple Layer 3 protocols such as IP, IPX, and AppleTalk.

An IS-IS routing domain is a series of interconnected routers (network) that are managed within the same administrative unit. This is also known as an autonomous system of routers or AS. All the routers in the domain run the Integrated IS-IS routing protocol to provide for intradomain exchange of routing information. This Integrated IS-IS network environment can be IP only, ISO CLNP only, or both.

The IS-IS protocol was initially meant to provide support for CLNP only. In RFC 1195, the original IS-IS specification (ISO 10589) is modified to support IP through the designated Integrated IS-IS.

In Table 6.2 you can review some of the most important terms and concepts related to IS-IS. You may want to return to this table throughout this chapter to reinforce your learning.

Table 6.2 Important Terms and Concepts for IS-IS	
Term or Concept	**Description**
Domain	A grouping of interconnected routers (network) that are managed under a shared administrative authority.
Circuit	An IS-IS interface that is uniquely identified with a circuit ID number (8 bytes).
Packet datagram unit (PDU)	Connectionless protocols, such as CLNP and IP, move data in chunks known as packets. In ISO 10589 terminology, packets are called protocol data units.
Link-state PDU (LSP)	This is the link-state packet used to flood information throughout the IS-IS routing domain.
Sequence number packets (SNP)	Control packets used with LSPs to successfully exchange IS-IS routing information.
Intermediate system (IS)	An IS simply represents the OSI term for a router.
Designated intermediate system (DIS)	The one elected router on the local network that is "logically" connected to all other nodes and sends the LSP information on behalf of its LAN. Dijkstra requires a pseudonode for broadcast media to compute shortest path.
End system (ES)	An ES represents the OSI term for a host.
Network service access point (NSAP)	The NSAP is the type of addressing scheme implemented by CLNS and IS-IS for identifying network devices and hosts.
Subnetwork point of attachment (SNPA)	The point at which subnetwork services are offered, usually a MAC address, Frame Relay DLCI, virtual circuit ID for X.25 or ATM, or HDLC.
End System–to–Intermediate xSystem (ES-IS)	A discovery protocol between IS-IS end systems, similar to the IP ARP protocol.
L1L2 IS	An IS, also called a router, that functions at Level 1 and Level 2 and maintains two separate link-state databases.

Types of IS-IS Routers and Their Role in Area Hierarchical Design

According to RFC 1195, pure IP domains are systems that use only IP as their primary routing protocol. Although IP domains route only IP traffic, they can also support the processing and forwarding of OSI packets necessary for IS-IS functionality. A pure ISO domain can transport only ISO traffic, which includes the traffic necessary to operate IS-IS. A dual domain, on the other hand, routes both IP and OSI CLNP traffic at the same time.

Integrated IS-IS is similar to many of the other routing protocols discussed in this BCSI course. Integrated IS-IS supports VLSM. Both the subnet mask and prefix are exchanged in routing updates. You can also redistribute routes in and out of IS-IS. It is feasible to configure a dual domain so that some areas route only IP and others route only CLNP. In addition, you can design other areas to route both IP and CLNP. The main objective, of course, is to have reliable routing information in an area by making sure that the databases are the same on all Level 1 link-state routers in the area. Therefore, at the area level, all the area routers must be identically configured either for IP only, CLNP only, or both protocols. In other words, an intermediate system is not permitted to have some connections devoted to IP only, another set dedicated to CLNP, and still another group configured for both protocols. At the domain level, however, there are no constraints on integrating IP-only areas with other CLNP-only or IP-CLNP areas. All links within an area must be configured in the same fashion, but backbone connections can configure the attached routers in a different way. An IS-IS area can be described as a contiguous group of Level 1 routers.

OSPF Area Borders Versus IS-IS Area Borders

Realize that with OSPF, the individual interfaces actually belong to the area. With Integrated IS-IS, the entire router is within the area and belongs to the area, not just the individual interfaces. Both IS-IS and OSPF use a hierarchical structure to facilitate design and addressing, yet IS-IS is a more scalable solution. As you learned in the previous two chapters, OSPF has a central Area 0 backbone to which all the other areas are physically attached. The border between the areas actually exists within the Area Border Routers (ABRs) so that each connection is in a particular area. This inherently introduces limitations in the network design. Integrated IS-IS builds its hierarchy with Level 1 and Level 2 routers, where the borders are in the connections as opposed to within the area routers themselves. In other words, every IS-IS router belongs to exactly one Level 2 area. This is different from OSPF, and permits an easier and more flexible solution to network scalability. With IS-IS you can extend the backbone area by simply adding more Level 2 routers.

An IS-IS network domain is the counterpart to an autonomous system (AS). A domain can be carefully planned or arbitrarily constructed into smaller units called areas. By choosing a hierarchical routing design, you can achieve more efficient intradomain routing. All routers in an IS-IS domain must be linked to a single physical area, which is designated by an area ID number in the network service address point (NSAP) address. (The NSAP is the point at which the OSI network services are made available to the Transport layer.) Routers are in the same area if they have an identical area ID number. In reality, an IS-IS router can have multiple NSAPs in multi-homing scenarios where the router is connected to multiple areas. We look closely at the NSAP addressing scheme later in this chapter. Multihoming combines all the areas into a single physical area. This is addressed later in this chapter.

Within the domain, a dual hierarchy exists where Level 1 routers (Intermediate Systems) perform the intra-area routing and Level 2 routers exchange data between areas (inter-area) only. Routers that operate at both levels (*L1L2*) perform routing services between the backbone and other areas, which include intra-area and inter-area routing.

An IS-IS L1L2 intermediate system is comparable to an area border router (ABR) in an OSPF autonomous system.

The Level 1 routers hold their own link-state database that stores the area topology and the exit points to other neighboring areas as well. In CLNP routing, for example, Level 1 routing engages in the collection of SysID (SysID is explained in the next section) and adjacency information from all routers and hosts in the local area. Level 2 routers have a different link-state topology database that contains the inter-area routing information. With CLNP Level 2 routing, routers exchange information such as area prefixes with their neighbors. Therefore, an L1L2 router will keep two separate databases so that they can perform L1 and L2 duties as if they were logically two separate routers, as shown in Figure 6.1.

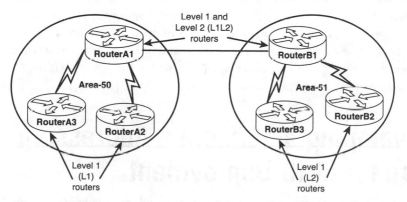

Figure 6.1   A sample physical IS-IS configuration between two areas linked by L1L2 routers.

An IS-IS backbone is different from an OSPF backbone in the sense that it is a group of areas that are linked by a chain of contiguous L1L2 and L2 routers, as shown in Figure 6.2.

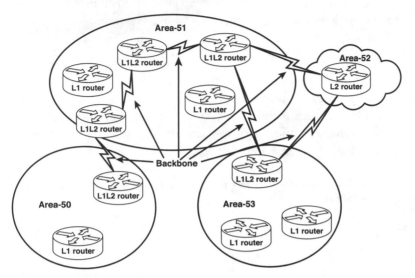

Figure 6.2 An IS-IS backbone linked by a chain of contiguous L1L2 and L2 routers.

IS-IS does not have the Area 0 backbone mechanism that is used by OSPF, but rather a dual-level hierarchy that propagates the Level 1 LSPs and the Level 2 LSPs separately. As mentioned in Table 6.2, the DIS sends the separate L1 and L2 LSPs for the network. In Figure 6.2, you can see that Area-51 has two Level 1 routers and three L1L2 routers that link the neighboring areas to form a "backbone path." The middle router has to provide Level 2 routing functions even though it does not directly connect to another area. If this router did not provide Level 2 routing or if it were to fail, the backbone would be brought down. Area-52 is a Level 2 area only because it has no intra-area routing to Level 1 routers within its area. This figure also reinforces the concept that IS-IS borders are maintained on the connections between the Level 2 routers, whereas OSPF creates the border within the ABRs connecting the multiple areas.

Developing an Effective Addressing Plan for IS-IS Deployment

Integrated IS-IS implements a CLNP node-based address structure to identify routers (even within pure IP environments). These CLNP addresses are called Network Service Access Points (NSAPs) and comprise three components: an area identifier (area ID) prefix, followed by a system identifier (SysID), and an N-selector, as shown in Table 6.3.

Table 6.3	The NSAP Addressing Structure				
IDP			**DSP**		
AFI	IDI		High Order DSP	SysID (6 bytes)	NSEL (1 byte)

The NSAP address shown in Table 6.3 is like a combination of an IP address and the upper-layer protocol in the IP header. The following list explains the different elements:

➤ *AFI*—This is the 1-byte authority and format ID that designates the formatting as well as the Internet authority that assigns the address.

➤ *IDI*—The interdomain ID identifies the domain and can be up to 10 bytes in length. The AFI and IDI together make up the interdomain part (IDP).

➤ *HODSP*—This is the high-order portion of the domain-specific part (DSP) of the address (similar to a major classful network address in IP) and is implemented to subdivide the domain into separate areas (such as an IP subnet).

➤ *SysID*—This ID defines an ES or IS device in an area. In OSI, a device has an address, as opposed to IP, where the interface has the address. Cisco, not OSI, implements a fixed length of 6 bytes for the SysID, and it must be consistent across all the devices in an area. Therefore, the MAC address is typically used for the system ID value.

➤ *NSEL*—The N-selector refers to the network service user, such as a transport protocol or the routing layer. (This is comparable to an IP port or socket.)

Each IS has a unique SysID, which together with the area ID and an N-selector value of 0×00 generates a special NSAP known as the node's network entity title (NET) or its network-level address. The HODSP, SysID, and NSEL work together to create the domain-specific portion of the NSAP address.

Although there are many different NSAP representations for disparate OSI systems, NSAPs are typically represented in a variable-length format up to 40 hex digits. IS-IS and ISO-IGRP, for instance, interpret the NSAP in different ways to add to the confusion. As you have seen, the IS-IS combines the IDP (AFI+IDI) and the High Order DSP to derive the Level 2 (area) address, and the SysID (MAC Address) is used for Level 1 routing. When you add on the 1-byte NSEL you get a three-part address for the IS-IS NSAP. OSI-IGRP routes, however, use a tri-level domain hierarchy where the IDP (AFI+IDI) represents the third level, the HODSP is Level 2, and the SysID is Level 3. In other words, where IS-IS uses the ASI+IDI+HODSP for the area ID, ISO_IGRP breaks this up into a Domain ID (AFI) and an Area ID, as shown in Table 6.4.

Table 6.4 The ISO-IGRP NSAP Addressing Structure is Different From IS-IS To Support a Tri-Level Hierarchy

IDP		DSP		
AFI	IDI	High Order DSP	SysID (6 bytes)	NSEL (1 byte)
Domain		Area	System ID	Unused

The area ID for ISO-IGRP is represented by the 2 bytes left of the SysID field to accommodate the allowable 65,535 IGRP areas. The remaining 1–11 bytes to the left of the area ID is the Domain ID field. That makes the minimum length for an ISO-IGRP NSAP equal to 10 bytes. In other words: 1-byte NSEL (fixed but unused) + 6-byte SysID (fixed) + 2-byte Area ID (fixed) + a minimum 1-byte Domain ID (variable) = 10 bytes.

If the NSEL value is set to 00 in a NSAP address, it is called a NET (network entity title).

IS-IS utilizes this node-based addressing scheme of CLNP, and standard NSAP prefixes must be used for routing data packets. It is a basic prerequisite that, even when Integrated IS-IS is used in an IP-only setting, the nodes must have ISO NSAP addresses (NETs). Addresses that begin with the AFI value of 49 are considered private internal addresses, similar to the ranges set aside for IP. (Refer to Chapters 1 and 2 to review IP addressing.) Although these addresses are routable, they should not be advertised outside the CLNS network.

The AFI value starting with 39 is used to designate the ISO data country code. An AFI value beginning with 47 specifies the international code. For example, look at the following NSAP:

```
49.0010.xxxx.yyyy.zzzz.00
```

For IS-IS, the area ID is `49.0010`, the SysID is `xxxx.yyyy.zzzz`, and the NSEL value is 00 (NET). However, if ISO-IGRP is being used, then the Domain is 49, the Area is 0010, the SysID is `xxxx.yyyy.zzzz`, and the NSEL value is unused.

When you enable Integrated IS-IS for IP routing on an interface, the IP subnets are automatically added to the router's LSP. The IP prefixes are then accumulated into an IP link-state database, which is used by the SPF algorithm to determine the best routes.

Identifying Systems and Establishing IS-IS Adjacencies

As you now know, an IS can be part of only one Level 2 area (as shown in Figure 6.2). It is the area ID and address that specifically identifies the area and system ID of each network node. Therefore, every IS in a particular area must use the same identifying area address (just as nodes in an IP subnet use the same subnetwork address). An adjacency is created between a host (end system) and a Level 1 router (IS) if they both have an identical area address. ESs create adjacencies only with ISs that have the same area addresses and with other ESs on their same subnetwork. Routing performed at Level 1 is based on SysID values (generally MAC addresses or an IP loopback address coded into the ID); therefore ES and IS devices must have unique SysIDs (as well as the uniform length) within the area. This is a mandatory 6 bytes when you're running the Cisco IOS.

Because all L2 ISs must be aware of the other ISs in the backbone, they need unique SysIDs as well (refer to Figure 6.3). As a matter of practice, you should ensure that the SysIDs are unique on a domainwide basis to prevent the possibility of conflicts. Referring back to Table 6.2, the SPNA number is the subnetwork point of attachment or Layer 2 mapping to the NET or NSAP address. This is something like a MAC address or DLCI number. A circuit ID is also used to identify the individual interfaces. This could be an 8-byte integer number on a WAN link such as 15, or an identifier attached to the end of the SysID of the DIS, such as `1820.5700.1003.15` where 15 represents the circuit ID number.

As you can see in Figure 6.3, all the ISs are in the same IS domain with the ID number of 40. Each IS also has a unique 3-byte area ID that corresponds to the area in which they are (Area 50, Area 51, and Area 52) and is shared by the other ISs within their respective areas. Third, each IS has a 6-byte SysID that is unique throughout the domain (`1111.1111.1111` to `8888.8888.8888`). Finally, each IS has an NSEL value of 00, which specifies this as a NETs.

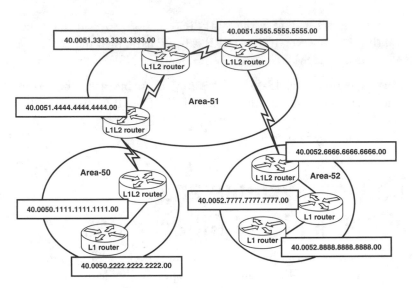

Figure 6.3 NSAP addressing on a physical IS-IS network.

Table 6.2 also defined the protocol data unit or PDU as the unit of data implemented by OSI. IS-IS and ES-IS data packets are encapsulated by a Data Link (Layer 2) PDU without an IP or CLNP header. Each IS-IS and ES-IS PDU contains the Type, Length, and Value fields (also referred to as TLV). The CLNP data packets, however, have a complete CLNP header placed between the Layer 2 header and the upper-layer CLNS routing information. Table 6.5 shows the four existing L1 and L2 packet types.

Table 6.5 IS-IS L1 and L2 Packet Types	
PDU Packet Type	**Description**
LSP	The link-state packet used to transport link-state information. LSP can be Broadcast (that is, LANs) or Nonbroadcast (that is, WAN point-to-point and multipoint—IS-IS does not understand NBMA networking topologies). LSP contains LSP header and variable-length TLV fields.
Hello	These Hello PDU packets are used to generate and manage adjacencies. ESHs hello packets are sent by an ES to an IS (ES to IS Hello), ISH hello packets are sent by an IS to an ES (IS to ES Hello), and IIH hello packets are used between two ISs (IS to IS Hello).
CSNP	This is the complete sequence number PDU that is utilized to propagate the IS's complete link-state topology database.
PSNP	This is the partial sequence number PDU that is utilized for link-state acknowledgements and requests.

NOTE

On LANs, IS-IS protocol data units are forwarded to the following well-known MAC layer broadcast addresses:

AllL1ISs at **01-80-C2-00-00-14**

AllL2ISs at **01-80-C2-00-00-15**

AllIntermediateSystems at **09-00-2B-00-00-05**

AllEndSystems at **09-00-2B-00-00-04**

IS-IS routers (ISs) use LSP sequencing to make sure that routers are getting the most up-to-date information for calculating routes. The LSP also has a Remaining Lifetime field to make sure that invalid or old LSPs get dropped from the database after a default interval of 20 minutes (1200 seconds). LSPs also store precise information about the ISs' attached peers. For example, an LSP knows the links to neighbor ISs and the interface metrics, as well as the links to end system peers.

IS-IS Metrics

One required metric and three optional metrics are associated with IS-IS. Regardless of the ones that you implement, they are all applied to the outbound interface of the peer IS. The default, required IS-IS metric value is cost. An interface cost is a 6-bit value between 1 and 63 and has a default value of 10. The total cost (total path metric) to a destination router is the sum of all the costs on *all* outbound interfaces on a precise path with the least cost being preferred. The maximum value is 1023, although Cisco supports a "wide metric" of 16,777,215 ($2^{24}-1$) with a total path value of one less than 2^{32}.

IS-IS LAN Adjacencies

You were also introduced to the term *designated intermediate system* (DIS) in Table 6.2. All routers on an IS-IS LAN create adjacencies through the elected DIS router. The DIS is also called a *pseudonode* because it creates a logical link to all the other nodes on the LAN. If the DIS fails, another election takes place because there is no backup DIS such as the OSPF BDR. The election is based on router priority with the MAC address as the last resort tiebreaker. The DIS creates and floods a new pseudonode LSP when a new neighbor is added or dropped or when the refresh interval timer expires. Each IS (router), on the other hand, generates and floods a new non-pseudonode LSP (non-DIS) when a new neighbor comes up or disappears, when new IP prefixes are added or removed, when the metric of a link changes, or when the refresh interval timer expires. This DIS pseudonode process works in concert with the IS LSPs to lower the number of adjacencies and the amount of flooding over LAN networks.

Separate adjacencies are created for Level 1 and Level 2 ISs and are stored in their own particular tables. On a LAN, these adjacencies are created with L1 and L2 IIH hello packets. The hello packet default interval is 10 seconds and the down timer is 30 seconds. Both of these timers are configurable. These separate IIH packets advertise L1 and L2 peers and establish adjacencies based on the inbound IIH and router type (L1L2 or L2). ISs within an area accept L1 IIH packets and establish adjacencies only within their own area ISs. Level 2 ISs or L1L2 routers accept Level 2 IIH packets and establish Level 2 adjacencies only.

IS-IS WAN Adjacencies

On a point-to-point connection, common IIH packets are used to advertise the level type and area ID information. For instance, two Level 1 routers connected by a WAN link in the same area would exchange IIH packets that designate Level 1 (level type) and establish a Level 1 adjacency. Level 2 ISs in the same area connected by a point-to-point link would designate a Level 2 type and establish a Level 2 adjacency. If two L1L2 ISs were in the same area, they would use a common IIH that would designate both types and adjacencies. In a nutshell, Level 1 ISs establish only Level 1 adjacencies, Level 2 ISs establish only Level 2 adjacencies between areas, and L1L2 ISs establish both.

If two routers were physically connected but in different areas, the IIH PDUs would be mutually ignored and no adjacencies would be established because the area IDs are inconsistent.

Database Synchronization and Routing Traffic Transport

To accomplish synchronization of the IS-IS link-state database, you use distinctive protocol data units referred to as CSNPs and PSNPs. They are often simply known as Sequence Number PDUs or SNPs. The goal of these special packets is to make sure that LSPs are exchanged in a reliable fashion. They do not actually carry the actual LSP data but rather LSP descriptors, or headers, that define the link-state packets.

Complete Sequence Number PDUs

Complete Sequence Number PDU (CSNP) packets contain an address range (a list of the LSPs held by the router), LSP ID, sequence number, checksum, and remaining lifetime value. The DIS multicasts them every 10 seconds so that the receiving ISs can compare the LSP list to their own database and subsequently request any missing LSPs if necessary. CSNPs are also sent out on point-to-point links whenever the connection comes up. Cisco enables you to configure periodic CSNPs on WAN links as well, if desired.

Partial Sequence Number PDU

Partial Sequence Number PDUs (PSNPs) are implemented to be exchanged for acknowledgement purposes to verify that an LSP was received on a LAN or a point-to-point WAN link. PSNPs are also used to request the transmission of the latest LSP. They usually contain only a single LSP descriptor block. Figure 6.4 gives an example of a PSNP in action.

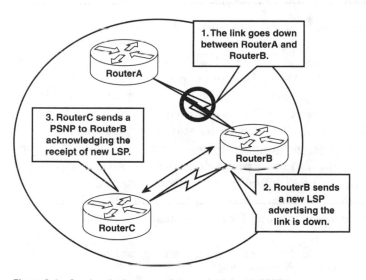

Figure 6.4 Synchronization on a point-to-point link with PSNPs.

Integrated IS-IS Routing Traffic Transport for IP and OSI

So far in this chapter we have focused on the behavior of IS-IS in an OSI-only (CLNS) implementation. Integrated IS-IS, however, has the flexibility to run

CLNS (OSI only), IP only, or a dual OSI and IP scenario. The link-state packets carried in an Integrated IS-IS topology can store several variable-length Type, Length, and Value fields (TLV) and there are IP-specific TLV fields to carry IP information. Although it is true that you can use Integrated IS-IS with only IP routing, you must still configure CLNS addresses because the OSI protocols are needed to generate the peer relationships between the routers. ISs still use the aforementioned IS-IS hello mechanisms to establish end system (host)–to–intermediate system (router) adjacencies. A NET address has to be configured to ID the Integrated IS-IS router, allow the SPF algorithm can do its magic, and facilitate Layer 2 forwarding processes.

Regardless of whether a router is running pure IS-IS or Integrated IS-IS, it has to build the CLNS routing/forwarding table to compute the SPF tree to the NETs or OSI addresses of the destination ISs. Cisco IP routers that use Integrated IS-IS as the routing protocol conform to the IP packet handling requirements as specified in RFC 1812 (Requirements for Internet Gateways). IP routers must process the ISO packets relevant to IS-IS operation, as well as other IP router functions such as ICMP and ARP.

The routing information base consists of two databases that are core to the IS-IS operation: the Link-State database and the OSI Forwarding database. The Link-State database is propagated with routing information learned from the update process. The update process produces local link-state information, based on the adjacency database built by the subnetwork-dependent functions mentioned previously. The router then advertises this information to all peers in link-state packets. The router also gets related link-state information from each adjacent neighbor, retains copies of received LSPs, and then re-advertises them to other peers. Routers in the same area will ultimately have identical Level 1 Link-State databases (matching views of the area topology), that are synchronized through the use of SNPs. This synchronization process is mandatory for routing stability within the area.

The Level 2 Link-State database contains area prefix information that combines the areas for Level 2 (inter-area) routing.

The Link-State database facilitates the decision making process by generating the Forwarding database, using the shortest path first (SPF) algorithm (also known as the Dijkstra algorithm). The shortest paths to the NETs or OSI addresses of the destination routers is computed by adding the link metrics along the routing path (chain).

On the BSCI exam, you must remember that an IS runs separate SPF processes and link-state databases for Level 1 and Level 2 routing. Therefore, a L1L2 IS runs the SPF algorithm twice and creates separate SPF trees for both levels.

The OSI Forwarding database is the CLNS routing table and consists of only the best IS-IS routes. These routes are used in packet-switching decisions. If a router has multiple sources of routing information, such as static routes and BGP, the Cisco router uses the administrative distance (AD) to prefer one routing source over another. As you know, the protocol with the lowest AD is preferred. The accepted best route is then installed in the routing table.

Intra-area Level 1 routing uses the SysID value in the destination NSAP. L1L2 routers send default routes to Level 1 ISs in their area. If the packet is going to a destination outside of the area, the Level 1 router forwards the packet to the nearest L1L2 router (the nearest exit point based on the best default route to L1L2 routers). Next, the L1L2 IS routes the packet across the Level 2 backbone by using the area ID of the destination area. Remember that Level 2 routing is based on the area ID value in the NSAP. Upon arrival, the packet is picked up by the Level 1 routing process in the destination area and delivered accordingly.

Take the IS-IS network in Figure 6.5, for example. Suppose that Router50A is sending packets to Router51D using Integrated IS-IS. The packets are first default routed to the Area-50 L1L2 router, Router50B, and then into the destination Area-51 at Router51A. Level 1 routing takes over as Router51A sends the packet through the L1L2 backbone router to the destination Router51D. The total cost on this path is 45. However, on the round trip, Router51D routes the packets back through its closest L1L2 IS, Router53B. This router determines that the lowest cost path to Area-50 is via another route altogether—through Area-53 via Router53A and over to Router50B to the round-trip destination. This is the nature of IS-IS packet switching and is not necessarily an unfavorable scenario for an internetworking environment.

As mentioned earlier in this chapter, a grouping of IS-IS is referred to as a domain, similar to an autonomous system. If you are running a pure CLNS network, you can use the Cisco-proprietary ISO-IGRP protocol to actually link multiple domains. ISO-IGRP deciphers the IDI part of the CLNS route to permit interdomain routing. If you are running IP in your environment, then an IP interdomain routing protocol is necessary. Typically, IS-IS is used in conjunction with BGP for routing IP packets. BGP injects external routes, where IS-IS functions as the IGP responsible for internal routing (mainly next-hop information for the BGP routes). As a result, there is very little overlap in routing information between either source. IS-IS and BGP routes can, therefore, coexist in the routing table.

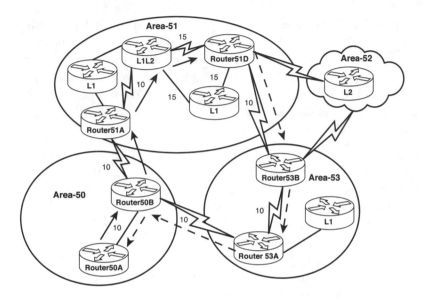

Figure 6.5 The IS-IS routing process can lead to asymmetric results.

Realize that IP information does not enter into the SPF equation when you run Integrated IS-IS, even though the IP information is included in the link-state packets. The SPF tree is constructed solely from CLSNS data. IP information is used locally for comparing things such as administrative distance and are tagged as coming through Level 1 or Level 2. This "separation of powers" from the key IS-IS networking mechanism is another factor that makes IS-IS a more scalable solution than OSPF. The SPF tree is unaffected, for instance, if an underlying IP subnet fails and link-state updates are flooded.

IS-IS NBMA Solutions in Switched WAN Networks

Integrated IS-IS recognizes three different types of WAN connections: point-to-point leased lines, dialup links, and switched WANs.

Point-to-Point WANs

This first category of WAN connection is usually a leased line solution between two ISs that exist on both sides of a HDLC or PPP circuit. In other words, IS-IS considers this an NBMA network with just two attached devices. A solitary IIH PDU is used to designate a Level 1, Level 2, or L1L2 adjacency on a point-to-point link. After adjacency is defined, the peers transmit CSNP (complete) packets detailing the contents of their link-state databases. PSNPs are then used to request missing LSPs and for acknowledgement as displayed earlier in Figure 6.4. This partial information exchange is another example of the superiority of link-state behavior versus distance-vector full table exchange.

Dialup Links

Dial-on-demand (DDR) solutions can be set up as either point-to-point or point-to-multipoint WANs. It is highly recommended by Cisco that you avoid an IS-IS over dialup scenario with the exception of backup purposes. Legacy DDR, dialer profiles, and dialer virtual profiles are not covered by the BSCI exam and are a remote access solution.

Switched WANs

If your network has been configured in a full-mesh topology, you can consider IS-IS over a multipoint network solution. The inherent possibilities of a full-mesh becoming a partial mesh because of link failures or poor configuration make this scenario problematic and one to be avoided. Cisco highly recommends that you opt for point-to-point subinterface solutions and steer clear of NBMA multipoint altogether when running IS-IS. The subinterface is normally on its own subnet with a 30-bit (/30) subnet mask, as shown in previous chapters for WAN links.

If you decide to deploy an Integrated IS-IS NBMA WAN solution, you will first invoke the IS-IS process and assign NETs. This is covered in detail in the next section, titled "Configuring Cisco Routers for Appropriate Integrated IS-IS Operation." Next, you must design a full (or partial) mesh among the neighbors and configure point-to-point interfaces for every NBMA virtual circuit, including IP addressing. You then need to map the Level 3 addresses/protocols to the virtual circuit, for instance using the `frame-relay map` commands. Finally, you can start the IS-IS process on each subinterface (not on the main interface!) with the `ip router isis` command explained in the following section.

Cisco IOS release 12.0 and higher enables you to use the **ip unnumbered** interface configuration command on point-to-point interfaces because Integrated IS-IS utilizes CLNS for route propagation.

Configuring Cisco Routers for Appropriate Integrated IS-IS Operation

To enable the IS-IS process, simply perform the following tasks while in global configuration mode:

```
Router50B(config)# router isis [tag]
```

This will start IS-IS routing and specify an IS-IS process for IP, placing you in router configuration mode. The [tag] is optional and is used to supply some unique and descriptive name for the routing process if more than one IS-IS process is configured on the router.

Your next step is to configure the NET for the routing process. The exact syntax for the net command is net *network-entity-title*. There is no network command as there is in IP. If you need to route CLNS packets as well, you also use the clns router isis [tag] interface configuration command. The parameter *network-entity-title* designates the area address and SysID for the IS-IS routing process. You can designate a name for a NET, as well as an address, with the following command:

```
Router50B(config-router)# net 00.000x.xyxy.xyxy.xyxy.00
```

The next step in the process is to go into interface configuration mode by using the following:

```
Router50B(config-router)# interface type number
```

For example:

```
Router50B(config-router)# int S1
```

Finally, you specify which interfaces will actively route IS-IS by using the following command in interface configuration mode:

```
Router50B(config-if)# ip router isis [tag]
```

Cisco enables both the Level 1 and Level 2 routing operations by default on routers running IS-IS. You can designate a router to run only Level 1 or Level 2 operations with the following router configuration commands:

```
Router50B(config-router)# is-type {level-1|level-1-2|level-2-only}
```

If you use the level-1 parameter, the IS functions solely as a "station" router for intra-area routing. It uses the nearest L1L2 router for inter-area routing. The is-type parameter level-1-2 is the default setting and tells the IS to operate as both a Level 1 station and an area router. As you have learned, this IS runs two instances of the link-state algorithm and database. The third option is to make the router an area router only as a part of the IS-IS backbone. It does not communicate with station routers within its own area. This is how you could configure the L2 router in Area-52, as shown in Figure 6.5.

The Cisco IS-IS implementation enables you to modify several interface-specific IS-IS parameters. Most interface configuration commands can be configured separately from other attached routers. You can perform the following tasks, described in the accompanying sections:

➤ Configure the IS-IS circuit type

➤ Configure the IS-IS link-state metrics

➤ Set the advertised Hello Interval

➤ Set the Retransmission Interval

➤ Set the LSP Transmissions Interval

➤ Set the Hello Multiplier

➤ Specify designated router election

➤ Assign a password for an interface

➤ Generate a default route

➤ Summarize address ranges

Configure the IS-IS Circuit Type

Even though your IS-IS router is functioning as a L1L2 router, you might need to control the type of adjacencies that are established on a per-interface basis. Remember that the default Cisco behavior is to function as an L1L2 router and attempt to generate both types of adjacencies, if possible. Here is the syntax to use in this situation:

```
Router50B(config-if)# isis circuit-type {level-1|level-1-2|level-2-only}
```

Configure the IS-IS Link-State Metrics

You can configure a cost for a specified interface by setting the default-metric for Level 1 or Level 2 routing. To configure the metric (or cost) for the specified interface, use the following command in interface configuration mode:

```
Router50B(config-if)# isis metric default-metric {level-1 | level-2}
```

Set the Advertised Hello Interval

You can designate the amount of time (in seconds) between hello packets that are sent on the interface. The hello interval can be configured independently for Level 1 and Level 2, except on serial point-to-point interfaces. (Because there is only a single type of hello packet sent on serial links, it is independent of Level 1 or Level 2.)

 Remember that Cisco recommends that your frame relay networks be configured with point-to-point subinterfaces as a best practice.

To specify the length of time, in seconds, between the hello packets that are sent on the specified interface, enter the following command in interface configuration mode:

```
Router50B(config-if)# isis hello-interval seconds {level-1 | level-2}
```

Set the Retransmission Interval

You can configure the number of seconds between retransmission of IS-IS link-state PDUs (LSPs) for point-to-point links. The value you choose should be an integer greater than the expected round-trip delay between any two ISs on the attached network. This parameter setting should be conservative, or unnecessary retransmissions will occur. The value should also be larger for serial lines. To configure the number of seconds between retransmission of IS-IS LSPs for point-to-point links, perform the following task in interface configuration mode:

```
Router50B(config-if)# isis retransmit-interval seconds
```

Set the LSP Transmissions Interval

To configure the delay between successive IS-IS link-state packet transmissions, you can perform the following task in interface configuration mode:

```
Router50B(config-if)# isis lsp-interval milliseconds
```

Set the Hello Multiplier

To designate the number of IS-IS hello packets a neighbor must miss before the router should declare the adjacency as "down," use the following command in interface configuration mode (the default value is 3):

```
Router50B(config-if)# isis hello-multiplier multiplier {level-1 | level-2}
```

Specify Designated Router Election

You can configure the priority used for designated router (DIS) election. Priorities can be configured separately for Level 1 and Level 2. To specify the designated router election, perform the following task in interface configuration mode:

```
Router50B(config-if)# isis priority value {level-1 | level-2}
```

Assign a Password for an Interface

You can assign different passwords for different routing levels as well. Specifying level-1 or level-2 configures the password for only Level 1 or Level 2 routing, respectively. If you do not designate a particular level, then the default is level-1. Authentication is automatically disabled. To configure a password for the specified level, perform the following task in interface configuration mode:

```
Router50B(config-if)# isis password password {level-1 | level-2}
```

Generate a Default Route

You can force a default route into an IS-IS routing domain. Whenever you specifically configure redistribution of routes into an IS-IS routing domain, the Cisco IOS software does not, by default, redistribute the default route into the IS-IS routing domain. The following feature enables you to force the boundary router to redistribute the default route or generate a default route into its L2 LSP. You can also use a route-map to advertise the default route conditionally, depending on the existence of another route in the router's routing table. To generate a default route, perform the following task in router configuration mode:

```
Router50B(config-router)# default-information originate [route-map map-name]
```

Summarize Address Ranges

You can create aggregate addresses that are represented in the routing table by a summary address. As you are aware, this process is called route summarization (or aggregation). One summary address can include multiple groups of addresses for a given level. Routes learned from other routing protocols can also be summarized. The metric used to advertise the summary is the smallest metric of all the more specific routes. To create a summary of addresses for a given level, perform the following task in router configuration mode:

```
Router50B(config-router)# summary-address address mask {level-1 | level-1-2
| ➡ level-2}
```

The Cisco IOS will try to summarize the area ID as much as and whenever it is feasible. If an IS-IS network was broken up into several subdivisions of a major area, then the area ID assignments reflect this design. For example, between the sub-areas the router routes according to the entire area ID, and between the major areas, the router summarizes the area ID up to the major boundary.

A Sample Dual Area Integrated IS-IS Environment

For a simple real-world configuration example, you can look at a subset of the internetwork shown in Figure 6.5. In Figure 6.6, we have an Integrated IS-IS scenario with an IS-IS process and NET configuration on a router serving as an IP-only L1L2 router.

Listing 6.1 shows a possible Integrated IS-IS configuration for Router50-2. It is a part of the area 49.0050, but it also links to the area 49.0051 through neighbor Router51-1 on an Ethernet connection. In this example, both Router50-2 and Router51-1 are L1L2 ISs, which is the default setting for the is-type command, so we do not need to include this in the router configurations.

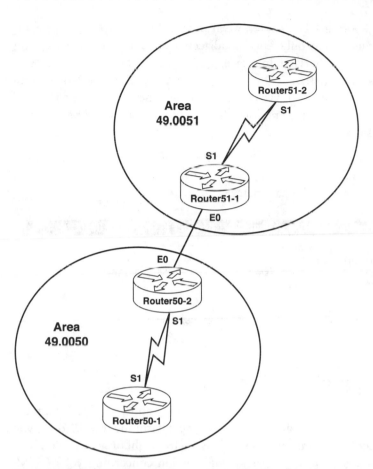

Figure 6.6   A simple Integrated IS-IS scenario between two areas.

Listing 6.1   The Configuration of Router50-2 As an L1l2 IS in Area 49.0050

```
Router(config)# hostname Router50-2
Router50-2(config)# int e0
Router50-2(config-if)# ip address 192.168.100.2 255.255.255.0
Router50-2(config-if)# ip router isis
Router50-2(config-if)# isis circuit-type level-2-only
!
Router50-2(config)# int S1
Router50-2(config-if)# ip address 192.168.200.2 255.255.255.0
Router50-2(config-if)# ip router isis
Router50-2(config-if)# isis circuit-type level-1
!
Router50-2(config)# router isis
Router50-2(config-router)# net 49.0050.1921.6820.0002.00
```

In Listing 6.1, we have configured IP for the Ethernet and Serial interfaces and enabled the Integrated IS-IS process. On the Ethernet 0 interface link with the neighboring L1L2 router, we also used the isis circuit-type command to designate that only Level 2 adjacency should be established with Router51-1. On the Serial 1 interface, we are using the isis circuit-type command to specify that a Level 1 adjacency is generated only with Router50-1 (see Figure 6.6). We could have issued the isis metric command as well to configure different metric values for the Ethernet and Serial interfaces, if necessary.

We don't want to forget the Level 1 router configuration for Router50-1. Listing 6.2 includes a sample configuration for that station router in Area 49.0050, where the is-type parameter is set to level-1:

Listing 6.2　The Configuration of Router50-1 As an L1 IS in Area 49.0050

```
Router(config)# hostname Router50-1
Router50-1(config)# int s1
Router50-1(config-if)# ip address 192.168.200.1 255.255.255.0
Router50-1(config-if)# ip router isis
!
Router50-1(config)# router isis
Router50-1(config-router)# net 49.0050.1921.6820.0001.00
Router50-1(config-router)# is-type level-1
```

Verifying and Troubleshooting IS-IS

Many commands are available for troubleshooting and verifying Integrated IS-IS. As you might have guessed, even if the environment is IP-only, you have to inspect CLNS information such as IS-IS neighbor adjacencies. The show clns command displays general information concerning your CLNS network, and the show clns protocol command can be issued at the EXEC-mode prompt, as well, to find out information about specific IS-IS processes on your router. Listing 6.3 shows the output for Router50-2 in Figure 6.6.

Listing 6.3　The show clns protocol Command

```
Router50-2# show clns protocol
IS-IS Router: <Null Tag>
  System Id: 1921.6820.0002.00  IS-Type: level-1-2
  Manual area address(es):
       49.0050
  Routing for area address(es):
       49.0050
  Interfaces supported by IS-IS:
       Serial1 - IP
       Ethernet0 - IP
  Redistributing:
    Static
  Distance: 110
```

The show clns interface command can be utilized to show individualized information on an interface-by-interface basis. For example, Listing 6.4 represents the output of this command on the Serial 1 interface of Router50-2.

Listing 6.4   The show clns interface Command Output

```
Router50-2# show clns interface s1
Serial1 is up, line protocol is up
  Checksums enabled, MTU 1500, Encapsulation HDLC
  ERPDUs enabled, min. interval 10 msec.
  RDPDUs enabled, min. interval 100 msec., Addr Mask enabled
  Congestion Experienced bit set at 4 packets
  CLNS fast switching enabled
  CLNS SSE switching disabled
  DEC compatibility mode OFF for this interface
  Next ESH/ISH in 18 seconds
    Routing Protocol: IS-IS
      Circuit Type: level-1
      Interface number 0x1, local circuit ID 0x100
      Level-1 Metric: 10, Priority: 64, Circuit ID: 1921.6820.0002.00
      Number of active level-1 adjacencies: 1
      Next IS-IS Hello in 3 seconds
```

You can also use the show ip route isis command to see just the IS-IS routes from the IP routing table. For instance, the output for Router50-2 would look like so:

```
Router50-2# show ip route isis
i*L1 0.0.0.0/0 [115/10] via 192.168.100.2, Serial1
```

Notice that the IP Administrative Distance for IS-IS routes is a default value of 115. Another EXEC-mode command that can come in handy is the show clns command. This command shows you how many interfaces have CLNS enabled, as well as the router IS level and area for which it is routing. The show isis route EXEC-mode command displays IS-IS Level 1 routes to all the other intra-area systems, and the show clns route command shows the IS-IS Level 2 routing table. If you wanted to get some quick neighbor information about your neighbors (similar to the show cdp nei command), you could issue the show clns neighbors or the show clns is-neighbors commands to discover information such as the number of neighbors, neighbor SNPA, state, hold time data, and neighbor level types. You can view the contents of the IS-IS link-state database with the show isis database EXEC-mode command. The show isis spf-log command shows you how often as well as the reasons that a router has run a full SPF calculation session.

Finally, you are likely to use a few of the debug commands on a very limited basis because of the router overhead and effect on other processes. However, the debug isis adj-packets verification command is used to print out IS-IS adjacency-related packets to your console. In addition, use the debug isis update-packets command to output any IS-IS update packets to your console session.

Exam Prep Questions

Question 1

Which of the following commands would you use to designate that an interface will actively route IS-IS?

- ○ A. **Router(config)# router isis**
- ○ B. **Router(config-if)# router isis**
- ○ C. **Router(config)# ip router isis**
- ○ D. **Router(config-if)# ip router isis**

Answer D is correct. You specify which interfaces will be actively routing IS-IS by using the `ip router isis` command in interface configuration mode. Answer A is incorrect because this is the `router isis` command in router configuration mode. This command simply enables the IS-IS process. Answer B is incorrect because it is the wrong command in interface configuration mode. Answer C is incorrect because it is the correct command at the wrong prompt.

Question 2

Which of the main Integrated IS-IS–recognized WAN connection types is highly recommended by Cisco over all others for reasons of network stability and consistency?

- ○ A. Point-to-point
- ○ B. Dial-on-demand
- ○ C. Switched WAN
- ○ D. NBMA multipoint

Answer A is correct. Cisco highly recommends that you opt for point-to-point subinterface solutions and do not use NBMA multipoint when running IS-IS. Answer B is incorrect because dial-on-demand should be used in rare backup situations only. Answer C is incorrect because a full-mesh topology is the only feasible IS-IS over a multipoint network solution. However, the inherent possibilities of a full mesh becoming a partial mesh because of link failures or poor configuration make this scenario problematic and one to be avoided. Answer D is incorrect because this is another type of switched WAN solution and point-to-point is the preferred method.

Question 3

Which PDU packet type is utilized specifically for link-state acknowledgements and requests?

- ○ A. Hello
- ○ B. CSNP
- ○ C. LSP
- ○ D. PSNP

Answer D is correct. This is the Partial Sequence Number PDU that is utilized for link-state acknowledgements and requests. Answer A is incorrect because these Hello PDU packets are used to generate and manage adjacencies. Answer B is incorrect because this is the Complete Sequence Number PDU that is used to propagate the IS's complete link-state topology database. Answer C is incorrect because the LSP is used to transport link-state information and contains an LSP header and variable-length TLV fields.

Question 4

Which one of the following statements is true concerning OSPF and IS-IS area design and configuration?

- ○ A. OSPF is a more scalable solution than OSI IS-IS.
- ○ B. OSPF builds its hierarchy with Level 1 and Level 2 routers where the borders are within the area routers themselves.
- ○ C. With Integrated IS-IS, the entire router is within the area and belongs to the area, not just to the individual interfaces.
- ○ D. IS-IS is designed around the backbone Area 0.

Answer C is correct. Integrated IS-IS builds its hierarchy with Level 1 and Level 2 routers where the borders are in the connections as opposed to within the area routers themselves. In other words, every IS-IS router belongs to exactly one Level 2 area. Answer A is incorrect because IS-IS is technically more scalable and flexible than OSPF. Answer B is incorrect because IS-IS uses Level 1 and Level 2 routers to build an area hierarchy. Answer D is incorrect because OSPF is built around the backbone Area 0.

Question 5

What is the term for the addressing scheme implemented by CLNS and IS-IS for identifying network devices and hosts?

○ A. SNPA

○ B. LSP

○ C. ES-IS

○ D. NSAP

Answer D is correct. The NSAP is the type of addressing scheme implemented by CLNS and IS-IS for identifying network devices and hosts. Answer A is incorrect because it is the Subnetwork Point of Attachment—the point at which subnetwork services are offered, usually a MAC address, Frame Relay DLCI, virtual circuit ID for X.25 or ATM, or HDLC. Answer B is incorrect because the LSP is the link-state packet used to flood information throughout the IS-IS routing domain. Answer C is incorrect because ES-IS is a discovery protocol and not an addressing scheme for identifying network devices.

Question 6

What acronym is used to represent the specific hello packet that is sent between two intermediate systems to establish adjacencies?

○ A. IIH

○ B. ISH

○ C. ESH

○ D. PDU

Answer A is correct. The IS-IS hello (IIH) is the hello packet utilized between two intermediate systems to establish adjacency. Answer B is incorrect because an ISH is a hello packet sent from an IS to an ES. Answer C is incorrect because ESH packets are sent by an ES to an IS (ES to IS Hello). Answer D is incorrect because a PDU is not a specific type of hello packet; rather a hello is a particular type of protocol data unit.

Question 7

Which of the following commands can be issued at the EXEC mode prompt to find out information about specific IS-IS processes on your router?

- ○ A. **show clns protocol**
- ○ B. **show clns interface**
- ○ C. **show ip route isis**
- ○ D. **show isis route**

Answer A is correct. The show clns command displays general information concerning your CLNS network, but the show clns protocol command can be issued at the EXEC-mode prompt to find out information about specific IS-IS processes on your router. Answer B is incorrect because the show clns interface command is used to see individualized information on an interface-by-interface basis. Answer C is incorrect because the show ip route isis command enables you to see just the IS-IS routes from the IP routing table. Answer D is incorrect because the show isis route EXEC-mode command displays IS-IS Level 1 routes to all the other intra-area systems.

Question 8

Which of the following represent the fields that are used to identify a router in an IS-IS environment? (Choose all that apply.)

- ❏ A. NSEL
- ❏ B. Area ID
- ❏ C. System ID
- ❏ D. Subnet ID

Answers A, B, and C are correct. An IS-IS router is signified by the 1-byte NSAP-selector (NSEL), the 6-byte System ID, and the variable-length (1- to 13-byte) area address or ID. Answer D is incorrect because there is no Subnet ID in IS-IS addressing.

Question 9

Which of the following statements are characteristics that are shared between OSPF and IS-IS? (Choose all that apply.)

❑ A. They are IGPs that are often hierarchical in their design.

❑ B. They use a Bellman-Ford algorithm.

❑ C. They establish adjacencies.

❑ D. They construct link-state databases.

❑ E. They are built around a core backbone supporting several areas.

Answers A, C, D, and E are correct. All four choices correctly describe the similarities between OSPF and IS-IS. Answer E addresses the fact that both protocols are structured around a backbone (or core) area, although IS-IS does not have an Area 0 like OSPF. Answer B is incorrect because both of these protocols use the same Dijkstra Shortest Path First algorithm; Bellman-Ford is a distance-vector algorithm.

Question 10

What do you call the NSAP when the NSEL field is set to 00 on a router configured with Integrated IS-IS?

○ A. PDU

○ B. NET

○ C. SNP

○ D. DIS

Answer B is correct. The NSAP becomes the NET when the NSEL field is set to 00. Answer A is incorrect because a PDU is a protocol data unit. Answer C is incorrect because the SNP is the control packet used with LSPs to successfully exchange IS-IS routing information. Answer D is incorrect because the DIS is the one elected router on the local network that is "logically" connected to all other nodes and sends the LSP information on behalf of its LAN.

Need to Know More?

 Martey, Abe and Sturgess, Scott. *IS-IS Network Design Solutions.* Indianapolis, IN: Cisco Press, 2002. ISBN 1578702208.

 Complete list of Requests for Comments: http://www.cis.ohio-state.edu/htbin/rfc/rfc-index.html.

 ISO 8473 covers the ISO CLNP: http://www.protocols.com/pbook/iso.htm.

 ISO/IEC 8348, Appendix A, covers NSAP addresses: http://www.protocols.com/pbook/iso.htm.

 ISO 9542 documents the ES-IS routing exchange protocol: http://www.protocols.com/pbook/iso.htm.

 ISO/IEC 10589 covers the IS-IS intradomain routing exchange protocol: http://www.protocols.com/pbook/iso.htm.

Employing Enhanced IGRP

Terms you'll need to understand:

✓ Diffusing update algorithm (DUAL)
✓ Smooth round trip time (SRTT)
✓ Retransmission timeout (RTO)
✓ Successor
✓ Feasible distance (FD)
✓ Feasible successor (FS)
✓ Stuck in active (SIA)
✓ Holdtime
✓ Uptime
✓ Reliability

Techniques you'll need to master:

✓ Learning how EIGRP discovers, chooses, and manages routes
✓ Configuring EIGRP for VLSM and route summarization
✓ Deploying EIGRP in several NBMA environments
✓ Configuring and verifying EIGRP operations

Cisco improved its proprietary Interior Gateway Routing Protocol with EIGRP by delivering a hybrid protocol that uses elements of distance-vector and link-state characteristics. EIGRP stands for Enhanced Interior Gateway Routing Protocol. Although EIGRP can be used to route IP, IPX, and AppleTalk packets, this book focuses exclusively on IP routing with EIGRP as covered on the Cisco BSCI exam. EIGRP functions like a distance-vector protocol to find the optimal path on a network and utilize link-state properties when discovering neighbors and managing changes in the topology.

EIGRP Features and Operation

EIGRP is rooted in the Cisco-compatible and adaptable nature of the distance-vector protocol IGRP. EIGRP offers several improvements and enhancements over IGRP, which make EIGRP a good choice for newer, growing network implementations. The opportunity for a reduction in bandwidth utilization is a primary benefit. EIGRP, like Open Shortest Path First (OSPF), uses multicast addresses as opposed to broadcast packets to propagate most of the operational traffic. EIGRP also has advantages that are due to its link-state behavior; for instance, EIGRP also offers route summarization at any bit position and route redistribution from other protocols. The algorithm used by EIGRP to provide a loop-free environment is called the *Diffusing Update Algorithm* (DUAL), which offers fast convergence. DUAL is the decision-making mechanism for determining what information will be stored in the topology table, as well as for performing all route computations. DUAL also keeps tabs on all of the advertised routes of the routers' peers, provides a loop-free circuit to every destination, and injects this information into the EIGRP routing table. In addition, EIGRP transmits incremental updates instead of the whole IP routing table.

The EIGRP router configuration **distance** command is used to manually configure the administrative distance value for an internal or external EIGRP route.

EIGRP uses IP packets to share routing information and uses protocol number 88 in its IP header. It is a very flexible routing protocol that operates over multiaccess topologies such as token ring and ethernet, as well as WAN technologies such as dedicated, point-to-point, and nonbroadcast multiaccess (NBMA) topologies. EIGRP supports hierarchical and variable-length subnet mask (VLSM) addressing, supernetting, and route summarization at major network boundaries by default. Here is a list of the most important features of Cisco's Enhanced Interior Gateway Routing Protocol:

➤ Bases metric on a composite of bandwidth, delay, and maximum transmission unit (MTU) sizes to offer the optimum path to a destination

➤ Enjoys a rapid convergence time and reduced use of bandwidth

➤ Sends only network changes instead of periodic changes

➤ Load balances up to six equal or unequal paths

➤ Provides support for multiple routed protocols

➤ Offers a loop-free, easy-to-configure environment

➤ Provides for VLSM, classless routing, and discontiguous networks

➤ Supports routing update authentication

➤ Is backward compatible with Cisco's IGRP protocol

As with any full-featured dynamic routing protocol, there is a wide range of concepts and terminology to digest from the outset. Table 7.1 describes much of the EIGRP terms and concepts necessary to master this powerful protocol.

Table 7.1 EIGRP Terms and Concepts	
EIGRP Term or Concept	**Description**
Neighbors	Routers that are connected and can exchange updates.
Neighbor table	A structure maintained by each EIGRP router that stores a list of adjacencies. An EIGRP router has a neighbor table for each supported routable protocol.
Hello	A multicast data packet that is used to discover and manage EIGRP neighbor relationships.
Query	A data structure that is used to address neighboring routers about a network path that is lost.
Reply	The answer to the query packet.
ACK	An acknowledgement that is typically made up of a Hello packet without data.
Holdtime	The amount of time that a router waits for a Hello packet before downing a neighbor relationship.
Topology table	A structure containing all the learned routes to a destination maintained per each configured routed protocol.
Routing table	A structure maintained for each routed protocol that is generated from the optimal routes to a destination and injected from the topology table.

Table 7.1 EIGRP Terms and Concepts *(continued)*

EIGRP Term or Concept	Description
Smooth round trip time (SRTT)	The amount of time in milliseconds necessary to transmit a packet reliably to a neighbor and receive the subsequent ACK packet.
Retransmission timeout (RTO)	The amount of time that an EIGRP router waits before retransmitting to a neighbor from the queue.
Feasible distance	The metric to a remote network.
Feasible successor	An EIGRP neighbor that does not represent the least-cost path and is not the router used for data forwarding.
Successor	A neighbor EIGRP router that meets the requirements for feasibility. The successor is the route from the topology table that will be inserted into the routing table because it possesses the best attributes for the destination.
Active	The time period when a router is querying neighbors for information regarding a network path.
Passive	The usual operating mode for finding a route to a destination.
Stuck in active (SIA)	A route that is abandoned and cleared when it takes too long for an EIGRP query to be answered.

EIGRP Discovery, Selection, and Route Maintenance

Routers that are loaded with the EIGRP routing protocol use the Hello protocol packets for the neighbor discovery process. The router discovery process is a dynamic activity via the Hello protocol. The Hello packets are sent to the 224.0.0.10 multicast address to determine whether a neighbor is available. An adjacency relationship is a formal agreement between EIGRP neighbor devices established for the goal of exchanging routing information. When EIGRP routers receive Hello packets from a router in the same autonomous system, they will establish an adjacency (neighbor relationship). EIGRP adjacencies must occur within the same AS; therefore neighbor relationships will not form if the devices are in different ASs. In addition, EIGRP uses the primary, not secondary, address on interfaces to build its adjacencies. The actual time interval of Hello packets is dependent on the media being used. For example, on an ethernet, token ring, fiber distributed data interface (FDDI) LAN, and on faster WAN links, Hello packets are sent every 5 seconds. Hello packets are generated every 60 seconds, however, on slower links such as ISDN BRI and multipoint serial interfaces.

Neighbor Table

The information that is learned from the contents of the Hello packets are subsequently stored in the neighbor table. EIGRP, like OSPF, uses multicast Hellos for neighbor discovery and route update trades. This table is responsible for maintaining the EIGRP holdtime value. The *holdtime* value is measured in seconds and represents the amount of time that a router waits to hear from a neighbor before declaring it "down." When you execute the show ip eigrp neighbors command, as shown in Listing 7.1, the holdtime value in the output determines a neighbor's availability. When a neighbor is affirmed as dead, the neighbor relationship is reset and any routes for which this neighbor is responsible are dropped from the table. If the dead neighbor becomes available again, the EIGRP routers exchange Hello packets and reestablish the neighbor relationship. The default EIGRP holdtime is three times the Hello interval. This results in a default holdtime of 15 seconds for LAN and faster WAN interfaces and 180 seconds (3 minutes) on slow WAN links. The holdtime value can be manually configured on a per-interface basis using the following command:

```
RouterA(config-if)# ip hold-time eigrp autonomous-system-number seconds
```

Listing 7.1 Sample Output from a show ip eigrp neighbors Command Showing Holdtime Values

```
RouterA# show ip eigrp neighbors
IP-EIGRP Neighbors for process 20
Address          Interface     Holdtime    Uptime    Q       Seq    SRTT
                               (secs)      (h:m:s)   Count   Num    (ms)
10.10.10.1       Ethernet1     9           0:00:33   0       13     6
10.10.20.2       Serial0       16          0:00:07   0       10     11
10.10.30.3       Ethernet0     12          0:00:09   0       6      3
```

In the previous neighbor table in Listing 7.1, the Address field shows the IP address of the EIGRP neighbor and the Interface field displays the interface on RouterA by which the neighbor can be reached. The Holdtime field is the maximum amount of time that the router will wait without receiving *anything*—not just a Hello packet—from this neighbor before regarding it as down. If it receives any subsequent packets, it resets this timer. *Uptime* is the elapsed time, in hours, minutes, and seconds, since the router first heard something from this neighbor. The field designated simply as Q refers to the queue count. The queue count is the number of packets sitting in the queue and waiting to be sent. A value greater than 0, on a regular basis, indicates a possible congestion issue.

The next field in the neighbor table is the sequence number of the last update, reply, or query that was obtained from this particular neighbor.

Smooth round trip time (SRTT) is the elapsed time, expressed in milliseconds, between the time that the local router sent its last update packet and when the acknowledgement was received from its neighbor. The router also uses the SRTT value to calculate the *retransmission timeout* (RTO) value. RTO is the length of time, expressed in milliseconds, that the router will wait between sending update packets to its neighbor. The exact order and format of these fields in the neighbor table may differ depending on the router model and IOS version, but the stored information is basically consistent.

Two EIGRP routers that have different Hello and holdtime values can still establish a neighbor relationship. However, if you modify the Hello interval on an individual router you must also manually configure the holdtime value to mirror the change. Setting these values independently may cause topology discrepancies. If a packet is not received before the hold time value expires, a topology change is detected and the neighbor adjacency can be dropped, affecting all the topology table entries learned from that particular neighbor.

Topology Table

EIGRP routers actually have three tables for each routable protocol that is configured on the router. We have just looked at the neighbor table, which catalogs the adjacent routers that are configured for EIGRP. When an EIGRP router discovers a new neighbor, it transmits an update to this neighbor and eventually obtains an update from this same neighbor. This information is used to construct an entity known as the topology table. The topology table stores all the learned routes to a destination. The third type of table, with which you are familiar, is the routing table, which keeps a record of the optimal routes to all destinations. These three tables are maintained separately for each protocol. Because EIGRP can support the IP, IPX, and AppleTalk routed protocols, an EIGRP router can maintain up to nine separate tables. In our scenario, the router maintains three tables: a neighbor table, a topology table, and a routing table for the IP protocol that is configured.

The topology table contains all the routes that it has gathered from neighboring routers, including the feasible distance to each destination network and the route status. The *feasible distance* (FD) is the lowest cost route to a particular destination. EIGRP uses bandwidth, delay, reliability, load, and Maximum Transmission Unit (MTU) as its metrics in determining the best path to a remote network. The metric that the router ultimately uses will be the sum of the best metric advertised by all the neighbors and the cost to reach the best neighbor router. Whenever a change takes place to a connected link or interface, or a peer advertises a change, the topology table is updated. The topology table also indicates whether the entry is static or passive. A route is passive if the router is not performing any recomputations on that route. The route is active, on the other hand, if recomputation activities are underway for that route entry.

The show ip eigrp topology EXEC-mode command is used to display the output shown in Listing 7.2.

Listing 7.2 Sample Output from a show ip eigrp topology Command

```
RouterA# show ip eigrp topology
IP-EIGRP Topology Table for process 20

Codes: P - Passive, A - Active, U - Update, Q - Query, R - Reply,
       r - Reply status

P 172.16.4.0/24, 1 successors, FD is 44132954
        via 10.1.1.1 (44132954/43620954), Serial0/0
P 172.16.2.0/24, 1 successors, FD is 22910732
        via 10.1.1.1 (22910732/20198510), Serial0/0
P 172.16.1.0/24, 1 successors, FD is 10797519
        via Connected, Seial0/0
```

In Table 7.2, you can observe the various contents of the EIGRP topology table or database.

Table 7.2 Contents of EIGRP Topology Table

Topology Table Item	Description
Codes:	The state or condition of this topology table entry.
P	Passive. No EIGRP calculations are being performed for this destination.
A	Active. EIGRP calculations are being performed for this destination.
U	Update. An update packet was sent to this destination.
Q	Query. A query packet was sent to this destination.
R	Reply. A reply packet was sent to this destination.
r	A reply status flag that indicates that the process has sent a query and is waiting for a reply packet.
172.16.4.0/24...	The destination IP network and subnet mask.
Successors	The number of successors.
FD	The total distance from the local router to the destination network. The feasible distance used in a feasibility condition check.
Replies	The number of outstanding reply packets for this destination while in the active state.
State	The precise state in which the destination is presently.
Via	The IP address of the neighbor that tells the process about this destination.

Table 7.2   Contents of EIGRP Topology Table *(continued)*

Topology Table Item	Description
(44132954/43620954)	The first number represents the EIGRP metric for cost to destination. The second is the EIGRP metric that this neighbor advertises.
Serial0/0	The interface from which this information was derived.

An EIGRP router extracts the best, or *successor*, routes to each destination network from the topology table and lists them in its routing table. The successor is the primary route from the topology table that is placed into the routing table because it has the best attributes for the particular destination. All successors are stored in the routing table. If you want to see all the IP entries in the topology table, you can issue the following command from the EXEC-mode prompt:

```
RouterA# show ip eigrp topology all-links
```

Routing Table

Like the topology table and the neighbor table, a separate routing table is maintained for each supported routable protocol. The routing table is basically a subset of the topology table, and the DUAL is the component that decides which information will be stored in the topology table. It enforces the decision-making process for all the routing calculations and traces routes advertised by EIGRP peers. The DUAL propagates the routing table by using the metric to determine the best loop-free path to every destination in the network. As mentioned earlier, the lowest cost route ends up being the cost between the local router and the next-hop router plus the advertised distance. Advertised distance is defined as the cost between the next-hop router and the destination. The resulting sum of these two distances is the FD. A successor, as defined in Table 7.1, is a neighboring EIGRP router that meets the requirements for forwarding packets because it has a loop-free least-cost path to a destination (feasibility). DUAL uses the detailed information from the topology table and ultimately adds all the successors to the routing table.

A next-hop router (or routers) that serves as a backup path is known as the *feasible successor* (FS). If a route is lost to a destination, the router looks in the topology table, not the routing table, for an FS. To qualify as an FS, a next-hop router must have an advertised distance less than the feasible distance of the current successor route, and you can have more than one feasible successor. If one is found, this FS is made the successor and injected into the routing table. If no feasible successors are found, then the router goes into active state and starts the process of calculating a new route topology. This process of recalculation has an effect on the overall convergence time. The show ip route command is used to view the EIGRP routing table.

EIGRP Discovery Process

When an EIGRP router, RouterA, comes up for the first time, it initializes and transmits a Hello packet out all its interfaces. As shown in Figure 7.1, RouterB receives the Hello packet from RouterA and responds with update packets that contain information about all routes in its routing table (metrics are also included). Because EIGRP uses the split horizon rule, it does not send information that it may have previously learned via that interface. This update packet from RouterB actually creates the neighbor relationship between the two routers. Returning to Figure 7.1, you can see that RouterA replies with an ACK packet and inserts the new information in its topology table. Next, RouterA shares this new information with its other neighbors in the form of an update message. Each router, in turn, acknowledges RouterA's update information. After all the information is added to all the router's topology tables, they can begin to select the routes to be added to the routing tables.

The topology table contains all the destinations learned from the adjacent routers, along with a listing of all the neighbors that can get to the particular destination. After all the updates have been exchanged and acknowledged, the router can select the primary (successor) route and backup (feasible successor) routes to store in the topology database.

Table 7.3 lists the five different EIGRP packets that have been discussed and a brief description of each.

Table 7.3 The Types of EIGRP Packets in Their Respective Order During the Discovery and Selection Process	
Packet Type	Description
Hello	A multicast packet used for neighbor discovery.
Update	A packet sent reliably to communicate routes used for convergence purposes. This packet is sent via multicast when new routes are discovered and if the route is passive when the convergence process is complete. Updates are sent as unicast packets during the EIGRP initial startup process to synchronize the topology database.
ACK	A unicast packet used for acknowledging EIGRP queries, replies, and updates.
Query	A reliable multicast packet sent when a router, performing computations, cannot find a feasible successor. This packet is sent to a neighbor looking for a feasible successor.
Reply	A unicast packet sent in response to a query.

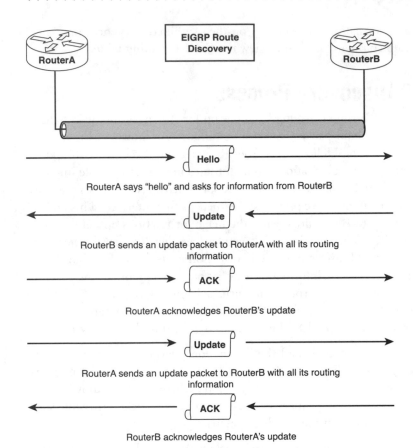

Figure 7.1 The initial EIGRP route discovery process.

EIGRP Selection Process

The characteristics surrounding EIGRP route selection are unique to this hybrid routing protocol. EIGRP chooses up to six routes (one primary [successor] and up to five backup [FD]) per destination and places them into the topology table, which is eventually moved into the routing table. Similar to OSPF, EIGRP also supports internal, external, and summary routes.

The EIGRP metric is fundamentally the same as IGRP except that it is multiplied by 256. Like IGRP, EIGRP uses the following five variables to compute the metric:

➤ *Bandwidth*—A value represented as the smallest bandwidth between the source and destination

➤ *Delay*—The collective delay of interfaces along the path

➤ *Reliability*—The lowest (worst) reliability along the network path (see the "Reliability" sidebar)

➤ *Load*—Represented by the worst load on a connection between the source and destination, in bps

➤ *MTU*—The smallest maximum transmission unit value in the path

Reliability

The EIGRP reliability variable supplies crucial information to neighbor routers to help maintain a consistent loop-free topology. EIGRP uses a sequence number to facilitate this process by requiring an acknowledgement for a specific sequence number. The component that is responsible for this orderly delivery is the Reliable Transport Protocol (RTP). EIGRP update packets are an example of a message that demands a reliable acknowledgement, and RTP makes sure that communication channels are maintained between peers. RTP keeps a retransmission list on the EIGRP router for each neighbor that lists the packets that have not yet been acknowledged by a neighbor. Reliable packets that are not acknowledged can be retransmitted up to 16 times or up to the holdtime, whichever is longer.

EIGRP adds the weighted values (K) of different link variables together to derive the metric. These K values are stored and transported in Hello packets throughout the network. By default, only bandwidth (K1) and delay (K3) are used to compute the metric value, as shown in the following mathematical operation. It is not recommended that you modify these values.

The values of the default constants are as follows:

K1 = K3 = 1

And

K2 = K4 = K5 = 0

The weights that are attributed to the variables are as follows:

➤ K1 = bandwidth

➤ K2 = load

➤ K3 = delay

➤ K4 = reliability

➤ K5 = MTU

When K5 = 0 during metric calculation, variables will be weighted according to the constants K1, K2, and K3 with the following formula:

Metric=(K1 x bandwidth)+[(K2 x bandwidth)÷(256–load)]+K3×delay

If these constant values are the same as their defaults, the formula will be:

Metric=1×bandwidth+[(0×bandwidth)÷(256–load)]+1×delay
Which evaluates to
Metric=bandwidth+[0]+delay
Which evaluates to
Metric=bandwidth+delay

The bandwidth value is computed by taking the minimum bandwidth link on the path divided into 10^7 and multiplied by 256. If K5 does not equal 0, you must perform this extra operation:

Metric=Metric×[K5÷(reliability+K4)]

 When you are injecting IGRP routes into your routing domain, you simply multiply the IGRP metric by 256 to get the equivalent EIGRP metric.

The EIGRP topology table subsequently stores all routes that have been learned by the router via the EIGRP routing updates. The topology table contains information such as the status of the routes, the number of successors to a destination network, and the FD to destination networks, as well as the IP address or interface number of the successor. Feasible distance is the router's best-calculated distance metric, or lowest-cost route, to a destination network. A successor is simply the best path to a route, and the successor route is the only route that is stored in both the topology database and the EIGRP routing table. EIGRP can store a total of six redundant routes in the topology table. The five backup routes are known as feasible successors.

Information regarding the router that is the best route for a particular destination, the successor, is maintained in the routing table. Backup routers, or feasible successors, are those routers that can be used to reach a specific destination, but do not represent the least-cost path to that destination. For instance, assume that a router has an established feasible distance value to a destination network 172.16.4.0 in its topology table. A newly advertised route by a neighbor has a lower advertised distance to network 172.16.4.0. Because the neighbor's advertised distance value is less than the router's FD to network 172.21.4.0, the new route becomes a feasible successor route and is stored only in the topology table. If the router holding the current successor route were to become unavailable, then the feasible successor with the next-lowest advertised distance would become the new successor route and would be added to the routing table.

A sample topology database table is shown in Listing 7.3.

Listing 7.3   A Sample Topology Database Table

```
RouterA# show ip eigrp topology
IP-EIGRP Topology Table for process 100

Codes: P - Passive, A - Active, U - Update, Q - Query, R - Reply,
       r - Reply status

P 172.16.4.0/24, 1 successors, FD is 44132954
          via 10.1.1.1 (44132954/43820954), Serial0/0
P 172.16.2.0/24, 1 successors, FD is 22910732
          via 10.1.1.1 (22910732/20198510), Serial0/0
P 172.16.1.0/24, 1 successors, FD is 10797519
          via Connected, Seial0/0
```

The first number that is displayed in brackets for each successor refers to the local router's distance metric to that destination network. The second number between the brackets designates the advertised distance. The advertised distance value is the next-hop routers reported or "advertised" distance metric to the destination network. Every time a route is newly advertised, the local EIGRP router conducts a feasibility check. If the neighbor router's advertised distance value is less than the local router's feasible distance to a destination network, the path will be selected as a feasible successor route. It is subsequently stored in the topology table as a backup route. Information about available feasible successors is kept in the topology table.

An EIGRP route is considered to be in a passive state when the router has a valid successor for that route and is not in the process of querying neighbors for any alternate paths. The term "query" refers to an EIGRP message that is sent to discover the status of network routes. If a route suddenly becomes unavailable because the successor route is no longer accessible via the local router's topology table, the router quickly queries other neighbors in an attempt to find another feasible successor for that route. During this time, the router recalculates in a state known as active mode.

Look back at Figure 7.1 and review the EIGRP process again with this new knowledge. When EIGRP RouterB receives an initial multicast Hello packet from RouterA, it sends unicast update packets that contain the contents of its routing table. Unlike OSPF routers, connected EIGRP routers establish a neighbor relationship (adjacency) after their initial exchange of Hello and update packets. After receiving the routing table contents from RouterA, RouterB acknowledges delivery by sending an ACK packet to RouterA. The process then reverses, with RouterB sending RouterA update packets that contain RouterB's routing table information, and RouterA returning an ACK packet to RouterB. When both routers have incorporated their neighbors' routing information, they select successor and feasible successor routes and inject them into their topology tables. Reply packets are reliable unicast packets that are sent by a router that has received query packets from an active state or stuck in active (SIA) state router (we will look at the SIA state in a moment) that is querying for an alternative network route.

EIGRP Support of VLSM and Route Summarization

EIGRP automatically summarizes routes at classful major network boundaries on attached interfaces. This is one of the attributes of its distance-vector behavior. Route summarization reduces the number of routing table entries that are advertised to neighbor routers, which results in fewer routing table lookups and enhances overall network performance. For example, routes for 10 contiguous Class C networks, such as 192.168.1.0/24 through 192.168.10.0/24, would be advertised by EIGRP with just a single summary route: 192.168.1.0/16.

EIGRP supports both automatic route summarization and manual summarization. EIGRP, like its predecessor IGRP, auto-summarizes at major network boundaries by default, although this behavior can be disabled. Manual summarization enables you to implement VLSMs and force a summary route from an interface at any bit boundary. This is a major advantage of EIGRP over older distance-vector routing protocols. The router configuration command auto-summary is used to enable automatic summarization of IP subnets at major network boundaries. Again, this is the default setting.

One negative issue that can arise with automatic classful route summarization is the potential for routing discrepancies when discontiguous network numbers are implemented on multiple routers. For example, EIGRP would automatically advertise the subnetted Class B network 172.16.5.0/24 as 172.16.0.0. If another subnet with the address 172.16.10.0 were to be deployed on a subnet connected to another router, EIGRP would also advertise the classful summary route 172.16.0.0. This could result in real problems when the router attempts to access some networks. In certain circumstances, you may want to disable the default EIGRP route summarization at classful boundaries. To enable variable-length subnet masking and route summarization at arbitrary network boundaries, you need to first disable auto-summary by issuing the no auto-summary command from the router configuration prompt:

```
RouterA(config-router)# no auto-summary
```

To configure manual route summarization, use the following command:

```
RouterA(config-router)# summary-address eigrp autonomous-system-number
➥address mask
```

The *autonomous-system-number* parameter is obviously the EIGRP AS number. This number is the global designator for all the routers within the EIGRP internetwork and must be identical on all the routers configured within the internetwork. The address keyword is the IP address that is being advertised as a summary (at any bit boundary). The mask keyword is the IP mask that is creating the summary address. To turn off the auto-summarization of EIGRP, execute the no auto-summary command. This router configuration command is used with EIGRP to support variable-length subnet masks and route summarization at classless network boundaries. Using no auto-summary disables automatic route summarization altogether for the EIGRP process. Any summarized routes, whether classful or classless, thereafter must be manually configured with the ip summary-address eigrp interface configuration command. In Listing 7.4, RouterA advertises a single summary route entry for all networks that match prefix 10.10.0.0/16. First, you select the interface that you want to propagate the route summary, in this case interface e0/0. Next, you use the proper command to designate the EIGRP process number and route summarization format.

Listing 7.4   A Sample Manual EIGRP Summarization

```
RouterA#config t
Enter configuration commands, one per line. End with CNTL/Z
RouterA(config)# router eigrp 10
RouterA(config-router)# no auto-summary
RouterA(config-router)# network 10.10.0.0
RouterA(config-router)# exit
RouterA(config)# interface e0/0
RouterA(config-if)# ip summary address eigrp 10 10.10.0.0 255.255.0.0
RouterA(config-if)# exit
RouterA(config)#
```

Remember that normal EIGRP routes have an administrative distance (AD) value of 90 and that external EIGRP routes have a much higher AD of 170. In addition, IP EIGRP summary routes have a default AD value of 5.

Routing Traffic Transport and Database Synchronization

The EIGRP routing protocol and autonomous system number is enabled by way of the global configuration command `router eigrp autonomous-system-number`. As mentioned, an AS is a logical grouping of routers that fall under a common administration. Here is the syntax for starting an EIGRP routing process on a router at the global configuration prompt:

```
RouterA(config)# router eigrp autonomous-system-number
```

The *autonomous-system-number* parameter is any number between 1 and 65,535 (16-bit). Make sure that you configure all the EIGRP routers in your network with the same AS number. Listing 7.5 will properly configure a serial interface on RouterBBR with an IP address of 10.1.1.1 and a 24-bit mask, as well as a bandwidth value of 128 Kbps. The EIGRP router process is enabled and defined with AS 100 as well.

Listing 7.5 A Sample EIGRP Serial Interface Configuration

```
RouterBBR(config)# interface s0
RouterBBR(config-if)# ip address 10.1.1.1 255.255.255.0
RouterBBR(config-if)# bandwidth 128

<Output Omitted>

RouterBBR(config)# router eigrp 100
RouterBBR(config-router)# network 10.0.0.0
RouterBBR(config-router)# network 172.168.0.0 255.255.0.0
```

The `network network-number` router configuration command is used on RouterBBR to identify the networks on which this EIGRP router will advertise routes.

We also used a bandwidth value of 128 for our serial interface in Listing 7.5. Realize that an EIGRP routing process will use up to 50% of the bandwidth of any interface on which it is configured. When configuring EIGRP on serial interfaces, you issue the `bandwidth kilobits` command while the router is still in interface configuration mode. Remember that the speed (bandwidth) of the link must be expressed in kilobits. This is an important step because EIGRP uses the bandwidth value when it computes the cost of the route.

If no bandwidth is designated, EIGRP assumes that the bandwidth on the serial link is 1.544Mbps (T1) and makes its routing decisions based on this default value.

Because EIGRP supposes that serial links operate at T1 speeds, it may be important to manually configure the bandwidth of the connection to prevent the link from being saturated with routing updates. EIGRP can be configured to use a set percentage of declared bandwidth on either an interface or subinterface by manually overriding the default. Setting the allocation percentage too high could result in a loss of EIGRP packets, whereas configuring the value too low increases convergence time and drastically reduces network performance. The command bandwidth 256, for example, allocates up to 50% (128Kbps) of the specified bandwidth.

If your present routing policy demands that you declare a low bandwidth value on an interface, this percentage of utilization can be adjusted to a value higher than 100%. To modify the default settings, you must first place the router in interface configuration mode by using the interface serial interface-number command. Then you can adjust the bandwidth on an interface or subinterface with the following syntax:

```
RouterA(config-if)# ip bandwidth-percent eigrp as-number percent
```

For example, the following entries configure EIGRP to utilize 200% of the configured bandwidth on the first subinterface connected to AS number 10. Here we have set the percent parameter to a value larger than 100% to overcome an unusually low bandwidth configured for the routing policy:

```
RouterA(config-if)# interface serial 0.1
RouterA(config-if)# ip bandwidth-percent eigrp 10 200
```

The interface number should be typed as a whole number that designates the interface that should be configured, or as two numbers that are separated by a period that corresponds to interface.subinterface.

In another example, we use the code from Listing 7.5 to set both the bandwidth and the bandwidth-percent parameter at the same time for a fractional T1:

```
RouterA(config)# interface s0
RouterA(config-if)# ip address 10.1.1.1 255.255.255.0
RouterA(config-if)# bandwidth 128
RouterA(config-if)# ip bandwidth-percent eigrp 100 200
```

In the preceding sample, we allow EIGRP to utilize the CIR for a fractional T1 of 256Kbps on the interface (200% of the configured 128Kbps bandwidth).

EIGRP can distribute traffic across four equal-cost paths, by default, to increase utilization and improve the effective network bandwidth. The maximum-paths router configuration command is implemented to increase the number of equal-cost routes to the same destination network. Using this command, you can ask for up to six equal routes to be stored in the EIGRP topology table. The default number of equal-cost paths that can be stored by EIGRP is four; the `maximum-paths` command increases that number to six.

The router configuration command `variance multiplier` enables you to load balance between two or more redundant routes with different metrics by assigning a multiplier value to a route's current feasible distance. This allows for the use of other routes to the same network but with higher metrics than the feasible successor route.

A separate variance table does not exist.

The *multiplier* keyword is an integer between 1 and 128 with a default value of 1. A value of 1 indicates that equal-cost load balancing will be performed by the router. When the multiplier value is increased, the router multiplies the value by the metric of the successor route for which multiple paths exist. Next, the router compares the metric of the redundant routes with the modified metric of the successor route. Any redundant routes that have a metric value less than the modified metric of the successor route are included in the load-balancing process and will be used by the router. The amount of traffic that the router will send over the unequal-cost paths is proportional to the degree by which the route's metric varies from the successor route's modified metric.

In Figure 7.2, RouterA declares RouterB as the successor to RouterD, instead of RouterC, because it has the lowest feasible distance value of 20 (10+10) as opposed to 50 (20+30). After you configure RouterA with a variance multiplier value of 2, RouterC may be used for unequal-cost load balancing if certain conditions are met. Figure 7.2 provides an example of when the two conditions are not met. Notice that the advertised distance value on RouterC to RouterD is 30. Because RouterC's advertised distance value of 30 is greater than RouterA's feasible distance of 20, it will not be considered for load balancing. More importantly, RouterC will not be considered because the feasible distance through RouterC (50) is more than twice (variance of 2) the feasible distance of the successor RouterB (20).

Figure 7.3 illustrates an example of when EIGRP load balances with a variance multiplier of 2.

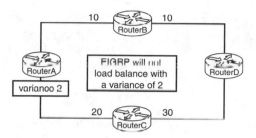

Figure 7.2 Using the **variance** keyword in EIGRP operations.

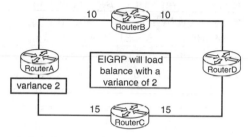

Figure 7.3 An EIGRP router load balancing using the **variance** keyword.

In this example, RouterC may be used for unequal-cost load balancing because two conditions are met. First, the advertised distance on RouterC to RouterD is 15. Because RouterC's advertised distance value of 15 is less than RouterA's feasible distance of 20, it will be considered for load balancing. More importantly, RouterC will be considered because the feasible distance through RouterC (30) is less than twice (variance of 2) the feasible distance (20) of the successor RouterB. This is a simple example. If you had four to six multiple paths, you could experiment with different variance multipliers to include or exclude certain unequal cost paths.

EIGRP Operation in an NBMA Environment and Large Networks

The Cisco EIGRP is a scalable option that provides support for point-to-point connections as well as NBMA point-to-point and multipoint links. This is another benefit of moving from IGRP to EIGRP and is a viable alternative to OSPF, depending on your environment.

As far as bandwidth is concerned, EIGRP looks at point-to-point Frame Relay interfaces just like any other serial interface and defaults to

1.544Mbps. Make sure that you configure your interfaces based on the Committed Information Rate (CIR) agreements with your vendor, corporate site, or area of your campus design.

Pure Multipoint Scenario

In a pure multipoint EIGRP WAN environment, one physical interface on the hub router is connected to two or more spoke routers that share identical CIRs for each circuit. In our first real-world scenario, we assume that you are setting the bandwidth for interface serial 1 on an EIGRP router configured in a pure multipoint frame relay topology. When configuring this environment, you must remember that the total bandwidth is shared equally among all the neighbors. For example, the hub router is connected to three remote sites and each is connected to the frame cloud by a 768Kbps CIR link (fractional T1) that is supplied by your service provider. When configuring the bandwidth of interface serial 1 on the EIGRP hub router, you use the `bandwidth 768` command divided by the number of frame relay virtual circuit neighbors. This configuration needs to be an accurate reflection of the percentages of actual available bandwidth on the cloud, as shown in Figure 7.4.

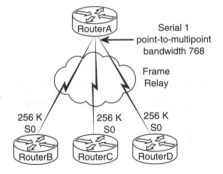

Figure 7.4 EIGRP in a pure multipoint frame relay environment.

Therefore, in this scenario, where three virtual circuits (VCs) have equal CIR values, you should issue the `bandwidth 768` command to set the bandwidth for interface serial 1 on your hub router. This will provide enough bandwidth to support intervals of peak usage when all three sites are consuming their full allotment of bandwidth. The configuration for serial interface 1 would be as follows:

```
RouterA(config-if)# interface serial 1
RouterA(config-if)# encap frame-relay
RouterA(config-if)# bandwidth 768
```

Hybrid Multipoint Scenarios

In our first hybrid multipoint scenario, an EIGRP hub router uses a single physical interface to connect three spoke routers that have unequal CIR values. In this case, you should multiply the number of VCs by the lowest CIR value when computing interface bandwidth to prevent the VCs with the smaller CIR value from being overloaded, as shown in Figure 7.5.

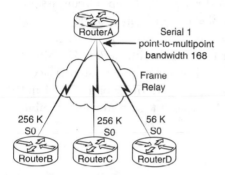

Figure 7.5 EIGRP hybrid multipoint with different CIR values.

In this situation, you want to multiply 56 (the lowest CIR value) by the number of virtual circuits (3) and configure the interface serial 1 with bandwidth 168 to prevent the slowest circuit from becoming saturated.

A better solution might be to configure your hybrid frame relay topology with a combination of multipoint and point-to-point operations. As shown in Figure 7.6, you can use subinterfaces on serial 1 to first configure the two higher CIR rates as a multipoint subinterface with a bandwidth equaling the total combined CIRs. Then you configure the single lower CIR (56Kbps) as a point-to-point interface with the bandwidth value being the total point-to-point circuit.

When determining a network type for a subinterface, only the multipoint and point-to-point keywords are valid. Listing 7.6 shows the configuration that you would perform on RouterA to accomplish this hybrid design.

Listing 7.6   A Sample Hybrid EIGRP Frame Relay Interface Configuration

```
RouterA(config)# interface serial 0.1 multipoint
RouterA(config-subif)# bandwidth 512
RouterA(config)# interface serial 0.2 point-to-point
RouterA(config-subif)# bandwidth 56
```

The EIGRP WAN configuration shown in Listing 7.6 and Figure 7.6 is an example of a hybrid multipoint topology. In situations in which different

VCs have different CIRs, you can create subinterfaces on a single physical interface to provide the maximum possible bandwidth to each virtual circuit in the network. In this case, issuing the global configuration command shown in Listing 7.6 defines a multipoint serial interface that can be used to allocate bandwidth evenly between RouterB and RouterC. In a multipoint configuration, subinterface bandwidth is calculated by multiplying the number of VCs by the shared CIR value of both circuits. Because RouterB and RouterC are both connected to RouterA through a 256Kbps circuit, issuing the interface configuration command `bandwidth 512` will provide sufficient bandwidth to both virtual circuits, even during times of peak usage when RouterB and RouterC are nearing their CIR bandwidth values. The slower circuit to RouterB is then placed on its own point-to-point subinterface as shown in Listing 7.6 above. You can then configure the subinterface bandwidth equal to the link's CIR by using the `bandwidth 56` command in subinterface configuration mode.

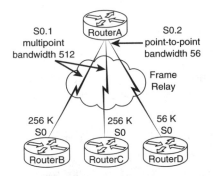

Figure 7.6 An EIGRP hybrid frame relay interface WAN configuration.

You should compute the bandwidth value for each subinterface by specifying a percentage of the physical interface's total link capacity. For example, six point-to-point subinterfaces on a single 768Kbps frame relay serial connection would each be configured with 128Kbps of bandwidth so that you do not saturate any one interface.

As previously mentioned, if your Frame Relay cloud is oversubscribed, you can implement the `ip bandwidth-percent` commands on individual subinterfaces to properly allocate bandwidth. This takes a lot of preplanning and foresight to get it right the first time. That should be your priority when building a scalable EIGRP internetwork. The key factors to keep in mind throughout the process of configuring EIGRP operations in a scalable internetwork environment are the level of traffic flowing between neighbors, the rate of change to the topology, the number of routers, and the number of substitute paths in your EIGRP internetwork.

Stuck-in-Active (SIA)

Sometimes a router will fail to receive a reply to an unresolved query within a certain time interval (3 minutes for EIGRP). If this is the case, an EIGRP route will be considered in a state of *stuck in active* (SIA). If a successor route is unavailable and a router is unable to locate a feasible successor in the EIGRP topology table, the failed route enters the active state and begins querying neighbor routers for another path to the destination network. If another neighbor does have an alternate path, then an update packet is sent to the active router and the querying process ends. However, if the SIA router fails to receive a response to an outstanding query within the 3-minute time interval, the route is considered SIA. A router responds to an SIA route by immediately entering the active state for all routes learned through the failed neighbor. A router remains in an SIA state for a maximum of 3 minutes by default, after which the DUAL clears the adjacency with the neighbor that failed to reply to the query.

If a router running EIGRP drops a successor route and no feasible successor exists, the router goes into the active state for that particular route. A router that has gone active on a route sends query messages to all its neighbors (other than the unavailable neighbor) for an alternative route to the destination network. Because it could take more than 3 minutes for a query message to negotiate a large EIGRP internetwork, the `timers active-time` router configuration command can be used to set the time duration that a router running EIGRP will wait before declaring a route SIA. Here is the syntax for this command:

```
RouterA(config-router)# timers active-time [time-limit | disabled]
```

The `time-limit` parameter is the threshold value (in minutes) that the querying router will remain in an active state before entering the SIA state. Some network engineers have attempted to lower the occurrence of SIA incidences by breaking an EIGRP AS into several autonomous systems to put boundaries on the query range. This does not necessarily solve the problem because the query can continue into the other AS where it can also go SIA.

The most effective approach for limiting the problem of SIA routes is to limit the range of EIGRP query propagation. Both route summarization and distribute lists can be implemented to place boundaries on the flood of query and update packets in an internetwork in which EIGRP is running. Distribute lists will be covered in detail in the chapters on BGP policy.

Verifying Enhanced IGRP Operation

The `show ip eigrp neighbors` EXEC-mode command is one of the main tools to use for EIGRP verification and maintenance. This command displays the contents of the EIGRP neighbor table and the peers that have been discovered. The EIGRP neighbor table contains the IP address of each neighbor, the local interface used for the connection, the holdtime value, the uptime value, and information regarding EIGRP packet updates, as shown in Listing 7.7.

Listing 7.7 A Sample Output from the `show ip eigrp neighbors` Command

```
RouterA# show ip eigrp neighbors
IP-EIGRP Neighbors for process 20
Address          interface   Holdtime  Uptime   Q      Seq   SRTT   RTO
                             (secs)    (h:m:s)  Count  Num   (ms)   (ms)
10.10.10.1       Ethernet1   9         0:00:33  0      13    6      22
10.10.20.2       Serial0     16        0:00:07  0      10    11     18
10.10.30.3       Ethernet0   12        0:00:09  0      6     3      8
```

The `eigrp log-neighbor-changes` EXEC-mode command allows you to enable logging of status changes that occur with EIGRP adjacencies. It is also useful for monitoring router stability and issues surrounding SIA, as mentioned in the previous section.

The `show ip route eigrp` command is used to view the records currently in the EIGRP routing table. This command presents only the EIGRP-derived routes that are stored in the routing table, as shown in the following sample snippet:

```
RouterA# show ip route eigrp
D     10.0.0.0/8 [90/20268800] via 172.16.1.18, 00:00:22, Serial0/0
      172.16.0.0/16 is variably subnetted, 3 subnets, 2 masks
D         172.16.1.20/30 [90/20268800] via 172.16.1.2, 00:00:22, Ethernet0/0
```

The privileged `show ip eigrp topology` EXEC-mode command offers the contents of the EIGRP topology table, as shown in Listing 7.8. EIGRP maintains a separate topology table for each routable protocol that is configured on the router. The topology table contains a list of all successor and feasible successor routes, as well as the active or passive status.

Listing 7.8 A Sample Output from the `show ip eigrp topology` Command

```
RouterA# show ip eigrp topology
IP-EIGRP Topology Table for process 20

Codes: P - Passive, A - Active, U - Update, Q - Query, R - Reply,
       r - Reply status

P 172.16.90.0 255.255.255.0, 2 successors, FD is 0
          via 172.16.80.28 (46251776/46226176), Ethernet0
```

Listing 7.8   A Sample Output from the show ip eigrp topology Command *(continued)*

```
          via 172.16.81.28 (46251776/46226176), Ethernet1
          via 172.16.80.31 (46277376/46251776), Ethernet0
P 172.16.81.0 255.255.255.0, 1 successors, FD is 307200
          via Connected, Ethernet1
          via 172.16.81.28 (307200/281600), Ethernet1
          via 172.16.80.28 (307200/281600), Ethernet0
          via 172.16.80.31 (332800/307200), Ethernet0
```

The successor routes are listed with both the local router's calculated distance metric and the next hop router's calculated distance metric to the destination network. The local router's distance metric represents the best-known path to the destination network. This again is known as the router's feasible distance. The next-hop router's distance metric is the route's advertised distance. The routers are listed as passive (P) in the topology table in Listing 7.8 because the routes are operational and EIGRP is not "actively" looking for alternate paths to reach the destination network. If RouterA were to determine that the neighbor advertising the successor route was not functioning, the route would be listed as active (A) and the router would start the query process to probe other EIGRP neighbors for an alternate route to that particular network. The show ip eigrp topology command also shows the number of successors for each route entry.

The show ip eigrp traffic command is used to establish the amount of control packet traffic that an EIGRP router has received and transmitted. This command displays the number of Hello, update, query, reply, and ACK packets that were sent to or received by a router.

The show ip protocols command illustrates the parameters for all routing protocols that were configured for use on a router. It also shows the current state of the EIGRP process, if applicable. You can also use this command to quickly get the EIGRP AS number, as well as any filtering or distribution numbers, distance, and neighbor data.

Using the passive-interface command in router configuration mode enables the designated interface to accept incoming routing updates and prevents the specified interface from advertising all outgoing routing updates. This also serves to prevent the establishment of a neighbor adjacency. The syntax for the passive-interface command is

```
RouterA(config-router)# passive-interface type number
```

The type and number keywords indicate the interface type and number (for example, Ethernet 0/1). The no passive-interface type number command is used to re-enable route updates for a specific interface. Listing 7.9 shows the correct command for preventing RouterA from advertising EIGRP routes on interface e0/0 for AS 20:

Listing 7.9 A Sample Output from the passive-interface Command

```
RouterA>en
RouterA#config t
Enter configuration commands, one per line. End with CNTL/Z
RouterA(config)# router eigrp 20
RouterA(config-router)# network 172.16.1.0
RouterA(config-router)# passive-interface e0/0
RouterA(config-router)# exit
RouterA(config)#
```

Link-state protocols, such as OSPF and EIGRP, neither send nor receive any routing updates for interfaces configured as passive because neighboring routers that run link-state protocols cannot establish bidirectional communication by using the Hello protocol. Using the `default` keyword with `passive-interface` sets all active interfaces to passive mode. The `default` keyword will not re-enable all the interfaces automatically.

The privileged `debug eigrp packets` EXEC-mode command is used to establish and diagnose end-to-end connectivity problems, such as abnormal session closures between EIGRP neighbor routers. When used without parameters, the `debug eigrp packets` command displays information regarding all types of communication packets exchanged between the local router and its neighbors. You use the `debug eigrp packets ?` command to display a list of the packet types that are used by EIGRP. The `?` parameter, used in conjunction with most IOS commands, displays content-sensitive help that demonstrates the 11 available parameters that can be used with this command. To display the individual packet types that are available for individual or group output, type the command shown in Listing 7.10.

Listing 7.10 The Results of the debug eigrp packets ? Command

```
RouterA# debug eigrp packets ?
  ack        EIGRP ack packets
  hello      EIGRP hello packets
  ipxsap     EIGRP ipxsap packets
  probe      EIGRP probe packets
  query      EIGRP query packets
  reply      EIGRP reply packets
  request    EIGRP request packets
  retry      EIGRP retransmissions
  terse      Display all EIGRP packets except Hellos
  update     EIGRP update packets
  verbose    Display all EIGRP packets
  <cr>
```

This display indicates the possible parameters and a brief description of the use of the parameter. Using the `debug eigrp packets` command with the `verbose` parameter would display traffic statistics for all EIGRP packets. The information derived from the `debug eigrp packets verbose` command can be used to diagnose end-to-end connectivity problems associated with the EIGRP neighbor routers.

Another command that you may want to use sparingly is the `debug ip eigrp` command. This prolific command generates a ton of valuable output about packets that are sent and received on an interface. The `debug ip eigrp summary` option generates a summary version of your EIGRP operations. This shows a similar result to the `show ip protocols` command.

Exam Prep Questions

Question 1

Which one of the following EIGRP terms can best be described as a packet that is specifically transmitted by EIGRP peer routers when a neighbor is newly discovered and when changes occur?

○ A. Hello packet

○ B. Update packet

○ C. ACK packet

○ D. Successor packet

Answer B is correct. An update packet is sent reliably to communicate routes used for convergence purposes. It is sent when new neighbors are discovered and changes occur. Answer A is incorrect because a Hello packet is a multicast packet used for neighbor discovery. Answer C is incorrect because an ACK packet is a unicast packet used for acknowledging EIGRP queries, replies, and updates. Answer D is incorrect because it is not a packet type.

Question 2

Which of the following statements are true regarding the difference between IGRP and EIRGP? (Choose all that apply.)

❑ A. They both provide support for VLSM, classless routing, and discontiguous networks.

❑ B. They both use the same computations for determining the metric, except that EIGRP's metric is multiplied by 256.

❑ C. They both use distance-vector characteristics to find the optimal path to a network.

❑ D. They are both hybrid routing protocols using elements of distance-vector and link-state algorithms.

❑ E. They both utilize the DUAL to provide a loop-free environment and fast convergence.

Answers B and C are correct. IGRP and EIGRP both use the same metric computations with the exception of multiplying the result by 256 for scalability and granularity. Cisco improved its proprietary IGRP with EIGRP by delivering a hybrid protocol that uses elements of distance-vector and link-state characteristics. Answer A is incorrect because only EIGRP offers support for VLSM, classless routing, and discontiguous networks. Answer D is incorrect because only EIGRP is a hybrid routing protocol using elements of distance-vector and link-state algorithms. IGRP is a distance-vector protocol. Answer E is incorrect because only EIGRP uses the DUAL algorithm.

Question 3

A feasible successor is a backup route to the primary route. When is a route marked as a feasible successor?

- ○ A. When the next hop router's FD value is lower than the advertised distance of the current successor route to the destination
- ○ B. When the next hop router's FD value is higher than the advertised distance of the current successor route to the destination
- ○ C. When the next hop router's advertised distance value is higher than the FD of the current successor route to the destination
- ○ D. When the next hop router's advertised distance value is lower than the FD of the current successor route to the destination

Answer D is correct. A feasible successor is a neighboring router with a lower advertised distance. Answers A and B are incorrect because the next hop router's advertised distance, not feasible distance, is considered. Answer C is incorrect; the next hop router's advertised distance value must be lower and not higher to be a feasible successor.

Question 4

Which one of the following terms best describes the amount of time that a router waits for a Hello packet before downing a neighbor relationship?

- ○ A. Holdtime
- ○ B. Smooth round trip time
- ○ C. Retransmission timeout
- ○ D. Stuck in active

Answer A is correct. Holdtime is the time duration that a router waits for a Hello packet before ending a neighbor relationship. Answer B is incorrect because SRTT is the amount of time in milliseconds necessary to transmit a packet reliably to a neighbor and receive the subsequent ACK packet. Answer C is incorrect because RTO is the amount of time that an EIGRP router waits before retransmitting to a neighbor from the queue. Answer D is incorrect because SIA is actually a route that is abandoned and cleared when it takes too long for an EIGRP query to be answered.

Question 5

The default EIGRP holdtime is dependent on the Hello interval and defaults to which values for a LAN connection and slow WAN link, respectively?

○ A. 5 seconds, 60 seconds

○ B. 10 seconds, 90 seconds

○ C. 15 seconds, 180 seconds

○ D. 20 seconds, 240 seconds

Answer C is correct. The default EIGRP holdtime is 3 times the Hello interval of 5 seconds. This results in the default holdtime of 15 seconds for LAN and faster WAN interfaces and 180 seconds (3 minutes) on slow WAN links. Answers A, B, and D are incorrect because both of the multiples are wrong.

Question 6

Which of the following pieces of information are stored in the topology table? (Choose all that apply.)

❑ A. All the routes collected from neighboring routers

❑ B. The feasible distance to each destination network

❑ C. The administrative distance of EIGRP

❑ D. The active or passive status of the route

Answers A, B, and D are correct. The topology table contains all the routes that it has gathered from neighboring routers, including the FD to each destination network and the route status. Answer C is incorrect because the administrative distance value of EIGRP is displayed in the routing table.

Question 7

Which of the following statements are *false* concerning the EIGRP routing protocol? (Choose two.)

❑ A. EIGRP supports variable-length subnet masking.

❑ B. EIGRP Hello interval values cannot be modified.

❑ C. An EIGRP router can maintain up to nine separate tables.

❑ D. EIGRP auto-summarization cannot be disabled.

Answers B and D are correct. Both Answers B and D are false statements concerning the EIGRP routing protocol. You can indeed change the Hello interval value as well as disable auto-summarization in EIGRP. Answer A is incorrect because it is true that EIGRP supports VLSM. Answer C is also true. Because EIGRP can support the IP, IPX, and AppleTalk routed protocols, an EIGRP router can have up to nine separate tables: three neighbor tables, three topology tables, and three routing tables.

Question 8

If you wanted to specifically see all the IP entries in the topology table, which one of the following commands would you execute from the EXEC-mode prompt?

- ○ A. **Router#show ip protocols**
- ○ B. **Router#show ip eigrp topology all-links**
- ○ C. **Router#debug ip eigrp summary**
- ○ D. **Router#show ip eigrp traffic**

Answer B is correct. You can issue the `show ip eigrp topology all-links` command from the EXEC-mode prompt to display all the IP entries in the topology table. Answer A is incorrect because the `show ip protocol` command shows the settings for all IP routing protocols that are configured for use on a router. It also shows the current state of the EIGRP process, if applicable. Answer C is incorrect because the `debug ip eigrp summary` command, similar to the `show ip protocols` command, generates a summary version of your EIGRP operations. Answer D is incorrect because the `show ip eigrp traffic` command is used to establish the amount of control packet traffic that an EIGRP router has received and transmitted. This command displays the number of Hello, update, query, reply, and ACK packets that were sent to or received by a router.

Question 9

You are configuring a point-to-point frame relay connection to your service provider with six equal virtual circuits over a T1 connection. What should the configured bandwidth value be for each point-to-point subinterface?

- ○ A. 56
- ○ B. 128
- ○ C. 256
- ○ D. 1544

Answer C is correct. If your subinterface has multiple VCs, you should configure the bandwidth value as the total CIR bandwidth divided by the number of VCs. In this case, the math would be 1.544Mbps÷6=256. Answers A, B, and D are incorrect because the math was wrong.

Question 10

You have configured an EIGRP hub router to use a single physical interface to connect three spoke routers with unequal CIR values. You multiplied the number of VCs by the lowest CIR value to calculate the interface bandwidth to prevent the circuit with the smaller CIR value from becoming overloaded. What is this topology known as?

- ○ A. Pure multipoint topology
- ○ B. DUAL topology
- ○ C. Broadcast multiaccess topology
- ○ D. Hybrid multipoint topology

Answer D is correct. This is an example of a hybrid multipoint topology in which unequal CIR values exist. You could also use subinterfaces and separate bandwidth value configurations to better manage the frame relay cloud. Answer A is incorrect because in a pure multipoint EIGRP WAN environment, one physical interface on the hub router is connected to two or more spoke routers that share identical CIRs for each circuit. Answer B is incorrect because there is no DUAL topology. The DUAL is the component that decides which information will be stored in the topology table. Answer C is incorrect because ethernet is a multiaccess broadcast topology where frame relay is a nonbroadcast medium.

Need to Know More?

 Pepelnjak, Ivan. *EIGRP Network Design Solutions: The Definitive Resource for EIGRP Design, Deployment, and Operation.* Indianapolis, IN: Cisco Press, 2000. ISBN 1578701651.

 Benjamin, Henry. *CCNP Practical Studies: Routing.* Indianapolis, IN: Cisco Press, 2002. ISBN 1587200546.

 Logilent—Leading the IT Industry in Live Hands-on Access to Real Network Devices: http://www.logilent.com/.

 Enhanced IGRP: http://www.cisco.com/univercd/cc/td/doc/cisintwk/ito_doc/en_igrp.htm.

Configuring Border Gateway Protocol

Terms you'll need to understand:

- ✓ Border Gateway Protocol version 4 (BGP-4)
- ✓ Exterior Gateway Protocol (EGP)
- ✓ BGP speakers
- ✓ BGP peers or neighbors
- ✓ Open message
- ✓ Notification message
- ✓ Update message
- ✓ Keepalive message
- ✓ Autonomous system number (ASN)
- ✓ Path vector protocol
- ✓ Interior Border Gateway Protocol (IBGP)
- ✓ Transit AS
- ✓ Multihomed AS
- ✓ Attributes
- ✓ Synchronization
- ✓ Black hole
- ✓ Peer group
- ✓ Community

Techniques you'll need to master:

- ✓ Understanding the process for connecting to other autonomous systems
- ✓ Knowing the basics behind BGP routing policy functions
- ✓ Understanding how BGP synchronization works
- ✓ Understanding BGP peering functions with peer groups and communities
- ✓ Configuring and verifying BGP

As you have learned so far, routing involves the transport of packets and the determination of optimal routing paths through an internetwork. A key protocol that addresses the mission of path determination in modern internetworks is the Border Gateway Protocol (BGP). Presently, four versions can run on a Cisco router. This chapter focuses on the default standard BGP as defined in RFC 1771—BGP version 4, or simply, BGP-4. BGP achieves interdomain routing in TCP/IP networks.

Routing protocols are often categorized according to whether they are exterior gateway protocols or interior gateway protocols. *Interior gateway protocols* (IGPs) are needed to share information within (intradomain) an autonomous system. Interior routing protocols are implemented to learn the internal network topology and IP subnet information to maintain loop-free networks. Some common examples of IGPs are RIP, IGP, OSPF, and EIGRP. *Exterior gateway protocols* (EGPs), on the other hand, are utilized to exchange information between (interdomain) multiple autonomous systems and to maintain loop-free paths. BGP is a prime example of an exterior gateway protocol.

BGP-4 offers a lot of improvements and enhancements over other routing protocols. This is the primary reason that it is used over the Internet to connect ISPs and enterprise internetworks. As you have learned, OSPF and EIGRP are interior routing protocols, whereas BGP is considered an exterior routing protocol. OSPF is a link-state protocol that uses cost for a metric, whereas EIGRP and BGP are in a category of advanced distance vector protocols with several enhancements. EIGRP uses a composite metric of bandwidth and delay. BGP uses network reachability information called path vectors (or *attributes*) for its metric. These attributes include an inventory of the full path that a route takes to reach a destination. Another comparison is that OSPF requires a hierarchical design for proper address summarization, whereas EIGRP and BGP do not need a hierarchy. OSPF uses cost, which on Cisco routers is based on bandwidth, as its metric. EIGRP uses a composite metric, similar to the IGRP metric.

The acronym EGP has a dual meaning in that it also stands for an obsolete protocol that was developed in the beginning phases of the Internet to isolate networks from each other. The BGP routing protocol is a chief successor to this Exterior Gateway Protocol (EGP). BGP was intended to replace the now obsolete Exterior Gateway Protocol (EGP), as the standard exterior gateway–routing protocol used in the global Internet. BGP solves serious problems with EGP and scales to Internet growth more efficiently. In this book, the acronym EGP refers to a generic exterior gateway protocol such as BGP.

Connecting to Other Autonomous Systems

Border Gateway Protocol is the only routing protocol in operation today that uses Transmission Control Protocol (TCP) for the reliable movement of its update information. TCP is the connection-oriented protocol defined at the Transport layer of the OSI reference model that provides reliable delivery of data. Routers that are configured with the BGP routing protocol are commonly called *BGP speakers*. Any two routers that have generated a TCP connection for sharing BGP routing information are called peers, or neighbors. These *BGP peers* exchange different types of messages to open and maintain the connection. BGP speakers exchange network reachability information in the form of the full paths (BGP AS numbers) that a route should take to get to a destination network. This information is vital for building a loop-free topology where routing policies can be used to manage the routing behavior.

BGP can route between multiple autonomous systems (or domains), as well as exchange routing and reachability information with other BGP systems. BGP is often referred to as a path-vector protocol because it transports a sequence of AS numbers in its packets for loop-avoidance and designates a path to a remote network. An AS utilizes BGP to find out about other routes' reachability by gathering information from other ASs.

The rules for maintaining and exchanging information are called *policies* and each AS can have specific policies for the different points to external networks. BGP provides for making decisions based on rules enforced at the AS level through policy-based routing. This mechanism controls how the data is transported through the AS and is based on BGP attributes covered throughout this chapter.

BGP peers exchange their full routing tables at the outset. After the initial exchange, peers send incremental updates whenever there is a change to the routing table. BGP also stores a version number of the BGP table, which should be identical for all its peers. Whenever BGP updates the table because of a routing information change, the version number is also changed. *Keepalive messages* are also used to make certain that the connection is alive between the BGP peers. *Notification messages* are sent to respond to network errors or special situations.

BGP has four different types of messages that are exchanged between BGP routers: open, keepalive, update, and notification. Table 8.1 displays the four message types that BGP-4 uses to guarantee that updates are transmitted and neighbors remain active.

Table 8.1 BGP-4 Message Types

BGP Message	Description
Open	This message is the first message sent after the TCP connection is established. It is used to establish BGP peer relationships and contains the following fields: version, AS number of the sender, Holdtime, BGP Identifier (Router ID), and optional parameters.
Keepalive	This message confirms that connections are active or established and are exchanged between peers so that holdtimes do not expire. If hold-time intervals are configured to zero, periodic keepalives won't be exchanged.
Update	This message is generated if a change occurs and has information on a single path only. Update messages can include a list of IP address prefixes for withdrawn routes, path attributes, and lists of IP address prefixes that are reachable by this single path. Multiple paths require multiple update messages.
Notification	These messages are sent to alert BGP peers about detected errors. Notifications include an error code, subcode, and other pertinent data.

Each enterprise network or ISP on the Internet is identified by an *autonomous system number* (ASN) that provides a hierarchy for managing route information. The Internet Assigned Numbers Authority (IANA) is the consortium that doles out ASNs to ISPs and other organizations that use BGP (or another EGP) to connect to the Internet. The ASN is a 16-bit number (1–65535). As with IP addresses, a range of ASNs is reserved for private use. These reside at the top of the address space from 64512 through 65535. The guidelines for ASNs are defined in RFC 1930.

Over 20 RFCs currently apply to Border Gateway Protocol version 4. For example, RFCs 1771 through 1774 define BGP-4 definition, application, and analysis. For a complete list of RFCs, navigate to **www.cis.ohio-state.edu/htbin/rfc/rfc-index.html**.

There are two modes of BGP: Interior Border Gateway Protocol (IBGP) and Exterior Border Gateway Protocol (EBGP). IBGP is used to exchange BGP information between BGP routers within the same AS. IGRP and OSPF are both IGPs that can be used within a BGP AS. Implementing an internal routing protocol within the AS removes the requirement that all BGP neighbors within the same AS be directly connected to one another. EBGP allows for the sharing of routing information between BGP neighbors across AS boundaries. EBGP demands that there be a direct link between neighbors that reside in different ASs, as shown in Figure 8.1.

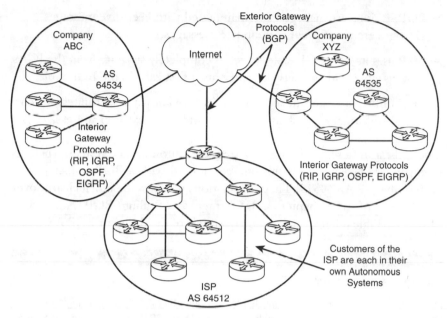

Figure 8.1 IGPs and EGPs operating together in an internetwork design.

Path Vector

Border Gateway Protocol is often categorized as an advanced distance vector routing protocol or a "path vector" protocol. The term *path vector* refers to the obligatory AS-path attribute that is located in BGP update messages. This AS-path attribute tracks the incrementing sequence of autonomous systems that the packet passes through on its way to the destination network. Only EBGP speakers modify the AS-path attribute. They do this by including the ID number of the local AS to any update messages that it sends to remote ASs. The AS-path attribute, with several other attributes, is discussed later in this chapter.

Here is a list of the most important features of BGP-4:

➤ BGP routers exchange network reachability data, termed path vectors (or attributes), that carry a list of the full path of BGP AS numbers that a route takes to reach a destination network.

➤ BGP offers support for VLSM and CIDR aggregation (summarization).

➤ BGP utilizes TCP port 179 as its transport (Layer 4) mechanism for reliable data exchange and loop-avoidance.

➤ BGP exchanges the full routing table only at the outset of the BGP session.

➤ BGP sessions are managed and maintained with keepalive messages. Changes are propagated with update messages.

➤ BGP uses its own BGP table, which is completely separate from the IGP's routing table, and any network entry must first exist in the BGP table.

➤ BGP utilizes a rather intricate set of metrics known as attributes, which include information such as the Origin and the Next-hop address.

There is a difference between a regular autonomous system, such as Company ABC AS 65534, and one configured with a BGP transit policy, such as the ISP AS 64512. These distinctions will become much clearer over the course of this chapter and Chapter 9, "Scaling BGP Networks." However, Table 8.2 provides a good overview of the different BGP AS types.

Table 8.2 BGP AS Types	
AS Type	Description
Stub AS	A stub AS is connected to only one other AS, such as a single-homed stub AS with a single connection to an ISP. These AS types often serve as enterprise BGP border ASs with a single entry and exit point linking it to an ISP's system. For that reason, stub ASs typically run an interior gateway protocol such as EIGRP or OSPF for routing internal traffic.
Transit AS	Transit ASs connect to more than one AS and operate as agents between multiple autonomous systems. For example, an ISP's AS will serve as a transit AS. The primary function of an ISP's AS is to deliver information to other ASs that belong to independent enterprise network systems. Typically, a transit AS will be configured in a fully meshed topology running only BGP as the routing protocol because no traffic is headed for intra-AS networks.
Multihomed AS	A multihomed AS is connected to multiple ASs; however, it does not operate as a transit or intermediate AS. These ASs typically link an AS to two or more ISPs to ensure that communications with Internet destinations are not interrupted if one ISP experiences a failure.

You should strongly consider implementing BGP when

➤ The inbound and outbound traffic flow of your network must be highly controlled.

➤ You need to allow traffic to pass through one AS to get to another AS.

➤ You are connecting multiple ISPs, network access points (NAPs), or autonomous systems.

➤ You are implementing a multihoming solution in an enterprise environment to connect to more than one ISP.

You should *not* use BGP when

➤ Your router does not have enough memory or processing power to handle the BGP update messages and large routing tables.

➤ You have only a single connection to another autonomous system or the Internet.

➤ You have limited knowledge of or no need for implementing routing policy or route selection and filtering techniques.

➤ You have low bandwidth channels between the autonomous systems.

Static routes or an IGP can be used if your organization cannot implement BGP for one of the preceding reasons.

The method for configuring static routes has already been addressed in this book. You should know the **ip route** command completely. For the BSCI exam, you need to know that static routing should be used instead of BGP if you meet one of the criteria in the preceding bulleted list for not using BGP. For review, the syntax for the **ip route** command is as follows:

Router(config)# ip route prefix mask {address | interface} [distance]

As you recall, when there are multiple routes to a destination network, it is the administrative distance value that determines what routes are ultimately injected into the routing table. The AD value of a static route is set to 1 if the route is designated with the `next-hop address` parameter. The AD value of a status route designated by the `interface` parameter is 0. A "floating" static route is often implemented to override a dynamically learned route. It can be used to generate a path of last resort that can be used when no dynamic route data exists. A floating static route is a sort of "path of last resort" that kicks in when no dynamic routing information is available. You can establish a floating static route by using an AD value that is higher than the default AD of the routing protocol being used. It is statically configured to be explicitly overridden by dynamically learned information.

A router running BGP maintains information concerning neighbor routers in the BGP routing table. In fact, a BGP router actually maintains two separate tables. It has the BGP routing table and the IP routing table. The BGP routing table is filled with routes obtained by the BGP protocol and the IP routing table is proliferated by routes that are obtained by IGPs running on the router. Even though these two tables are managed independently, your BGP router can be configured to exchange information between the tables. If you want to display detailed information about BGP neighbor routers, you can use the following EXEC-mode command:

```
RouterA(config)# show ip bgp neighbors.
```

Listing 8.1 shows an example of the show ip bgp neighbors command on a Cisco router running BGP.

Listing 8.1   A Sample show ip bgp neighbors Command

```
Router#show ip bgp neighbors
BGP neighbor is 172.16.11.1,  remote AS 1, external link
  Index 3, Offset 0, Mask 0x8
   BGP version 4, remote router ID 172.16.15.1
   BGP state = Established, table version = 1, up for 01:07:28
   Last read 00:00:28, hold time is 180, keepalive interval is 60 seconds
   Minimum time between advertisement runs is 30 seconds
   Received 70 messages, 0 notifications, 0 in queue
   Sent 70 messages, 0 notifications, 0 in queue
   Prefix advertised 0, suppressed 0, withdrawn 0
   Default weight 10
   Connections established 1; dropped 0
   Last reset never
   0 accepted prefixes consume 0 bytes
   0 history paths consume 0 bytes
Connection state is ESTAB, I/O status: 1, unread input bytes: 0
Local host: 172.16.11.2, Local port: 11000
Foreign host: 172.16.11.1, Foreign port: 179
Enqueued packets for retransmit: 0, input: 0  mis-ordered: 0 (0 bytes)
Event Timers (current time is 0x18AE8E0):
Timer         Starts    Wakeups           Next
Retrans          71         0             0x0
TimeWait          0         0             0x0
AckHold          70        45             0x0
SendWnd           0         0             0x0
KeepAlive         0         0             0x0
GiveUp            0         0             0x0
PmtuAger          0         0             0x0
DeadWait          0         0             0x0
iss: 1359248693  snduna: 1359250034  sndnxt: 1359250034      sndwnd:    15044
irs: 1979028943  rcvnxt: 1979030284  rcvwnd:        15044 delrcvwnd:    1340
SRTT: 300 ms, RTTO: 607 ms, RTV: 3 ms, KRTT: 0 ms
minRTT: 20 ms, maxRTT: 300 ms, ACK hold: 200 ms
Flags: higher precedence, nagle
Datagrams (max data segment is 1460 bytes):
Rcvd: 97 (out of order: 0), with data: 70, total data bytes: 1340
Sent: 117 (retransmit: 0), with data: 70, total data bytes: 1340
BGP neighbor is 172.16.40.2,  remote AS 2, external link
  Index 2, Offset 0, Mask 0x4
   BGP version 4, remote router ID 0.0.0.0
   BGP state = Idle, table version = 0
   Last read 00:00:11, hold time is 180, keepalive interval is 60 seconds
   Minimum time between advertisement runs is 30 seconds
   Received 0 messages, 0 notifications, 0 in queue
   Sent 0 messages, 0 notifications, 0 in queue
   Prefix advertised 0, suppressed 0, withdrawn 0
   Connections established 0; dropped 0
   Last reset never
   0 accepted prefixes consume 0 bytes
   0 history paths consume 0 bytes
   External BGP neighbor not directly connected.
   No active TCP connection
RouterB#
```

BGP information is transported inside of TCP segments with the default TCP port designator of 179. BGP routers that have generated a BGP TCP connection-oriented communication are peers or neighbors, either internal or external. IBGP peers are routers running BGP and exchanging information within a single AS to be eventually passed on to other ASs.

BGP routers communicating between disparate ASs are directly connected and run EBGP. Before it exchanges routing table or BGP table information with a peer in an external AS, BGP makes certain that networks within the AS are reachable. This is done by a combination of internal BGP peering among routers within the AS and then redistributing BGP routing information to IGPs running within the AS, such as IGRP, IS-IS, RIP, or OSPF, as shown in Figure 8.2.

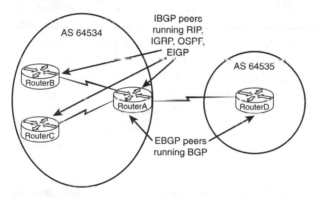

Figure 8.2 Internal and external BGP neighbors.

BGP Policy-Based Routing Functions Within an Autonomous System

Border Gateway Protocol mandates that a BGP router can advertise only routes that it uses itself to peers in an AS. This is exactly the way that routing hops function on the Internet. BGP is well suited for the modern Internet because it supports any implemented policy that abides by the current "hop-by-hop" routing mechanism. You cannot change how your peer AS will route your packets. You can affect only the manner in which your packets get to your peer ASs.

When a BGP router stores multiple routes to the same destination network in its routing table, it uses a complex sequence of configurable metrics known as attributes to choose the optimal path. Path attributes fall into one of the following four categories:

➤ Well-known, mandatory

➤ Well-known, discretionary

➤ Optional, transitive (only these can be marked as "partial")

➤ Optional, non-transitive

Well-known mandatory attributes, as the name signifies, must appear in all BGP update messages. These attributes are implemented and recognized by all compliant BGP implementations. These attributes are sent to BGP peers and must appear in the route description data. A well-known, discretionary attribute does not have to exist in a route description. It may or may not be included. An optional attribute could be some special attribute that is supported by only certain BGP implementations. A BGP speaker might not recognize an optional transitive attribute and it is not expected to because it is destined for some private BGP network. If the BGP router fails to recognize an optional transitive attribute, it will mark it as a partial message and will continue to propagate it to its peers untouched (transitive). An optional non-transitive attribute must be dropped (deleted) by the non-compliant router. Table 8.3 shows the four main categories of attributes and the associated attribute item.

Table 8.3 Path Attribute Categories and Associated Attributes	
Category	**Associated Attributes**
Well-known, mandatory	AS-path, Next-hop, Origin
Well-known, discretionary	Local preference, Atomic aggregate
Optional, transitive	Aggregator, Community
Optional, non-transitive	Multi-exit-discriminator (MED)

AS_path Attribute

The AS-path attribute is BGP type code 2 and is a well-known mandatory attribute. Every BGP has an associated type code as will be shown throughout this chapter. Whenever a route update passes through an AS, the AS number is prepended to that update. The AS-path attribute is actually a list of AS numbers that a route has traversed to reach a destination. An AS-set is an ordered mathematical set of all the ASs that have been traversed. If the route (or routes) does not originate from the local router, it will take the path with the shortest AS-path attribute. If the routes share the same AS path value, the router will give preference to the route with the lowest Origin attribute. Origin codes are displayed next to entries in the BGP routing table in a similar fashion to the code entries in the routing tables for other IP routing protocols.

In Figure 8.3, an update message exits AS 65510 and transits AS 65520 on its way to AS 65520. RouterB then prepends its AS number to the AS-path list so that RouterD has an AS path to 172.16.10.0 of (65520,64510).

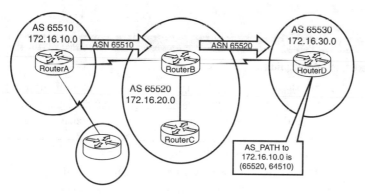

Figure 8.3 The AS-path attribute at work.

Next-hop Attribute

The Next-hop attribute is BGP type code 3 and is a well-known mandatory attribute. The BGP Next-hop attribute is simply the next hop IP address that is going to be used to reach a certain destination. For EBGP, the next hop is always the IP address of the neighbor specified with the `neighbor` command. The following code snippet shows a BGP router specifying a neighbor with the `neighbor` command:

```
RouterA#config t
Enter configuration commands, one per line.  End with CNTL/Z.
RouterA(config)#router bgp 65500
RouterA(config-router)#network 172.16.0.0 mask 255.255.255.0
RouterA(config-router)#network 10.1.10.0 mask 255.255.255.0
RouterA(config-router)#network 10.1.20.0 mask 255.255.255.0
RouterA(config-router)#neighbor 172.16.11.1 remote-as 65000
```

Origin Attribute

The Origin attribute is BGP type code 1 and is a well-known, mandatory attribute. The Origin attribute defines the origin of the path information.

The origin code is an indication of whether the route originated from internal BGP (IBGP) or external BGP (EBGP). If the routes have the same origin code, the route with the lowest multi-exit-discriminator (MED) is preferred. The Origin attribute can assume three values as described in Table 8.4.

 BGP transmits routing update messages that contain Network layer reachability information (NLRI) to portray a particular route and how to get there. An NLRI is a prefix or assigned ASN that needs to be advertised over the Internet. A BGP update message holds one or more NLRI prefixes, as well as the attributes of a route for the NLRI prefixes. Route attributes include such elements as a BGP next hop address, Origin attribute, and more.

Table 8.4   Origin Attribute Values

Origin Attribute Value	Description
IGP	The Network layer reachability information (NLRI) is internal to the originating AS. When the **bgp network** command is used or when IGP is redistributed into BGP, the Origin attribute value is IGP. When the origin of the path information is IGP, the indicator **i** appears in the BGP table.
EGP	The NLRI is discovered through an EGP such as Border Gateway Protocol. This value will be represented by an **e** in the BGP table.
INCOMPLETE	In this case the NLRI is unknown or is learned by some other method such as a redistributed static route into BGP where the origin of the route is incomplete. This is indicated with a **?** in the BGP table.

Local Preference Attribute

The Local preference attribute is BGP type code 5 and is a well-known discretionary attribute. It is an inverse value of the MED attribute described later in this section. EBGP neighbors use the Local preference attribute to guide outbound update traffic through a specific router. A path with higher Local preference value will be preferred over paths with lower Local preference values. An example of this is shown in Figure 8.4, in which the update message bound for AS 65504 will exit AS 65501 RouterA because of the higher Local preference value.

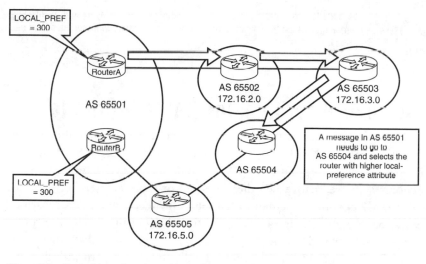

Figure 8.4   RouterA is preferred over RouterB because of the higher Local preference attribute.

Atomic Aggregate Attribute

The Atomic aggregate value is BGP type code 6. It is a well-known discretionary attribute that notifies BGP routers of policy routing choices made when there are overlapping routes. It is used to decide that a prefix will or will not be used.

Aggregator Attribute

The Aggregator attribute has a BGP type code of 7. It is an optional transitive attribute made up of the AS number and the identifying IP address for a total of 48 bits. This attribute is often appended to messages that are performing aggregation (route summarization) to designate the AS and the BGP router performing the aggregation.

Community Attribute

The Community attribute is BGP type code 8 and is an optional transitive attribute. This value has a range of 0 to 4,294,967,200 and is a method for clustering destinations into a particular community and employing routing decisions accordingly. You can use route maps to set the Community attributes. This is addressed in detail in Chapter 9.

You need to know that a route map is a technique for modifying and maintaining routing information by defining certain conditions for redistributing routes from one protocol to another.

Multi-exit-discriminator (MED) Attribute

The Multi-exit-discriminator attribute is type code 4 and is an optional non-transitive attribute. Multi-exit-discriminator, formerly the inter-AS attribute, is a metric incorporated into BGP updates to give external (EBGP) neighbors a favored path when there are two or more entry points into the local AS. MED is implemented to tell, or influence, remote ASs regarding the best path(s) into the local AS. If identical MED values exist, the router chooses a path through an interior BGP (IBGP) peer rather than through an exterior BGP peer (EBGP). The router finally selects the path with the lowest BGP peer Router ID value if the route is available only via an EBGP peer.

As you can see in Figure 8.5, RouterA has the MED value set to 200 and RouterB has the MED value configured to 300. RouterC will choose RouterA as the optimal next hop when it receives updates from RouterA and RouterB, because it prefers the lower MED metric. In situations where there are multiple entry points into the local AS and you want to direct inbound EBGP updates to a preferred EBGP route, set a lower MED attribute for the preferred route. A route map is used to configure the MED value for a route. Although route maps are covered in later chapters, it is important to realize that they are mechanisms used to manage and change routing information by determining conditions for redistributing routes from one protocol (or AS) to another. By using the MED metric, BGP will be the only set of rules that will attempt to influence how routes are injected into an AS.

Know the difference between the Local preference attribute and the MED. To help you remember, the term "local" represents information used inside the AS (intra-AS). Therefore, the Local preference attribute is exchanged only between internal BGP peers to determine preferred paths to exit the AS. It is not passed on to EBGP neighbors. MED, on the other hand, is shared among ASs. The metric is transported to a peer AS and used for decision making without being further passed to the next autonomous system.

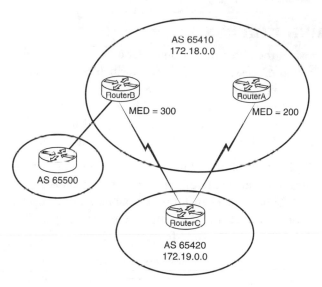

Figure 8.5 The MED attribute at work.

Weight Attribute

Cisco also has a proprietary defined Weight attribute for BGP. Weight is a locally stored and manually assigned attribute used to designate the desirability of a route. If a next-hop router is available for multiple routes, the router will choose the one with the highest Weight value. If the multiple routes have the same weights, the router will pick the route with the highest Local preference value. Local preference also serves as a guide to route desirability, but it is shared among all IBGP neighbors in an AS. When paths have identical Local preference values, a route generated from the local router is favored over a route resulting from a remote router. The following sample output shows the Weight values in the **show ip bgp** output:

```
RouterA# show ip bgp

BGP table version is 583644, local router ID is 172.28.124.90
Status codes: s suppressed, d damped, h history, * valid, > best, i -
internal
Origin codes: I - IGP, e - EGP, ? - incomplete

     Network          Next Hop         Metric    LocPrf   Weight  Path
*>   10.24.0.0        172.20.32.2          0        100      200   481  i
*>   10.33.0.0        172.24.20.1          0        100      200   140  i
*    10.55.0.0        172.23.1.10          0        300      100   360  i
s                     192.168.5.2          0        450      150   200  i
*>                    192.168.6.10         0        500      200   100  i
*                     192.168.7.4          0        150      180   200  i
```

Here is the syntax to configure the proprietary Weight value:

```
 neighbor {ip-address | peer-group-name} weight weight
```

The parameter **ip-address** is the IP address of the designated neighbor router and **weight** is an integer value between 1 and 65,535. If unspecified, the router defaults to 32,768 for all routes.

Route Selection Process

Now that you have a grasp of the different attributes, let us see how they play into the BGP route selection process. BGP determines which path to choose to reach a certain destination network as soon as it receives updates about different destinations from other autonomous systems. BGP ultimately selects only one optimal path to a particular destination. BGP chooses the best route for routing traffic toward the destination, based on the following steps:

1. If the route is not in the IGP routing table (the route is not synchronized and synchronization is enabled), or the next hop address is unreachable, ignore it. When synchronization is enabled, a BGP router will not use or advertise a route learned by IBGP to an external BGP peer unless the route is local or is learned from the IGP.

2. Use the route with the highest Cisco-proprietary Weight attribute (Weight is local to the router only). If multiple routes have the same Weight, use the route with the highest Local preference attribute (Local preference is used intra-AS).

3. If the multiple routes have identical Local preference values then the route generated by the local router is selected. If multiple routes have the same local preference, or if the local router did not generate a route, use the route with the shortest AS-path attribute value.

4. If the AS-path length is identical, use the route with the lowest Origin code value. IGP is lower than EGP, which is lower than incomplete. If all the Origin codes are the same, choose the path with the lowest MED attribute. (Remember that the MED value was sent from another AS. Refer to Figure 8.5.) This step occurs only when the neighboring AS is the same for all the routes that are being considered.

5. If the routes have an identical MED attribute then give preference to external paths (EBGP) over internal paths (IBGP).

6. If you have disabled synchronization (see the synchronization section later in this chapter) and only internal paths remain, the shortest internal path within the AS to the destination (the closest IGP neighbor) will be chosen. If the remaining paths are EBGP paths, choose the oldest route to counteract flapping routes. This last step is proprietary behavior in Cisco routers.

7. Next, select the route with the lowest neighbor BGP router ID value. Loopback addresses are typically used to influence this decision. If the IDs are identical, then choose the route with the lowest neighbor IP address.

This is a generalized summary example of the process that BGP goes through before it injects a route into the routing table and propagates it to its peers.

BGP Synchronization

Synchronization is a technique for automatically redistributing routes between the BGP and your IGPs. The main goal of BGP synchronization is to prevent routing inconsistencies. It serves to guarantee that only entries that exist in the IGP's IP routing table are included in the BGP routing tables. The BGP rule of synchronization states that if your autonomous system is passing traffic from another AS to a third AS, BGP should not advertise a route until the entire collection of local AS routers has learned about the route via an IGP routing protocol. BGP will wait until IGP has propagated the route within the AS before advertising it to external neighbor routers.

For example, suppose that a BGP router advertised a route to external network 10.10.10.0 without first allowing IGP to flood this route information throughout the local AS. If another BGP router received a packet destined for network 10.10.10.0 without receiving the update, this second router would discard the packet. BGP synchronization can be disabled, but it is only safe to do so when full mesh connectivity exists between all IBGP routers within the AS. After the entries between the tables are synchronized, routes can be redistributed between the protocols without the risk of black holes.

NOTE

BGP synchronization helps to prevent the phenomenon of a non-existent route known as a *black hole*. A black hole occurs when a destination is advertised to an EBGP peer before all the internal AS routers can reach that destination.

Current Cisco IOS releases all have synchronization enabled by default, although in future releases it will probably be disabled because most ISPs are running BGP on all their routers. Disabling synchronization can reduce convergence time between routers because fewer routes need to be advertised by each protocol. However, it should be disabled only if all routers in the BGP transit path run BGP or if no traffic moves through the AS to another AS (in other words, the AS is not serving as a transit AS). In these cases, disabling synchronization reduces the number of routes that must be stored by IGP and increases IBGP convergence time. Because of the cost and complexity of maintaining direct connections for all BGP routers in an AS—a requirement of IBGP peer interactions—most BGP ASs use an IGP for intra-AS communications. Usually, only ISP-related transit ASs run BGP on all routers in the transit path because the only purpose of the AS is to route traffic between other connected ASs from a fully meshed topology.

BGP Peering Functions with Peer Groups and Communities

BGP *peer groups* are administrative units that are deployed to simplify the maintenance of several BGP routers. Technically speaking, a peer group must consist of two or more BGP neighbor routers. BGP peers in a peer group have identical update policies and are administered as a single entity. Because all peer group members inherit all peer group settings, you might create one routing update policy and apply it to a peer group rather than configure a routing policy for each individual peer router. After you have properly configured a peer group, all changes on one member router will be dynamically applied to all the BGP routers within the peer group. Each member of the peer group routinely shares the policy information. All EBGP members of a peer group must be able to be accessible over the same interface so that the Next-hop attribute is different for the EBGP peers on different interfaces. Loopback addresses can be used as a workaround for this limitation. Peer group members can also be configured to override options if they do not affect outbound updates. You can override only peer group options that are set on the inbound.

Another structure that can be established to simplify administration of BGP routers is a Community. A *Community* is an attribute that can be assigned to a route to make route filtering, redistribution, and/or path selection easier. It is fundamentally a set of destination networks that have a common property and to which the same or similar policy rules can be applied. The administrative benefits of a Community pales in comparison to peer groups, but they can provide a suitable way to create a reliable route-selection policy when using route maps. (Route maps are covered in the next chapter.) The Community attribute is a 32-bit number. The first 16 bits represent the local AS and the second 16 bits identify the community number itself. BGP routers can use the Community attribute to flag routes that are entering and exiting interfaces during route updates. Any other router configured to support the Community attribute can then make routing decisions based upon the Community identifier. The Community attribute has an advantage over other types of routing policy because only a single attribute must be checked on incoming route update traffic, rather than entire packets, which must be processed using access list technology. Table 8.5 offers some commonly used Community types.

Table 8.5 Some Well-Known Community Types	
Community Types	**Description**
No-export	This Community tells the router not to advertise to EBGP peers; keep this route within an AS.
No-advertise	This Community tells the router not to advertise the route to any peer, whether internal (IBGP) or external (EBGP).
internet	This Community tells the router to advertise the route to the Internet community, or any router that belongs to it.
Local-AS	This Community tells the router to advertise this route to IBGP peers only. Also uses confederation scenarios to prevent sending packets outside the local AS. (Confederations are covered in the next chapter.)

Configuring and Verifying External and Internal BGP

Basic BGP configuration is relatively simple on a Cisco router between two BGP peers. Figure 8.6 shows a basic BGP configuration.

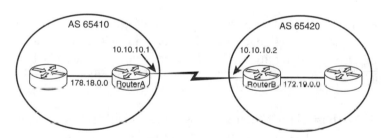

Figure 8.6 A sample of a basic BGP configuration.

RouterA in AS 65410 and RouterB in AS 65420 are BGP peers (or neighbors) and will begin to advertise networks 172.18.0.0/16 and 172.19.0.0/16 respectively. Listing 8.2 shows the Cisco configuration commands.

Listing 8.2 A Sample Configuration for Basic BGP Neighbors

```
RouterA(config)# router bgp 65410
RouterA(config-router)# neighbor 10.10.10.2 remote-as 65420
RouterA(config-router)# network 172.18.0.0

RouterB(config)# router bgp 65420
RouterA(config-router)# neighbor 10.10.10.1 remote-as 65410
RouterA(config-router)# network 172.19.0.0
```

Sometimes, in a frame relay environment, you may need to modify the Next-hop attribute to force a router to advertise itself as the next hop. This can be accomplished with the `neighbor next-hop-self` router configuration command when a single path exists to the neighbor AS.

In other situations you may not need synchronization. If you are not passing traffic from another AS through your AS, or if all your AS routers are running BGP (full mesh), you can disable synchronization. Disabling this feature enables you to carry fewer routes in your IGP and enables BGP to converge more quickly. This process is not automatic. If all the routers in your AS are running BGP and you are not running any IGP, the router has no way of knowing it. Your router will be stuck waiting for an IGP update about a certain route before it can send it on to an external neighbor. You would need to manually disable synchronization in this case for routing to function properly.

You use the BGP configuration command `no synchronization` to disable the synchronization of routing information between the IGPs and BGP within a fully meshed, non-transit AS. Now your router can use and advertise a route learned by IBGP to an EBGP peer before they are learned within the IGP. The following snippet shows this command on a router running BGP:

```
RouterA(config-router)#no synchronization

RouterA(config-route-map)# set community {community-number [additive]} | none}
```

The `set community` command is used to create a BGP Community. The optional keyword `additive` designates that this Community should be added to the already existing communities to which a destination belongs. The keyword `none` deletes the Community attribute from the specified destination network.

After you have established the Community, use the following `router` configuration command to send a Community attribute to a BGP neighbor:

```
Router(config-router)# neighbor {ip-address | peer-group-name} send-community
```

The `send-community` attribute enables BGP routers to filter incoming or outgoing updates to manage the "flaggable" entries in a route map to keep the route from being advertised by a certain router. Commands should be used to create and manage communities within the unique route-map configuration mode after the route map is established.

To configure multiple, connected BGP routers to act as a peer group (a single administrative entity sharing routing update policies) named MyPeerGroup, you would use the following command:

```
RouterA(config-router)# Neighbor MyPeerGroup peer-group
```

Use the `maximum-paths` router configuration command when your router has two parallel paths to two different routers in the same remote autonomous system. Without the `maximum-paths` command, you will not have more than one path to a destination in the routing table. For example, if you use the `maximum-paths 2` command, two paths can appear in the routing table, although only one path is ultimately selected as the best one in the BGP table. This is indicated by the > symbol.

The `clear ip bgp` privileged EXEC command activates the configuration changes by resetting specific BGP connections. There are several possible connection parameters for this command, including `ip address`, which resets the connection with the specified neighbor and *, which resets all connections with all neighbors.

To reset the configuration for a peer group, use the following syntax:

```
Router# clear ip bgp peer-group peer-group-name
```

You can use several important commands to verify BGP operations. Table 8.6 shows some of the more important commands. You should refer back to this table when reading Chapter 9, as well as know this information for your BSCI exam.

Table 8.6 BGP Routing Protocol Verification Commands

BGP Command	Description
show ip route	Will display the IP routing table. Other keywords can follow for more granular investigation.
show ip bgp	Shows the BGP routing table. You can also designate a network number for more granular information concerning a specific network.
show ip bgp summary	Displays the status of all BGP connections.
show ip bgp neighbors	Shows details concerning TCP and BGP neighbor connections.
debug ip bgp updates	Invokes a console display of BGP update messages. Because of its use of router resources, it should be run for only a short time and then shut off. Other options for **debug ip bgp** include *dampening*, *events*, and *keepalives*.

Exam Prep Questions

Question 1

> Which of the following is the correct protocol and port combination that is used for BGP connection services?
>
> ○ A. TCP, port 69
> ○ B. UDP, port 23
> ○ C. TCP, port 179
> ○ D. UDP, port 179

Answer C is correct. BGP uses TCP port 179 as its transport Layer 4 mechanism for reliable data exchange and loop-avoidance. Answer A is incorrect because TCP port 69 is for Trivial File Transfer Protocol (TFTP). Answer B is incorrect because BGP uses TCP and port 23 is for Telnet services. Answer D is incorrect because although the port number is correct, BGP uses TCP for its update messages.

Question 2

> Which of the following command sets represents a valid way to configure a BGP router with an external peer?
>
> ○ A. `router bgp 65520`
>   `neighbor 10.10.10.1 remote-as 65510`
>
> ○ B. `router bgp 65550`
>   `neighbor 10.10.10.1 remote-as 65560`
>
> ○ C. `router bgp 65520`
>   `neighbor 10.10.10.1 as 65510`
>
> ○ D. `ip bgp 65520`
>   `neighbor 10.10.10.1 remote-as 65510`

Answer A is correct. The `router bgp` command starts the process, and the `neighbor remote-as` combination creates a peer relationship with the BGP neighbor. Answer B is a trick because the AS numbers are invalid. The ASN must be between 1 and 65,535, a 16-bit number. Answer C is incorrect because the `remote-as` command was not used. Answer D is incorrect because the command to start the process is `router bgp`, not `ip bgp`.

Question 3

In which of the following BGP scenarios would it be acceptable to implement static routes? (Choose 2.)

- ❑ A. Your router does not have enough memory or processing power to handle the BGP update messages and large routing tables.
- ❑ B. You are implementing a multihoming solution in an enterprise environment to connect to more than one ISP.
- ❑ C. You have only a single connection to another autonomous system or the Internet.
- ❑ D. The inbound and outbound traffic flow of your network must be highly controlled through route policy and route selection.

Answers A and C are correct. Static routes would be appropriate to use when your router has inadequate resources to handle the BGP update messages and large routing tables, when you have only a single connection to another autonomous system or the Internet, when you have no need to implement routing policy, and when you have low bandwidth channels between the autonomous systems. Answers B and D are incorrect because these are examples of situations in which you should strongly consider BGP routing instead of static routing.

Question 4

Which one of the following types of BGP attributes might not be recognized nor expected because it is destined for some private BGP network but will be marked as "partial" and sent on its way to its peers untouched?

- ○ A. Well-known, mandatory
- ○ B. Well-known, discretionary
- ○ C. Optional, transitive
- ○ D. Optional, non-transitive

Answer C is correct. A BGP router might not recognize an optional transitive attribute and it is not expected to because it is headed for some private BGP network. If the BGP speaker fails to recognize an optional transitive attribute, it marks it as a "partial" message and continues to propagate it to its peers untouched (transitive). Answer A is incorrect because well-known mandatory attributes must appear in all BGP update messages and are recognized by all compliant BGP implementations. Answer B is incorrect because although a well-known, discretionary attribute does not have to exist in a route description, it doesn't meet the other stated criteria. Answer D is incorrect because a non-compliant router must drop an optional non-transitive attribute.

Question 5

Which of the following displays the proper order of preference for the MED, Local-preference, and Weight attributes?

○ A. Local preference, MED, Weight

○ B. Weight, MED, Local preference

○ C. MED, Local preference, Weight

○ D. Weight, Local preference, MED

Answer D is correct. The correct preference order is Weight, Local preference, then MED. The route with the highest Weight attribute is preferred. If multiple routes have the same Weight, then the route with the highest Local preference attribute is used. MED is farther down the chain of preferences as sent from other ASs.

Question 6

You are not passing traffic from another AS through your AS and all your AS routers are running BGP. What command could you run to carry fewer routes in your IGP and allow BGP to converge more quickly?

○ A. **no auto-summary**

○ B. **no synchronization**

○ C. **disable auto-summary**

○ D. **disable synchronization**

Answer B is correct. You will use the BGP configuration command `no synchronization` to disable the synchronization of routing information between the IGPs and BGP within a fully meshed, non-transit AS. Now your router can use and advertise a route learned by IBGP to an EBGP peer before the routes are learned within the IGP as well as improve convergence. Answer A is incorrect because `no auto-summary` disables the automatic route summarization for EIGRP. Answer C is incorrect because it is neither a valid command nor applicable to BGP. Answer D is incorrect because you use the `no` command, not `disable`, to turn off BGP synchronization.

Question 7

> Which one of the following is *not* a valid BGP message type?
> - A. Notification
> - B. Keepalive
> - C. Update
> - D. Hello

Answer D is correct. The Hello protocol message is not one of the BGP message types. Answers A, B, and D are incorrect because they are actually valid message types. BGP has four different types of messages that are exchanged between BGP routers: open, keepalive, update, and notification. The open message is the first message sent after the TCP connection is established. The keepalive message confirms that connections are active or established and is exchanged between peers so that hold times do not expire. The update message is generated if a change occurs and has information on a single path only. Notification messages are sent to alert BGP peers about detected errors.

Question 8

> Which of the following is a valid BGP Origin attribute value that displays in the BGP table as a question mark (?) because the NLRI is unknown?
> - A. UNKNOWN
> - B. INCOMPLETE
> - C. NONTRANSITIVE
> - D. MISSING

Answer B is correct. The INCOMPLETE Origin value shows up as a question mark in the BGP table because the NLRI is unknown or is learned by some other method such as a redistributed static route into BGP where the origin of the route is incomplete. Answer A is incorrect because UNKNOWN is not a valid Origin attribute value. Answer C is incorrect because NONTRANSITIVE is not a valid Origin attribute value. Answer D is incorrect because MISSING is not a valid Origin attribute value.

Question 9

Which of the following attributes is a well-known mandatory attribute with BGP type code 3 and represents the next IP address that will be used to reach a particular destination?

- ○ A. Origin
- ○ B. Next-hop
- ○ C. AS-path
- ○ D. Local preference
- ○ E. Aggregator

Answer B is correct. The Next-hop attribute is BGP type code 3 and is a well-known mandatory attribute. The BGP next hop attribute is simply the next hop IP address that is going to be used to reach a certain destination. Answer A is incorrect because the Origin attribute is BGP type code 1 and is a well-known, mandatory attribute. Answer C is incorrect because the AS-path attribute is BGP type code 2 and is a well-known mandatory attribute. Answer D is incorrect because the Local preference attribute is BGP type code 5 and is a well-known discretionary attribute. Answer E is incorrect because the Atomic aggregate value is BGP type code 6. It is a well-known discretionary attribute that notifies BGP routers of policy routing choices made when there are overlapping routes.

Question 10

Which one of the following commands can invoke a console display of BGP update messages?

- ○ A. **debug ip bgp**
- ○ B. **show Ip bgp summary**
- ○ D. **show ip bgp neighbors**
- ○ E. **show ip bgp**

Answer A is correct. The `debug ip bgp` updates command invokes a console display of BGP update messages. Answer B is incorrect because the `show ip bgp summary` command displays the status of all BGP connections. Answer C is incorrect because the `show ip bgp neighbors` command displays details about TCP and BGP neighbor connections. Answer D is incorrect because the `show ip bgp` command shows the BGP routing table.

Need to Know More?

Halabi, Sam, et al. *Internet Routing Architectures (2nd Edition)*. Indianapolis, IN: Cisco Press, 2000. ISBN 157870233X.

Huitema, Christian. *Routing in the Internet, 2nd Edition*. Indianapolis, IN: Prentice Hall PTR, 2000. ISBN 0130226475.

Loshin, Peter. *Big Book of Border Gateway Protocol (BGP) RFCs*. San Diego, CA: Morgan Kaufmann, 2000. ISBN 0124558461.

Parkhurst, William R. *Cisco BGP-4 Command and Configuration Handbook*. Indianapolis, IN: Cisco Press, 2001. ISBN 158705017X.

Stewart, John W. *BGP4 Inter-Domain Routing in the Internet*. Reading, MA: Addison-Wesley Pub Co, 1998. ISBN 0201379511.

RFC 1654: A Border Gateway Protocol (BGP-4): www.faqs.org/rfcs/rfc1654.html.

Scaling BGP Networks

Terms you'll need to understand:

✓ Route reflectors
✓ Route reflector client
✓ Cluster
✓ Cluster ID
✓ Originator ID
✓ Cluster list
✓ BGP split horizon rule
✓ Confederation
✓ Distribute lists
✓ Prefix lists
✓ Multihoming
✓ Redistribution

Techniques you'll need to master:

✓ Calculating connections needed for IBGP
✓ Designing and configuring a route reflector
✓ Using the **show ip bgp** command
✓ Implementing distribute lists and prefix lists
✓ Connecting multiple ISPs with BGP
✓ Redistributing routes between BGP and IGPs
✓ Verifying a multihomed environment

In this chapter, you build upon the knowledge gained in Chapter 8 about the Border Gateway Routing protocol version 4 (BGP-4). Now that you understand the basic characteristics, configuration, and verification methods of BGP, we look at concepts such as BGP scalability through route reflectors and managing policy using prefix lists. You will also learn how to connect to multiple Internet service providers (ISPs) via BGP, as well as how to configure and verify multihomed BGP scenarios. We also explore the methods for redistributing routes between BGP and interior gateway protocols.

Scalability Issues with Internal BGP

Before exploring the scalability issues of internal BGP, you should make certain that you have valid reasons for even implementing the BGP routing protocol in the first place. Your router's hardware capacity and the bandwidth between the ISP's AS and your AS is a key consideration for implementing BGP. Because of the system overhead involved in handling Internet routing updates, you should make sure that the prospective BGP router has sufficient CPU and memory resources. In addition, adequate bandwidth must be in place between your AS and the ISP's AS to handle the traffic loads created by BGP. Without ample bandwidth, the link between the ASs may get clogged up, and the subsequent routing updates may produce out-of-date routing tables. Also, you do not need to deploy BGP when your internetwork AS has only one route to the ISP's AS. Taking advantage of a simpler static route configuration between ASs is a more logical choice because the local AS has only one route to the ISP's AS. BGP is most suitable to put into service when an AS has several connections to other ASs. When operating in this capacity, BGP can effectively be used to influence inbound and outbound route update traffic between the local and remote ASs.

Before implementing BGP, revisit Chapter 8 to make sure that you adequately understand the BGP path selection process. Proper path election involves cautious management and well-chosen route filtering techniques because BGP routing updates from ISPs can quickly devastate your local AS boundary routers. Your local AS may not be adequately outfitted to handle the 80,000+ routes that exist on the current Internet.

Just to refresh your memory, BGP speakers that exchange routing information and belong to the same AS are known as IBGP peers. BGP speakers that belong to different ASs and exchange routing information are called Exterior BGP (EBGP) peers. EBGP peers, as opposed to IBGP peers, are most often directly connected to each another. Both IBGP peers and EBGP peers, however, use reliable TCP session connections to launch and maintain neighbor (peer) relationships. The *BGP split horizon rule* dictates that IBGP-learned routes never get sent to neighbors. The BGP split horizon rule assuages the number of routing loops that would occur if non-meshed IBGP peers sent routing information to all connected peers. A full-mesh topology between IBGP peers is necessary because the rule prevents IBGP routers from propagating their derived routing table to other IBGP peers within an AS. In Figure 9.1, the BGP split horizon rule prevents RouterB from forwarding information learned from RouterA to RouterC. Instead, RouterA should be directly connected to RouterC, creating a full mesh.

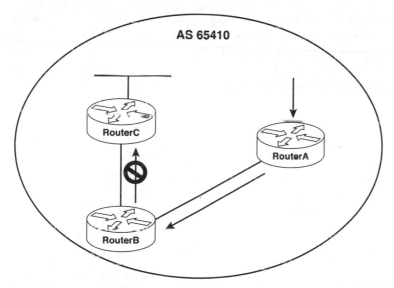

Figure 9.1 RouterB will not forward routes learned from RouterA to RouterC because of the BGP split horizon rule.

As explained in Chapter 8, IBGP peer relationships need a connection-oriented TCP session to operate. As an IBGP network increases in size, so will the number of TCP sessions required. Therefore, a full mesh IBGP topology will maximize, not minimize, the number of TCP sessions required in the AS. This is a scalability issue. The number of BGP sessions can be determined by the following formula:

```
N * (n-1) ÷ 2 = connections needed
```

If you only had 10 routers, then the number of connections would be 45 or 10(10–1)÷2. To carry this example one step further, 1,000 routers would demand roughly 500,000 BGP sessions to fulfill the full mesh requirement. Because BGP uses TCP, another problem arises. A large amount of replication traffic and bandwidth consumption results in a large BGP autonomous system. Route reflectors can be used to decrease the number of TCP sessions and routing update traffic created in an IBGP full mesh AS.

BGP Route Reflectors

A *route reflector* is a BGP router configured to forward routing updates to peers within the same AS. Route reflectors reduce the problems that are caused by fully meshed IBGP topologies. This is accomplished by lowering the number of IBGP neighbor relationships needed in an AS. BGP route reflectors alleviate the scalability problem of internal BGP (IBGP) full mesh topologies by reducing the number of IBGP sessions that must be configured between routers. They serve to tweak the BGP split horizon rule by permitting a BGP router, configured as a route reflector, to send out IBGP-learned routes to other IBGP neighbors. This change in behavior can be seen in Figure 9.2.

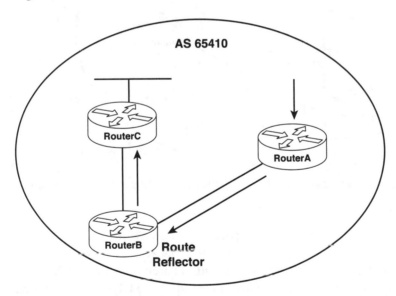

Figure 9.2 RouterB is configured as a route reflector to propagate routes from RouterA to RouterC.

Not only does a route reflector alter the split horizon rule by allowing IBGP-learned routes to be flooded to other IBGP peers, but the number of BGP TCP sessions is lessened considerably and BGP routing traffic is reduced. Because the route reflector propagates any IBGP routes learned from its configured clients, client-to-client peering is not necessary. Table 9.1 shows the main terminology needed to understand Route Reflectors.

Table 9.1   Route Reflector Terminology

Route Reflector Term	Description
Route reflector	A router that is set up to reflect or advertise IBGP-learned routes to other IBGP neighbors.
Client	Routers that have neighbor relationships with the route reflector. The number of clients that a reflector can have is limited only by memory.
Cluster	A grouping of the route reflector and its respective clients.
Cluster ID	An identifier that enables a route reflector to see updates from other routers in the same cluster.
Non-clients	IBGP peers of the route reflector that are not configured as clients.
Originator ID	An optional and non-transitive BGP attribute that is generated by a route reflector. The attribute is the Router ID of the originating route reflector of the route in the local AS.
Cluster-list	An optional and non-transitive attribute that represents a sequence of cluster IDs that are passed along with the route. The local cluster ID is appended to the cluster list when a route reflector advertises a route from its clients to non-clients outside the cluster.

The following list demonstrates the many benefits and advantages of implementing route reflectors:

➤ You do not need to implement a full mesh topology.

➤ The route reflector propagates routes to IBGP peers.

➤ The number of BGP peer relationships is reduced.

➤ You can employ multiple route reflectors for redundancy and session reduction.

➤ Route reflectors need minimal configuration.

➤ Regular BGP routers can coexist with route reflectors.

A *route reflector client* is an IBGP router specifically set up to be given routing updates from a reflecting router. The term that describes the collective unit of a route reflector and the clients it communicates with is called a *cluster*. An AS can be separated into multiple clusters containing a route reflector and its clients. The route reflectors have to be configured in a full mesh topology with IBGP. You still utilize an IGP, for example EIGRP or OSPF, to transport local route and next-hop address information. A broad example of this concept is demonstrated in Figure 9.3.

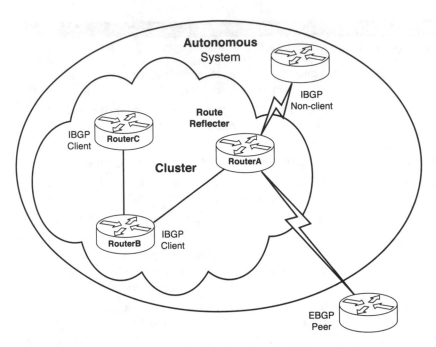

Figure 9.3 A sample router topology showing the main route reflector concepts.

You should know that multiple route reflectors can be deployed within a large autonomous system for purposes of redundancy.

If an update packet comes from a client peer, the route reflector will forward the update to all client and non-client peers, except for the peer that sent the original route. (The route reflector and its clients will still adhere to the normal split horizon rule.) If an IBGP route reflector receives a routing update from a non-client IBGP peer, it forwards the update to all IBGP clients in the cluster. If the update comes from an EBGP peer from outside the AS, then the route reflector forwards the update to all client and non-client peers within the AS. Figure 9.4 shows an example of a route reflector with three clients in a cluster.

To establish a route reflector, you would configure RouterA normally and then configure a `neighbor` statement on RouterA for each BGP neighbor with which it is to communicate. In this case, the BGP neighbors are RouterB, RouterC, and RouterD. Route reflector configuration is done only on the route reflector and the clients are set up as normal IBGP neighbors. Updates are sent from the route reflector directly to all clients, and the clients receive only updates from the reflector. All the updates have the originator-ID attribute included. This is to assure a loop-free environment as the route reflector disregards an update with itself as the originator. There must be at least one route reflector per cluster, and the routers that are not part of the cluster (non-clients) still need to be in a full mesh topology for full connectivity. You should configure the route reflector in Figure 9.4 by using the following command:

```
neighbor ip address route-reflector-client
```

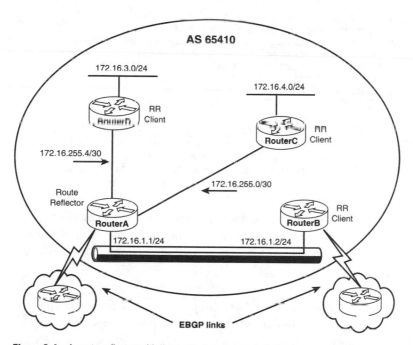

Figure 9.4 A route reflector with three client routers in a cluster.

Refer to Figure 9.4 and notice that RouterA is the central distribution point for the BGP route updates. RouterB, RouterC, and RouterD are route reflector client peers that send all route updates that they learn to RouterA. RouterA then propagates the route to all its client peers, as well as to any non-client peers to which it is connected. This combination of a route reflector and its client peers is what we call a *cluster*. Route reflectors, clients, and non-clients all send and receive updates strictly with IBGP.

Listings 9.1 and 9.2 show the actual configuration for RouterA in Figure 9.4.

Listing 9.1   Configuring IBGP Peers for RouterA

```
RouterA> enable
RouterA# config t
Enter configuration commands, one per line.  End with CNTL/Z
RouterA(config)# router bgp 65410
RouterA(config-router)# neighbor 172.16.1.2 remote-as 65410
RouterA(config-router)# neighbor 172.16.255.6 remote-as 65410
RouterA(config-router)# neighbor 172.16.255.2 remote-as 65410
```

Listing 9.2   Configuring RouterA As a Route Reflector

```
RouterA> enable
RouterA# config t
Enter configuration commands, one per line.  End with CNTL/Z
RouterA(config-router)# neighbor 172.16.1.2 route-reflector-client
RouterA(config-router)# neighbor 172.16.255.6 route-reflector-client
RouterA(config-router)# neighbor 172.16.255.2 route-reflector-client
RouterA(config-router)# exit
RouterA(config)#
```

On the BSCI exam you may see a simulator question that demands that you perform all the steps to configure a route reflector in the proper order and with the correct syntax, shown in Listings 9.1 and 9.2. Also remember that in the simulator sections of the test, the question mark (?) is available to assist you with the syntax of the commands.

The router configuration command `bgp cluster-id` is used to assign a *cluster ID* when a cluster contains more than one route reflector for purposes of redundancy. The correct syntax for the `bgp cluster-id` command is as follows:

```
RouterA(config-router)# bgp cluster-id cluster-id
```

The `cluster-id` parameter is a four-byte integer value. You cannot change the cluster ID after you have configured the route reflector clients. Route reflector clients are also incompatible with peer groups because a peer group router has to send out policy updates to each and every member of its peer group.

The following router configuration command is used to selectively disable route reflection between clients:

```
RouterA(config-router)# no bgp client-to-client reflection
```

The `show ip bgp ?` command offers a number of parameters for viewing information about your cluster. Listing 9.3 shows the output of this powerful command.

Listing 9.3 The show ip bgp ? Command

```
RouterA# show ip bgp ?
  A.B.C.D            IP prefix <network>/<length>, e.g., 35.0.0.0/8
  A.B.C.D            Network in the BGP routing table to display
  cidr-only          Display only routes with non-natural netmasks
  community          Display routes matching the communities
  community-list     Display routes matching the community-list
  dampened-paths     Display paths suppressed due to dampening
  filter-list        Display routes conforming to the filter-list
  flap-statistics    Display flap statistics of routes
  inconsistent-as    Display only routes with inconsistent origin ASs
  neighbors          Detailed information on TCP and BGP neighbor connections
  paths              Path information
  peer-group         Display information on peer-groups
  regexp             Display routes matching the AS path regular expression
  summary            Summary of BGP neighbor status
  <cr>
```

For example, the `show ip bgp neighbors` command can be used to display the status of TCP connections to BGP neighbors, including which neighbors are configured as route reflector client routers. The abbreviated command `sh ip bgp nei` displays the same information. Also, the `show ip bgp summary` command displays the three peer routers from Listing 9.1 and Listing 9.2 in a table format with statistics for data such as the AS number, messages received, messages sent, and so on.

BGP Confederations

A BGP *confederation* is a BGP configuration in which a single AS is divided into multiple logical ASs that run EBGP between them. It is another way of handling the sudden and rapid growth of an IBGP network. A confederation reduces the number of IBGP peers in an AS by dividing the AS into multiple smaller ASs (sub-autonomous systems), each with its own logical AS number. Each sub-AS sends and receives route updates internally with IBGP and communicates with other sub-ASs in the confederation by using EBGP. The BGP confederation looks like a single AS to the outside world.

Policy Control in BGP Using Prefix Lists

Distribute lists, prefix lists, and route maps are BGP advertisement control mechanisms that can be used to normalize the propagation of BGP advertisements throughout the internetwork. They all function in much the same way as access lists in that they can be tweaked to regulate how data is sent through the network. *Distribute lists* use access lists to decide what routing information will be filtered to govern whether a certain router will send or receive BGP route advertisements with a particular peer. You basically configure a distribute list to permit or deny a router to send or receive BGP advertisements with the `distribute-list in` or the `distribute-list out` commands. In addition to update traffic filtering, you can also use distribute lists to filter inbound and outbound protocol traffic by configuring and applying access lists.

Prefix lists are easier to configure than traditional routed protocol access lists because the entries are sequentially numbered. This allows for the insertion, deletion, and modification of specific statements. Mechanically, however, they use the same rules for reading and application as a traditional access list.

NOTE: This chapter looks at distribute lists and primarily prefix lists as tools to implement BGP policy. Route maps are covered in greater detail in the next chapter on optimizing routing updates.

To apply a distribute list to an IP interface, you should use the `neighbor distribute-list` command. The complete syntax of the command is as follows:

```
RouterA(config-router)# neighbor distribute-list {ip-address | peer-group-
➥name} distribute-list access-list-number in | out
```

The `ip-address` parameter is the IP address of the BGP neighbor for which routes will be filtered. The `peer-group-name` parameter, if applicable, is the name of the peer group. The `access-list-number` parameter provides the IP standard or extended access list to be applied (1 to 199). The keywords `in` or `out` determine whether the access list is to be applied to inbound or outbound advertisements from the specified neighbor. A snippet of sample code to configure a distribute list could look like this:

```
RouterA(config) router bgp 65410
RouterA(config-router)# network 192.168.10.0
RouterA(config-router)# neighbor 10.1.1.2 remote-as 65420
RouterA(config-router)# neighbor 10.1.2.2 remote-as 65430
RouterA(config-router)# neighbor 10.1.1.2 distribute-list 1 out
RouterA(config-router)# exit
RouterA(config) access-list 1 deny 172.16.0.0  0.0.255.255
RouterA(config) access-list 1 permit any
```

In the preceding sample listing, the distribute list prevents any traffic to major network 172.16.0.0 from being sent outbound to the BGP neighbor at address 10.1.1.2. The last line permits all the rest of the traffic to circumvent the implicit `deny` statement at the end of every access list.

On BGP routers, you can also achieve filtration by implementing a *prefix list*. Prefix lists offer a combination of the protocol filtration of access lists with the route filtration capability of distribute lists based on network access prefixes. Distribute lists have effectively become obsolete because of the extensive use of prefix lists in Cisco IOS 12.0 and later. Prefix lists work the same way as access lists, except that they offer several important benefits over access lists. Prefix lists are

➤ Not as processor-intensive as access lists because they are better at loading and performing lookups of large lists

➤ More flexible than access lists because they can add and delete individual lines and perform incremental changes

➤ More user-friendly than the typical access list

Prefix lists do have some functional rules that should be adhered to for optimal performance. Consider carefully the following list:

➤ An empty prefix list essentially allows (permits) all route prefixes.

➤ If a prefix is allowed (permitted), the route is utilized.

➤ If a prefix is not allowed (denied), the route is not used.

➤ Prefix lists are made up of a list of sequenced statements. The router starts at the top of the list and searches down until a match is made. The statement with the lowest sequence number is at the top of the list.

> Consider placing the most common permit or deny matches towards the top of the list by applying lower sequence numbers to them.

➤ If a provided prefix does not match any prefix list statements then a tacit implicit deny applies, just as in an access list.

➤ Sequence numbers are automatically generated unless explicitly disabled.

To configure a prefix list, use the following command:

```
ip prefix-list prefix-list-name [permit | deny] network-address/len
```

The parameter `network-address/len` indicates the network prefix and mask length for which the configured action should be used. Use the `no ip prefix-list prefix-list-name` command to delete an existing prefix list.

Figure 9.5 uses a prefix list to force RouterA to send only network prefix (supernet) 169.0.0.0/8 to AS 65410, but not the route to network 169.254.0.0/16. Listing 9.4 lists the RouterA prefix list configuration commands.

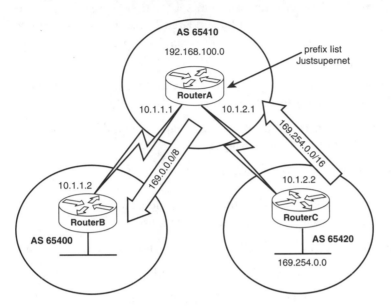

Figure 9.5 A sample prefix list scenario.

Listing 9.4   The Prefix List Configuration for RouterA

```
RouterA(config)# ip prefix-list justsupernet permit 169.0.0.0/8
RouterA(config)# router bgp 65410
RouterA(config-router)# network 192.168.100.0
RouterA(config-router)# neighbor 10.1.1.2 remote-as 65400
RouterA(config-router)# neighbor 10.1.2.2 remote-as 65420
RouterA(config-router)# aggregate-address 169.0.0.0 255.0.0.0
RouterA(config-router)# neighbor 10.1.1.2 prefix-list justsupernet out
RouterA(config-router)# exit
RouterA#
```

As shown in Figure 9.5, RouterA is a peer with RouterB at address 10.1.1.2 in AS 65400, and RouterC at 10.1.2.2 in AS 65420. The neighbor prefix-list command dictates that RouterA is to use the prefix list named justsupernet to decide which update messages are pushed to BGP peer RouterB. Only the route 169.0.0.0/8 gets sent to RouterB because the implicit deny stops the rest of the routes.

You cannot combine the **neighbor prefix-list** command with the **neighbor distribute-list** command to configure the same BGP peer.

If you want to delete a prefix list, use the following syntax:

```
RouterA(config)# no ip prefix-list list-name
```

The `show ip prefix-list` command is used with a wide array of keywords and parameters to display information regarding the prefix list policy that is configured on a router. The full syntax for the `show ip prefix-list` command is as follows:

```
show ip prefix-list [detail-summary] name [network/len] [seq seq-num]
➥[longer][first-match]
```

When you opt for the `detail` keyword, it displays information for all prefix lists configured on a router, as well as the description and the number of times the entry has matched a route (hit count). If you issue the `show ip prefix-list detail name` command, it displays information for the specified prefix list only. The *[network/len]* parameter displays the policy that is associated with a certain prefix/len value (for example, 169.254.0.0/16) in a prefix list. The seq *seq-num* parameter denotes a specific prefix list entry's sequence number.

The `clear ip prefix-list` command can be used to clear and reset the hit count that is displayed for a particular prefix-list whenever the `show ip prefix-list [detail | summary] prefix-list-name` command is run. The full syntax is

```
clear ip prefix-list prefix-list-name
```

In spite of the methods used for filtering, particular consideration needs to be given to the size and number of lists that are configured on your router. Because all pertinent traffic is compared to applied access lists and extended access lists line by line, CPU usage increases in proportion to the number and size of applied lists.

Connecting Multiple ISPs Using BGP

The generic term, *multihomed*, is often used to depict a host linked to two or more networks or having two or more network addresses. For instance, a server might be connected to a serial line and a LAN. For the purposes of Cisco routing, generating multiple connections between an autonomous system and two or more ISPs is referred to as *multihoming*. The technique of multihoming is often used to establish redundant connections between ASs and the Internet to increase the stability and reliability of the connection or to utilize preferable paths to particular destinations with which it often communicates. By generating links with more than one ISP, an organization can ensure that communications with Internet destinations are not broken if a particular ISP experiences a failure.

 BGP Multihoming is technically not a configuration of multiple links to a single ISP, such as an ISDN fault-tolerant connection. Although multiple links to an ISP do help in the event of a link failure, they do not protect your organization against a communications failure at the ISP itself.

By establishing connections to more than one ISP, you can also improve performance between the AS and common network destinations. For example, if your two most common destinations used different ISPs and a separate link was established with each ISP, then certain routes could be established through each ISP between the AS and common destinations. This offers more possibilities for policy control than would be possible with only a single link to one service provider. For example, a company could use a particular provider for multicast conferencing services and instant messaging while using another provider for email services.

Three common ways exist to configure multiple connections to the ISPs. One method entails all ISPs passing only default routes to your AS. A second method is to have all ISPs pass default routes *and* selected routes to your AS (the selected routes, for example, of certain high-traffic customers). Third, all ISPs can pass all routes to your AS. The following sections look at each of the scenarios in detail.

All ISPs Pass Only Default Routes

If only default routes are passed from each ISP to the AS, for example, then memory and CPU utilization are held to a minimum. Your autonomous system passes all its routes to the multiple ISPs, who in turn apply policy and forward them on to other ASs as necessary. Inbound packets coming into the AS are managed by the ISPs and other ASs, whereas the outbound packets going to the ISPs are managed according to the metrics of the IGP, such as RIP, EIGRP, or OSPF, which are used to reach the default route configured internally at the local AS. The route to the ISP depends upon the metric of the routing protocol used as the IGP. At this point, you should be well aware of how to use the `ip route` command to configure a default route. However, here is a quick example of configuring interface Serial 0 as your default route:

```
RouterA(config)# ip route 0.0.0.0 0.0.0.0 S0
```

All ISPs Pass Default and Selected Routes

Establishing specific routes to common destinations demands additional router overhead (processor and memory) because both default routes and specific routes to other destinations are being processed. You want to choose only customers with whom you exchange a substantial amount of traffic to pass selected routes. The ISP that a router in your AS selects to reach a customer network is most likely the one with the shortest AS path value (however, this could be rigged with a Local-preference attribute, for example). The default route configured and used by the IGP will be used to get to all the other external networks. As in the previous scenario, the ISPs and other ASs control inbound packets coming into the AS.

All ISPs Pass All Routes

A multihomed AS can be configured to receive all routes from each ISP. Obviously, this significantly increases the overhead for each router in your AS because all external routes have to be processed. Your AS sends all its routes to each ISP, which in turn applies policy and forwards them when applicable to other ASs. The ISP that a router in your AS selects to reach an external network is most likely the one with the shortest AS path value, although attributes such as Weight and Local-preference can be used to influence this decision-making process.

Weight and Local-preference Revisited

Some of the most common methods for manipulating the path chosen to reach external networks are the Weight and Local-preference attributes. The following snippet shows the syntax used to designate a weight attribute:

```
RouterA(config-router)# neighbor {ip-address | peer-group-name} weight
weight
```

The ip-address parameter is the IP address of a BGP peer, and peer-group-name is the name of the BGP peer group. Although either the ip-address or peer-group-name parameters can be used, neither are required. The weight keyword is, of course, the assigned weight value, which can be between 1 and 65535 (16-bit). The default weight value is 32768 for routes that originate from the local router. The default weight value for other routes is 0. The weight value influences only the local router.

You can modify the default local preference value from 100 to another number between 1 and 4,294,967,295, where the higher value is preferred. This value is local to the autonomous system and is utilized to influence routes that have equal weights. It influences other routers within the AS. The command syntax looks like this:

```
RouterA(config-router)# bgp default local-preference value
```

Although there are several other BGP commands that can be used to manipulate and influence router policy, the rest of these options typically utilize route maps. Route maps are explored in greater detail in Chapter 10, "Optimizing Routing Updates."

Route Redistribution Between BGP and IGPs

As you are aware, a router running the BGP routing protocol handles its own routing table separately from the IP routing table. An AS uses three primary methods to inject route information into BGP: using the network command, redistributing static routes to null 0, and redistributing dynamic routes into BGP.

Using the **network** Command

First, the network command is used to manually configure BGP to advertise a network that already exists in the IP routing table. The list of network command entries must contain all the networks in the AS that you want to advertise. For example:

```
RouterA(config) router bgp 65410
RouterA(config-router)# network 192.168.10.0
RouterA(config-router)# network 10.10.0.0
```

If summary routes need to be advertised into BGP, then the redistribution of static routes can be used to bypass the requirement that the route exist in the IP routing table. One technique is to use the network command. The network router configuration command advertises a particular IGP network and generates a corresponding entry in the router's BGP routing table.

Know the basic definition of redistribution. The redistribution process happens when a router is running multiple routing protocols and it advertises the routing information that is received between the protocols. The process enables routing information learned from one protocol to be "disseminated" in the update messages of another routing protocol.

Routes that are advertised by the use of the `network` command are shown with the origin code IGP (I) in the BGP routing table. The preferred method for advertising a summary route, however, is via the `aggregate-address` router configuration command. The `aggregate-address` command generates a single route entry for a range of network addresses if at least one specific route entry that is contained within the aggregate address range exists in the BGP routing table.

As discussed in Chapter 2, "Routing Principles," classless interdomain routing (CIDR) is a mechanism developed to help alleviate the problem of exhaustion of IP addresses and the growth of routing tables. The idea behind CIDR is that blocks of multiple addresses can be combined, or aggregated, to create a larger classless set of IP addresses. These multiple addresses can then be summarized in routing tables, resulting in fewer route advertisements. Earlier versions of BGP did not support CIDR; BGP-4 does, however, and BGP-4 support includes the following:

➤ The BGP update message carries both the prefix and the prefix length (len). Previous versions of BGP included only the prefix, and the length was assumed from the address class.

➤ Addresses can be aggregated (summarized) when advertised by a BGP router.

➤ The AS-path attribute can include a combined unordered list of all ASs through which all the aggregated routes have passed. This combined unordered list should always be measured to ensure that the route is loop-free and stable.

Two BGP attributes are related to aggregate addressing. The well-known discretionary Atomic-aggregate attribute tells the peer AS that the originating router has summarized the routes. The optional transitive Aggegator attribute designates the BGP router ID and AS number of the router that carried out the route aggregation.

By default, the aggregate route is advertised as coming from the AS that did the aggregation and has the Atomic-aggregate attribute set to show that information may be missing. The Autonomous System numbers from the non-aggregated routes are not included in the list. The router can be configured to include the unordered list of all autonomous systems contained in all paths that are being summarized. Aggregate addresses are not used in the Internet as much as they could or should be because most multihomed ASs want to make certain that their routes are advertised, without being aggregated into a summarized route.

Redistributing Static Routes into BGP Using Null 0

Another recommended method for advertising an IGP network into BGP is to redistribute static routes into BGP by using the null 0 interface. Creating a static route by using the null 0 interface advertises a single aggregate address for IGP networks instead of multiple single IGP addresses for each network. This is actually a way of tricking the process into thinking that a route actually exists for the aggregate. (If you use the network command for a network that already exists in the IP routing table, the static route to null 0 is altogether unnecessary.) Although routing to null 0 literally means "discard the packet to this network," pointing a static route to the null 0 virtual interface is acceptable. The BGP router already has specific routes to all networks inside the local AS and ignores the static route in favor of a more specific path.

You create a static route with a null 0 interface by using the ip route global configuration command and the redistribute static router configuration command. For example:

```
RouterA(config)# router bgp 65410
RouterA(config-router)# redistribute static
RouterA(config-router)# exit
RouterA(config)# ip route 0.0.0.0 0.0.0.0 null0
```

Redistributing Dynamic IGP Routes into BGP

Although not really recommended, a third option is to redistribute dynamic routing IGP routes into BGP. The redistribution of dynamic IGP routes into BGP should rarely be configured because subsequent changes in IGP routing information may not be indicated in the BGP updates. A BGP update is generated every time a change is detected in the IGP route topology, such as when a link becomes unavailable. This increase in BGP routing updates may lead to instability in the BGP routing tables within an AS. Only local routes should be distributed. To avoid routing loops, routes learned from other ASs must not be re-sent from the IGP. Using a redistribute command into BGP results in the (?) incomplete Origin attribute entry for the BGP route to show up in the show ip bgp output. A sample of show ip bgp output is shown in Listing 9.5

Listing 9.5   A Sample show ip bgp Output

```
RouterA show ip bgp
BGP table version is 583644, local router ID is 172.16.157.32
Status codes: s suppressed, d damped, h history, * valid, > best, i -
internal
Origin codes: I - IGP, e -EGP, ? - incomplete

      Network         Next Hop           Metric     LocPref   Weight  Path
*>   10.1.0.0         172.20.36.2           0          100       0     480  i
*>   10.2.0.0         172.24.20.1           0          100       0     140  i
*    10.3.0.0         172.23.1.10           0          100       0     340  i
*>                    192.168.2.1           0          100       0     200  i
*                     192.168.3.1           0          100       0     100  i

RouterA(config-router)# exit
RouterA#
```

Looking at Listing 9.5, RouterA sends traffic destined for network 10.3.0.0 to the next-hop router 192.168.2.1 (notice the > symbol) because it determines that the path through AS 200 is the optimal path. In a BGP routing table, the first column displays the status of each stored route based on the codes in the legend above the table. Even though BGP can store several routes to the same destination, a BGP router has only one best, or preferred, route. The optimal path for each route is specified by a > symbol in the first status column. Table 9.2 describes each field found in the BGP routing table.

Table 9.2   The BGP Routing Table As Seen Via the show ip bgp Command

BGP Routing Table Field	Description
BGP table version	An internal version number that is incremented each time a routing change occurs.
Local Router ID	An internal identification number for the router; derived from the highest IP address configured for the router, often a loopback address.
Status Codes	Identifies the status of each route in the routing table: *Suppressed*—Inactive route. *Valid*—Active route. *Best*—Best route to that network. *Internal*—Route learned from the IBGP peer. *Damped*—Route is currently reachable and is used, but has an instability metric from previous bad behavior. *History*—Route has been withdrawn and is currently unreachable.

Table 9.2 The BGP Routing Table As Seen Via the show ip bgp Command *(continued)*

BGP Routing Table Field	Description
Origin Codes	Identifies the source of each route in the routing table. *IGP*—Source of route originated with IGP and was advertised by means of the **network** command *EGP*—Source of the route originated with EGP *?*—Source of the route is unknown, most likely distributed into BGP by means of IGP
Network	IP address of the destination network.
Next Hop	IP address of the next router along the path to the destination network.
Metric	The inter-autonomous system metric value.
LocPref	The configured local preference attribute for this route entry.
Weight	The configured weight attribute for this route entry.
Path	Listing of AS(s) traversed on the way to the destination network.

Verifying Multihomed BGP Environment

By this point at the end of these two BGP-related chapters, you should already be familiar with many of the Cisco IOS commands to configure and verify a BGP implementation. You need to practice extensively on real routers or simulators so that you are proficient with the commands used to configure, verify, and debug basic BGP operations, route reflectors, and prefix lists.

Don't forget that you can also use the `show ip protocols` command to display a list of protocols operating on a router and the interfaces to which the protocols are bound. Furthermore, the `show ip protocols` command displays information concerning the redistribution of routing table updates communicated between all active routing protocols. To verify end-to-end connectivity on the network you can use the `ping` command. To verify optimal routing path usage, you can use the `traceroute` command.

Exam Prep Questions

Question 1

Which one of the following statements is *false* concerning route reflectors?

○ A. Route reflectors change the BGP split horizon rule by letting the route reflector propagate routes learned by IBGP to other IBGP peers.

○ B. A route reflector cluster is the grouping of the route reflector and its clients.

○ C. Route reflectors do not have to be in a full mesh configuration with IBGP.

○ D. When a route reflector gets an update from a client, it sends it to all non-client peers except the route originator.

Answer C is correct. The route reflectors must be fully meshed with IBGP to ensure that all routes learned will be sent throughout the AS. Answers A, B, and D are all accurate statements concerning route reflectors.

Question 2

Which one of the following terms describes a unit containing a route reflector and the configured route reflector clients?

○ A. Area

○ B. Connection

○ C. Cluster

○ D. Confederation

Answer C is correct. This combination of a route reflector and its client peers is called a cluster. Answer A is incorrect because an area is a logical grouping of network segments and their connected devices. Answer B is incorrect because a connection is merely a link between two network devices. Answer D is incorrect because a confederation is a BGP configuration in which a single AS is divided into multiple logical ASs that run Exterior BGP (EBGP) between them.

Question 3

Which of the following commands generates the following table output?

```
BGP table version is 583644, local router ID is
➥172.16.157.32
Status codes: s suppressed, d damped, h history, * valid, >
➥best, i -
internal
Origin codes: I - IGP, e -EGP, ? - incomplete

    Network          Next Hop          Metric      LocPref
➥Weight  Path
```

○ A. **show ip bgp**

○ B. **show ip prefix-list**

○ C. **show ip protocols**

○ D. **debug ip bgp neighbors**

Answer A is correct. In this BGP routing table generated by show ip bgp, the first column displays the status of each stored route based on the codes in the legend above the table. Even though BGP can store several routes to the same destination, a BGP router has only one best, or preferred, route. The optimal path for each route is specified by a > symbol in the first status column. Answer B is incorrect because the show ip prefix-list command displays all information on all prefix lists. Answer C is incorrect because show ip protocols displays all IP protocol information on the Cisco router. Answer D is incorrect because debug ip bgp neighbors outputs the detailed BGP neighbor status.

Question 4

You have 20 peers in your IBGP network. How many TCP peer sessions do you need if you do not implement route reflectors?

○ A. 380

○ B. 190

○ C. 100

○ D. 20

Answer B is correct. The answer is derived from the formula $n(n-1) \div 2$, where n is the number of IBGP peer routers; therefore, the answer is 190. Answers A, C, and D are incorrect because the calculations are wrong.

Question 5

Which one of the following sets of commands is the proper syntax to configure a route reflector client?

○ A. RouterA(config)# neighbor 172.16.1.2 as-remote 65410
       RouterA(oonfig)# neighbor 172.16.1.2 route-reflector-client

○ B. RouterA(config)# neighbor 172.16.1.2 remote-as 65410
       RouterA(config)# neighbor 172.16.1.2 route-reflector-client

○ C. RouterA(config-router)# neighbor 172.16.1.2 as-remote 65410
       RouterA(config-router)# 172.16.1.2 route-reflector-client

○ D. RouterA(config-router)# neighbor 172.16.1.2 remote-as 65410
       RouterA(config-router)# neighbor 172.16.1.2 route-reflector-client

Answer D is correct. In router configuration mode, the `neighbor remote-as` syntax is used to create the peer relationship and the `neighbor route-reflector-client` command generates the peer relationship. Answer A is incorrect because it is not in router configuration mode and the command is not `as-remote`. Answer B is incorrect because although the syntax is perfect, the configuration mode is wrong. Answer C is incorrect because it is not `as-remote` and the `neighbor` command is missing from the second line.

Question 6

Which keyword needs to follow the **show ip bgp** command to display detailed information on TCP and BGP peer connections?

○ A. **peer-group**
○ B. **summary**
○ C. **neighbors**
○ D. **community**

Answer C is correct. The `neighbors` keyword shows detailed information on TCP and BGP neighbor connections. Answer A is incorrect because the `peer-group` keyword displays information on peer groups. Answer B is incorrect because the `summary` keyword shows a synopsis of BGP neighbor status. Answer D is incorrect because the `community` keyword displays routes matching the communities.

Question 7

Which of the following statements identifies a benefit of prefix lists over access lists? (Choose all that apply.)

❑ A. Prefix lists are not as processor-intensive as access lists because they are quicker loading and better at performing lookups of large lists.

❑ B. The rules of prefix lists are somewhat different from access lists, including the lack of an implicit **deny** statement at the end of the list.

❑ C. Prefix lists are more flexible than access lists because they enable you to add and delete individual lines and perform incremental changes.

❑ D. Prefix lists are generally more user-friendly than the typical access list.

Answers A, C, and D are correct and represent benefits of prefix lists over access lists. Answer B is incorrect because the functionality of prefix lists are similar to access lists yet enhanced. Prefix lists do indeed have an implicit deny statement at the end of the list.

Question 8

You would like to reset the hit count that is displayed for a particular prefix list whenever the **show ip prefix-list detail** command is run. Which one of the following commands would you run?

○ A. **ip clear prefix-list**

○ B. **clear prefix-list**

○ C. **clear ip prefix list**

○ D. **clear ip prefix-list**

Answer D is correct. The clear ip prefix-list command can be used to clear and reset the hit count that is displayed for a particular prefix list whenever the show ip prefix-list [detail | summary] prefix-list-name is run. The full syntax is clear ip prefix-list prefix-list-name. Answer A is incorrect because the keyword ip comes after the clear command. Answer B is incorrect because the keyword ip is missing. Answer C is incorrect because the hyphen is missing between prefix and list.

Question 9

Which one of the following is *not* a common method for configuring multiple connections to the ISPs (multihoming)?

○ A. All ISPs pass only a few selected routes to your AS.

○ B. All ISPs pass only default routes to your AS.

○ C. All ISPs pass default routes and selected routes to your AS.

○ D. All ISPs pass all routes to your AS.

Answer A is correct. Building an environment where all the ISPs pass only a few selected routes to the AS is not a typically used multihoming method. There are basically three common ways to configure multiple connections to the ISPs. One method entails all ISPs passing only default routes to your AS. A second method is to have all ISPs pass default routes and selected routes to your AS (for example, certain high-traffic customers). Thirdly, all ISPs can pass all routes to your AS.

Question 10

Which of the following are primary methods that an AS uses to inject route information into BGP? (Choose all that apply.)

❑ A. Using the **network** command.

❑ B. Redistributing static routes to the null 0 interface.

❑ C. Redistributing dynamic routes into BGP.

❑ D. Using the **aggregate-address** router configuration command.

Answers A, B, and C are correct. An AS uses three primary methods to inject route information into BGP: using the network command, redistributing static routes to null 0, and redistributing dynamic routes into BGP. Answer D is incorrect because the aggregate-address router configuration command is the preferred method for advertising a summary route.

Need to Know More?

Halabi, Sam, et al. *Internet Routing Architectures, 2nd Edition.* Indianapolis, IN: Cisco Press, 2000. ISBN 157870233X.

Huitema, Christian. *Routing in the Internet, 2nd Edition.* Indianapolis, IN: Prentice Hall PTR, 2000. ISBN 0130226475.

Loshin, Peter. *Big Book of Border Gateway Protocol (BGP) RFCs.* San Diego, CA: Morgan Kaufmann, 2000. ISBN 0124558461.

Parkhurst, William R. *Cisco BGP-4 Command and Configuration Handbook.* Indianapolis, IN: Cisco Press, 2001. ISBN: 158705017X.

Stewart, John W. *BGP4 Inter-Domain Routing in the Internet.* Reading, MA: Addison-Wesley Pub Co, 1998. ISBN 0201379511.

RFC 1654: A Border Gateway Protocol (BGP-4): `http://www.faqs.org/rfcs/rfc1654.html`.

Routing Update Optimization and Redistribution

Terms you'll need to understand:

- ✓ Redistribution
- ✓ Administrative distance (AD)
- ✓ Policy-based routing
- ✓ Filtering
- ✓ Switching
- ✓ Core
- ✓ Backbone
- ✓ Edge
- ✓ Distribute lists
- ✓ Access lists
- ✓ Seed metric
- ✓ Route maps

Techniques you'll need to master:

- ✓ Influencing the optimal path
- ✓ Understanding the guidelines for route redistribution
- ✓ Configuring and verifying route redistribution
- ✓ Using different mechanisms to resolve path selection
- ✓ Verifying route redistribution and route map policy
- ✓ Configuring policy-based routing with route maps

Cisco Policy-based Routing

Policy-based routing was introduced to Cisco administrators in IOS release 11.0 and affords network load-sharing capacities and traffic shaping by letting you have granular control of the movement of network traffic through a router. For instance, you can generate a route map that sends high-bandwidth, high-priority traffic through a high-speed interface, while sending the rest of the network traffic through a lower-bandwidth interface. Policy-based routing can also enable you to flag packets with different TOS (type of service) values so that specific types of traffic can be given special treatment. ISPs, for example, deploy policy-based routing to control different Internet links over policy routers. Quality of service (QoS) mechanisms can configure precedence or TOS values in IP headers at borders to utilize queuing techniques for prioritizing traffic in the network backbone.

You can also force bulk traffic activities toward a higher-cost bandwidth link for a brief time period while allowing normal traffic to flow over the lower-cost bandwidth connection. Policy-based routing can also be used for load-sharing activities to better distribute network packets across several paths based on the patterns and attributes of the particular traffic. When enabled, policy-based routing works on inbound packets that are received on an interface.

The packets are passed through enhanced packet filters called route maps. Depending upon on the defined statements of the route maps, the packets are then routed to the suitable next hop. Each item in a route map statement has a mixture of `match` and `set` commands. The `match` commands determine the conditions to be met, and the `set` commands give details on how the packets will be routed after they meet the criteria set forth in the `match` clauses. For every grouping of `match` and `set` clauses in a route map entry, all the sequential match clauses must simultaneously be met by the packet for the `set` commands to be applicable. There can be many groups of `match`/`set` combinations in a complete route map statement. Route map statements can also be marked as `permit` or `deny`. An important concept to remember is that if the statement is flagged as `deny`, the packets that conform to the `match` criteria are simply sent back through the normal routing channels. This is what you know as typical destination-based routing. Only if the statement is marked as `permit` and the packets meet the `match` criteria are the `set` clauses applicable. Likewise, if the route map statement is flagged as `permit` and the packets do not meet the `match` criteria, the packets also proceed through the usual routing channel (or destination-based routing). Be aware that policy routing is designated only on the interface that receives the packets, as opposed to the interface that sends the packet.

Route maps employ either standard *access lists* to filter a packet's source address or extended access lists to filter a packet's source and destination address. An access list is a grouping of conditions that are maintained by Cisco routers to determine which traffic qualities for filtering, rules, and other network services. Route maps can match on various criteria, including the source system, various running programs, protocol being used, and even the packet size.

The syntax for configuring your route map policy is

```
RouterA(config)# route-map map-tag [permit | deny] [sequence number]
```

The map-tag parameter has a friendly name that defines its purpose. The permit and deny keywords determine whether the matched datagrams are permitted or denied for policy-based routing. If denied, they are destination routed. The sequence-number parameter is the value that signifies the position that new statements will have in the list of statements previously configured under the same map-tag name, and also determines the order of testing.

An advantage of route maps is that they can contain several route-map statements, and each statement can have multiple match conditions. This is also something that makes route maps different from access lists, even though the two mechanisms serve different functions. Each route-map statement is acknowledged by its sequence number and is processed from the top of the list down just like an access list.

The following represents the logic of a route map:

```
sequence 10
match a, b, c,
match x
set y

sequence 20
match a
Match b
Match c
Set y
Set z
```

This can be interpreted as follows:

```
For sequence 10, EITHER a, OR b, OR c AND x MUST BE TRUE TO SET y
For sequence 20, a, b, AND c, MUST BE TRUE TO SET y AND z.
```

The first match condition that is met for a route is applied, and there is an implicit deny at the end. The default setting of a route-map command is permit and has a sequence number of 10 unless otherwise configured. Another advantage of route maps is that the number sequencing enables you to delete and insert certain statements as necessary in the route map.

The two main components of a route map are the `match` and `set` clauses. The syntax of these commands is as follows:

```
RouterA(config-route-map)# match {condition}
RouterA(config-route-map)# set {condition}
```

The `match` clause usually leverages an access list, or access lists, to do packet testing. What the packet tests do depends on how the access list is applied. For example, when applied to the interface via the `access-group` command, traffic is filtered as defined in the access list. Access lists can packet-test network traffic based on such factors as IP address, running applications, TCP ports, and packet length.

The `set` clause actually establishes the destination of traffic that meets the `match` clause(s) criteria. Particularly, the `route-map` configuration command `set-interface` specifies the output interface for the packet and `set-ip-next-hop` designates the next hop through which to route the packet.

In Figure 10.1 and Listing 10.1, we have applied policy-based routing on RouterA so that packets that come from 192.168.101.1 should be forwarded to RouterC on address 172.18.1.2. The `ip policy route-map` command was configured on interface Serial 1 of RouterA, which receives packets from 192.168.101.1. The route map tests the IP addresses in the packets against access list 2 to decide which packets will have policy-based routing applied to them. Access list 2 determines that packets from 192.168.101.1 will be policy-based routed and matching packets will be forwarded to the next-hop address of 172.18.1.2 on RouterC. The other packets will be destination routed as usual, unless other access lists are applied on the interface.

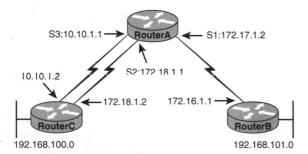

Figure 10.1 Applying policy-based routing on RouterA to direct packets from RouterB to 172.18.1.2 on RouterC.

Listing 10.1   Sample Configuration of a Route Map on RouterA

```
RouterA(config)# int S1
RouterA(config-if)# ip address 172.17.1.2 255.255.255.0
RouterA(config-if)# ip policy route-map sample
```

Listing 10.1 Sample Configuration of a Route Map on RouterA *(continued)*

```
RouterA(config)# route-map sample permit 10
RouterA(config-route-map)# match ip address 2
RouterA(config-route-map)# set ip next-hop 172.18.1.2
RouterA(config-route-map)# exit
RouterA(config)# access-list 2 permit 192.168.101.1 0.0.0.0
```

As we have established, a route map can have several match and set state-ments. You first use the match ip address command to create your standard or extended access lists to be implemented to establish the matching policy.

The match ip address Command

Here is the syntax of the match ip address command:

```
RouterA(config-route-map)# match ip address {access-list-number | name}
➥ [...access-list-number | name]
```

The access-list-number | name parameter is the name or number of the standard or extended access list used to test inbound packets. Policy-based routing is always configured on a router's inbound interface, and therefore analyzes incoming packets only. This is critical because the purpose of policy-based routing is to have control over the path of any particular datagram. To do this, packets must be "tagged" (or permitted) for policy routing before they are route processed.

The match length Command

You can also use the route-map configuration command match length to create *filtering* rules based on the length of the packet. Filtering is the process of allowing only certain types of traffic to pass through a router. For example, you could use this as part of a policy for distinguishing between email or messaging traffic and the larger-sized file transfer packets. The syntax for the match length command is

```
RouterA(config-route-map)# match length min max
```

The *min* parameter designates the minimum IP datagram length of the packet and the *max* value matches against the maximum Network layer packet length (in hex).

The set ip default next-hop Command

A default route is a route that is used when the router has no explicit path to a destination network listed in its IP routing table. When configuring policy-based routing through route maps, an administrator can use standard or extended access lists and match statements to establish the conditions that IP traffic must meet to determine whether matched datagrams are policy routed or destination routed (the default). The set statement is used to specify the destination of traffic that meets the criteria of the route map's match statements.

The set ip next-hop route map configuration command offers a list of IP addresses that designate the adjacent next-hop router on the way to the packet destination. The syntax would be:

```
RouterA(config-route-map)# set ip next-hop ip-address [...ip-address]
```

You could use the route-map configuration command set ip default next-hop 172.16.32.1 to designate that traffic be forwarded to router 172.16.32.1 in case the local router does not have an explicit entry for the route in its IP routing table, like so:

```
RouterA(config-route-map)# set ip default next-hop 172.16.32.1
```

You could also specify a list of several default addresses so that the first adjacent next-hop is used and then the others are attempted in order.

The set default interface Command

This route-map configuration command presents a list of default interfaces that can be used when no explicit route exists for the destination address of the reviewed packet. This set command routes to the next hop only when there is no specified route for the packet destination address in the routing table. The set default interface command has the following syntax:

```
RouterA(config-route-map)# set default interface type number
➡ [...type number]
```

The type number parameter is the interface type (serial) and number (0/0, for example) where the packets are being sent.

The set ip tos Command

This route-map configuration command configures the 8-bit IP TOS (type of service) field in the IP header. Five bits are used to set the class of service (COS) value, which is accomplished through the set ip tos command. Here is the syntax:

```
RouterA(config-route-map)# set ip tos [number | name]
```

The *number* parameter can be a service value from 0 to 15. The *name* parameter is used instead to set the services of minimum delay [*min-delay* (8)], maximum throughput [*max-throughput* (4)], maximum reliability [*max-reliability* (2)], cost [*min-monetary-cost* (1)], and the [*normal* (0)] parameters.

The **set ip precedence** Command

This command is used to set the other three bits of the IP TOS value. These IP precedence bits are used to control QoS services such as weighted fair queuing and weighted random early detection. The syntax of this route-map configuration command is as follows:

```
RouterA(config-route-map)# set ip precedence [number | name]
```

The *number* parameter can be a precedence value from 0 to 7 (3 bits) that corresponds to *name* parameter values in Table 10.1. The *name* parameter can be used instead as shown in Table 10.1.

Table 10.1 set ip precedence Name Parameter Values	
Command Parameter	**Description**
critical	Set the critical precedence (5)
flash	Set the flash precedence (3)
Flash-override	Set the flash override precedence (4)
immediate	Set the immediate precedence (2)
Internet	Set the internetwork control precedence (6)
network	Set the network control precedence (7)
priority	Set the priority precedence (1)
routine	Set the routine precedence (0)

The **ip policy route-map** Command

Finally, when you want to designate a route map to be used for *policy-based routing* on a certain interface, you will use the interface configuration command ip policy route-map with the following syntax:

```
RouterA(config-if)# ip policy route-map map-tag
```

The map-tag parameter represents the identifier for the route map that is being used for routing policy. This value must match up to a map tag designated by the accompanying route-map command mentioned earlier.

The **ip route-cache policy** Command

The `ip route-cache policy` interface configuration command is implemented to allow fast switching for policy-based routing. Fast-switching policy-based routing was introduced in IOS Release 11.2F. *Switching* refers to a router's capability to receive packets in from an inbound interface and send (switch) them out via an exit interface. *Fast switching* accelerates the speed at which policy-based routing functions because it caches and reuses exit interface information for policy-routed packets instead of repeatedly performing lookups. The switching method that was previously used, which fully processed every packet before sending it out, is called *process switching*. Process switching is much slower and more CPU-intensive than fast switching. For fast switching to be implemented, policy-based routing that uses route maps must already be configured on the router. The fast-switching feature is disabled by default on Cisco routers. The `ip route-cache policy` command, with the following syntax, must be used on each entry interface that will participate in policy-based routing:

```
RouterA(config-if)# ip route-cache policy
```

Verifying Policy-Based Routing

After you have configured your route maps, you should test the configuration of policy routing on the router's interfaces by using the EXEC command `show route-map`. The syntax is a follows:

```
RouterA# show route-map [map-name]
```

The `map-name` parameter is an optional parameter that can be used if you want to see a certain route map. If the `show route-map` command is used without the `map-name` parameter, the command lists information regarding all route maps that are configured on the router. Here is a snippet of what the output could look like:

```
RouterA# show route-map
route-map policy, permit, sequence 10
  Match clauses:
    ip address (access-lists): 123
  Set clauses:
    ip next-hop 172.16.1.1
  Policy routing matches: 3 packets, 163 bytes
```

The `show ip policy` EXEC-mode command enables you to succinctly view all route maps that are configured on a router. It also displays the interfaces to which they are assigned. The `show ip policy` command has no optional parameters. You must use the EXEC-mode command `show route-map [map-name]`, explained earlier, if you want to view specific contents of a configured route map. The following snippet shows a sample output from the show ip policy command:

```
RouterA# show ip policy
Interface       Route map
Serial0         policy
```

The debug ip policy EXEC command is useful for showing policy routing packet activities on the router. It shows you whether the packet matches the criteria and the effect it is having on the packet. Again, any debugging commands should be used only in off-peak hours and very sparingly because of excessive router overhead. Here is the syntax for this command:

```
RouterA# debug ip policy
```

Redistribution of Routing Update Traffic

The term *redistribution* is technically defined as the exchange of routing update packets from one routing protocol domain to another routing domain. All the Cisco-supported routing protocols support route redistribution. Route redistribution may be necessary in any of several scenarios where an organization may be implementing multiple protocols. One may be that you are using products from several vendors, including Cisco devices. You are using a common open standard protocol such as RIP or OSPF for the non-Cisco devices and perhaps IGRP and EIGRP for the Cisco routers. Or perhaps you are migrating to a new routing protocol altogether, yet you need to retain the older protocol for awhile to accommodate certain areas of your network that are unable to migrate at the same time. You may have to implement several redistribution boundaries until the migration has been completed. Some areas may simply never migrate to a newer IGP for a variety of reasons. Some business units might require RIP for host-based routing and want to keep it for their LAN networking. Also, if a department's filtering policy does not fit into the long-term network infrastructure, you might need to isolate that department from the other routing protocols on your internetwork.

In the context of this chapter, an autonomous system represents internetworks running different routing protocols—IGPs or EGPs. Do not confuse this with the Autonomous System as an entity used with Border Gateway Protocol.

Selecting the Optimal Path

Because routing metrics and algorithms are inherently incompatible, the process of determining the best route when multiple routing protocols are in use is tantamount. There are actually two steps involved. First, if there is more than one source (static or dynamic) for any destination network, the router decides which of the two sources has the lowest administrative distance. Secondly, after the routing process is selected (usually a dynamic routing protocol), the route provided by that particular routing protocol with the best metric is selected.

Cisco utilizes two mechanisms for choosing the best path when one or more routing protocols are in play. The first is the *administrative distance* (AD) value. It is proper to re-emphasize why administrative distance is so important. The worst thing that can happen in a routing domain is a routing loop, which can cause data black holes and a nightmare for the network engineer. The easiest solution for preventing routing loops is to avert route feedback through route filtering. This is ineffective, however, because it can prevent less desirable, though useable, routes from being implemented in the event of a primary path failure. The next easy solution is to change the metric for all routes being redistributed. Although this is a good solution, it is subject to failure under various (remotely possible) circumstances.

The most elegant way to prevent routing loops for redistributed routes is to change the administrative distance of those redistributed routes to be worse (higher) than the administrative distance of the protocol that is offering the best path. For example, you can change the AD of routes (originally in IGRP) to 150, which is worse than the AD of RIP (120). Even though IGRP provides superior metric calculation, because these routes are being redistributed, the metric value is typically inaccurate and can lead to suboptimal path selection. By making one or more redistributed IGRP routes less desirable, you ensure that the more accurate (shorter) RIP routes get used. However, you also ensure that in the event of a primary path failure, the less desirable (but fully useable) backup path can be used. The administrative distance is an integer value between 1 and 255 that designates the trustworthiness of a certain route's source. The AD value is generated from the metric of a dynamic routing protocol or is manually overridden by the administrator. A router trusts, and then injects into the routing table, routes with lower AD values before routes with higher AD values. You can see the default AD values of routing protocols in Table 10.2.

Table 10.2 Default Administrative Distance Values of the Cisco-Supported Routing Protocols

Source of Route	Default Administrative Distance
Connected interface	0
Static route outbound on interface	0
Static route to next hop	1
EIGRP summary route	5
External BGP	20
Internal EIGRP	90
IGRP	100
OSPF	110
IS-IS	115
RIPv1, RIPv2	120
EGP	140
External EIGRP	170
Internal BGP	200
Unknown	255

The second mechanism for selecting the optimal path is the routing metric. This value measures the path—usually hop count or cost—between the source router and the destination network. Because routing protocols implement different metrics, you modify the metric when redistributing routes. For instance, when going from RIPv2 to OSPF, you need to translate the metric from an RIP hop count to an OSPF cost.

Implementing Successful Route Redistribution

Although we have covered a variety of routing protocols in great detail, you need to consider in depth the techniques for connecting multiple networks running different routing protocols. In today's dynamic environment, mergers, acquisitions, corporate politics, security, and multiple protocols often require that more than one routing protocol be used, at least for a short time. A common misconception is that if you simply connect two disparate networks together, the router automatically redistributes routes between them. Although redistribution occurs automatically between IGRP and EIGRP if the autonomous system numbers are identical, this is not the case for the other routing protocols covered in this book. Redistribution is a necessary task that the network engineer must accomplish when connecting systems that use multiple routing protocols.

NOTE

Redistributed routes must have a seed value (default or manually configured). For routers with directly connected networks, metric costs are determined by the routing protocol activated on the interface connected to the network. For redistributed networks (and subnets), there is no "direct connection"; therefore, a metric value must be assigned (seed value) to redistributed routes, to allow propagation to provide appropriate (not necessarily shorter) route selection. A router that is directly connected to the destination network typically derives the *seed metric*. Because a redistributed route is not physically connected to an ASBR, however, and different routing protocols have different metric values, you may need to configure the seed metric manually when distributing RIP or IGRP by using the **default-metric** router configuration command.

After the seed metric is configured for a redistributed route, the metric is incremented in a normal manner (unless it is the Type 2 external route in OSPF) as the route moves through the autonomous system. To prevent route feedback (loops), it is preferable to set the seed metric value higher for redistributed routes than the one used for a redundant route that originated in the core routing AS. It is rare for a preferred path to be through an external AS; therefore, the seed metric should be less desirable than the longest path in the receiving AS.

It is important to realize, however, that redistribution raises the level of complexity considerably for managing an internetwork and should be implemented only after much planning and forethought. The number of routing loops can increase when you integrate redistribution on boundary routers. The goal of this section of the chapter is to learn how to ensure optimized routing while eliminating routing loops. You also have to consider that different routing protocols have different convergence times and the impact that this will have on updates and the smooth flow of data packets. The impact is suboptimal path selection or a routing loop. Finally, redistributed routes introduce suboptimal path selection because the seed metric value (either correctly or incorrectly configured) can make a redistributed (and less desirable) route look more attractive to the router logic. This potential for network complexity should lead you to the conclusion that route redistribution should be used only when absolutely necessary.

Even though all the Cisco-supported routing protocols support route redistribution, generally speaking, you can redistribute only protocols that support the same protocol software. For example, you can redistribute between OSPF and IP RIP because both protocols support TCP/IP. Attempting to exchange routes between IPX RIP and OSPF is a different story because OSPF does not support the IPX/SPX protocol stack necessary to run IPX RIP.

The most important principle to follow is to be familiar with your network design, traffic, and business model. This includes being cognizant of impending changes in the infrastructure such as mergers or acquisitions.

Because IGRP and EIGRP have such a similar metric, redistribution will be automatic (if AS numbers are the same) when migrating to EIGRP. This fact led some organizations to prematurely rush into an EIGRP migration when, for business purposes, OSPF may have been the better long-term choice.

Another good piece of advice is to avoid running multiple routing protocols in the same internetwork. It is imperative that you draw distinct boundaries between *routing domains* (networks) that are implementing different routing protocols.

As mentioned earlier in this chapter, one-way redistribution is less complex to administer and troubleshoot. If you decide to implement a complex two-way redistribution design, as shown in Figure 10.2, you need to implement policy mechanisms such as default routes for a one-way redistribution, route filtering, metric tweaking, and the modification of administrative distance to prevent routing loops.

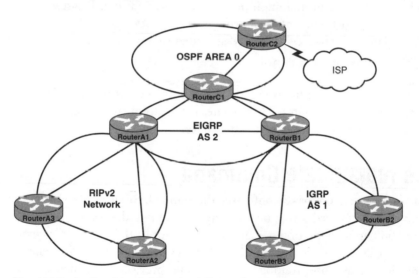

Figure 10.2   A rather elaborate internetwork that requires planning to prevent routing loops and convergence issues.

Some specific circumstances dictate when to avoid route redistribution. For example, in redistributed situations in which both the *core* (*backbone*) and the *edge* routing protocols (the protocols from which you are redistributing) advertise paths to the same destination network, you are likely to apply methods for avoiding certain routes from being exchanged and propagated between domains, such as filtering network packets as they enter a router's inbound interface. However, access lists alone are not meant to be used as route update filters. Both *distribute lists* and *route maps* use standard or extended access lists to control route update traffic. You can also influence route selection by modifying the administrative distance values or using passive interfaces, default routes, or static routes.

Configuring Route Redistribution

There are many variables to deal with when discussing the process of configuring route redistribution. The level of complexity and the command structures depend on the routing protocols being distributed. You should first find the router or routers that are on the edge of the different autonomous systems or routing domains. These are the routers that you will configure for route redistribution. Next, you must determine what the core (or backbone) protocol will be. This is typically EIGRP or OSPF in today's internetworking environments because they are classless routing protocols. Now, you should decide which routing protocol is at the edge. This could also be the short-term migration protocol or a static route. Begin with the core, such as OSPF, and enter into router configuration mode for the routing protocol that is to receive the redistributed routes; for example:

```
RouterA(config)# router ospf 100
```

The final action for configuring redistribution is to configure the boundary router to redistribute routes. These routes can be from any dynamic routing protocol supported by Cisco or a static route.

The redistribute Command

The `redistribute` command configures the redistribution, or translation, of routing protocols used within one routing domain into the routing protocols used within another routing domain. In other words, the `redistribute` command actually engineers the injection of routes learned by any one routing source into a dynamic routing protocol. The precise syntax depends on whether you are redistributing into OSPF or EIGRP, the two routing protocols into which you are concerned with redistributing for the BSCI exam. We first look at the process of redistributing routes into an OSPF system. This is the complete syntax for redistributing updates into OSPF:

```
RouterA(config-router)# redistribute protocol [process-id] [metric
➥metric-value] [metric-type type-value][route-map map-tag][subnets]
➥[tag tag-value]
```

Here is a sample of this command at work:

```
RouterA(config)# router ospf 100
RouterA(config-router)# redistribute igrp 1 metric 30 subnets
```

With these commands, all subnets contained within the IGRP routing process are injected into OSPF as external Type 2 routes with a metric (cost) of 30, rather than the default cost of 20. The parameter combination of `protocol [process-id]` signifies the protocol that is being redistributed and, if necessary, the process ID of the instance of that protocol (an EIGRP process in this case). The protocol value could be any of the following: `connected`, `bgp`, `eigrp`, `egp`, `igrp`, `isis`, `iso-igrp`, `mobile`, `odr` (on-demand routing), `static`, or `rip`. The optional parameter `metric` `metric-value` designates the metric or cost used for the redistributed route. The default metric value for routes that are redistributed into OSPF is 20. The metric value is applied as a seed value to all those routes being injected into the receiving routing protocol, in this example, OSPF. Routes with lower cost values are used before routes with higher cost values. The optional parameter `metric-type` `type-value` determines whether the redistributed route should be classified as an external Type 1 or external Type 2 OSPF route. The default type value is 2. This is critical. With Type 2 external routes, the cost metric does not aggregate and with Type 1 it does aggregate. The default is Type 2. Use Type 1 if there is more than one path to the external (edge) network because you want metric calculations to actually reflect actual path cost. The `route-map` `map-tag` parameter pair is the optional identifier of the route map that is queried for filtering policies. This subject is addressed in the "Resolving Path Selection Issues in Redistributed Networks" section later in this chapter.

The keyword `subnets` is another optional OSPF parameter that designates that subnetted network routes, in addition to non-subnetted network routes, should be redistributed. If the `subnets` keyword is not used, only the routes that are not subnetted are redistributed. This command is critical if you want any subnets of the other routing process to be qualified for redistribution. Without the `subnets` keyword, one may find that no routes are injected into the receiving routing process.

The `tag` `tag-value` parameter is an optional 32-bit decimal value assigned to every external route. This is not used by OSPF but rather between ASBRs. The following example configures redistribution of EIGRP routes from AS 500 into OSPF, using a default cost of 60 and assigning the E1 external type code.

```
RouterA(config-router)# redistribute eigrp 500 metric 60 metric-type 1
➥subnets
```

The `metric` `60` parameter specifies the metric of the core protocol, which in this case is OSPF. Therefore, the metric value `60` denotes the cost that is assigned to EIGRP redistributed routes. EIGRP uses a composite metric based on bandwidth and delay (and optionally reliability, load, and MTU). The optional `metric-type` `type-value` parameter specifies the OSPF external link type. OSPF external Type 2 routes, which are given the E2 origin code in the routing table, use only external cost as their metric. If no metric type is assigned, then the router considers the redistributed routes as E2 external routes by default. The optional subnets keyword specifies that OSPF will redistribute routes from subnets of the major network that is shared by the EIGRP routing domain and the OSPF routing domain. The subnets keyword should be used for classful routing protocols such as RIP and IGRP. EIGRP is special in that it is a converted classful routing protocol and still possesses many of the characteristics of IGRP. If you redistribute a classless protocol into another classless protocol, the subnets keyword is not an option.

The following redistribute command looks slightly different from the redistribute command shown previously because you are redistributing OSPF into EIGRP:

```
RouterA(config-router)# redistribute protocol [process-id] [match
➥{internal | external 1 | external 2}] [metric metric-value]
➥ [route-map map-tag]
```

The parameter protocol designates the protocol that is being redistributed. This value could be any of the following: connected, bgp, eigrp, egp, igrp, isis, iso-igrp, mobile, odr (on-demand routing), static, or rip. The [process ID] in this case is the EIGRP, BGP, EGP, or IGRP autonomous system number for the instance of that protocol. You use the match keyword to determine which types of OSPF routes will be distributed into other routing domains. This is vital because it enables you to block external routes (which have already been redistributed) from being redistributed into the receiving routing process. Again, the goal is to help prevent routing loops and optimize your scalable internetwork. The match keyword can have one of the following values:

➤ *internal*—Routes that are internal to the designated autonomous system

➤ *external 1*—Routes that are external to the autonomous system and injected into OSPF as Type 1 external

➤ *external 2*—Routes that are external to the autonomous system and injected into OSPF as Type 2 external

The metric metric-value parameter is an option used to designate the seed metric for the redistributed route. The route-map map-tag parameter pair is the optional identifier of the route map that is queried for filtering policies.

The default-metric Command

One of the ways that you can influence how routes are redistributed is by modifying the default metric of the route or routes being redistributed. There are a couple of ways to do this. You can specifically designate it with the default-metric command or you can use the metric parameter in the redistribute command shown previously. If you use the metric parameters in the redistribute command, you have more granularity if you set a different default metric for every protocol into which you are redistributing. When using the default-metric command, the specified default is applicable to all the protocols into which you redistribute. You must use the default-metric command separately rather than as part of the redistribute command.

The command syntax for redistributing default metrics into IGRP and EIGRP is as follows:

```
RouterA(config-router)# default-metric bandwidth delay reliability
↪loading mtu
```

Table 10.3 is a review of the metrics for IGRP and EIGRP, which also serve as parameters for the default-metric command for IGRP and EIGRP. It is important to note here that EIGRP multiplies what IGRP would calculate by a factor of 256, because EIGRP uses a 32-bit metric field, versus the 24-bit field for IGRP.

Table 10.3 The default-metric Command to Be Used with IGRP and EIGRP	
Command Parameter	**Description**
bandwidth	The minimum bandwidth value of the route in Kbps.
delay	The route delay value in tens of milliseconds.
reliability	A numerical value between 1 and 255, where 255 represents a route that is 100% reliable.
loading	A numerical value between 1 and 255, where 255 represents a route that is 100% loaded.
mtu	The maximum transmission unit (MTU) is the maximum packet size on the route in bytes.

In the following example, you want RouterA to redistribute RIPv2 and EIGRP routes. The network 192.168.100.1 is redistributed into the RIPv2 network with a metric of 3 hops and EIGRP routing in AS 2 is learning routes from RIPv2. Listing 10.2 shows how you would configure redistribution with the default-metric command.

Listing 10.2   Sample Configuration of Redistribution Using the default-metric Command

```
RouterA(config)# router rip
RouterA(config-router) network 172.16.0.0
RouterA(config-router) redistribute eigrp 2
RouterA(config-router) default-metric 3
!
RouterA(config)# router eigrp 2
RouterA(config-router) network 192.168.100.0
RouterA(config-router) redistribute rip
RouterA(config-router) default-metric 64 2500 255 1 1500
```

In Listing 10.2, the router configuration command `redistribute eigrp 2` allows redistribution of routes that are learned from EIGRP AS 2 into the RIPv2 network. The command `default-metric 3` designates that the EIGRP learned routes are to be injected as three hops away. The router configuration command `redistribute rip` allows for the redistribution of RIP-learned routes into the EIGRP AS 2. The command `default-metric 64 2500 255 1 1500` indicates that the bandwidth metric is 64Kbps, the delay metric is to be 2500 tens of microseconds, the reliability metric is 100%, the loading metric is less than 1%, and the MTU is 1500 bytes.

Use the following, and slightly different, command syntax for configuring the seed metric when redistributing into the OSPF, RIP, EGP, and BGP routing protocols:

```
RouterA(config-router)#default-metric number
```

Do not confuse this discussion with the **ip default-gateway** command. This command is used on servers or routers that have IP routing disabled. They are functioning as just another host on the internetwork.

Resolving Path Selection Issues in Redistributed Networks

Now that you have an understanding of the commands to redistribute into OSPF and EIGRP, you next need to configure the router to redistribute into the edge (or interim) protocol. This edge protocol is often, but not exclusively, an IGP such as RIPv2, IGRP, and EIGRP in Cisco implementations. The process entails going into global configuration mode for the edge routing process and taking one of several approaches. You can redistribute a default route for the core AS (backbone) into the edge AS, or redistribute several static routes to the backbone into the edge system. Whenever there is two-way redistribution, however, filtering is often a necessary component of redistribution strategy. You can also tweak the administrative distance value assigned to the routes received so that they are not selected when more than one route exists to a destination network.

The **passive-interface** Command

You may remember the `passive-interface` command from your CCNA studies. It is commonly used to keep routing updates from being sent out of an interface, while still allowing the designated interface to receive update messages. The `passive-interface` command is also often used in the redistribution process with the OSPF to stop the router from establishing an adjacency with another router connected on the same interface as the link identified in the `passive-interface` command. You should not activate OSPF on the interfaces that should not be participating in OSPF. With EIGRP, all a router has to see is a hello packet from a peer, and it begins sending out its routing table through update packets. There is no requirement for two-way communications in EIGRP as there is in OSPF.

Because the Hello protocol is used to confirm the two-way exchange between the routers, an adjacency relationship is not created. A router that is configured to refrain from sending updates does not take part in the two-way communication process of link-state protocols or EIGRP. After you determine which router protocol and interfaces from which you want to prevent the sending of updates, you use the following sample syntax in router configuration mode:

```
RouterA(config-router)# passive-interface Serial0.1
```

If your network is using a single major network IP address, a static route to 0.0.0.0 is probably your best option. A default route is a route that a Cisco router utilizes when no entry exists for a destination network in the routing table. The router to which the default route points is called the *gateway of last resort*.

The **ip default-network** Command

You can also configure a default route for protocols on a Cisco router by issuing the global configuration `ip default-network` command. The `ip default-network` command is used specifically to let other internal routers know how to get to networks outside the internetwork through another major network. The command doesn't offer any real functionality for the configured router.

When you use the `ip default-network` command, you specify a network that is in your current routing table as the default path to take. The syntax for the `ip default-network` command is

```
RouterA(config)# ip default-network network-number
```

The configuration of the RIP router could look something like this:

```
Router rip
  network 10.10.0.0
  network 172.16.0.0
!
ip classless
ip default-network 10.10.0.0
```

As a result, RIP sources a default route in the routing table which appears as `0.0.0.0 0.0.0.0` to its RIP neighbors. For example, assuming the IP address of the next-hop router was 10.20.1.2, the output snippet from the `show ip route` command would look like something like this:

```
<Output Omitted>
Gateway of last resort is 10.20.1.2 to network 0.0.0.0

<Output Omitted>
R*  0.0.0.0/0 [120/1] via 10.20.1.2, 00:00:17, Ethernet0
```

You can use **ip default-network** to distribute a default route to other internal RIP routers. However, if this were a router running IGRP, the default route (**0.0.0.0 0.0.0.0**) would not be redistributed by default. You need to add the **network 0.0.0.0** command to the configuration of the IGRP process on the router.

The number of redistribution scenarios is almost unlimited. However, a typical configuration might be EIGRP running as the backbone (core) routing protocol with RIPv2 as the edge (or transitional) protocol, as shown in Figure 10.3.

In the following scenario represented in Figure 10.4, you want the OSPF core network (the backbone) to be aware of all the routes in every AS, so you configure redistribution on RouterA1 and RouterB1 so that two summarized routes, 10.10.0.0/24 and 192.168.0.0/24, are redistributed into OSPF. Both these routes are summaries of the many smaller subnets contained in the RIP areas. You also want the RIPv2 routing domains to know about only their internal edge areas and a default route to get to the backbone. Therefore, you have the ASBR's RouterA1 and RouterB1 running both routing protocols and injecting the default route into the RIP domains.

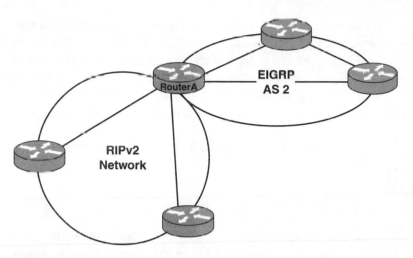

Figure 10.3 A typical redistribution scenario with an EIGRP backbone and RIPv2 at the edge.

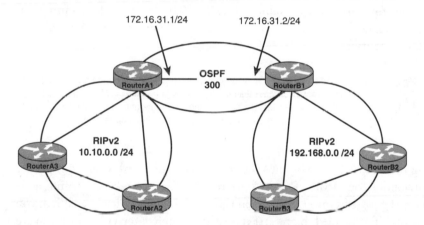

Figure 10.4 A more elaborate redistribution scenario with an OSPF backbone and RIPv2 at the edge.

The internal RIP routers in networks 10.10.0.0/24 and 192.168.0.0/24 (A2 and A3, B2 and B3) do not need any redistribution configured because they are only loaded with RIPv2. We do not need these routers to learn any specific external route because the default gateway will do.

It is important to mention that extreme care should be taken when redistributing from a classful protocol, such as RIPv1 or IGRP, to a classless protocol, such as OSPF. As you know, classful protocols are not capable of VLSM and are unable to advertise subnet mask information.

You must issue the classless global configuration command `ip classless` on all the RIP routers if they are not already so configured. By default, classful routing protocols, such as RIP and IGRP, throw out packets that are intended for unrecognized or non-connected subnets of a classful network to which they are directly attached. If the RIP router has no entry in its routing table for the non-connected subnet, then the destination network is considered nonexistent. As a result, the router ignores any default route in its routing table and drops the packet. Classful routing protocols take for granted that any subnets of a directly attached major network should appear in its routing table.

The **ip classless** command is enabled by default in Cisco IOS release 12.0 and higher.

In classless routing mode, a RIP router uses the default route when it is unable to reach subnets that do not appear in the routing table. In Figure 10.4, the ip classless command enables the Cisco IOS to forward data packets meant for unrecognized subnets (the 10.10.0.0 subnets, for example) of directly connected networks to the optimal supernetted route, possibly the default route itself.

One-way redistribution is the recommended method for preventing routing loops and convergence issues because it allows for routes to be exchanged in a single direction only. Realize, however, that if a primary and only route goes down, the backup (suboptimal) path will be unknown because of the one-way redistribution.

Along these same lines, you must use the subnets keyword when configuring redistribution on ASBR RouterA to redistribute all subnetted and non-subnetted networks into OSPF. Even though it is automatically enabled, you do not specifically need the ip classless setting on RouterA1 because you are running OSPF. You can see the configuration of ASBR RouterA1 from Figure 10.4 in Listing 10.3.

Listing 10.3   Configuration for ASBR RouterA1

```
<Output Omitted>
!
RouterA1(config)# router ospf 300
RouterA1(config-router)# redistribute rip metric 30 subnets
RouterA1(config-router)# network 172.16.31.1 0.0.0.0 area 0
!
RouterA1(config)# router rip
RouterA1(config-router)#  network 10.0.0.0
!
RouterA1(config)# no ip classless
RouterA1(config)# ip default-network 10.0.0.0
!
<Output Omitted>
```

In Listing 10.3, the statement redistribute rip metric 30 subnets specifies that route updates originating from the RIP routing domain should be assigned an OSPF cost value of 30. The subnets keyword tells the router to consider subnets (in the RIP domain) as qualified for redistribution. The ip default-network command is intended to relieve administrators of the necessity of manually configuring static default routes on every router in a routing domain. After you configure redistribution on ASBR RouterA1, you can issue the show ip route command on RouterA1 and see something similar to Listing 10.4.

Listing 10.4 Routing Table of ASBR RouterA1 After Configuring Redistribution

```
RouterA1# show ip route
<Output Omitted>

*      10.10.0.0/24 is subnetted, 6 subnets
C         10.10.3.0 is directly connected, Serial0
O E2      10.20.1.0 [110/30] via 172.16.31.2, 00:23:42, Ethernet0
C         10.10.2.0 is directly connected, Serial1
R         10.10.1.0 [120/1] via 10.10.3.1, 00:00:07, Serial0
                    [120/1] via 10.10.2.1, 00:00:15, Serial1
O E2      10.20.2.0 [110/30] via 172.16.31.2, 00:23:42, Ethernet0
O E2      10.20.3.0 [110/30] via 172.16.31.2, 00:23:42, Ethernet0
       172.16.0.0/24 is subnetted, 1 subnets
C         172.16.31.0 is directly connected, Ethernet0
```

We need to follow up on the previous discussion of the ip default-network command. The internal RIPv2 routers in network 10.10.0.0/24 have a default entry to external networks through the internal interface 10.10.2.2 on RouterA1, as follows:

```
R*   0.0.0.0/0 [120/1] via 10.10.2.2, 00:00:17, Serial0
```

Implementing Route Filters

You can leverage the Cisco IOS access list technology to filter inbound and outbound updates. The router goes through a five-step process to filter routes.

1. The router considers the interface that is preparing to send (outbound) a routing update or is in the process of receiving (inbound) a message.

2. The router resolves whether a filter is applied to the interface or not.

3. If not, the route entry is then processed as it normally would be.

4. If there is an applicable filter, the router scrutinizes the access list to see whether there is a match for the particular update packet. If a match exists, then the route entry is either permitted or denied based on the filtering rules.

5. If there is an applicable filter, but no match is found, then the implicit deny all at the end of the access list discards the packet into the bit bucket.

You can use both the access-list and distribute-list commands to filter inbound and outbound IP routes. One commonly used technique of route filtering involves identifying the network addresses that you want to filter, generating an access list to define the packet test for routing information, and then using the distribute-list command to implement the filtering policy. The complete syntax for the distribute-list out command is as follows:

```
RouterA(config-router)# distribute-list {access-list-number | name}
➥out [interface-name | routing-process [autonomous-system-number]
```

The access-list-number | name parameter designates the standard access list number or name. The out keyword binds the access-list to outbound routing update messages. The interface-name parameter is an optional parameter that represents the interface name on which updates are filtered. *OSPF outbound updates cannot be filtered on the way out of an interface.* The routing-process parameter can be either a routing process number for OSPF or an AS number for IGRP/EIGRP.

In Figure 10.5, the finance department in network 10.0.0.0 needs to be hidden (filtered) from the sales department at network 192.168.100.0.

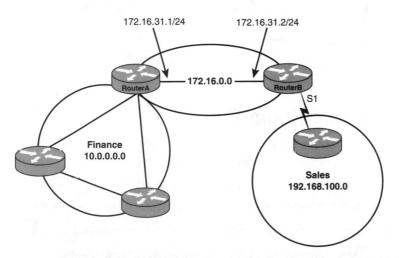

Figure 10.5 Using route redistribution filtering to hide the finance LAN from the sales LAN.

You can use the following snippet to filter out network 10.0.0.0 on RouterB:

```
RouterB(config)# router eigrp 10
RouterB(config-router)# network 172.16.0.0
```

```
RouterB(config-router)# network 192.168.100.0
RouterB(config-router)# distribute-list 1 out s1
!
RouterB(config)# access-list 1 permit 172.16.1.1 0.0.255.255
```

The router configuration command `distribute-list 1 out s1` applies access list number 1 to filter route redistribution of EIGRP updates sent outbound on Serial 1 to the sales LAN. The global configuration command `access-list 1 permit 172.16.0.0 0.0.255.255` gives the access-list number, enables routes that match the parameters of the list, and provides the network and wildcard mask that is used to see which (the first two octets in this case) source addresses are qualified. This is not the only method that could be used for filtering out the finance LAN, but it shows how you can use the `access-list` and `distribute-list` in combination effectively.

Use the **ip prefix-list** command to create a BGP prefix list. Prefix lists are the preferred alternative to distribute lists when filtering BGP route updates. Prefix lists are more flexible and easier to configure than distribute lists.

The **distance** Command

You can also use the `distance` command instead of the `default-metric` command to make sure that a router chooses an optimal path over a suboptimal path for redundant network routes. You can assure the selection of routes from the preferred protocol by assigning the other redundant route(s) a larger AD through the router configuration `distance` command. This also serves to reduce the incidence of loops between routing domains. The command syntax is a bit different for the EIGRP and BGP routing protocols. The syntax of the `distance` command for any supported routing protocol other than EIGRP or BGP is as follows:

```
RouterA(config-router)# distance weight
↪[address mask [access-list-number | name]] [ip]
```

The syntax for the EIGRP routing protocol, as follows, is somewhat different and is fully explained in Table 10.4:

```
RouterA(config-router)# distance eigrp internal-distance
↪external-distance
```

The `distance` command is also different for the BGP routing protocol, with more similarity to EIGRP, as shown here:

```
RouterA(config-router)# distance bgp internal-distance
↪external-distance local-distance
```

Tables 10.4 through Table 10.6 show the definitions of the various parameters for the `distance` command for the routing protocols mentioned previously. You may refer back to Table 10.1 as a reference as well.

Table 10.4 distance Command Syntax Parameters for the BGP Routing Protocol

Command Parameter	Description
external-distance	This parameter is the AD for BGP external routes (routes learned from an external peer of the AS). Values range from 1 to 255 with a default value of 20.
internal-distance	This parameter is the AD for BGP internal routes (routes learned from another peer within the AS). Values range from 1 to 255 with a default value of 200. Refer to Table 10.1.

Table 10.5 distance Command Syntax Parameters for the EIGRP Routing Protocol

Command Parameter	Description
internal-distance	This parameter is the AD for EIGRP routes discovered from another routing device within the same AS.
external-distance	This parameter is the AD for EIGRP routes where the optimal path is discovered from a peer that is external to the AS.

Table 10.6 distance Command Syntax Parameters for All Other Cisco-Supported Routing Protocols

Command Parameter	Description
weight	This parameter is the assigned AD number with a value ranging from 10 to 255.
address	This is an optional IP address used to filter networks based on the Layer 3 address of the router that generated the route.
mask	This optional parameter is the wildcard mask for the address parameter.
access-list-number I name	This optional parameter is the name or number of a standard access list attached to inbound packets to filter advertised networks.
ip	This keyword is an optional value to specify IP-derived routes for the IS-IS protocol.

A route with an administrative distance number of 255 should not be injected into a routing table of any routing protocol.

For instance, if you want to assign a default administrative distance of 160 to routes that match an access list number of 30, and that come from any other router, you can issue the following command in router configuration mode:

```
RouterA(config-router)# distance 160 0.0.0.0 255.255.255.255 30
```

The parameter of 160 represents the AD that designated routes are assigned. The 0.0.0.0 255.255.255.255 represents the source address (any router) of the device providing the routing update. Finally, the number 30 at the end of the command stands for access list number 30. This list filters incoming routing updates to decide which ones will have their AD numbers modified.

Verifying Route Redistribution

The most important aspect of verifying and confirming the proper redistribution of your routes is to know your network topology intimately. This is even more critical when you have redundant routes to destination networks. The command show ip protocols lists the routing protocols that are configured for use on your router and exhibits the routing processes that the router is redistributing. The show ip route command shows the IP routing table of the router, including all the known network routes and the precise routing protocols that generated them. The ping command verifies end-to-end connectivity between your network devices; however, ping does not offer information about the specific path that the ICMP echo packets are taking as they move through the internetwork. Therefore, you should use the traceroute command to verify that optimal paths are being used between the core (backbone) network and the edge network(s). The traceroute command can be found in the Cisco IOS documentation simply as "trace." The traceroute command sends ICMP echo packets to a destination hostname or IP address, whereas the screen outputs the name and round-trip time in milliseconds of each gateway encountered throughout the internetwork. The traceroute command can also assist you in diagnosing routing devices that are congested or even offline, as well as verify that the best routing paths are being utilized. You can also run the various debug commands for a short period to view the router activity and traffic on your ASBRs and internal routers. Because the debug process is so processor intensive, it is not a recommended practice except for extreme circumstances.

Exam Prep Questions

Question 1

> You are in a networking environment where a border router is configured with both OSPF and EIGRP dynamic routing protocols. Which path to a remote network is the preferred selection if EIGRP and OSPF have both discovered it?
>
> ○ A. IGRP
>
> ○ B. EIGRP
>
> ○ C. OSPF
>
> ○ D. Gateway of last resort

Answer B is correct. The AD is the first priority given by the Cisco IOS, and EIGRP has a lower AD (90) than OSPF (110). Answer A is incorrect because IGRP is not running on this router. Answer C is incorrect because OSPF has a higher AD value and is therefore less trustworthy than EIGRP. Answer D is incorrect because, although valid, the gateway of last resort would be a factor only if no route existed in the routing table to the remote network.

Question 2

> Which of the following are valid ways to manipulate routing updates and filtering in a Cisco internetwork? (Choose all that apply.)
>
> ❏ A. Route maps
>
> ❏ B. Default gateways
>
> ❏ C. Access lists
>
> ❏ D. Passive interfaces

Answers A, C, and D are correct. Policy-based routing was introduced to Cisco administrators in IOS release 11.0 and affords network load-sharing capacities and traffic shaping by letting you have granular control of the movement of network traffic through a router with route maps. Also, access list technology is used with a variety of mechanisms to filter interfaces. The `passive-interface` command is also often used in the redistribution process with a link-state protocol or EIGRP to stop the router from establishing a peer (adjacency) with another router connected on the same interface as the link identified in the `passive-interface` command. Answer B is incorrect because the `default-gateway` command is used on servers or routers that have IP routing disabled. In other words, they are functioning as just another host on the internetwork.

Question 3

Which one of the following commands prevents updates from being sent, yet allows updates to still be received and processed?

- ○ A. **ip classless**
- ○ B. **default-network**
- ○ C. **passive-interface**
- ○ D. **default-gateway**

Answer C is correct. The `passive-interface` command is commonly used to keep routing updates from being sent out of an interface while still allowing the designated interface to receive update messages. Answer A is incorrect because `ip classless` mode enables a classful protocol router, such as RIP, to use the default route when it is unable to reach subnets that do not appear in the routing table. Answer B is incorrect because the `default-network` command is intended to relieve administrators of the necessity of manually configuring static default routes on every router in a routing domain, not to prevent updates from being sent. Answer D is incorrect because the `default-gateway` command is used on routers that have IP routing disabled.

Question 4

Which one of the following scenarios is *not* a reason to deploy and operate multiple routing protocols in your internetworking environment?

- ○ A. You need to migrate from IGRP to EIGRP over a period of months.
- ○ B. You are about to acquire two small companies that have a number of non-Cisco routing devices and your network is currently running only EIGRP.
- ○ C. Because of politics between the sales, finance, and developers departments, a company-wide router upgrade and redesign is impossible. The sales group must migrate to EIGRP because of a vendor relationship with the call center. The finance and developers need to be isolated as well.
- ○ D. You are going to perform a weekend migration of all your routing devices from EIGRP to OSPF because there is a more cost-effective vendor solution.

Answer D is correct. This quick 72-hour migration to OSPF does not necessitate deploying and operating a multi-protocol solution. Answers A, B, and C are all excellent representations of scenarios in which a multiple protocol environment would be applicable.

Question 5

You have configured a DDR ISDN WAN link between your main headquarters and a branch office, which both run EIGRP. You would like to keep extra routing update traffic from traversing this connection while still having your ASBRs aware of the remote networks. Which of the following solutions would be the best choice?

- ○ A. Configure the **ip classless** command.
- ○ B. Configure the **passive-interfaces** command.
- ○ C. Configure the **ip default-network** command on the ASBR.
- ○ D. Configure the router with the **ip prefix-list** command.

Answer B is correct. The `passive-interface` command can be implemented to designate certain routes to use when more than one AS needs to exchange updates rather than pass along the whole routing table of information. Answer A is incorrect because `ip classless` routing mode would simply allow a router to use the default route when it cannot reach subnets that do not appear in the routing table. Answer C is incorrect because you would generally use `ip default-network` to distribute a default route to other internal RIP routers. Even with this router running EIGRP, and if this command met the criteria of the question, the default route would not be redistributed by default. Answer D is incorrect because the `ip prefix-list` command is primarily used to create a BGP prefix list.

Question 6

Which of the following is the correct route map configuration that can be used to establish guidelines based on designated minimum and maximum values?

- ○ A. **match length min max**
- ○ B. **match ip address**
- ○ C. **match ip min max**
- ○ D. **match as-path**

Answer A is correct. You can use the route-map configuration command `match length` to create filtering rules based on the length of the packet. Answer B is incorrect because you first create your standard or extended access lists to be implemented to establish the matching policy via the `match ip address` command. Answer C is incorrect because that syntax is `match length`, not `match ip`. Answer D is incorrect because, although a valid command, it filters based on the AS-path attribute and not the packet length.

Question 7

You want to assign a default administrative distance of 165 to routes that match an access list number of 10, and that are generated from any address on any network. Which of the following would be the correct command to issue?

- ○ A. RouterA(config-router)# distance 10 0.0.0.0 255.255.255.255 165
- ○ B. RouterA(config-if)# distance 165 0.0.0.0 255.255.255.255
- ○ C. RouterA(config-router)# distance 165 0.0.0.0 255.255.255.255 10
- ○ D. RouterA(config-route-map)# distance 165 0.0.0.0 255.255.255.255 10

Answer C is correct. The parameter of 165 signifies the AD that designated routes will be assigned. The 0.0.0.0 255.255.255.255 represents the source address (any router) of the device providing the routing update. The number 10 at the end of the command stands for access list 10, which filters incoming routing updates to decide which ones should have their AD numbers modified. Answer A is incorrect because the AD weight value and the access list number are reversed in the syntax. Answer B is incorrect because configuration mode is wrong and the access list number is missing at the end. Answer D is incorrect because although the syntax is correct, the router is in the wrong configuration mode.

Question 8

Which of the following statements are true concerning policy-based routing? (Choose 2.)

- ❑ A. By putting policy-based routing into practice, you can achieve cost savings and load-sharing capabilities.
- ❑ B. Companies can set the TOS values in IP headers at the network boundaries to provide TQM.
- ❑ C. Policy-based routing is always applied to outbound packets only.
- ❑ D. Policy-based routing was introduced in Cisco IOS release 11.0.

Answers A and D are correct. Policy-based routing, introduced in Cisco IOS release 11.0, provides the benefits of enabling ISPs to route traffic more efficiently, provide Quality of Service (QoS), generate cost-saving measures, and implement load-sharing techniques. Answer B is incorrect because you can set the TOS values in IP headers at the network boundaries to provide QoS, not TQM. Answer C is incorrect because policy-based routing is always applied to inbound packets only, not outbound ones.

Question 9

Which of the following command sets enable you to filter outbound routing update traffic effectively?

- ○ A. **RouterA(config)# distribute-list {access-list-number I name} in interface-name**
- ○ B. **RouterA(config-router)# distribute-list {access-list-number I name} in interface-name**
- ○ C. **RouterA(config)# distribute-list {access-list-number I name} out interface-name**
- ○ D. **RouterA(config-router)# distribute-list {access-list-number I name} out interface-name**

Answer D is correct. This is the proper syntax and configuration mode of the `distribute-list` command when used in conjunction with an access-list number. Answer A is incorrect because the configuration mode is wrong. In addition, the `in` keyword is used rather than the `out` keyword. Answer B is incorrect because the `in` keyword is used rather than the `out` keyword. Answer C is incorrect because although the syntax is correct, the configuration mode is wrong.

Question 10

Which of the following EXEC-mode commands would you run if you wanted to display the specific contents of a configured route map?

- ○ A. **show route-map map-name**
- ○ B. **show ip policy**
- ○ C. **debug ip policy**
- ○ D. **show route map**

Answer A is correct. You must use the EXEC-mode command `show route-map [map-name]` if you want to view specific contents of a configured route map. Answer B is incorrect because the EXEC-mode command `show ip policy` is used to succinctly view *all* route maps configured on a router. Answer C is incorrect because `debug ip policy` is to be used rarely and is useful simply for showing policy routing packet activities on the router. Answer D is incorrect because `show route map` is used without the `map-name` parameter. The command displays information regarding all route maps that are configured on the router.

Need to Know More?

Parkhurst, William R. *Cisco OSPF Command and Configuration Handbook*. Indianapolis, IN: Cisco Press, 2002. ISBN 1587050714.

Thomas, Tom. *OSPF Network Design Solutions, Second Edition*. Indianapolis, IN: Cisco Press, 2003. ISBN 1587050323.

Halabi, Sam, et al. *Internet Routing Architectures, Second Edition*. Indianapolis, IN: Cisco Press, 2000. ISBN 157870233X.

Huitema, Christian. *Routing in the Internet, Second Edition*. Indianapolis, IN: Prentice Hall PTR, 2000. ISBN 0130226475.

Complete list of Requests for Comments: http://www.cis.ohio-state.edu/htbin/rfc/rfc-index.html.

Practice Exam 1

In this chapter, I provide pointers to help you develop a successful test-taking strategy, including how to choose proper answers, how to decode ambiguity, how to work within the Cisco testing framework, how to decide what you need to memorize, and how to prepare for the test. At the end of the chapter, I include 60 questions on subject matter pertinent to Cisco Exam 640-901, "Building Scalable Cisco Internetworks." In Chapter 12, you'll find the answer key to this test. Good luck!

Questions, Questions, Questions

There should be no doubt in your mind that you are facing a test full of specific and pointed questions. If the version of the exam that you take is fixed-length, it will include 50 questions, and you will be allotted 90 minutes to complete the exam. If it's an adaptive test (the software should tell you this as you begin the exam), it will consist of somewhere between 25 and 35 questions (on average) and take somewhere between 30 and 60 minutes.

Whichever type of test you take, exam questions belong to one of five basic types:

➤ Multiple choice with a single answer

➤ Multiple choice with multiple answers

➤ Multipart with a single answer

➤ Multipart with multiple answers

➤ Simulations whereby you click on a GUI screen capture to simulate using the Cisco IOS interface

You should always take the time to read a question at least twice before selecting an answer, and you should always look for an Exhibit button as you examine each question. Exhibits include graphics information related to a question. An *exhibit* is usually a screen capture of program output or GUI information that you must examine to analyze the question's contents and formulate an answer. The Exhibit button displays graphics and charts used to help explain a question, provide additional data, or illustrate page layout or program behavior.

Not every question has only one answer; many questions require multiple answers. Therefore, you should read each question carefully, determine how many answers are necessary or possible, and look for additional hints or instructions when selecting answers. Such instructions often appear in brackets immediately following the question itself (for multiple-answer questions).

Picking Proper Answers

Obviously, the only way to pass any exam is to select enough of the right answers to obtain a passing score. However, Cisco's exams are not standardized like the SAT and GRE exams; they are far more diabolical and convoluted. In some cases, questions are strangely worded, and deciphering them can be a real challenge. In those cases, you may need to rely on answer-elimination skills. Almost always, at least one answer out of the possible choices for a question can be eliminated immediately because it matches one of these conditions:

➤ The answer does not apply to the situation.

➤ The answer describes a nonexistent issue, an invalid option, or an imaginary state.

➤ The answer may be eliminated because of information in the question itself.

After you eliminate all answers that are obviously wrong, you can apply your retained knowledge to eliminate further answers. Look for items that sound correct but refer to actions, commands, or features that are not present or not available in the situation that the question describes.

If you're still faced with a blind guess among two or more potentially correct answers, reread the question. Try to picture how each of the possible remaining answers would alter the situation. *Be especially sensitive to terminology*; sometimes the choice of words ("remove" instead of "disable") can make the difference between a right answer and a wrong one.

Only when you've exhausted your ability to eliminate answers but remain unclear about which of the remaining possibilities is correct should you guess at an answer. An unanswered question offers you no points, but guessing gives you at least some chance of getting a question right; just don't be too hasty when making a blind guess.

 If you're taking a fixed-length test, you can wait until the last round of reviewing marked questions (just as you're about to run out of time or out of unanswered questions) before you start making guesses. If you're taking an adaptive test, you have to guess to move on to the next question (if you can't figure out an answer some other way). Either way, guessing should be a last resort.

Decoding Ambiguity

Cisco exams have a reputation for including questions that can be difficult to interpret, confusing, or ambiguous. In my experience with numerous exams, I consider this reputation to be completely justified. The Cisco exams are tough, and they're deliberately made that way.

The only way to beat Cisco at its own game is to be prepared. You'll discover that many exam questions test your knowledge of things that are not directly related to the issue raised by a question. This means that the answers you must choose from, even incorrect ones, are just as much a part of the skill assessment as the question itself. If you don't know something about most aspects of Cisco IOS, you may not be able to eliminate answers that are wrong because they relate to an area of the IOS other than the one that's addressed by the question at hand. In other words, the more you know about the software, the easier it will be for you to tell right from wrong.

Questions often give away their answers, but you have to be Sherlock Holmes to see the clues. Often, subtle hints appear in the question text in such a way that they seem almost irrelevant to the situation. You must realize that each question is a test unto itself and that you need to inspect and successfully navigate each question to pass the exam. Look for small clues, such as the mention of times, group permissions and names, and configuration settings. Little things such as these can point to the right answer if they're properly understood; if missed, they can leave you facing a blind guess.

Another common difficulty with certification exams is vocabulary. Cisco has an uncanny knack for naming some utilities and features entirely obviously in some cases and completely inanely in other instances. Be sure to brush up on the key terms presented at the beginning of each chapter of this book. You may also want to read the glossary at the end of this book the day before you take the test.

Working Within the Framework

The test questions appear in random order, and many elements or issues that are mentioned in one question may also crop up in other questions. It's not uncommon to find that an incorrect answer to one question is the correct answer to another question, or vice versa. Take the time to read every answer to each question, even if you recognize the correct answer to a question immediately. That extra reading may spark a memory or remind you about a Cisco router feature or function that helps you on another question elsewhere in the exam.

If you're taking a fixed-length test, you can revisit any question as many times as you like. If you're uncertain of the answer to a question, check the box that's provided to mark it for easy return later. You should also mark questions that you think may offer information you can use to answer other questions. On fixed-length tests, I usually mark somewhere between 25–50% of the questions. The testing software is designed to let you mark every question if you choose; use this framework to your advantage. Everything you'll want to see again should be marked; the testing software can then help you return to marked questions quickly and easily.

For fixed-length tests, I strongly recommend that you first read the entire test quickly, before getting caught up in answering individual questions. Doing this will help to jog your memory as you review the potential answers and can help you identify questions that you want to mark for easy access to their contents. You can also identify and mark the tricky questions for easy return. The key is to make a quick pass over the territory to begin with so that you know what you're up against, and then survey that territory more thoroughly on a second pass, when you can begin to answer all questions systematically and consistently.

If you're taking an adaptive test and you see something in a question or in one of the answers that jogs your memory on a topic, or that you feel you should record if the topic appears in another question, write it down on your piece of paper. Just because you can't go back to a question in an adaptive test doesn't mean you can't take notes on what you see early in the test, in hopes that it might help you later in the test.

For adaptive tests, don't be afraid to take notes on what you see in various questions. Sometimes, what you record from one question can help you on other questions later, especially if it's not as familiar as it should be or it reminds you of the name or use of some utility or interface details.

Deciding What to Memorize

The amount of memorization you must undertake for an exam depends on how well you remember what you've read and how well you know the software by heart. If you're a visual thinker and can see the commands in your head, you won't need to memorize as much as someone who's less visually oriented. However, the exam will stretch your abilities to memorize product features and functions, interface details, and proper application design, development, and maintenance approaches, as well as how they all relate to the Cisco IOS.

If you work your way through this book while sitting at a console and a router and try to perform the functions as they're discussed throughout, you should have little or no difficulty mastering this material. Also, don't forget that the Cram Sheet at the front of the book is designed to capture the material that's most important to memorize; use this to guide your studies as well.

Preparing for the Test

The best way to prepare for the test—after you've studied—is to take at least one practice exam. I've included one here in this chapter for that reason; the test questions are located in the pages that follow. (Unlike the questions in the preceding chapters in this book, the answers don't follow the questions immediately; you'll have to flip to Chapter 12 to review the answers separately.)

Give yourself 105 minutes to take the exam, and keep yourself on the honor system—don't look at earlier text in the book or jump ahead to the answer key. When your time is up or you've finished the questions, you can check your work in Chapter 12. Pay special attention to the explanations for the incorrect answers; these can also help to reinforce your knowledge of the material. Knowing how to recognize correct answers is good, but understanding why incorrect answers are wrong can be equally valuable.

Taking the Test

Relax. As soon as you're sitting in front of the testing computer, there's nothing more you can do to increase your knowledge or preparation. Take a deep breath, stretch, and start reading that first question.

You don't need to rush, either. You have plenty of time to complete each question, and if you're taking a fixed-length test, you'll have time to return to the questions that you skipped or marked for return. On a fixed-length test, if you read a question twice and you remain clueless, you can mark it; if you're taking an adaptive test, you'll have to guess and move on. Both easy and difficult questions are intermixed throughout the test in random order. If you're taking a fixed-length test, don't cheat yourself by spending too much time on a hard question early in the test, thereby depriving yourself of the time you need to answer the questions at the end of the test. If you're taking an adaptive test, don't spend more than five minutes on any single question—if it takes you that long to get nowhere, it's time to guess and move on.

On a fixed-length test, you can read through the entire test, and, before returning to marked questions for a second visit, you can figure out how much time you've got per question. As you answer each question, remove its mark. Continue to review the remaining marked questions until you run out of time or complete the test.

On an adaptive test, set a maximum time limit for questions, and watch your time on long or complex questions. If you hit your limit, it's time to guess and move on. Don't deprive yourself of the opportunity to see more questions by taking too long to puzzle over individual questions, unless you think you can figure out the answer. Otherwise, you're limiting your opportunities to pass.

Question 1

You are studying scalable network design practices in preparation for implementing a medium-scale Enterprise routed network. Regarding hierarchical network designs, which layer typically features the highest possible bandwidth links and often includes redundancy mechanisms?

- ○ A. Distribution
- ○ B. Core
- ○ C. Access
- ○ D. Workgroup

Question 2

You are using the following command in the configuration of your router at the central office:

```
ip route 10.20.16.0 255.255.255.0 10.10.1.1 200
```

What is the purpose of the 200 parameter in the command?

- ○ A. This parameter forces the metric value to 200.
- ○ B. This parameter forces the administrative distance to 200.
- ○ C. This parameter specifies the amount of time the route stays in the routing table.
- ○ D. This parameter specifies the number of TCP sessions that are able to use the route.

Question 3

Which of the following is not a valid reason for using static routes in your enterprise network?

- ○ A. Several of your routers do not possess powerful CPUs or memory resources.
- ○ B. You desire total control over routes in your environment.
- ○ C. You want a route to appear to be directly connected.
- ○ D. You desire a small degree of administrative overhead.

Question 4

Which of the following statements are true regarding the **network** command?

- ❏ A. Use classful **network** statements with RIP and IGRP.
- ❏ B. For all routing protocols except BGP, the **network** statement indicates an advertisement concerning that route.
- ❏ C. Integrated IS-IS does not use a **network** statement.
- ❏ D. IGRP and OSPF permit the use of a wildcard mask in the **network** statement.

Question 5

Which of the following statements regarding On-Demand Routing are true? (Choose all that apply.)

- ❏ A. ODR is a classful routing technology.
- ❏ B. ODR is used in hub and spoke topologies.
- ❏ C. Spoke routers send a default route to the hub while the hub sends information regarding networks in the core to the spoke routers.
- ❏ D. Spoke routers send information about networks to the hub while the hub sends default route information to the spoke routers.

Question 6

You are interested in configuring ODR in your network topology. Which of the following are valid ODR configuration steps? (Choose all that apply.)

- ❏ A. All routers that are to participate in ODR must have the **router odr** global configuration command.
- ❏ B. The hub router needs the **router odr** global configuration command.
- ❏ C. The spoke routers need default routes configured that point to the hub router.
- ❏ D. CDP must be enabled on the links between the spoke routers and the hub.
- ❏ E. The hub router must also be running a classless dynamic protocol.

Question 7

Which of the following statements regarding classful routing protocols are true? (Choose all that apply.)

☐ A. Classful routing protocols do not carry subnet mask information in routing updates.

☐ B. RIP V1 and IGRP are examples.

☐ C. Network boundary summarization is not performed automatically.

☐ D. If a routing update is received and a different major network is indicated than the network address in use on the interface, the router applies the subnet mask configured on the receiving interface.

Question 8

Your RIP version 1 router contains the following entries in the ip routing table.

```
R     10.1.1.0/24    [120/1]    via    10.1.1.2,    00:00:16,
➥Ethernet0
C     10.1.2.0/24    is directly connected,    Ethernet0
R     10.1.3.0/24    [120/2]    via    10.1.2.2,    00:00:05,
➥Ethernet0
R*    0.0.0.0/0      [120/3]    via    10.1.2.2,    00:00:16,
➥Ethernet0
```

Your router has received traffic destined for the IP address 10.2.2.2. You are not using the **ip classless** command. Where will the traffic be routed?

○ A. The traffic uses the first entry in the routing table to route via 10.1.1.2.

○ B. The traffic uses the third entry in the routing table to route via 10.1.2.2.

○ C. The traffic uses the default route entry to route via 10.1.2.2.

○ D. The traffic will be discarded.

Question 9

You are using RIP version 2 in your enterprise network. You are interested in controlling the summarization process between two of your routers in the network. What two commands are required to configure manual summarization with RIP version 2? (Choose 2.)

☐ A. **ip rip send-version-2**

☐ B. **no auto-summary**

☐ C. **network** command with a summarized prefix

☐ D. **ip summary-address rip**

Question 10

What is the administrative distance assigned to external BGP by default?

○ A. 20

○ B. 90

○ C. 5

○ D. 100

○ E. 110

Question 11

Which of the following routing protocols feature automatic route summarization by default? (Choose all that apply.)

❑ A. RIPv2

❑ B. EIGRP

❑ C. IS-IS

❑ D. OSPF

❑ E. BGP

Question 12

Which of the following IS-IS routers is equivalent to an ABR in OSPF?

○ A. Level 1

○ B. Level 2

○ C. Level 1/2

○ D. Level 3

Question 13

Which of the following statements regarding IS-IS metrics are true? (Choose all that apply.)

❑ A. The Cisco IOS supports the default metric component by default.

❑ B. The Cisco router assigns a default metric of 1 to an interface.

❑ C. If not adjusted, the Cisco metric approach is similar to RIP.

❑ D. Narrow metrics are limited to a 24-bit interface and 32-bit path metrics.

Question 14

You are considering using IS-IS as your IGP. You are confused by the different levels of routing that IS-IS defines, however. What level of IS-IS routing is also known as area routing?

- ○ A. L0
- ○ B. L1
- ○ C. L2
- ○ D. L3

Question 15

You have been asked to provide a comparison between IS-IS and OSPF. Which of the following statements are true regarding IS-IS in comparison to OSPF? (Choose all that apply.)

- ❑ A. IS-IS is more extensible.
- ❑ B. Documentation and experienced engineers are easier to find for IS-IS.
- ❑ C. IS-IS metrics scale automatically.
- ❑ D. IS-IS is more customized to IP, providing advanced features such as area types.
- ❑ E. IS-IS detects network changes more quickly.

Question 16

Which portion of the IS-IS NSAP address structure identifies a process on the device, and corresponds roughly to a port or socket in IP?

- ○ A. Area address
- ○ B. NSEL
- ○ D. System ID
- ○ D. HODSP

Question 17

Which of the following statements is true regarding system IDs?

- ○ A. System IDs must be unique.
- ○ B. System IDs are 6 bytes.
- ○ C. System IDs are 8 bytes.
- ○ D. System IDs are not used in IS-IS.

Question 18

You are troubleshooting an IS-IS network. Under this IGP, what does the SNPA employ for an HDLC interface?

- ○ A. MAC address
- ○ B. Virtual Circuit ID
- ○ C. DLCI
- ○ D. HDLC

Question 19

Which of the following IS-IS PDU types is used to acknowledge and request missing pieces of link-state information?

- ○ A. IIH
- ○ B. LSP
- ○ C. PSNP
- ○ D. CSNP

Question 20

You are troubleshooting your IS-IS network and you would like to view the IS-IS L2 routing table. Which command should you use?

- ○ A. **show clns route**
- ○ B. **show ip route**
- ○ C. **show isis database**
- ○ D. **show isis route**

Question 21

You are configuring Integrated IS-IS in your Cisco internetwork. How do the Cisco routers identify which interfaces are participating in the IS-IS routing process?

○ A.   The **network** router configuration command

○ B.   The **ip router isis** interface configuration command

○ C.   The NET configured on the router

○ D.   The **isis** interface map statements

Question 22

You are studying IP version 6 in preparation for deploying it in your Cisco network. You are interested in the autoconfiguration capabilities built into the protocol. Using this technology, a client station automatically learns its network address. Which part of the address is sent from the router to the host?

○ A.   Network prefix

○ B.   Entire network address

○ C.   MAC address

○ D.   Host address

Question 23

The new IPv6 header contains 40 octets in contrast to the 20 octets in IPv4. This header contains several new or modified fields. Which field is used for special multilayer switching techniques and faster packet-switching performance mechanisms?

○ A.   Version

○ B.   Traffic Class

○ C.   Flow Label

○ D.   Next Header

Question 24

Which command might you use when troubleshooting NAT?

○ A. **show nat events**

○ B. **debug nat events**

○ C. **show ip nat translations**

○ D. **show ip nat events**

Question 25

Which of the following elements of NAT terminology describes the IP address of an inside host as it appears to the outside network?

○ A. Inside local IP address

○ B. Inside global IP address

○ C. Outside global IP address

○ D. Outside local IPaddress

Question 26

Which of the following is the best summary route for the 172.24.4.0/24 through 172.24.14.0/24 range of subnets?

○ A. 172.24.4.0/20

○ B. 172.24.4.0/22

○ C. 172.24.4.0/23

○ D. 172.24.8.0/22

○ E. 172.24.14.0/23

Question 27

If you are using a prefix of /20, how many additional subnetworks are gained when you take one of your subnets and use a prefix of /24?

○ A. 2

○ B. 4

○ C. 8

○ D. 16

○ E. 32

Question 28

You are going to employ VLSM. You have a network address of 192.168.2.0. Which mask would be best to use with a point-to-point serial WAN connection?

○ A. 255.255.255.224

○ B. 255.255.255.240

○ C. 255.255.255.248

○ D. 255.255.255.252

Question 29

Which of the following protocols does not support VLSM?

○ A. EIGRP

○ B. RIP V2

○ C. IGRP

○ D. OSPF

○ E. IS-IS

Question 30

Which of the following statements about variable length subnet masking is true? (Choose all that apply.)

- ❏ A. It is supported in classless routing protocols.
- ❏ B. It enables you to create multiple logical interfaces on a single physical router interface.
- ❏ C. It enables you to allocate IP addressing in an efficient manner, and allows for more summarization.
- ❏ D. It is supported in all standard routing protocols.

Question 31

In the EIGRP dynamic routing protocol, the best next hop router to reach a given destination is referred to as what?

- ○ A. Feasible successor
- ○ B. Successor
- ○ C. Primary
- ○ D. Designated

Question 32

In EIGRP, what term refers to the cost between your source router and the destination network?

- ○ A. Advertised distance
- ○ B. Feasible distance
- ○ C. Successor distance
- ○ D. Feasible successor

Question 33

What is the correct criteria for a route to become a feasible successor?

- A. The feasible distance of the route must be equal to the feasible distance of the successor.
- B. The advertised distance of the next hop router must be less than the feasible distance of the successor.
- C. The advertised distance of the next hop router must be greater than the feasible distance of the successor.
- D. The advertised distance of the next hop router must be equal to the feasible distance of the successor.

Question 34

Which of the following statements are true regarding the EIGRP metric calculation? (Choose all that apply.)

- A. The default K values are as follows: K1 = 1; K2 = 0; K3 = 0; K4 = 0; K5 = 1.
- B. The default key values indicate that the metric is composed of bandwidth and delay.
- C. EIGRP does not form a neighbor relationship if K values do not match.
- D. When using redistribution to integrate IGRP routes into an EIGRP domain, the router multiplies the IGRP metric by 256 to compute the EIGRP-equivalent metric.

Question 35

Which packet types used by EIGRP must be explicitly acknowledged? (Choose all that apply.)

- A. ACK
- B. hello
- C. reply
- D. query
- E. update

Question 36

EIGRP features a unique treatment of WAN bandwidth by default. What percentage of WAN bandwidth does EIGRP use by default?

- ○ A. 25
- ○ B. 50
- ○ C. 75
- ○ D. 100

Question 37

Which of the following is not an advantage that OSPF possesses over RIP?

- ○ A. OSPF features faster convergence in most circumstances.
- ○ B. OSPF does not impose a hop count limit.
- ○ C. OSPF features decreased CPU utilization when compared to RIP.
- ○ D. OSPF uses cost as a metric to make routing decisions.

Question 38

All OSPF routers in the same area possess identical _____ databases.

- ○ A. Link state
- ○ B. Routing
- ○ C. Neighborship
- ○ D. Area

Question 39

In which of the following states are routers considered synchronized?

- ○ A. Loading State
- ○ B. Exstart state
- ○ C. Init State
- ○ D. Two-way state
- ○ E. Full State

Question 40

You have three routers on a network segment. One is set to a priority of 2, another is set to 0, and the third is left in the default configuration. Which router becomes the DR?

○ A. The router with a priority of 0

○ B. The router with a priority of 1

○ C. The router with a priority of 2

○ D. The router with a loopback interface

Question 41

Your router is configured with a serial interface (172.16.8.1), an Ethernet interface (172.16.16.1), and two loopback addresses (10.1.1.1 and 10.2.2.2). What is the Router ID for this router?

○ A. 172.16.8.1

○ B. 172.16.16.1

○ C. 10.1.1.1

○ D. 10.2.2.2

Question 42

Which of the following is an RFC mode of operation for OSPF in a NBMA topology?

○ A. Broadcast

○ B. Point-to-point

○ C. Point-to-multipoint

○ D. Point-to-multipoint nonbroadcast

Question 43

Which of the following is not a field found in an OSPF Hello packet?

○ A. Router ID

○ B. Stub area flag

○ C. Router priority

○ D. DR address

○ E. BDR address

○ F. Link-state update

Question 44

You are the administrator for a very large Cisco network running the OSPF routing protocol. You want to ensure that a specific router never participates in DR or BDR elections. What is the best course of action?

○ A. Set the priority values of the router to a very high value.

○ B. Set the priority values of the router to 0.

○ C. Create a loopback interface on the router.

○ D. Use the command **no election-process**.

Question 45

You would like to configure your full mesh frame relay topology in NBMA mode. Which of the following statements is true?

○ A. There is no DR/BDR election.

○ B. You must manually configure the neighbors.

○ C. Each interface pair must be placed In Its own unique subnet.

○ D. This configuration is unique to Cisco equipment.

Question 46

Which of the following OSPF network statements configures OSPF to function with all interface addresses on the router?

○ A. network all all area 0

○ B. network any any area 0

○ C. network area 0

○ D. network 0.0.0.0 255.255.255.255 area 0

Question 47

You need to identify the OSPF priority value of the router to which you are currently logged in. What command should you use?

○ A. **show ip ospf**

○ B. **show ip ospf border-routers**

○ C. **show ip ospf database**

○ D. **show ip ospf interface**

Question 48

Which of the following is an advantage of using multiple areas with OSPF?

○ A. SPF calculations increase, yet the neighbor table size is reduced.

○ B. Router table size is increased, yet SPF calculations are reduced.

○ C. Topology tables are increased in size, yet router tables decrease in size.

○ D. Smaller routing tables are possible, and SPF calculations are reduced.

Question 49

Because multiple areas can be used to configure OSPF, it is a _____ routing protocol.

○ A. Distance vector

○ B. Link State

○ C. Hierarchical

○ D. Reliable

Question 50

This OSPF router type has at least one interface attached to an external network (another AS):

○ A. ABR

○ B. Internal

○ C. Backbone

○ D. ASBR

Question 51

This LSA type originates at the ASBR and describes routes to destinations external to the AS:

○ A. Type 1

○ B. Type 2

○ C. Type 3

○ D. Type 4

○ E. Type 5

Question 52

What type of LSA is blocked from a totally stubby area?

○ A. Type 1

○ B. Type 2

○ C. Type 3

○ D. Type 4

○ E. Type 5

○ F. Types 1 and 2

○ G. Types 3, 4, and 5

Question 53

Which of the following statements regarding redistribution is true?

- ○ A. Redistribution is an excellent design technique and should be used whenever possible.
- ○ B. Redistribution is not possible between IGRP and EIGRP.
- ○ C. Hop count is always used as the metric when routes are redistributed.
- ○ D. Redistribution occurs automatically between IGRP and EIGRP when they have the same AS number.

Question 54

Which of the following match statements would you use if you are interested in matching packet length?

- ○ A. **match length min max**
- ○ B. **match layer 3 length min max**
- ○ C. **match size min max**
- ○ D. **match min max**

Question 55

Which of the following statements regarding BGP is *not* correct?

- ○ A. Periodic keep-alives are sent to verify TCP connectivity.
- ○ B. Reliability in BGP stems from the use of Transmission Control Protocol.
- ○ C. Periodic updates are used to ensure full topological awareness.
- ○ D. BGP uses path vectors for routing decisions.

Question 56

Which statement about two routers connected via EBGP is true?

- ○ A. They are typically directly connected.
- ○ B. They are not typically connected.
- ○ C. Keep-alive mechanisms are not used.
- ○ D. UDP is used to transfer information with EBGP.

Question 57

What is the BGP synchronization rule?

- ○ A. Do not use or advertise a route learned by IBGP until a matching route has been learned from an IGP.
- ○ B. Do not use or advertise a route learned by EBGP until a matching route has been learned from an IGP.
- ○ C. Do not use or advertise a route learned by IBGP.
- ○ D. Do not use or advertise a route learned by EBGP.

Question 58

How do you configure a BGP neighbor that is in your same AS of 65000?

- ○ A. neighbor 10.1.1.2 as 65000
- ○ B. neighbor 10.1.1.2 65000
- ○ C. neighbor 10.1.1.2 as IBGP 65000
- ○ D. neighbor 10.1.1.2 remote-as 65000
- ○ E. neighbor 10.1.1.2

Question 59

What does a route reflector do when it receives an update from one of its clients?

- ○ A. The route reflector sends the update to all nonclient peers and all clients.
- ○ B. The route reflector sends the update to all nonclient peers and all clients with the exception of the originator.
- ○ C. The route reflector sends the update to all client peers.
- ○ D. The route reflector sends the update to all other route reflectors.

Question 60

What is the correct syntax to configure route reflectors in your BGP AS?

- ○ A. route-reflector self
- ○ B. neighbor 172.16.10.10 route-reflector-client
- ○ C. route-reflector 172.16.10.20
- ○ D. neighbor 172.16.10.10 reflector-client

Answer Key 1

1. B	21. B	41. D
2. B	22. A	42. C
3. D	23. C	43. F
4. A, C	24. C	44. B
5. B, D	25. B	45. B
6. B, D	26. A	46. D
7. A, B	27. D	47. D
8. D	28. D	48. D
9. B, D	29. C	49. C
10. A	30. A, C	50. D
11. A, B, E	31. B	51. E
12. C	32. B	52. G
13. A, C	33. B	53. D
14. B	34. B, C, D	54. A.
15. A, E	35. C, D, E	55. C
16. B	36. B	56. A
17. A, B	37. C	57. A
18. D	38. A	58. D
19. C	39. E	59. B
20. A	40. C	60. B

Answer Key Explanations

Question 1

Answer B is correct. The Core layer must feature the fastest and most efficient transmissions of data between other divisions of the network. As such, this layer often features the circuits with the largest bandwidth and often implements redundancy mechanisms. Answer A is incorrect because the Distribution layer is the consolidation point for the various Access layers in the hierarchical design. Answer C is incorrect because the Access layer is the entry point onto the network for end station systems and servers. Sometimes the Access layer is referred to as the Desktop layer. Answer D is incorrect because in the classic hierarchical network design from Cisco, there is no Workgroup layer.

Question 2

Answer B is correct. Administrative Distance is forced to 200. You can force the administrative distance used for a static route by setting the value in the `ip route` command. Doing so enables you to create a floating static route that is used as a backup route in the event the dynamic routing protocol fails to provide the necessary information. Answer A is incorrect because the metric value is not forced in the `ip route` command. Answer C is incorrect because this command does not specify the amount of time the route stays in the routing table. Answer D is incorrect because this value cannot designate the number of sessions that may use the route.

Question 3

Answer D is correct. Static routes are a heavy administrative task. The use of static routes in your enterprise network typically increases the administrative overhead required to maintain the network. As the network changes, you must manipulate the static routes manually. Answer A is incorrect because resource shortages are in fact a valid reason for the creation of static routes. Many routers do not possess enough CPU or memory to be wasteful. Answer B is incorrect because static routes also enable an administrator to have absolute control over the flow of traffic in the network, more so than dynamic routing. Answer C is incorrect because the use of static routes enables the administrator to have remote networks appear as if they are directly connected.

Question 4

Answer A is correct because RIP and IGRP use only major classful networks to determine the interfaces participating in the protocol. Answer C is also correct because integrated IS-IS does not use a network statement. Interface configuration mode is used to configure interfaces participating in the IS-IS routing process. Answer B is incorrect because BGP is the only dynamic routing protocol that uses the network statement to indicate an advertisement for the listed network. Answer D is incorrect because EIGRP and OSPF—not IGRP and OSPF—allow the specification of a wildcard mask.

Question 5

Answer B is correct because ODR is used in hub and spoke environments: Spoke routers send information to the hub and the hub sends default route information the spokes. ODR is appropriate only within a hub and spoke topology. In this design, the stub routers use CDP to send IP prefixes to the hub router. Answer D is also correct because the hub router sends default routes to the spoke routers. Answer A is incorrect because CDP does carry subnet mask information; therefore ODR is a classless routing technology. Answer C is incorrect because spoke routers do not send default routes—they receive default routes from the hub router.

Question 6

Answer B is correct because the hub router needs the router odr global configuration command. Also answer D is correct because the spoke routers must feature CDP on the links between the spoke routers and the hub router. Answer A is incorrect because all routers participating in ODR do not require the router odr global configuration command. Answer C is incorrect because only the hub router requires default routes. The spoke routers do not need default routes configured; these routes are automatically injected from the hub router that is configured for ODR. Answer E is incorrect because the hub router does not need to be running any other routing protocol, although it often is. ODR information can be injected into other dynamic routing protocol information.

Question 7

Answer A is correct because by definition, classful routing protocols do not carry subnet mask information in routing updates. Answer B is correct because RIP v1 and IGRP are examples of early classful routing protocols. Answer C is incorrect because subnet mask information is not carried in routing updates within the same network; consistency of the mask is assumed. Network boundary summarization is performed automatically. Answer D is incorrect because if routing update information contains a different major network than the one configured on the receiving interface, the router applies the default classful mask by IP address class.

Question 8

Answer D is correct because the traffic is bound for an unknown subnet of the 10 network. Therefore, the traffic is discarded. This behavior is a result of the lack of the `ip classless` command. Answer A is incorrect because the 10.2.2.2 destination does not match the first entry, nor does it match the third entry, Answer B, in the routing table. Answer C is incorrect because the default route entry would be used to route the traffic only if the `ip classless` command is used.

Question 9

Answer B is correct because in RIP version 2 you turn off auto summarization by using the `no auto-summary` command under the RIP process. Answer D is also correct because you can use the `ip summary-address rip` interface command and define a network number and mask that meets the particular requirements. Answers A and C are incorrect because neither is capable of configuring manual summarization.

Question 10

Answer A is correct because the administrative distance value of 20 assigned to external BGP enables it to be preferred over most other dynamic protocols. These other values are assigned to the following protocols: Answer B is incorrect because internal EIGRP is 90; Answer C is incorrect because EIGRP summary route is 5; Answer D is incorrect because IGRP is 100; and Answer E is incorrect because OSPF is 110.

Question 11

Answers A, B, and E are correct because even though they are classless protocols, RIPv2, EIGRP, and BGP all exhibit automatic route summarization by default. Answers C and D are incorrect because IS-IS and OSPF do not automatically summarize IP address information. Summarization must be manually configured if it is to be used.

Question 12

Answer C is correct because the Level 1/2 router learns about paths both within and between areas. L1/2 routers are equivalent to ABRs in OSPF. Answer A is incorrect because L1 routers learn about paths within the areas to which they connect. Answer B is incorrect because L2 routers learn about paths among areas. Answer D is incorrect because L1/2 routers learn about paths within and between areas.

Question 13

Answer A is correct because even though IS-IS metrics can consist of default, delay, expense, and error components, Cisco supports only the default value. Answer C is also correct because if not manipulated, this default value has the IS-IS metric function very similar to RIP in that it is a simple measure of hop count. Answer B is incorrect because the Cisco router assigns a default metric value of 10 to each IS-IS interface. Answer D is incorrect because *Narrow* metrics are limited to a 6-bit interface and 10-bit path metric. Cisco has addressed this in post 12.0 IOS routers by using a wide metric value.

Question 14

Answer B is correct because Level 1 routing is also called area routing. It deals with IS moving data within an area. Answer A is incorrect because Level 0 routing deals with moving data from an end system to an IS. Answer C is incorrect because Level 2 routing is known as inter-area routing. Answer D is incorrect because Level 3 routing deals with moving data between domains.

Question 15

Answer A is correct because IS-IS is easy to extend through the Type, Length, and Value mechanism. Also, answer E is correct because based on the default timers, IS-IS detects a failure in the network faster than OSPF. Answer B is incorrect because OSPF does have the advantage of more engineers and documentation being available. Answer C is incorrect because the metric of OSPF automatically scales to represent bandwidth by default. The default metric for IS-IS used by Cisco does not. Also answer D is incorrect because OSPF has more customized features for IP because the protocol was designed to run IP.

Question 16

Answer B is correct because the NSEL identifies a process on the device. It is roughly the equivalent to a port or socket in IP. Answer A is incorrect because the area address is used to identify areas in the IS-IS routing domain. Answer C is incorrect because the system ID identifies an individual OSI device. Answer D is incorrect because the HODSP subdivides the domain into areas. It is roughly equivalent to a subnet in IP.

Question 17

Answer A is correct because each IS-IS router requires a unique system ID. Answer B is correct because on Cisco routers, this value must be 6 bytes. Typically, administrators use the MAC address of a LAN interface for this value. This ensures uniqueness throughout the domain. An IP address from an interface can also be used. Answer C is incorrect because System IDs are not 8 bytes, and answer D is incorrect because System IDs are used in IS-IS.

Question 18

Answer D is correct because for HDLC interfaces, the SNPA is simple HDLC. Answer A is incorrect because the MAC address is used as the SNPA for a LAN interface. Answer B is incorrect because the Virtual Circuit ID is used for X.25 or ATM interfaces. Finally, answer C is incorrect because the DLCI is used for Frame Relay interfaces.

Question 19

Answer C is correct because partial sequence number PDUs are used to acknowledge and request missing pieces of link-state information. Answer A is incorrect because IS-IS `Hellos` are used to maintain adjacencies between neighboring routers. Answer B is incorrect because link-state PDUs are used to distribute link-state information. Answer D is incorrect because complete sequence number PDUs are used to describe the complete list of LSPs in a router's link-state database.

Question 20

Answer A is correct because the `show clns route` command displays the IS-IS routing table. Answer B is incorrect because the `show ip route` command displays the IP IS-IS routes in the IP routing table. Answer C is incorrect because the `show isis database` command displays the contents of the IS-IS LSDB. Answer D is incorrect because the `show isis route` command displays the IS-IS L1 routing table, which includes all other system IDs in the area.

Question 21

Answer B is correct because when configuring Integrated IS-IS, you must configure the interfaces that are to participate by entering interface configuration mode and using the `ip router isis` command. Answer A is incorrect because the `network` command is not used with IS-IS. Answer C is incorrect because the NET configured on the router does not dictate what interfaces actually route traffic. Answer D is incorrect because there is no such thing as an `isis` interface map statement.

Question 22

Answer A is correct because during autoconfiguration, the router sends a network prefix to enable the autoconfiguration of the host. The prefix also contains a lifetime. Answers B, C, and D are incorrect because the information that the router sends includes one or more prefixes to use on the link, the lifetime information, flags, default router information, and other types of host information. Entire network addresses, MAC addresses, and host addresses are not sent.

Question 23

Answer C is correct because the Flow Label field tags flows of IP packets. It can be used for multilayer switching and faster packet switching. Answer A is incorrect because the Version field indicates the version of IP in use. Answer B is incorrect because the Traffic Class field is similar to the ToS field in IPv4. Answer D is incorrect because the Next Header value determines the type of information following the basic IPv6 header.

Question 24

Answer C is correct because the `show ip nat translations` command enables you to examine the IP NAT translation table. Answers A, B, and D are incorrect. All other commands listed here produce syntax errors.

Question 25

Answer B is correct because the inside global IP address is the IP address of an inside host as it appears to the outside network. Answer A is incorrect because the inside local IP address is the IP address of an internal host prior to any translation. Answer C is incorrect because the outside global IP address is the ISP-configured IP address configured on an external host. Answer D is incorrect because the outside local IP address is the external address of a host as it appears on the inside network.

Question 26

Answer A is correct because the best summary route is 172.24.4.0 with a 20 bit mask. This masks off all the bits that are identical in the 11 networks. Answers B, C, D, and E are incorrect. No other address in the options masks off all the bits that are identical in all the addresses.

Question 27

Answer D is correct because 16 additional subnetworks are gained when you use one of your subnets from the /20 mask scheme and use a mask of /24. This happens because 4 additional bits are "borrowed." Plugging these 4 bits into the formula 2^n yields 16 subnets. Answers A, B, C, and E are incorrect because no other number of subnets provided is the appropriate result of the formula.

Question 28

Answer D is correct because VLSM enables a very efficient use of IP address space. For point-to-point serial connections that require only two addresses, the 255.255.255.252 subnet mask meets the requirement ideally. Answers A, B, and C are incorrect because all other subnet masks presented result in address space waste. More host addresses are possible than can be used.

Question 29

Answer C is correct because IGRP is a "first-generation" routing protocol. It is classful in nature and as such does not support VLSM. Answers A, B, D, and E are incorrect. These are all classless and support VLSM.

Question 30

Answer A is correct because VLSM is supported in classless routing protocols and allows for efficient use of IP address space. Answer C is correct because VLSM designs also allow for more use of route summarization. Answer B is incorrect because subinterfaces allow the creation of additional logical interfaces in a single physical interface. Answer D is incorrect because not all routing protocols support VLSM—classful routing protocols do not, for example.

Question 31

Answer B is correct because the term *successor* refers to the best next-hop router to reach a given network destination. Answers A, C, and D are incorrect. Feasible successor refers to an EIGRP backup route. Primary and designated are not terms that apply to EIGRP routes.

Question 32

Answer B is correct because the feasible distance is the distance from the local router to the destination. Answer A is incorrect because the advertised distance is the EIGRP metric for an EIGRP neighbor to reach a particular network. Answer C is incorrect because the feasible successor is the backup route to a destination. Answer D is incorrect because there is no such term as "successor distance."

Question 33

Answer B is correct because the mathematical formula to ensure that the feasible successor is loop-free requires that the AD of the second-best route be less than the FD of the successor. Answers A, C, and D are incorrect because they do not properly state the mathematical formula as it exists.

Question 34

Answers B, C, and D are correct. With K values at their defaults, the default metric for EIGRP consists of bandwidth and delay. EIGRP does not form a neighbor relationship with another router if that router uses different K values. IGRP-to-EIGRP conversions are simple: The metric of IGRP is multiplied by 256. Answer A is incorrect because the default K value settings are K1=1; K2=0; K3=1; K4=0; K5=0.

Question 35

Answers C, D, and E are correct because EIGRP reliable packets are packets that require explicit acknowledgement. These packets are Update, Query, and Reply packets. Answers A and B are incorrect. Hello and ACK packets are unreliable and do not require explicit acknowledgement.

Question 36

Answer B is correct because by default, EIGRP uses up to 50% of the bandwidth of an interface or subinterface. This bandwidth amount is set with the bandwidth interface parameter. Answers A, C, and D are incorrect. To change the bandwidth that EIGRP can use on a WAN interface, use the `ip bandwidth-percent eigrp` interface configuration command.

Question 37

Answer C is correct because OSPF does require additional router resources, including CUP and memory. Answer A is incorrect because OSPF tends to converge faster than most distance vector–based dynamic routing protocol approaches. Answer B is incorrect because there is no simple hop count limitation in the protocol. Answer D is incorrect because cost is the default metric. By default, cost calculations are based on bandwidth.

Question 38

Answer A is correct because two routers belonging to the same area have identical LSDBs for that area. Answer B is incorrect because each router may maintain a unique routing database with unique entries toward particular destinations. Answers C and D are incorrect because each maintains a neighborship and area database that also may be unique.

Question 39

Answer E is correct because after all LSRs have been satisfied for a given router, the adjacent routers are considered synchronized and in the full state. Answers A, B, C, and D are incorrect. The process of sending LSRs is called the loading state. After the DR and BDR have been selected, the routers are considered to be in the `exstart` state.

Question 40

Answer C is correct because the router with the highest priority wins the role of DR. Answers A, B, and D are incorrect. All other routers must have higher priority values to be considered the DR.

Question 41

Answer D is correct because the router ID is the highest loopback interface address configured on a router. Answers A, B, and C are incorrect. Loopback interfaces receive immediate priority over other interfaces for router ID selection.

Question 42

Answer C is correct because the point-to-multipoint mode treats the non-broadcast network as a collection of point-to-point links. Answers A, B, and D are incorrect. These are not the correct operation mode.

Question 43

Answer F is correct because link-state update information is not found in a Hello packet. Answers A, B, C, D, and E are incorrect. The Hello packet contains routerID, hello and dead intervals, neighbors, area ID, router priority, DR and BDR IP addresses, authentication password, and stub area flag.

Question 44

Answer B is correct because setting the priority to a value of 0 ensures that the router never wins the DR election. Answer A is incorrect because setting the priority value to a high value ensures that the router wins the election process. Answer C is incorrect because creating a loopback interface on the router ensures the router ID value. Answer D is incorrect because there is no `election` command.

Question 45

Answer B is correct because the `neighbor` command is used to statically define adjacent relationships in NBMA networks. Answers A, C, and D are incorrect. A DR and BDR are elected. All serial ports are part of the same IP subnet. NBMA is an RFC-compliant mode.

Question 46

Answer D is correct because using the address and wildcard mask of 0.0.0.0 255.255.255.255 matches all interfaces on the router. Answers A, B, and C are incorrect. `All` and `any` are not valid keywords for use with the `network` statement.

Question 47

Answer D is correct because you can use the `show ip ospf interface` command with no arguments to display summarized OSPF information about all interfaces and composite links. Answers A, B, and C are incorrect. No other command provided gives information about OSPF priority values.

Question 48

Answer D is correct because using multiple areas enables routing tables to be reduced in size, thanks to summarization. Also, SPF calculations can be reduced because network details can be hidden from different areas. Answers A, B, and C are incorrect. SPF calculations do not tend to increase in size, nor do routing tables increase in size. Topology tables are not increased in size.

Question 49

Answer C is correct because hierarchical routing protocols are OPSF and IS-IS. They allow for the creations of areas to increase the scalability of the routing protocol. Answers A, B, and D are incorrect. Answer A is incorrect because distance vector approaches are first-generation technology. Answer B is incorrect because link-state routing protocols do not provide a hierarchical approach by default. Answer D is incorrect because there is no such category as "reliable protocols."

Question 50

Answer D is correct because an autonomous system boundary router makes a connection to another AS. Answers A, B, and C are incorrect. An ABR makes connections between two areas. An internal router exists in only one area. A backbone router makes a connection to Area 0.

Question 51

Answer E is correct because the external LSA type that describes routes to networks outside the OSPF AS is type 5. Answers A, B, C, and D are incorrect. No other LSA types describe these external networks.

Question 52

Answer G is correct. Types 3, 4, and 5 are blocked from a totally stubby area. Totally stubby areas do not accept information about routes external to the ASs or summary routes from other areas internal to the AS. Answers A, B, C, D, E, and F are incorrect. Totally stubby areas do not block Type 1 and 2 LSAs.

Question 53

Answer D is correct because IGRP and EIGRP are compatible. In fact, redistribution is automatic when the same AS number is used. Answer A is incorrect because redistribution should be used only when absolutely necessary. Answer B is incorrect because redistribution is possible between IGRP and EIGRP. Answer C is incorrect because hop count is not always the metric; the metric depends on the metric of the receiving protocol.

Question 54

Answer A is correct because you can use the `match length` command to specify the match criteria. You can specify one or both of the following: matches the Level 3 length of the packet and/or matches the source and destination IP address that is permitted by one or more standard or extended access lists. If you do not specify a `match` command, the route map applies to all packets. Answers B, C, and D are incorrect. All these command examples produce syntax errors.

Question 55

Answer C is correct because periodic updates are not used to ensure topological awareness. Triggered updates are used. Answers A, B, and D are incorrect. All these statements are indeed valid.

Question 56

Answer A is correct because these systems are typically directly connected. Answers B, C, and D are incorrect. All these statements regarding EBGB are false.

Question 57

Answer A is correct because the synchronization rule prevents "black holes"—the route must be learned from an IGP first. Answers B, C, and D are incorrect because all these responses are invalid.

Question 58

Answer D is correct because you should use the `neighbor remote-as` command. This looks strange if the neighbor is in your AS, but the configuration is valid. Answers A, B, C and E are incorrect. The syntax is incorrect in all of these.

Question 59

Answer B is correct because after receiving an update from a client, the route reflector sends the update to all nonclient peers and all clients with the exception of the originator. Answers A, C, and D are incorrect. None of these statements accurately describe route reflector behavior.

Question 60

Answer B is correct because of the use of the `route-reflector-client` syntax with the `neighbor` command. This command is part of the `neighbor` statement. It tells the route reflector to start "reflecting" IBGP routes to and from the client. Answers A, C, and D are incorrect. None of these syntax examples are valid.

13

Practice Exam 2

Question 1

Which layer of the Cisco hierarchical network model often features the use of access lists and features consolidation from other layers?

- ○ A. Access layer
- ○ B. Core layer
- ○ C. Distribution layer
- ○ D. Desktop layer

Question 2

Which of the following are valid benefits to using VLSM? (Choose all that apply.)

- ❑ A. Helps to reduce IP address space waste
- ❑ B. Is supported by every major dynamic routing protocol
- ❑ C. Helps reduce the size of IP routing tables
- ❑ D. Enables the design of hierarchical networks that feature route summarization

Question 3

You have a router that is capable of route summarization. What is the best summary route for the following networks:

$$192.16.12.0/24$$
$$192.16.13.0/24$$
$$192.16.14.0/24$$
$$192.16.15.0/24$$

- ○ A. 192.16.12.0/22
- ○ B. 192.16.15.0/22
- ○ C. 192.16.12.0/23
- ○ D. 192.16.15.0/23

Question 4

Which of the following statements about the IPv6 frame format are true? (Choose all that apply.)

❑ A. It contains half of the previous IPv4 header fields

❑ B. It enables direct routing data storage.

❑ C. It permits faster routing data retrieval with 64-bit aligned fields.

❑ D. It contains fewer header fields because it handles fragmentation.

Question 5

Which of the following IPv6 addresses are valid? (Choose all that apply.)

❑ A. 2031:0:130F:0:0:9C0:876A:130B

❑ B. 2031:0000:130F:0000:0000:09C0:876A:130B

❑ C. 2031::130F::9C0:876A:130B

❑ D. FF01::1

Question 6

You are contemplating the use of NAT in your Cisco network. How do you refer to the IP address of an inside host as it appears to the outside network?

○ A. Inside local

○ B. Outside local

○ C. Outside global

○ D. Inside global

Question 7

What is the benefit of using route maps in conjunction with your NAT implementation in your Cisco network?

- ○ A. Route maps promote reduced overhead as a result of the NAT process on the router.
- ○ B. Route maps provide security for the NAT system.
- ○ C. Route maps simplify the translation table and therefore reduce overhead on the router as a result of the NAT process.
- ○ D. Route maps permit fully-extended translation entries in the translation table.

Question 8

You are interested in manipulating the timers that are used with on-demand routing. How do you do this?

- ○ A. Use the **timers basic** command in router configuration mode.
- ○ B. Use the **timers basic** command in global configuration mode.
- ○ C. Use the **cdp timers** command in router configuration mode.
- ○ D. Use the **cdp timers** command in interface configuration mode.
- ○ E. Timers cannot be manipulated for on-demand routing.

Question 9

Which of the following dynamic routing protocols are considered classless? (Choose all that apply.)

- ❑ A. IGRP
- ❑ B. EIGRP
- ❑ C. RIP v1
- ❑ D. OSPF
- ❑ E. IS-IS
- ❑ F. BGP
- ❑ G. RIP v2

Question 10

Which of the following statements are true regarding EIGRP? (Choose all that apply.)

- ❑ A. EIGRP is considered a hybrid routing protocol.
- ❑ B. EIGRP is a classful routing protocol.
- ❑ C. EIGRP behaves in a classful manner by default regarding automatic summarization.
- ❑ D. EIGRP uses path attributes as a metric.

Question 11

You are running RIP version 2 in your enterprise network. You are interested in creating a summary route and advertising this route out the Serial 2 interface of one of your routers. The summary address is 10.10.0.0 255.255.0.0. What is the correct command to use to configure this summary address?

- ○ A. Manual address summarization is not possible with RIP.
- ○ B. **Router(config-router)#ip summary-address 10.10.0.0 255.255.0.0**
- ○ C. **Router(config-if)#ip summary-address 10.10.0.0 255.255.0.0**
- ○ D. **Router(config-if)#ip summary-address rip 10.10.0.0 255.255.0.0**

Question 12

Which of the following route sources features the best administrative distance value?

- ○ A. RIP v2
- ○ B. OSPF
- ○ C. IGRP
- ○ D. External EIGRP

Question 13

You are examining the reliability of various routing protocols. Which of the following protocols features TCP windowing to assist with reliability?

○ A. IGRP

○ B. EIGRP

○ C. OSPF

○ D. BGP

Question 14

How often are hello messages sent by EIGRP on Ethernet media by default?

○ A. Every 2 seconds

○ B. Every 5 seconds

○ C. Every 30 seconds

○ D. Every 60 seconds

Question 15

EIGRP functions at which layer of the OSI model?

○ A. Data Link

○ B. Network

○ C. Transport

○ D. Session

Question 16

You are troubleshooting your EIGRP-based network and you issue the **show ip elgrp neighbors** command. What is the meaning of the SRTT value that appears in the output from this command?

○ A. Displays the time in milliseconds that the router waits for an acknowledgement before it retransmits the reliable packet.

○ B. Indicates the average time it takes to send and receive packets from a neighbor.

○ C. Specifies the time to wait without receiving anything from a neighbor before considering the neighbor unavailable.

○ D. Indicates the number of packets waiting in the queue to be sent.

Question 17

You are interested in viewing information about the receipt and generation of EIGRP packet types. You also want to inspect sequence numbers and serial numbers, but you do not want to view the contents of packets. What command should you use?

○ A. **debug ip eigrp**

○ B. **debug eigrp packets**

○ C. **show ip eigrp topology**

○ D. **show ip eigrp interface**

Question 18

You have had a failure of a key EIGRP router in your network. The EIGRP routing process is unable to determine a feasible successor and the successor route is no longer available. How does the EIGRP process respond?

○ A. The EIGRP process ceases on the router to ensure routing loops are not introduced.

○ B. The successor route is removed and the router waits for updates from other EIGRP speaking routers.

○ C. The router actively queries for an alternate pathway, and when a loop-free path is found, it is installed in the routing table.

○ D. The route with the lowest feasible distance is automatically utilized.

Question 19

You are configuring EIGRP on your Cisco router. You issue the **ip default-network** command and you specify a network number with the command. What effect does this have on your router? (Choose all that apply.)

❑ A. The command has no direct effect on your router.

❑ B. The command causes your router to advertise this default route information to other EIGRP routers.

❑ C. The router configures its gateway of last resort with that network information.

❑ D. The router advertises EIGRP information on all interfaces falling in that network range.

Question 20

You have learned that EIGRP routers do not form an adjacency in your network if K values do not match. What command should you use to quickly view the settings of your K values?

○ A. **show ip protocols**

○ B. **show ip route**

○ C. **show ip route eigrp**

○ D. **show ip eigrp topology**

Question 21

OSPF relies upon a hello protocol to establish and maintain relationships for bidirectional communication between neighbors. How does OSPF send these hello packets?

○ A. Broadcast to all routers

○ B. Multicast using 224.0.0.5

○ C. Multicast using 224.0.0.8

○ D. Unicast using the lowest IP address of each router

Question 22

OSPF includes a "paranoid update" feature. This helps to ensure convergence of routing information. How often does this process occur?

- ○ A. Every 2 minutes
- ○ B. Every 5 minutes
- ○ C. Every 20 minutes
- ○ D. Every 30 minutes
- ○ E. Every 60 minutes

Question 23

Which of the following statements regarding the following command are true? (Choose all that apply.)

router ospf 10

- ❑ A. It is a global configuration command.
- ❑ B. It is a router configuration command.
- ❑ C. The number 10 must match the number used on other routers.
- ❑ D. The command should be followed with one or more network commands.

Question 24

You would like to ensure that the Serial interface 0/0 with an IP address of 10.30.12.1/16 participates in OSPF advertisements and is a member of area 1. What network statement should you use?

- ○ A. **network 10.30.0.0 area 1**
- ○ B. **network 10.30.12.1 0.0.0.0 area 1**
- ○ C. **network 10.30.12.1 255.255.255.255 area 1**
- ○ D. **network 10.30.12.1 255.255.0.0 area 1**
- ○ E. **network 10.30.0.0 255.255.0.0 area 1**

Question 25

What is the preferred procedure for setting the router ID of an OSPF speaking router?

○ A. Use a loopback interface.

○ B. Use an internal-use only address on a physical interface.

○ C. Use the **ip ospf router id** command.

○ D. Use the **router-id** command.

Question 26

You need to verify the router ID assigned to one of your OSPF speaking routers. What command accomplishes this?

○ A. **show ip interface brief**

○ B. **show ip ospf**

○ C. **show ip ospf neighbors**

○ D. **show ip ospf interfaces**

Question 27

You have configured the priority value of one of your OSPF routers as 0. What is this router called in OSPF terms?

○ A. DR

○ B. BDR

○ C. DROTHER

○ D. DIS

Question 28

Which of the following **ip ospf network** command options utilizes one IP subnet, does not require a DR or BDR and is typically used in a partial mesh topology?

○ A. **broadcast**

○ B. **nonbroadcast**

○ C. **point-to-multipoint**

○ D. **point-to-point**

Question 29

Which of the following LSA types are known as network link advertisements?

○ A. 1
○ B. 2
○ C. 3
○ D. 4
○ E. 5
○ F. 6
○ G. 7

Question 30

Which of the following types of external OSPF routes calculates the cost by adding the external cost to the internal cost of each link the packet crosses?

○ A. E1
○ B. E2
○ C. E3
○ D. E4

Question 31

Which level of routing in IS-IS deals with routing information within an area?

○ A. Level 1
○ B. Level 2
○ C. Level 3
○ D. Level 0

Question 32

Which portion of the following IS-IS address is the System ID?

49.0001.0000.0C22.2222.00

- ○ A. 49.0001
- ○ B. 00
- ○ C. 0000.0C22.2222
- ○ D. 49.0001.0000

Question 33

What is the typical IS-IS SNPA for a Frame Relay connection?

- ○ A. MAC address
- ○ B. HDLC
- ○ C. DLCI
- ○ D. NET

Question 34

What is the recommended configuration of IS-IS in a NBMA network such as frame relay?

- ○ A. broadcast
- ○ B. point-to-multipoint
- ○ C. point-to-point
- ○ D. static map

Question 35

You are examining a point-to-point IS-IS link. You notice that a CSNP is sent once when the link comes up. Following this transmission, you notice LSPs are sent on the link to describe topology changes. What is sent in acknowledgement to these LSPs?

- ○ A. An ACK
- ○ B. An IIH
- ○ C. A PSNP
- ○ D. An LSP

Question 36

You need to verify the CLNS prefix routing table, as well as the local NET configured on your router. You are concerned about the L2 path that might be chosen to reach a particular remote area. What is the appropriate **show** command to initiate?

- ○ A. **show clns route**
- ○ B. **show isis route**
- ○ C. **show clns protocol**
- ○ D. **show clns neighbors**

Question 37

What is the correct command to use to configure the NSAP on an IS-IS router?

- ○ A. **Router(config-router)#network**
- ○ B. **Router(config)#network**
- ○ C. **Router(config-if)#net**
- ○ D. **Router(config-router)#net**

Question 38

You would like to optimize your IS-IS configuration by proactively configuring your device as a Level 2 router. What command should you use?

- ○ A. **Router(config)#is-circuit-type level-2-only**
- ○ B. **Router(config-if)#is-type level-2**
- ○ C. **Router(config-router)#is-type level-2-only**
- ○ D. This configuration is not possible.

Question 39

What is the appropriate NSEL for the configuration of an NSAP address on a Cisco router?

- ○ A. 00
- ○ B. 100
- ○ C. 200
- ○ D. 01

Question 40

A single router interconnects Area 0, Area 10, and a non-OSPF external network. How can the router be described in pure OSPF terms? (Choose all that apply.)

- ❑ A. ABR
- ❑ B. ASBR
- ❑ C. Backbone router
- ❑ D. Internal router
- ❑ E. External router

Question 41

Which of the following best describes the BGP synchronization rule?

- ○ A. Peer routers are established by TCP only.
- ○ B. Routing processes do not begin until all forwarding databases are synchronized.
- ○ C. Do not advertise destination routes with inconsistent MEDs.
- ○ D. BGP routers should not use, nor advertise to an external neighbor, routes learned via IBGP until a matching route has been learned via an IGP.

Question 42

What is the protocol and port used by BGP? (Choose 2.)

- ❑ A. TCP
- ❑ B. ICMP
- ❑ C. UDP
- ❑ D. SNMP
- ❑ E. IP
- ❑ F. 100
- ❑ G. 24
- ❑ H. 89
- ❑ I. 179

Question 43

Which of the following are accurate descriptions of the connection characteristics between BGP peers functioning as neighbors? (Choose all that apply.)

- ❑ A. The routers must be directly connected.
- ❑ B. The routers must be in the same AS.
- ❑ C. The routers must have established a TCP connection.
- ❑ D. The routers must use the same metric attributes.

Question 44

You are configuring redistribution into EIGRP. Which of the following are valid parameters for the **redistribute** command? (Choose all that apply.)

- ❏ A. **match**
- ❏ B. **metric**
- ❏ C. **level**
- ❏ D. **route-map**

Question 45

Which of the following factors can become the basis for route filtering with distribute lists? (Choose all that apply.)

- ❏ A. The incoming interface of the advertisement
- ❏ B. The routing protocol originating the advertisement
- ❏ C. The outgoing interface of the advertisement
- ❏ D. The administrative distance of the route

Question 46

Which of the following are valid match criteria for a **route-map**? (Choose all that apply.)

- ❏ A. **match type**
- ❏ B. **match interface**
- ❏ C. **match length**
- ❏ D. **match ip next-hop**

Question 47

You are using a route map to assist in the redistribution of RIP into OSPF in your network. You are using the following set command:

set metric 10

What is the meaning of this command?

○ A.   Set the cost value of 10 for all routes redistributed into OSPF.

○ B.   Set a hop count value of 10 for all routes redistributed into RIP.

○ C.   Add 10 to the hop count for RIP routes.

○ D.   Add 10 to the cost value for OSPF routes.

Question 48

How do you configure an internal BGP neighbor at an IP address of 192.168.1.2?

○ A.   **Router(config-router)#neighbor 192.168.1.2 as 65000**

○ B.   **Router(config-router)#neighbor 192.168.1.2 65000**

○ C.   **Router(config-router)#neighbor 192.168.1.2 remote-as 65000**

○ D.   Internal BGP neighborships are formed automatically and cannot be statically configured.

Question 49

You have changed the outbound policy of a BGP router. You need to force a routing table update without resetting the TCP session. You also need to flag all routes as withdrawals or inserts to the neighbor 192.168.1.1. Which command should you use?

○ A.   **clear ip bgp ***

○ B.   **clear ip bgp 192.168.1.1**

○ C.   **clear ip bgp 192.168.1.1 soft in**

○ D.   **clear ip bgp 192.168.1.1 soft out**

Question 50

You would like to manually create a summary address in your BGP routing topology. What command do you use to accomplish this?

○ A. **summary-address**

○ B. **summary**

○ C. **aggregate-address**

○ D. **ip summary-address**

Question 51

Which of the following are valid reasons for the use of BGP? (Choose all that apply.)

❏ A. An AS has multiple connections to other Autonomous Systems.

❏ B. There is a single connection to the Internet that requires the highest level of availability.

❏ C. You require strict routing policy and route selection for traffic entering your AS.

❏ D. You are forced to run low bandwidth connections between your Autonomous Systems.

Question 52

Which of the following components are included in a BGP open message? (Choose all that apply.)

❏ A. Version number

❏ B. Holdtime

❏ C. Router ID

❏ D. Error code

Question 53

You must override the default next-hop behavior of a router and force it to advertise itself as the next-hop address. What command should you use?

- ○ A. **neighbor ip-address**
- ○ B. **neighbor ip-address next-hop-self**
- ○ C. **neighbor ip-address no summary**
- ○ D. **neighbor ip-address peer-group name**

Question 54

Which of the following are BGP well-known, mandatory attributes? (Choose all that apply.)

- ❏ A. **AS-path**
- ❏ B. **Local preference**
- ❏ C. **Aggregator**
- ❏ D. **Origin**
- ❏ E. **Next-hop**

Question 55

Which of the following are valid components of the BGP route selection decision process? (Choose all that apply.)

- ❏ A. Prefer the lowest weight value
- ❏ B. Prefer the shortest AS path
- ❏ C. Prefer the lowest MED
- ❏ D. Prefer the path with the lowest neighbor BGP router ID

Question 56

You are examining the BGP table on your Cisco router. You notice that several of the entries are flagged with a ? symbol. What does this indicate?

- ○ A. The network command has been used to advertise the route via BGP.
- ○ B. The route has been learned via EGP.
- ○ C. The route has been redistributed from an IGP.
- ○ D. The route values cannot be verified by the BGP routing process as the true shortest path.

Question 57

You are interested in manipulating the local preference value for BGP on your Cisco router. What command should you use?

- ○ A. **bgp default local-preference**
- ○ B. **ip bgp local-preference**
- ○ C. **bgp local-preference**
- ○ D. **ip bgp default local-preference**

Question 58

What is the default MED value for a Cisco router running BGP?

- ○ A. 0
- ○ B. 1
- ○ C. 10
- ○ D. 100

Question 59

Which configuration for multihomed BGP creates the least memory usage and CPU utilization on the non-ISP Autonomous System?

- ○ A. Full routes from all providers
- ○ B. Customer routes and default routes from all providers
- ○ C. Default routes from all providers
- ○ D. None of the above

Question 60

Prefix lists can be used to control updates in your BGP network. What default numbering is applied to a prefix list if line numbers are not specified?

○ A. Numbering starts at 10 and automatically increments by 10.

○ B. Numbering starts at 5 and automatically increments by 5.

○ C. Numbering starts at 15 and automatically increments by 15.

○ D. Numbering starts at 20 and automatically increments by 20.

Answer Key 2

1. C	21. B	41. D
2. A, C, D	22. D	42. A, I
3. A	23. A, D	43. C
4. A, B, C	24. B	44. A, B, D
5. A, B, D	25. D	45. A, B, C
6. D	26. B, D	46. B, C, D
7. D	27. C	47. A
8. A	28. B	48. C
9. B, D, E, F, G	29. B	49. D
10. A, C	30. A	50. C
11. D	31. A	51. A, C
12. C	32. C	52. A, B, C
13. D	33. C	53. B
14. B	34. C	54. A, D, E
15. C	35. C	55. B, C, D
16. B	36. A	56. C
17. B	37. D	57. A
18. C	38. C	58. A
19. A, B	39. A	59. C
20. A	40. A, B, C	60. B

Answer Key Explanations

Question 1

Answer C is correct. The Distribution layer is the consolidation point for Access layer devices. Security and QoS are often found at this layer. Answer B is incorrect because the Core layer features redundancy and the largest bandwidth connections. Answer A is incorrect because the Access layer is also known as the desktop layer. This layer features the devices that require access to the network. Answer D is incorrect because there is no Desktop layer in the Cisco Model.

Question 2

Answers A, C, and D are correct. The use of VLSM helps to eliminate IP address waste. For example, if only two IP addresses are needed for a point-to-point serial interface, an appropriate mask can be used that provides just two addresses. VLSM promotes route summarization, which reduces the size of IP routing tables. VLSM also promotes hierarchical network designs that feature summarization. Answer B is incorrect because VLSM is not supported by all dynamic protocols. It is supported only in "second generation" classless routing protocols.

Question 3

Answer A is correct. 192.16.12.0/22 enables the 4 networks described to be summarized. The 22 bit mask masks all the "common bits" in the four networks. Answers B and D are incorrect because the network number would not encompass the 12, 13, and 14 networks. Answer C is incorrect because it would encompass only the 12 and 13 networks.

Question 4

Answers A, B, and C are correct. IPv6 features half of the previous IPv4 header fields. This promotes easier packet processing, enhanced performance, and greater routing efficiency. The IPv6 headers enable direct routing data storage and faster routing data retrieval with 64-bit aligned fields. Answer D is incorrect because IPv6 routers no longer perform fragmentation.

Question 5

Answers A, B, and D are correct. Colons separate a series of 16-bit hexadecimal fields that represent IPv6 addresses. Leading 0s are optional. Successive fields of 0s can be represented as "::" only once in an address. Answer C is incorrect because the address in option c attempts to substitute the "::" notation too many times.

Question 6

Answer D is correct. An inside global IP address is an address of an inside host as it appears to the outside network. Answer A is incorrect because the inside local address is the IP address of an inside host, as it appears on the inside network. Answer B is incorrect because the outside local address is an address of a host in the outside network as it appears to the inside network. Answer C is incorrect because the outside global address is the address of the external host as it appears on the outside network.

Question 7

Answer D is correct. If you configure a route map to use in conjunction with an access list for NAT, an extended translation entry is generated in the NAT translation table. Answer A is incorrect. Route maps do not reduce the overhead that NAT adds to the routing process. Answer B is incorrect because these maps provide no additional means of security. Answer C is incorrect. Route maps do not simplify the translation table—in fact, they make it more complex.

Question 8

Answer A is correct. To adjust ODR network timers, use the `timers basic` router configuration command. To restore the default timers, use the no form of this command.

Answer B is incorrect. Notice that `timers basic` is a router configuration command, not a global configuration command. Answers C and D are incorrect because there is no such command as `cdp timers`. Answer E is incorrect because it is possible to modify the default timers.

Question 9

Answers B, D, E, F, and G are correct. Classless protocols transmit the subnet mask information with routing updates. As a result, VLSM may be utilized. EIGRP, OSPF, IS-IS, BGP, and RIP v2 are all classless. Answer A and C are incorrect. IGRP and RIP v1 are classful routing protocols. They do not pass subnet mask information in their updates.

Question 10

Answers A and C are correct. EIGRP is an advanced distance vector routing protocol. Because it exhibits some link state behaviors, it is considered a hybrid protocol. EIGRP engages in automatic summarization by default. Answer B is incorrect because EIGRP is a classless routing protocol that behaves as if it were classful. Answer D is incorrect because it relies upon a composite metric. BGP relies upon path attributes as a metric.

Question 11

Answer D is correct. To configure manual summarization in RIP v2, use the `ip summary-address rip` command, followed by the network address and mask. Answer A is incorrect because manual summarization is possible in RIP v2. It is not possible in RIP v1. Answer B is incorrect. You do not configure manual summarization in config-router mode. Answer C is incorrect. The correct interface configuration command is `ip summary-address rip`, not `ip summary-address`.

Question 12

Answer C is correct. IGRP features the best (lowest) administrative distance at 100. Answers A, B and D are incorrect. RIPv2 features an administrative distance of 120. OSPF is 110. External EIGRP is 170.

Question 13

Answer D is correct. BGP uses TCP as its transport protocol. As such, it takes advantage of TCP windowing for reliability. Answer A is incorrect.

IGRP uses simple best-effort delivery. Answers B and C are incorrect because EIGRP and OSPF both require a one-to-one window mechanism; there is one update and one acknowledgement required.

Question 14

Answer B is correct. The default hello time for EIGRP over Ethernet media is 5 seconds. Answer D is incorrect. The default hello time for EIGRP over multipoint circuits with bandwidth less than or equal to T1 is 60 seconds. Answers A and C are incorrect because 2 seconds and 30 seconds are not valid default helot times.

Question 15

Answer C is correct. EIGRP functions at the Transport layer and uses protocol number 88. Answers A and D are incorrect. EIGRP does not function at the Data Link Layer, nor the Session layer. Answer B is incorrect. EIGRP does use the Network layer to exchange routing information, but it is still considered a Transport layer protocol.

Question 16

Answer B is correct. The SRTT stands for smooth round trip timer. This indicates the average time it takes to send and receive packets from a neighbor. Answer A is incorrect. The RTO is the time in milliseconds that the router waits for an acknowledgement before retransmission. Answer C is incorrect. The hold time value specifies the maximum time to wait without receiving anything from a neighbor. Answer D is incorrect. The queue value indicates the number of packets in the queue.

Question 17

Answer B is correct. The `debug eigrp packet` command traces transmission and receipt of EIGRP packets. Answer A is incorrect. The `debug ip eigrp` command displays packets that the router sends and receives—including content information. Answer C is incorrect. The `show ip eigrp` topology displays entries in the EIGRP topology table. Answer D is incorrect. Use the `show ip eigrp interfaces` command to determine on which interfaces Enhanced IGRP is active, and to find out information about Enhanced IGRP relating to those interfaces.

Question 18

Answer C is correct. When there is no feasible successor route, a discovery process that uses EIGRP queries and replies is used to find a loop-free alternate pathway. Answer A is incorrect. The EIGRP process does not stop in response to the loss of any route. Answer B is incorrect. The router does not wait for updates from other routers in this situation; it proactively begins a discovery process. Answer D is incorrect. The route with the lowest feasible distance is not automatically utilized.

Question 19

Answers A and B are correct. The `ip default-network` command can be used to distribute default route information to other routers via EIGRP. It has no functionality for the router on which it is configured. Answer C is incorrect because the router on which this command is issued does not adjust its gateway of last resort information. Routers that receive the advertisements do. Answer D is incorrect because this command does not control which interfaces participate in EIGRP advertisements.

Question 20

Answer A is correct. The `show ip protocols` command enables you to verify EIGRP settings. This includes the current K value settings. Answer B is incorrect. The `show ip route` command enables you to view the current routing table, but it does not provide K value information—only final metric calculations for routes. Answer C is incorrect. The `show ip route eigrp` command shows you the same information as `show ip route`, except the routes are exclusively EIGRP routes. Answer D is incorrect because `show ip eigrp topology` lists the networks known by the router, but does not provide K value information.

Question 21

Answer B is correct. OSPF relies upon multicasts to send updates. This is more efficient than broadcast approaches like those used in RIP version 1. Answer A is incorrect because OSPF does not rely on broadcasts to send updates. Answer D is incorrect. OSPF uses multicasts, not unicasts to send updates. Answer C is incorrect. It uses the multicast address 224.0.0.5 for this purpose.

Question 22

Answer D is correct. The "paranoid update" process occurs every 30 minutes by default. Answers A, B, C, and E are incorrect. The default time of the update is 30 minutes. Every other interval presented here is incorrect.

Question 23

Answers A and D are correct. The `router ospf` command is a global configuration command. After you are in router configuration mode for OSPF, it is common to "train" the router regarding which interfaces are to participate in the routing protocol. This is done with the `network` command. Answer B is incorrect. The `router ospf` is not a router configuration mode command. In fact, the command causes the router to enter router configuration mode. Answer C is incorrect. The number 10 is the process ID. It does not have to match the value configured on other routers. It is an internal use–only value.

Question 24

Answer B is correct. The command `network 10.30.12.1 0.0.0.0 area 1` specifies that the 10.30.12.1 interface participates in OSPF and is in area 1. The all-zeros wildcard mask ensures that the specific interface address is matched. Answer A is incorrect because it fails to specify the wildcard mask. Answers C and D are incorrect because they use the wrong wildcard mask. Answer E is incorrect because it specifies the network and also uses an inappropriate wildcard mask.

Question 25

Answer D is correct. The `router-id` command enables you to force the `router-ID` value of an OSPF router and is the preferred configuration for this value. Answer A is incorrect. Using a loopback interface is the most common method of setting the value, but it is not the most preferred method. Answer B is incorrect. Cisco does not recommend setting this value through the use of a physical interface address. Answer C is incorrect. There is no such command as `ip ospf router id`, as presented in option C.

Question 26

Answers B and D are correct. To display general information about OSPF routing processes, use the `show ip ospf` command in EXEC mode. The use of this command enables you, among other things, to view the local router ID value. The `show ip ospf interfaces` command provides OSPF-related details for each interface and includes router ID information. Answer A is incorrect. The `show ip interface brief` command provides summary information for all IP interfaces, but does not provide router ID information. Answer C is incorrect. You use `show ip ospf neighbors` to verify OSPF adjacencies in your network.

Question 27

Answer C is correct. When you configure a router priority of 0, the router does not participate in OSPF as a DR or BDR. The router does appear as DROTHER. Answers A and B are incorrect. Because the router has a priority of 0, it cannot function as DR or BDR. Answer D is incorrect because DIS is a router role in IS-IS.

Question 28

Answer B is correct. The nonbroadcast `ip ospf network` command option utilizes one IP subnet; neighbors must be manually configured; DR and BDR are elected; they must have connectivity with all other routers; this mode is typically used in a partial-mesh topology. Answer A is incorrect. The broadcast option makes the WAN interface appear to be a LAN. This configuration requires a full mesh topology. Answer C is incorrect. In the point-to-multi-point configuration, the DR and BDR are not required. Answer D is incorrect. The point-to-point configuration also does not feature a DR or BDR election.

Question 29

Answer B is correct. Type 2 LS Types are network link advertisements. Answer A is incorrect. LS Types of 1 are router link advertisements. Answer C is incorrect. LS Types of 3 or 4 are summary link advertisements. Answer D is incorrect. An LS Type 5 is an AS external link advertisement. Answer E is incorrect. LS Type 6 advertisements are multicast OSPF LSAs. Answer F is incorrect. LS Type 7 is defined for not-so-stubby areas.

Question 30

Answer A is correct. Type O E1 external routes calculate the cost by adding the external cost to the internal cost of each link that the packet crosses. Answer D is incorrect. The external cost of O E2 packet routes is always the external cost only. Answers C and D are incorrect. There are no E3 and E4 routes.

Question 31

Answer A is correct. Level 1 routing deals with IS-IS routing within an area. Answer B is incorrect. Level 2 routing involves routing between areas within the same domain. Answer C is incorrect. Level 3 routing involves routing between domains. Answer D is incorrect. Level 0 routing involves routing from an ES to an IS system.

Question 32

Answer C is correct. A fixed length of six octets is used for the system ID in Cisco software. In this NSAP, the system ID is 0000.0C22.2222. Answer A is incorrect. 49.0001 is the AFI and the IDI portion of the address. Answer B is incorrect. 00 is the NSEL. Answer D is incorrect. 49.0001.0000 is the AFI, the IDI, and a portion of the system ID.

Question 33

Answer C is correct. For frame relay connections the DLCI is used as the SNPA. Answer A is incorrect. The MAC address is the SNPA for Ethernet interfaces. Answer B is incorrect. HDLC is the default SNPA for serial interfaces. Answer D is incorrect. The NET is not a SNPA type.

Question 34

Answer C is correct. IS-IS is not designed with NBMA networks in mind. As such, a point-to-point design is most appropriate. Answer A is incorrect. The use of broadcast mode assumes full mesh and requires static mappings; it is not recommended for NBMA networks. Answers B and D are incorrect. There is no such representation as the point-to-multipoint in IS-IS, nor is there a static map mode.

Question 35

Answer C is correct. A partial sequence number packet is used to acknowledge LSPs in IS-IS. Answer A is incorrect. ACKs are not used in IS-IS. Answer B is incorrect. The IIH is a hello packet in IS-IS. Answer D is incorrect. A LSP is not used to acknowledge another LSP.

Question 36

Answer A is correct. The `show clns route` command displays the CLNS prefix routing table and the local NET entry. Answer B is incorrect. The `show isis route` command displays the level 1 IS-IS routing table. Answer C is incorrect. The `show clns protocol` command is often used to display the system ID and area ID. Answer D is incorrect. The `show clns neighbors` command enables you to view adjacencies information.

Question 37

Answer D is correct. To configure the NSAP address on the Cisco router, use the `net` router configuration mode command. Answers A and B are incorrect.

The `network` command is not used in IS-IS. Answer C is incorrect. The `net` command is not an interface configuration mode.

Question 38

Answer C is correct. You can use the `is-type level-2-only` command to pre-configure the IS-IS level on a router. Answer A is incorrect. The `circuit-type` command enables you to control adjacencies, not control the level of the router. Answer B is incorrect. Level-2 is not a valid `is-type` keyword. Answer D is incorrect because this configuration actually is possible.

Question 39

Answer A is correct. The appropriate NSEL value is 00. Answers B, C, and D are incorrect. 00 is the only acceptable NSEL value for a NET on a Cisco router.

Question 40

Answers A, B, and C are correct. Any router connected to area 0 is considered a backbone router. A router that connects two areas is an ABR. Finally, a router that connects to a non-OSPF area is an ASBR. Answers D and E are incorrect because there are no such terms as internal router and external router in OSPF.

Question 41

Answer D is correct. The synchronization rule states that BGP routers should not use, nor advertise to an external neighbor, routes learned via IBGP until a matching route has been learned via an IGP. Answers A, B, and C are incorrect. All other definitions stated here of the synchronization rule are not accurate.

Question 42

Answers A and I are correct. BGP relies upon TCP port 179. Answer B is incorrect. ICMP is used for ping and other mainly diagnostic functions. Answer C is incorrect. UDP is an unreliable protocol and as such is not used by BGP. Answer D is incorrect. SNMP is used for network management. Answer E is incorrect. IP is the Network layer protocol for the TCP packet. Answer F, G, and H are incorrect. The correct port number is 179.

Question 43

Answer C is correct. The only requirement for adjacencies is the establishment of a direct TCP connection. Answer A is incorrect. BGP routers do not require direct connectivity. Answer B is incorrect because the routers do not need to exist in the same AS. Answer D is incorrect. BGP relies upon a complex set of metrics that do not need to match on adjacent routers.

Question 44

Answers A, B and D are correct. `Match`, `metric`, and `route-map` are all valid parameters for the `redistribute` command. Answer C is incorrect. `Level` is a valid attribute for the `redistribute` command when used with IS-IS.

Question 45

Answers A, B, and C are correct. Distribute lists are powerful methods for manipulating the default routing behavior. The incoming interface of the advertisement, the routing protocol originating the advertisement, and the outgoing interface of the advertisement are all possible criteria for manipulating the default behavior. Answer D is incorrect. The administrative distance of a route is not a valid criteria component for distribute lists.

Question 46

Answers B, C, and D are correct. Route maps enable you to match traffic by interface, length, and even next-hop information. Answer A is incorrect. There is no match type possibility.

Question 47

Answer A is the correct answer. The value of 10 sets the metric for incoming routes in this case. Answer B is incorrect. Here the redistribution is into OSPF, not RIP. Answers C and D are incorrect. The metric value used in redistribution is not added to the metric value of the injected route; it resets the metric value to the specified parameter.

Question 48

Answer C is correct. Here you use the `neighbor 192.168.1.2 remote-as 65000` command to configure the neighbor. The `remote-as` keyword is always used, even in the configuration of an "internal" neighbor. Answers A and B are incorrect and will produce syntax errors. Answer D is incorrect because the configuration is possible.

Question 49

Answer D is correct. The `clear ip bgp soft out` option allows a "soft" reset for outbound updates. Answer A is incorrect. The `clear ip bgp *` command resets all BGP connections with this router. Answer B is incorrect. Using an IP address with the command resets only a single router. Answer C is incorrect.

Question 50

Answer C is correct. You use the `aggregate-address` command to manually summarize addressing. Answers A, B, and D are incorrect. All other commands presented here are invalid for use with BGP.

Question 51

Answers A and C are correct. BGP is appropriate when multiple connections exist to other autonomous systems and routing control is required. It is also appropriate when you need strict controls over traffic entering the AS. Answer D is incorrect. It is not appropriate when bandwidth levels are low. Answer B is incorrect. BGP is not required when you have a single connection to the Internet.

Question 52

Answers A, B, and C are correct. An open message includes version number, AS number, holdtime, and router ID. Answer D is incorrect. Notification messages include an error code.

Question 53

Answer B is correct. You may use the `neighbor ip-address next-hop-self` command when you need to control the default next-hop behavior of BGP. Answers A, C, and D are incorrect. All other commands here produce a syntax error, or are inappropriate for use with BGP.

Question 54

Answers A, D, and E are correct. Well-known mandatory attributes include `AS-path`, `next-hop`, and `origin` values. Answer B is incorrect. `Local preference` is a well-known discretionary attribute, whereas answer C is incorrect. `aggregator` is a optional transitive attribute.

Question 55

Answers B, C, and D are correct. All these options are valid criteria for best path decisions in BGP. Answer A is incorrect. BGP prefers the highest weight value.

Question 56

Answer C is correct. Entries flagged with a ? have an unknown value or have been injected by an IGP. Answer A is incorrect because `i` entries indicate iBGP. Answer B is incorrect because `e` indicates eBGP. Answer D is incorrect. There is no indication for a lack of verification.

Question 57

Answer A is correct. To manipulate the local preference value on a Cisco router, use the bgp default local-preference command. Answers B, C, and D are incorrect, and will produce a syntax error.

Question 58

Answer A is correct. The default MED for a Cisco router is 0. Answers B, C, and D are incorrect. All other values here for the default MED are incorrect.

Question 59

Answer C is correct. Injecting default routes from all providers minimizes the impact on resources for the non-ISP equipment. Answer A is incorrect. Full routes from all providers require the greatest number of resources on the non-ISP equipment. Answer B is incorrect. Customer routes and default route information require nominal overhead, but still more than default routes only. Answer D is incorrect because there is an answer.

Question 60

Answer B is correct. If prefix list numbering is not assigned by the administrator, the numbering begins at 5 and increments by 5. Answers A, C, and D are incorrect. All other options here are incorrect. To increment by any number other than 5, an administrator must configure the new value.

Commands in the BSCI Exam Cram 2

Table A.1 is a list of the commands that are pertinent to the BSCI exam, along with several other valuable configuration and verification commands. The parameters are not included, only the core commands. For more information and details about the commands, see the Command Reference Manuals on Cisco's Web site at www.cisco.com.

Table A.1 Core Commands for the BSCI Exam

Command	Meaning
access-list	Defines an access list on a Cisco router.
area range	Defines route summarization for intra-area routes on an OSPF area border router.
area stub	Identifies the OSPF area as a stub area.
area virtual-link	Identifies the OSPF virtual link over a transit area to another OSPF router.
Bandwidth	Configures the bandwidth of an interface that is used by certain routing protocols for metric calculation.
bgp default local-preference	Designates the default local-preference attribute value.
clear ip bgp	Deletes the entries from the BGP routing table and resets the BGP sessions.
clear ip prefix-list	Resets the hit count that is displayed on IP prefix list entries.
clear ip route	Clears out the IP routing table entries.
configure terminal	Places the router in global configuration mode.
copy running-config startup-config	Copies (overwrites) the configuration from RAM to NVRAM.
debug	Prints the router events to the console display.
debug eigrp neighbors	Prints the EIGRP neighbor events to the console display.
debug eigrp packets	Prints the sent and received EIGRP packets to the console display.
debug ip bgp	Invokes the output of BGP events to the router console, using various options.
debug ip bgp updates	Invokes the display of BGP updates to the router console.
debug ip eigrp	Invokes the output of IP EIGRP advertisements and modifications to the IP routing table.
debug ip eigrp neighbors	Begins the process of showing the neighbors discovered by IP EIGRP, including the hello packet contents.
debug ip eigrp summary	Invokes the display of a summary report of IP EIGRP routing activity to the router console.
debug ip ospf	Invokes the display of OSPF-related events to the router console.

Table A.1 Core Commands for the BSCI Exam *(continued)*

Command	Meaning
debug ip ospf adj	Invokes the display of OSPF-related adjacency events to the router console.
debug ip ospf events	Invokes the display of OSPF-related events to the router console. Event types include adjacency relationships, flooding information, DR and BDR selection, and SPF calculations.
debug ip policy	Displays IP policy routing events to the router console.
debug ip routing	Displays IP routing events to the router console.
default-information originate always	Propagates a default route into an OSPF routing domain.
default-metric	Designates the seed metric that is used by a routing protocol before route redistribution.
distance	Specifies the administrative distance (AD) used for a particular routing protocol (except EIGRP and BGP).
distance bgp	Specifies the AD used for BGP.
distance eigrp	Specifies the AD used for EIGRP.
interface	Enters interface configuration mode.
interface serial multipoint I point-to-point	Enters the subinterface configuration mode for a serial interface and designates it as a multipoint or point-to-point link.
ip address	Allocates an IP address and mask to a particular interface.
Ip bandwidth percent eigrp	Determines the maximum percentage of bandwidth that EIGRP packets are to use on a specific interface.
ip classless	Designates that if packets are received with a destination address in an unknown subnet of a directly attached network, the address will be matched to the default route and forwarded to the next hop indicated by the configured default route.
ip default-gateway	Designates a default router to use on routing devices when IP routing is disabled.
ip default-network	Determines a default route.
ip helper-address	Defines the address that a router uses to forward certain broadcasts that are sent to a specific interface.

Table A.1   Core Commands for the BSCI Exam *(continued)*

Command	Meaning
ip ospf cost	Designates the cost of an outbound OSPF interface.
ip ospf network	Designates the OSPF mode configuration as either non-broadcast, point-to-multipoint non-broadcast, broadcast, or point-to-point.
ip ospf priority	Identifies the OSPF priority value on an interface that is used to determine the DR on a multi-access network.
ip policy route-map	Identifies a route map to implement on a specific interface for routing policy.
ip prefix-list	Identifies a prefix list on a router.
ip route	Identifies a static route to a destination IP address or network.
ip router isis	Enables the IS-IS routing process on interfaces to distribute IP information.
ip subnet-zero	Permits the utilization of subnets where all the subnet bits are equal to 0.
ip summary-address eigrp	Determines route summarization (aggregation) on an EIGRP protocol interface.
ip unnumbered	Invokes the IP process on a serial interface without having to assign a specific IP address.
is-type	Determines the type of IS-IS level on which a router will operate.
isis-priority	Modifies the IS-IS router priority value to rig the DR election process.
isis circuit-type	Determines the type of IS-IS adjacency that will be created on an interface.
isis metric	Determines the type of IS-IS metric that will be used on an interface.
match	Determines the conditions to be checked within a particular route map.
match ip address	Defines the IP addresses to be matched for a particular route map via an IP standard or extended access list.
maximum-paths	Determines the greatest number of parallel routes that the IP routing protocol will support.
neighbor	Identifies an OSPF peer router connecting over a non-broadcast network environment.

Table A.1 Core Commands for the BSCI Exam *(continued)*

Command	Meaning
network	In RIP, IGRP, EIGRP, and OSPF networks, determines the networks that the routing protocols will run. In OSPF, the command also defines the area in which the interface is. With BGP, the **network** command enables BGP to advertise a route that is in its routing table and can determine the subnet mask of that route.
no auto-summary	Disables the automatic route summarization process in EIGRP.
no-summary	This keyword is used on an ABR to define a totally stubby area.
no synchronization	Disables the BGP synchronization process.
passive-interface	Stops routing updates from being generated out of a particular interface.
ping	Transmits an echo with the expectation of receiving an echo reply packet.
redistribute	Determines the specific protocol that will be redistributed into the present routing protocol, including connected and static routes.
reload	Reloads the Cisco OS.
route-map	Creates a route map and enters the route map configuration mode.
router bgp	Designates BGP as an IP routing protocol and invokes the protocol configuration mode on the router.
router eigrp	Designates EIGRP as an IP routing protocol and invokes the protocol configuration mode on the router.
router isis	Designates IS-IS as an IP routing protocol and invokes the protocol configuration mode on the router.
router ospf	Designates OSPF as an IP routing protocol and invokes the protocol configuration mode on the router.
set	Defines the actions to use to match values within a route map.
set community	Sets the BGP **communities** attribute in a route map.

Table A.1 Core Commands for the BSCI Exam *(continued)*

Command	Meaning
set interface	Designates the interface to which packets should be forwarded from a route map.
set metric	Configures the BGP metric (MED) value from a route map.
show access-lists	Shows the contents of all configured access lists on the router.
show clns	Presents the common information concerning a CLNS network.
show clns route	Presents the CLNS destinations to which the router knows how to route packets.
show eigrp traffic	Presents the types of EIGRP packets that are sent and received.
show interfaces	Shows information concerning interface(s).
show ip access-list	Shows the configured IP access lists on the router.
show ip bgp	Shows the BGP routing table.
show ip bgp neighbors	Shows the data concerning the TCP and BGP peer connections.
show ip bgp summary	Presents the summary status of all BGP connections.
show ip eigrp topology	Displays the IP EIGRP topology table.
show ip eigrp traffic	Shows the number of IP EIGRP packets that are sent and received.
show ip interface	Presents the IP-related information on the interface, including access-list information.
show ip ospf	Displays OSPF-related parameters on a router.
show ip ospf border-routers	Shows the internal OSPF routing table entries to ABRs and ASBRs.
show ip ospf database	Presents the contents of the OSPF topology table maintained by this router.
show ip ospf interface	Shows the detailed information regarding OSPF on the interface, including area, state, timers, neighbors, router ID, and type.
show ip ospf neighbor	Presents a list of OSPF neighbors.
show ip ospf virtual-links	Presents a list of the OSPF virtual links.
show ip policy	Displays information regarding route maps that are configured on the interfaces.
show ip prefix-lists	Shows the information concerning all prefix lists.

Table A.1   Core Commands for the BSCI Exam *(continued)*

Command	Meaning
show ip protocols	Presents the running IP routing protocols and basic information concerning each.
show ip route	Presents the IP routing table.
show ip route eigrp	Shows the current entries in the IP EIGRP routing table.
show isis database	Presents the contents of the IS-IS link-state database.
show isis topology	Shows a list of the paths to all connected IS-IS routers.
show isis route	Presents the IS-IS Level 1 forwarding table with all the IS-IS routes.
show route-map	Shows the route maps and number of matches configured on the router.
show running-config	Shows the running configuration that is active in RAM.
show startup-config	Shows the backup configuration in NVRAM.
show version	Shows the system hardware, software versioning, and configuration register settings of the router.
summary-address	Defines the route summarization (aggregation) for external routes on an OSPF ASBR.
variance	Specifies the unequal cost load balancing methods when using EIGRP (and IGRP).

Resources

Print Resources

The following list of print resources includes eight publications that will make an important contribution to the library of any network engineer and/or prospective CCNA/CCDP/CCIE. Many of these books can be found on the World Wide Web from various online booksellers.

Colton, Andrew. *Cisco IOS for IP Routing*. Tempe, AZ: Rocket Science Press, 2002. ISBN 0972286209.

Comer, Douglas E. *Internetworking with TCP/IP Vol. I: Principles, Protocols, and Architecture, 3rd Edition*. Indianapolis, IN: Prentice Hall PTR, 1995. ISBN 0132169878.

Doyle, Jeff. *Routing TCP/IP Volume I (CCIE Professional Development)*. Indianapolis, IN: Cisco Press, 1998. ISBN 1578700418.

Doyle, Jeff. *Routing TCP/IP, Volume II (CCIE Professional Development)*. Indianapolis, IN: Cisco Press, 2001. ISBN 1578700892.

Halabi, Sam, et al. *Internet Routing Architectures, 2nd Edition*. Indianapolis, IN: Cisco Press, 2000. ISBN 157870233X.

Huitema, Christian. *Routing in the Internet, 2nd Edition*. Indianapolis, IN: Prentice Hall PTR, 2000. ISBN 0130226475.

Parkhurst, William R. *Cisco OSPF Command and Configuration Handbook*. Indianapolis, IN: Cisco Press, 2002. ISBN 1587050714.

Thomas, Tom. *OSPF Network Design Solutions, 2nd Edition*. Indianapolis, IN: Cisco Press, 2003. ISBN 1587050323.

Online Study Resources

This section contains several valuable Web resources that BSCI candidates can use to supplement their studies.

 Bitpipe, a leading syndicate of comprehensive IT content that includes white papers, Webcasts, case studies, and product literature from over 3,500 leading IT vendors and over 60 top analyst firms: www.bitpipe.com

 A newsgroup related to general networking topics: news:comp. networks

 A newsgroup dedicated to miscellaneous and general computer protocols: news:comp.protocols.misc

 A newsgroup revolving around topics related to the Point-to-Point protocol: news:comp.protocols.ppp

 Cisco Systems IP Routing Web site (an invaluable Web portal that is Cisco's starting place for information about Cisco routing protocols and operations): www.cisco.com/en/US/tech/tk365/tech_topology_ and_network_serv_and_protocol_suite_home.html

 IP addressing tutorial: www.avaya.co.uk/Resource_Library/downloads/ ip_addr_tutor.pdf

Relevant Standards and Specifications

A great number of Requests for Comments are referenced throughout this *Exam Cram 2*, as well as various ISO standards. The first URL in the following list is your launching point into all the published RFCs; the other links take you directly to information on specific ISO standards.

 Complete list of Requests for Comments: www.cis.ohio-state. edu/htbin/rfc/rfc-index.html

 ISO 8473 covers ISO CLNP: www.protocols.com/pbook/iso.htm

 ISO/IEC 8348, Appendix A, covers NSAP addresses: www.protocols. com/pbook/iso.htm

ISO 9542 covers ES-IS: www.protocols.com/pbook/iso.htm

 ISO/IEC 10589 covers IS-IS: www.protocols.com/pbook/iso.htm

Octet Calculation Table

The following table shows the breakdown of a binary octet from the left-most high-order bit to the right-most low-order bit. Also included is the exponential representation of each bit in the octet. This table can be used to help understand the binary-to-decimal conversion table, which immediately follows this table.

Bit in Octet	1		1	1	1	1	1	1	1
	(high- order bit)								(low- order bit)
Decimal value	128		64	32	16	8	4	2	1
Expo-nential value	2^7		2^6	2^5	2^4	2^3	2^2	2^1	2^0

Decimal-to-Binary Conversion Chart

The following table displays binary equivalents for decimal numbers.

0	00000000	64	01000000	128	10000000	192	11000000
1	00000001	65	01000001	129	10000001	193	11000001
2	00000010	66	01000010	130	10000010	194	11000010
3	00000011	67	01000011	131	10000011	195	11000011
4	00000100	68	01000100	132	10000100	196	11000100
5	00000101	69	01000101	133	10000101	197	11000101
6	00000110	70	01000110	134	10000110	198	11000110
7	00000111	71	01000111	135	10000111	199	11000111
8	00001000	72	01001000	136	10001000	200	11001000
9	00001001	73	01001001	137	10001001	201	11001001
10	00001010	74	01001010	138	10001010	202	11001010
11	00001011	75	01001011	139	10001011	203	11001011
12	00001100	76	01001100	140	10001100	204	11001100
13	00001101	77	01001101	141	10001101	205	11001101
14	00001110	78	01001110	142	10001110	206	11001110
15	00001111	79	01001111	143	10001111	207	11001111
16	00010000	80	01010000	144	10010000	208	11010000

17	00010001	81	01010001	145	10010001	209	11010001
18	00010010	82	01010010	146	10010010	210	11010010
19	00010011	83	01010011	147	10010011	211	11010011
20	00010100	84	01010100	148	10010100	212	11010100
21	00010101	85	01010101	149	10010101	213	11010101
22	00010110	86	01010110	150	10010110	214	11010110
23	00010111	87	01010111	151	10010111	215	11010111
24	00011000	88	01011000	152	10011000	216	11011000
25	00011001	89	01011001	153	10011001	217	11011001
26	00011010	90	01011010	154	10011010	218	11011010
27	00011011	91	01011011	155	10011011	219	11011011
28	00011100	92	01011100	156	10011100	220	11011100
29	00011101	93	01011101	157	10011101	221	11011101
30	00011110	94	01011110	158	10011110	222	11011110
31	00011111	95	01011111	159	10011111	223	11011111
32	00100000	96	01100000	160	10100000	224	11100000
33	00100001	97	01100001	161	10100001	225	11100001
34	00100010	98	01100010	162	10100010	226	11100010
35	00100011	99	01100011	163	10100011	227	11100011
36	00100100	100	01100100	164	10100100	228	11100100
37	00100101	101	01100101	165	10100101	229	11100101
38	00100110	102	01100110	166	10100110	230	11100110
39	00100111	103	01100111	167	10100111	231	11100111
40	00101000	104	01101000	168	10101000	232	11101000
41	00101001	105	01101001	169	10101001	233	11101001
42	00101010	106	01101010	170	10101010	234	11101010
43	00101011	107	01101011	171	10101011	235	11101011
44	00101100	108	01101100	172	10101100	236	11101100
45	00101101	109	01101101	173	10101101	237	11101101
46	00101110	110	01101110	174	10101110	238	11101110
47	00101111	111	01101111	175	10101111	239	11101111
48	00110000	112	01110000	176	10110000	240	11110000
49	00110001	113	01110001	177	10110001	241	11110001
50	00110010	114	01110010	178	10110010	242	11110010
51	00110011	115	01110011	179	10110011	243	11110011
52	00110100	116	01110100	180	10110100	244	11110100

53	00110101	117	01110101	181	10110101	245	11110101
54	00110110	118	01110110	182	10110110	246	11110110
55	00110111	119	01110111	183	10110111	247	11110111
56	00111000	120	01111000	184	10111000	248	11111000
57	00111001	121	01111001	185	10111001	249	11111001
58	00111010	122	01111010	186	10111010	250	11111010
59	00111011	123	01111011	187	10111011	251	11111011
60	00111100	124	01111100	188	10111100	252	11111100
61	00111101	125	01111101	189	10111101	253	11111101
62	00111110	126	01111110	190	10111110	254	11111110
63	00111111	127	01111111	191	10111111	255	11111111

IP Address Classes

The following table displays the three main IP address classes, along with their decimal address ranges, number of networks per class, and the number of available hosts in each class.

Class	Address Range	Number of Networks	Number of Hosts
A	1.0.0.0 to 126.0.0.0	128	16,777,214
B	128.0.0.0 to 191.255.0.0	16,386	65,532
C	192.0.0.0 to 223.255.255.0	~2 million	254
D	224.0.0.0 to 239.255.255.254	Reserved for multicast	-
E	240.0.0.0 to 254.255.255.255	Reserved for research	-

IP Address Default Subnet Masks

The following table displays the three main IP address classes, along with their default masks in binary and decimal formats, respectively.

Class	Default Mask in Binary	Default Mask in Decimal
A	11111111.00000000.00000000.00000000	255.0.0.0
B	11111111.11111111.00000000.00000000	255.255.0.0
C	11111111.11111111.11111111.00000000	255.255.255.0

Subnet Mask Examples

The following table offers some examples of different addresses and prefixes, along with the decimal and binary representations of the associated subnet mask.

Address/Prefix	Subnet Mask in Decimal	Default Mask in Binary
192.168.112.0/21	255.255.248.0	11111111.11111111.11111000.00000000
172.16.0.0/16	255.255.0.0	11111111.11111111.00000000.00000000
10.1.1.0/27	255.255.255.224	11111111.11111111.11111111.11100000

What's on the CD-ROM

This appendix is a brief rundown of what you'll find on the CD-ROM that comes with this book. For a more detailed description of the *PrepLogic Practice Tests, Preview Edition* exam simulation software, see Appendix D, "Using *PrepLogic, Preview Edition* Software."

PrepLogic Practice Tests, Preview Edition

PrepLogic is a leading provider of certification training tools. Trusted by certification students worldwide, PrepLogic is, we believe, the best practice exam software available. In addition to providing a means of evaluating your knowledge of the Training Guide material, *PrepLogic Practice Tests, Preview Edition* features several innovations that help you to improve your mastery of the subject matter.

For example, the practice tests allow you to check your score by exam area or domain to determine which topics you need to study more. Another feature allows you to obtain immediate feedback on your responses in the form of explanations for the correct and incorrect answers.

PrepLogic Practice Tests, Preview Edition exhibits most of the full functionality of the *Premium Edition* but offers only a fraction of the total questions. To get the complete set of practice questions and exam functionality, visit PrepLogic.com and order the Premium Edition for this and other challenging exam titles.

Again for a more detailed description of the *PrepLogic Practice Tests, Preview Edition* features, see Appendix D.

Using *PrepLogic, Preview Edition* Software

This Training Guide includes a special version of *PrepLogic Practice Tests*—a revolutionary test engine designed to give you the best in certification exam preparation. PrepLogic offers sample and practice exams for many of today's most in-demand and challenging technical certifications. This special Preview Edition is included with this book as a tool to use in assessing your knowledge of the Training Guide material while also providing you with the experience of taking an electronic exam.

This appendix describes in detail what *PrepLogic Practice Tests, Preview Edition* is, how it works, and what it can do to help you prepare for the exam. Note that although the Preview Edition includes all the test simulation functions of the complete, retail version, it contains only a single practice test. The Premium Edition, available at PrepLogic.com, contains the complete set of challenging practice exams designed to optimize your learning experience.

Exam Simulation

One of the main functions of *PrepLogic Practice Tests, Preview Edition* is exam simulation. To prepare you to take the actual vendor certification exam, PrepLogic is designed to offer the most effective exam simulation available.

Question Quality

The questions provided in the *PrepLogic Practice Tests, Preview Edition* are written to the highest standards of technical accuracy. The questions tap the content of the Training Guide chapters and help you review and assess your knowledge before you take the actual exam.

Interface Design

The *PrepLogic Practice Tests, Preview Edition* exam simulation interface provides you with the experience of taking an electronic exam. This enables you to effectively prepare for taking the actual exam by making the test experience a familiar one. Using this test simulation can help eliminate the sense of surprise or anxiety you might experience in the testing center because you will already be acquainted with computerized testing.

Effective Learning Environment

The *PrepLogic Practice Tests, Preview Edition* interface provides a learning environment that not only tests you through the computer, but also teaches the material you need to know to pass the certification exam. Each question comes with a detailed explanation of the correct answer and often provides reasons the other options are incorrect. This information helps to reinforce the knowledge you already have and also provides practical information you can use on the job.

Software Requirements

PrepLogic Practice Tests requires a computer with the following:

➤ Microsoft Windows 98, Windows Me, Windows NT 4.0, Windows 2000, or Windows XP.

➤ A 166MHz or faster processor is recommended.

➤ A minimum of 32MB of RAM.

➤ As with any Windows application, the more memory, the better your performance.

➤ 10MB of hard drive space.

Installing *PrepLogic Practice Tests, Preview Edition*

Install *PrepLogic Practice Tests, Preview Edition* by running the setup program on the *PrepLogic Practice Tests, Preview Edition* CD. Follow these instructions to install the software on your computer.

1. Insert the CD into your CD-ROM drive. The Autorun feature of Windows should launch the software. If you have Autorun disabled, click Start and select Run. Go to the root directory of the CD and select setup.exe. Click Open, and then click OK.

2. The Installation Wizard copies the *PrepLogic Practice Tests, Preview Edition* files to your hard drive; adds *PrepLogic Practice Tests, Preview Edition* to your Desktop and Program menu; and installs test engine components to the appropriate system folders.

Removing *PrepLogic Practice Tests, Preview Edition* from Your Computer

If you elect to remove the *PrepLogic Practice Tests, Preview Edition* product from your computer, an uninstall process has been included to ensure that it is removed from your system safely and completely. Follow these instructions to remove *PrepLogic Practice Tests, Preview Edition* from your computer:

1. Select Start, Settings, Control Panel.

2. Double-click the Add/Remove Programs icon.

3. You are presented with a list of software installed on your computer. Select the appropriate *PrepLogic Practice Tests, Preview Edition* title you want to remove. Click the Add/Remove button. The software is then removed from your computer.

Using *PrepLogic Practice Tests, Preview Edition*

PrepLogic is designed to be user friendly and intuitive. Because the software has a smooth learning curve, your time is maximized because you start practicing almost immediately. *PrepLogic Practice Tests, Preview Edition* has two major modes of study: Practice Test and Flash Review.

Using Practice Test mode, you can develop your test-taking abilities as well as your knowledge through the use of the Show Answer option. While you are taking the test, you can expose the answers along with a detailed explanation of why the given answers are right or wrong. This enables you to better understand the material presented.

Flash Review is designed to reinforce exam topics rather than quiz you. In this mode, you will be shown a series of questions but no answer choices. Instead, you will be given a button that reveals the correct answer to the question and a full explanation for that answer.

Starting a Practice Test Mode Session

Practice Test mode enables you to control the exam experience in ways that actual certification exams do not allow:

➤ *Enable Show Answer Button*—Activates the Show Answer button, enabling you to view the correct answer(s) and full explanation(s) for each question during the exam. When not enabled, you must wait until after your exam has been graded to view the correct answer(s) and explanation.

➤ *Enable Item Review Button*—Activates the Item Review button, allowing you to view your answer choices, mark questions, and facilitate navigation between questions.

➤ *Randomize Choices*—Randomize answer choices from one exam session to the next. Makes memorizing question choices more difficult, therefore keeping questions fresh and challenging longer.

To begin studying in Practice Test mode, click the Practice Test radio button from the main exam customization screen. This enables the options detailed in the preceding list.

To your left, you are presented with the option of selecting the preconfigured Practice Test or creating your own Custom Test. The preconfigured test has a fixed time limit and number of questions. Custom Tests enable you to configure the time limit and the number of questions in your exam.

The Preview Edition included with this book includes a single preconfigured Practice Test. Get the compete set of challenging PrepLogic Practice Tests at PrepLogic.com and make certain you're ready for the big exam.

Click the Begin Exam button to begin your exam.

Starting a Flash Review Mode Session

Flash Review mode provides you with an easy way to reinforce topics covered in the practice questions. To begin studying in Flash Review mode, click the Flash Review radio button from the main exam customization screen. Select either the preconfigured Practice Test or create your own Custom Test.

Click the Best Exam button to begin your Flash Review of the exam questions.

Standard *PrepLogic Practice Tests, Preview Edition* Options

The following list describes the function of each of the buttons you see. Depending on the options, some of the buttons will be grayed out and inaccessible or missing completely. Buttons that are appropriate are active. The buttons are as follows:

➤ *Exhibit*—This button is visible if an exhibit is provided to support the question. An exhibit is an image that provides supplemental information necessary to answer the question.

➤ *Item Review*—This button leaves the question window and opens the Item Review screen. From this screen you can see all questions, your answers, and your marked items. You also see correct answers listed here when appropriate.

➤ *Show Answer*—This option displays the correct answer with an explanation of why it is correct. If you select this option, the current question is not scored.

➤ *Mark Item*—Check this box to tag a question you need to review further. You can view and navigate your Marked Items by clicking the Item Review button (if enabled). When grading your exam, you are notified if you have marked items remaining.

➤ *Previous Item*—View the previous question.

➤ *Next Item*—View the next question.

➤ *Grade Exam*—When you have completed your exam, click to end your exam and view your detailed score report. If you have unanswered or marked items remaining you are asked whether you would like to continue taking your exam or view your exam report.

Time Remaining

If the test is timed, the time remaining is displayed on the upper-right corner of the application screen. It counts down minutes and seconds remaining to complete the test. If you run out of time, you are asked whether you want to continue taking the test or end your exam.

Your Examination Score Report

The Examination Score Report screen appears when the Practice Test mode ends—as the result of time expiration, completion of all questions, or your decision to terminate early.

This screen provides you with a graphical display of your test score with a breakdown of scores by topic domain. The graphical display at the top of the screen compares your overall score with the PrepLogic Exam Competency Score.

The PrepLogic Exam Competency Score reflects the level of subject competency required to pass this vendor's exam. Although this score does not directly translate to a passing score, consistently matching or exceeding this score does suggest you possess the knowledge to pass the actual vendor exam.

Review Your Exam

From Your Score Report screen, you can review the exam that you just completed by clicking on the View Items button. Navigate through the items, viewing the questions, your answers, the correct answers, and the explanations for those questions. You can return to your score report by clicking the View Items button.

Get More Exams

Each *PrepLogic Practice Tests, Preview Edition* that accompanies your training guide contains a single PrepLogic Practice Test. Certification students worldwide trust PrepLogic Practice Tests to help them pass their IT certification exams the first time. Purchase the Premium Edition of *PrepLogic Practice Tests* and get the entire set of all new challenging Practice Tests for this exam. PrepLogic Practice Tests—Because You Want to Pass the First Time.

Contacting PrepLogic

If you would like to contact PrepLogic for any reason, including information about our extensive line of certification practice tests, we invite you to do so. Please contact us online at www.preplogic.com.

Customer Service

If you have a damaged product and need a replacement or refund, please call the following phone number:

800-858-7674

Product Suggestions and Comments

We value your input! Please email your suggestions and comments to the following address:

feedback@preplogic.com

License Agreement

YOU MUST AGREE TO THE TERMS AND CONDITIONS OUT-LINED IN THE END USER LICENSE AGREEMENT ("EULA") PRESENTED TO YOU DURING THE INSTALLATION PROCESS. IF YOU DO NOT AGREE TO THESE TERMS, DO NOT INSTALL THE SOFTWARE.

Glossary

ABR (area border router)
An OSPF routing device that is situated at the border of the backbone area and one or more other OSPF areas.

access list
A set or grouping of conditions that are maintained by routers to determine which traffic qualifies for filtering, rules, and other network services.

access rate
The designated bandwidth of a particular network circuit, such as 1.544Mbps for a T1 link.

acknowledgement
A notification packet (ACK) sent from one node to another node to verify that a message has been received or a certain event has transpired.

AD (administrative distance)
A numerical value between 0 and 255, with a higher value being preferred, that specifies the degree of trustworthiness or integrity for the source of routing information.

address resolution
A mechanism for determining and resolving the disparities between computer system addressing schemes such as Layer 3 (Network) addresses and Layer 2 (Data Link) MAC addresses.

adjacency
A bond formed between end nodes and select peer routers on a common media for the purpose of exchanging routing information.

administrative domain (AD)
A group of hosts, network devices, and network segments that function as a single organizational unit.

AFI (Authority and Format Identifier)

The 1-byte portion of the OSI NSAP address that defines the format and authority that assigned the address. It also distinguishes the type and format of the IDI part of an ATM address.

aggregation

See *route summarization*.

algorithm

A collection of rules or mechanisms for solving a particular problem. In networking, algorithms are typically used for optimal path determination in routing traffic from a source to a destination device.

area

A logical collection of network segments and their devices, which are usually linked to other areas to form a single autonomous system.

AS (autonomous system)

A collection of networks that are under common administrative control and share identical routing information. An AS is designated by a 16-bit numerical identifier assigned by the Internet Assigned Numbers Authority (IANA).

ASBR (autonomous system boundary router)

An area border router that resides on the border of an OSPF autonomous system and a non-OSPF network running another routing protocol in addition to OSPF.

ASN (autonomous system number)

A 16-bit number used to identify an autonomous system. Public ASNs are allocated by the Internet Assigned Numbers Authority (IANA).

ATM (Asynchronous Transfer Mode)

An international networking standard that implements a fixed-length 53-byte cell for transmitting multiple data types such as voice, video, and regular data packets. ATM leverages high-speed transmission media such as E3, T3, SONET, and OC carriers.

attribute

An attribute is a characteristic. BGP update messages have information about BGP metrics, which are called path attributes.

backbone

The primary bus or wire that connects networking devices. The term is often used to describe the core network connections of the Internet. In an internetwork, the backbone is the main path for traffic sent to and received from other networks.

bandwidth

A range in a band of frequencies or wavelengths. In networking, bandwidth is a measurement of the amount of data that can be transmitted in a finite amount of time and is typically expressed in bits per second (bps) or bytes per second (Bps).

BBR (backbone router)

The routers that are part of the main network connections that compose an internetwork. In OSPF, a backbone router is a part of Area 0.

BDR (backup designated router)

The backup designated router (BDR) accepts all the same information as the designated router (DR), but does not conduct any synchronization or forwarding functions unless the DR fails. See *DR (designated router)*.

BGP (Border Gateway Protocol)

An interdomain routing protocol that replaces the obsolete EGP. BGP shares reachability information with other BGP domains. BGP version 4 is the principal interdomain routing protocol implemented on the Internet.

BGP peers

Also known as BGP neighbors.

BGP speakers

Routers that run the BGP protocol and exchange routing information.

BGP-4 (Border Gateway Protocol version 4)

The dominant interdomain routing protocol used on the Internet.

black hole

In routing, a destination that shows up in routing tables, but when traffic is sent to that destination, the traffic is discarded.

border router

Within OSPF, a router that links one area to backbone Area 0.

broadcast

The process of simultaneously sending the same message to multiple destination nodes. In networking, a distinction is made between broadcasting and multicasting. Broadcasting floods a message to each node on the network, whereas multicasting transmits a message to a select group of destination nodes.

buffer

A temporary data storage area, typically in dynamic RAM (DRAM) memory. Most buffers serve as a holding area while the CPU manipulates data packets before sending them to a network device.

CIDR (Classless Inter-Domain Routing)

Also called supernetting, an IP addressing scheme that replaces an older system based on classes A, B, and C. A single IP address is used to designate many unique IP addresses. A CIDR IP address has the appearance of a typical IP address, except that it ends with a slash followed by a number known as the IP prefix, such as 172.16.0.0/16.

CIR (committed information rate)

A designated amount of guaranteed bandwidth (measured in bits per second) on a frame relay service.

circuit
A communication pathway between two or more endpoints.

Cisco IOS
The Internetwork Operating System (IOS) is the software module that represents the kernel of the Cisco router and switch operating system.

Class A network
The portion of the IP hierarchical addressing scheme where the first 8 bits define the network and the remaining 24 bits represent the hosts on the network.

Class B network
The portion of the IP hierarchical addressing scheme where the first 16 bits define the network and the remaining 16 bits represent the hosts on the network.

Class C network
The portion of the IP hierarchical addressing scheme where the first 24 bits define the network and the remaining 8 bits represent the hosts on the network.

classful routing
A routing process used by protocols such as RIP and IGRP, which do not send any information about the prefix length.

classless routing
A routing process used by protocols such as RIPv2, EIGRP, and OSPF, which send subnet mask information in the routing updates.

CLI (command-line interface)
The interface of a Cisco router or switch that enables you to configure them from a console session.

client
A network host, node, or program that requests services from a server.

CLNP (Connectionless Network Protocol)
The OSI equivalent of IP.

CLNS (Connectionless Network Service)
One of two types of OSI Network layer services available to OSI Layer 4 (Transport). CLNS does not demand that a circuit be created before transmitting data. This service routes messages to destinations independently of other messages.

cluster
In BGP, the amalgamation of a route reflector and its clients.

cluster ID
In BGP, an identifier that enables a route reflector to recognize updates from other route reflectors in the same cluster.

cluster list
In BGP, a list or sequence of cluster IDs through which the route has passed.

CMNS (Connection-Mode Network Service)
One of two types of OSI Network layer services available at OSI Layer 4 (transport).

community
A BGP attribute that is used to organize BGP speakers according to shared destinations and common policies.

composite metric
The process of using more than one metric to determine the optimal path to a remote network, for example, bandwidth and delay with IGRP and EIGRP.

confederation
An extension of using route reflectors that enables one to divide an AS into sub-ASs running EBGP between them.

connectionless
Network protocols that enable a host to transmit a message without establishing a connection with the destination host. Examples of connectionless protocols include Ethernet, Internetwork Packet Exchange (IPX), and UDP.

connection-oriented
Network protocols that require a communication channel to be established between the sender and receiver before any messages are sent.

CONP (Connection-Oriented Network Protocol)
An OSI Network layer protocol that transports upper-layer information and error messages over connection-oriented links.

convergence
The amount of time that it takes for a router to update its routing tables.

core
See *backbone*.

cost
An arbitrary value used by the routing protocol to compare paths through an internetwork. This value is often assigned by a network administrator.

count to infinity
A network problem that happens with slowly converging algorithms where the hop count keeps increasing.

CSNP (Complete Sequence Number PDU)
A list of the link-state packets stored by the router, which in IS-IS is implemented to distribute the router's complete Link-State database.

DDR (Dial-on-Demand Routing)
A Cisco routing process that permits a user to use existing telephone lines to generate a WAN.

default route
A static routing table entry that sends frames that do not have a next-hop entry in the routing table to a default destination.

delay
The time between the start of a transaction by a sender and the first reply received by the sender. Delay is also defined as the time it takes to transport a packet from source to destination over a particular path.

destination address
The physical or logical address of a device that is the recipient of data.

DIS (designated intermediate system)
The elected designated router for an IS-IS network. The DIS is configurable by priority value and then MAC address.

distance vector
A category of routing algorithm that demands that each router send all or part of its routing table to its directly connected neighbors. Also known as a Bellman-Ford algorithm.

distribute list
An access list that is used to filter inbound and outbound route table entries on a router.

DR (designated router)
A router running an OSPF process that is elected to generate the LSAs for a multi-access network, such as Ethernet. See *BDR (backup designated router)*.

DUAL (diffusing update algorithm)
The algorithm used by Cisco's EIGRP. DUAL offers a loop-free environment because it engages in constant route recomputation.

dynamic address resolution
The process of implementing an address resolution protocol to establish and maintain address information that is to be available on demand.

dynamic routing
A process of adaptive routing that automatically adjusts to traffic or physical network changes.

E1
An autonomous system external type 1 entry that originates from the ASBR and describes routes to the destination external system.

E2
An autonomous system external type 2 entry that originates from the ASBR and describes routes to destinations external to the autonomous system.

EBGP (External BGP)
The scenario in which BGP is operating between routers in different autonomous systems.

edge device
A routing device that enables packets to be forwarded between legacy interfaces and ATM or Frame Relay interfaces based on Layer 2 and Layer 3 processes. Edge devices do not run Layer 3 routing protocols.

EGP (Exterior Gateway Protocol)
A general term for Internet protocol that exchanges routes among autonomous systems.

EIGRP (Enhanced Interior Gateway Routing Protocol)
An advanced version of Cisco's IGRP. EIGRP offers better convergence and efficient routing with a combination of characteristics of link-state and distance vector protocols.

encapsulation
The process in which data is wrapped inside a protocol header. In networking, the equivalent of tunneling.

encryption
The translation of data into a secret format. This is the most effective way to secure data over a network.

ES (end system)
Any non-routing host or node in an OSI IS-IS environment.

ES-IS (End System–to–Intermediate System)
A discovery protocol that performs functions between end systems (ESs) and intermediate systems (ISs), commonly referred to as Level 0 routing. ES-IS is similar to the ARP protocol used in IP.

ESH (end system hello)
Sent by ESs in an IS-IS environment.

exterior routing protocol
A particular type of routing protocol that links two autonomous systems.

FD (feasible distance)
In EIGRP, the lowest-cost route to a destination.

filter
A mechanism or device that screens or filters network traffic for specific characteristics and decides whether to forward or drop the packets based on established rules.

flapping
A situation in which an advertised route between two devices "flaps" back and forth between two paths because of the intermittent failure of an interface.

flash update
An asynchronous update packet sent in response to a change in the network topology.

floating static route
A static route with a higher AD value that can be overridden by a route entry learned from a dynamic routing protocol.

flooding
The process of passing traffic out of all interfaces of a networking device, with the exception of the interface on which the data was received.

frame relay

A packet-switching protocol that links network devices on a WAN and supports data transfer speeds of T1 (1.544Mbps) and T3 (45Mbps).

FS (feasible successor)

A route stored in the topology table and injected into the routing table if the current successor fails.

full mesh

A topology in which every node in a network has a link connecting it to every other node. Full mesh is expensive to implement but offers the highest degree of redundancy. Full mesh is typically used in backbone networks.

gateway

A node on a network that serves as an entry point to another network.

HDLC (High-level Data Link Control)

A protocol used at OSI Layer 2 (Data Link) for data communications. HDLC embeds information into a data frame so that network devices can control data flow and correct errors.

header

In network transmissions, the portion of the data packet that contains transparent information about the data or the transmission controls.

hello

A protocol used by OSPF routing devices for establishing, selecting, and maintaining neighbor relationships and adjacencies.

hello packet

A multicast data packet used for neighbor discovery, maintenance, and recovery.

hello PDU

A data packet used in IS-IS to generate and maintain peer adjacencies using ESH, ISH, or IS-IS Hello messages.

hierarchical addressing

An addressing scheme that uses a logical sequence of commands to determine a network's location. IP addresses consist of a hierarchy of network numbers, subnet numbers, and host numbers that send data packets to the proper destination.

hierarchical network

A network configuration of multiple segments that offers a single path from source segments through intermediate segments on to destination segments.

hold-down

A router state that is characterized by the fact that it can neither advertise a route nor accept updates about a route for a particular period of time. This process is used to prevent bad information from propagating through the network.

hold time
In EIGRP, the amount of time in seconds that a router waits to hear from its neighbor before designating it as down.

hop
A segment of the trip a data packet takes between any two nodes on a network.

hop count
A type of routing metric used by RIP in which the distance is calculated between a source and a destination.

host address
The logical address that is configured on a host device by an administrator and that logically identifies the device on a network.

IETF (Internet Engineering Task Force)
A governing body that consists of more than 80 groups working together to develop Internet standards.

IGP (Interior Gateway Protocol)
Any protocol, such as RIP, IGRP, and OSPF, used by the Internet to exchange routing data packets within a networking system.

IGRP (Interior Gateway Routing Protocol)
A proprietary distance vector protocol designed by Cisco.

inter-area routing
The process of routing between two or more logical areas.

internetwork
Generally speaking, a collection of networks that are interconnected by networking devices to function as a single network. Although an internetwork is sometimes referred to as an internet, it is not to be confused with the global Internet.

internetworking
The general process of connecting networks to each other. For example, when networks are connected to a router, an internetwork is technically created.

intra-area routing
Routing processes that take place within a single logical area.

IP (Internet Protocol)
A Network layer protocol that is a core component of the TCP/IP networking stack, allowing for connectionless service. IP provides addressing, type-of-service specification, fragmentation, and security.

IP address
This 32-bit address, also called an Internet address, uniquely defines any device (host) on the Internet or TCP/IP network.

IP multicast
A mechanism used for routing IP traffic from a single source to a logical group of endpoints, or from multiple sources to many destinations.

IP unnumbered
A Cisco proprietary protocol that permits two point-to-point connections to communicate without using an IP address.

IPv6 (Internet Protocol version 6)
The current official name of the next generation of IP is IPv6, where the v6 stands for version 6. The existing version of IP is version 4, sometimes referred to as IPv4.

IR (internal router)
A router that resides completely inside an IS-IS and does not have a link on the boundary between areas.

IS (intermediate system)
The term used for a router in OSI ES-IS and IS-IS protocols.

ISO-IGRP (International Organization for Standardization—Interior Gateway Routing Protocol)
The Cisco proprietary version of a protocol implemented in a pure OSI (CLNS) environment.

LAN (local area network)
Generally, any network linking two or more nodes within a limited geographical area.

latency
The amount of time that it takes for a data packet to get from one location to another. In the context of networking, it can be the elapsed time (delay) between the execution of a device's request for access to a network and the time the mechanism actually is permitted transmission. It can also be defined as the elapsed time between when a mechanism receives a frame and the time that frame is forwarded out of the destination port.

leased lines
Permanent links between two endpoints leased from a telephone company.

Level 1 IS
The IS-IS equivalent of an OSPF internal non-backbone area router that has the duty of routing to ESs within an area.

Level 2 IS
The IS-IS equivalent of an OSPF backbone router that can route only between areas.

Level 1–2 IS (L1L2)
The IS-IS equivalent of an OSPF ABR that routes between the backbone and other areas.

link state
The condition or state of a connection or link between two networking devices.

link-state router
A type of routing device that uses a protocol that incrementally sends partial route updates.

link-state routing algorithm
A routing algorithm that enables a router to broadcast (or multicast) information about the cost of reachability of all its neighbors to every node in the internetwork. Link-state algorithms offer a constant picture of the network topology and are not vulnerable to routing loops.

load
In networking, load is the amount of data (traffic) being carried by a network.

loopback interface
A virtual interface created and configured with Layer 3 addressing that remains active for router operations even if an individual physical interface goes down.

LSA (link-state advertisement)
A message stored inside a link-state packet. These are typically multicast packets that contain information about neighbors and path costs, which is used by link-state protocols.

LSAck (LSA acknowledgement)
A packet exchanged with OSPF neighbors and the originating OSPF router to acknowledge receipt of an LSA.

LSA flooding
The OSPF rapid convergence process where the network is flooded with LSAs when a change occurs in the network.

LSU (link-state update)
A term used in OSPF to describe link-state advertisements that are exchanged when a change occurs in the topology.

MAC address
A data-link layer hardware address that every port or device uses to connect to a LAN segment. MAC addresses are defined by the Institute of Electrical and Electronics Engineers (IEEE) standard and have a length of 6 bytes.

metric
A standard gauge of measurement used in routing to determine whether the primary goals of network maintenance have been met. For instance, this can be a performance factor or a path determination factor.

multicast
Any communication between one sender and multiple receivers. Multicast messages are sent to a defined subset of the network address, defined in the packet's destination address field.

multicast address
A single address that identifies more than one device on a network. Creating a multicast address is accomplished by designating a special nonexistent MAC address for the particular multicast protocol.

multihomed AS
The term used to describe an AS that is connected to two or more Internet service providers (ISPs).

multihoming
The scenario of being linked to two or more networks or having two or more network addresses. For example, a network server may be connected to a serial line and a LAN or to multiple LANs.

multiplexing
A method of converting multiple logical signals into a single physical signal for transmission over a single physical channel.

neighbor
A network device that shares a common network with another network device. See *neighboring routers*.

neighboring routers
Two OSPF routers that both have interfaces linked to a common network.

network address
The portion of the logical address used to identify the network segment of an internetwork.

Network layer
Layer 3 of the OSI reference model. This is the layer where routing is implemented, enabling connections and path selection between two end systems.

non-stub area
In OSPF routing, a resource-consuming area carrying a default route, intra-area routes, inter-area routes, static routes, and external routes.

notification message
In BGP, a type of message that a router transmits when an error state is detected. Notification messages include error codes, subcodes, and error data.

NSAP (network service access point)
A hierarchical address used at the OSI Network layer that consists of a conceptual point between the Transport and Network layers.

NSSA (not-so-stubby area)
An OSPF area that allows the injection of a limited set of external routes, that is, only the routes needed to provide connectivity to backbone areas.

open message
The first message sent by each speaker in a BGP network after a TCP connection has been established.

originator ID
A BGP identifier that designates the router that originated the message.

OSI (Open Systems Interconnection)

An international program designed by the International Organization for Standardization (ISO) and International Telecommunication Union-Telecommunication Standardization Sector (ITU-T) to develop data networking standards that facilitate multi-vendor equipment interoperability.

OSI reference model

A seven-layer conceptual archetype by which the ISO defines how any combination of devices can be connected for the purpose of communication.

OSPF (Open Shortest Path First)

A link-state, hierarchical IGP routing algorithm resulting from an earlier version of the IS-IS protocol. The characteristics include multipath routing, load balancing, and least-cost routing.

OSPF areas

Subsets within an autonomous system that share routing information.

packet

The essential logical unit of data information being transferred. A packet consists of a certain number of data bytes, encapsulated with headers and/or trailers containing information such as packet source and destination.

packet switching

A network mechanism involving the exchange of data packets. By dividing a continuous stream of data into smaller units, data can be simultaneously transferred through multiple devices on a network along the same communication channel.

partial mesh

A form of networking topology where some network nodes constitute a situation where every node has either a physical or a virtual circuit linking it to every other network.

path determination

The process of selecting the optimal route to a destination network or host. With RIP, routing decisions are made according to hop count. OSPF, on the other hand, uses a cost value based on the speed of the connection.

path vector protocol

Protocols such as BGP are known as path vector protocols because they exchange network reachability information called path vectors (or attributes).

PDU (protocol data unit)

The designation of the data process at each layer of the OSI model. For example, a PDU at the Network layer is a packet or datagram.

peer group

In BGP, neighbors that are logically grouped together through configuration commands based on a common routing policy.

pinhole congestion

Two links to the same remote network with equal hops but with different bandwidths. As a result, a distance-vector routing protocol attempts to load balance and therefore waste bandwidth by utilizing the slower link as well.

point-to-multipoint link

A communication path that connects a single root node to systems at multiple points of a destination called leaves.

point-to-point link

A communication channel that can be directed either one way or two ways between two end systems.

poison reverse updates

Update messages that are transmitted by a router back to the originating device (and that ignore the split-horizon rule) when route poisoning has occurred. Routes are poisoned when a neighbor router is deemed to be down. Typically used by distance vector routing algorithms to overcome routing loop problems. See *route poisoning*.

prefix length

The number of bits used to represent the network and subnet in a CIDR address.

prefix list

A mechanism available in Cisco IOS release 20.0 and later that is used as an alternative to access lists for filtering BGP routes.

prefix routing

A routing protocol used in classless routing that includes subnet mask information with route update transmission.

process switching

The process that ensues when a packet to be forwarded arrives at a router and is copied to the router's process buffer. The router performs a lookup on the network address. The route table associates an exit interface with the destination address. The processor then forwards the packet, along with the additional information, to the exit interface. Subsequent packets, destined for the same target address, follow the same path at the first packet.

protocol

The designation and standardization of a set of rules for a certain type of network communication. This term is also used to reference the software that implements a particular protocol.

Proxy ARP (Proxy Address Resolution Protocol)

Used to permit redundancy if a failure with the configured default gateway on a host occurs. With Proxy ARP, an intermediate device sends an ARP response on behalf of an end node to the requesting host.

Pseudonode

Another name for a DIS.

redistribution
A command that is used on a Cisco router to inject one routing protocol path into another type of routing protocol.

redundancy
The duplication or replication of links, devices, or services that are used as failsafe solutions in case the primary connections, devices, or services fail.

relay system
Another term for a routing device.

reliability
A measurement of the quality of a network link and one of the possible metrics for making routing decisions.

RFC (Request for Comments)
A published Internet document that is used to put forward and define networking industry standards.

RIP (Routing Information Protocol)
A distance vector interior gateway protocol that uses hop count as a routing metric for optimal path determination.

RIP version 2
A newer, more up-to-date, and full-featured version of the original RIP.

route map
A mechanism that is used to manage and modify routing information by defining conditions for redistributing routes from one protocol to another in BGP.

route poisoning
A mechanism used by distance vector protocols to overcome routing loops and provide explicit information concerning the times when a subnet or network is not accessible. Route poisoning is usually accomplished by setting the IP count value to one greater than the maximum.

routed protocol
A routed protocol, such as IP, IPX, or AppleTalk, that can be routed by a Network layer device. This device must be able to understand the logical internetwork as designated by the rules of the particular routed protocol. The protocol also includes the underlying addressing scheme that a routing protocol uses to determine the best path to a destination.

route redistribution
The translation and conversion of routing information from one routing protocol to another.

route reflector
BGP routers that are configured to propagate routes learned by IBGP to other IBGP neighbors (clients) to lower TCP sessions and reduce routing traffic.

route reflector client
IBGP neighbors that have a partial peering relationship with route reflectors to receive advertisements. See *route reflector*.

route summarization
The aggregation of publicized sub-network addresses so that a single summary route is advertised to other areas by an area border router. It is implemented in several dynamic routing protocols, such as OSPF, EIGRP, and IS-IS.

router
A network (Layer 3) software or hardware mechanism that uses one or more metrics to determine the best path to use for transmission of network traffic. This device has historically been referred to as a gateway.

router ID
In OSPF, the identifying factor of a router, which is typically the highest configured IP address of an active interface or a loopback address on the router.

routing
The method used for transmitting logically addressed packets from a local subnetwork to a destination network host. In large internetworks, a packet may travel through a complex array of intermediary devices and destinations before reaching the ultimate destination.

routing domain
A group of end systems and intermediate systems that function under a common administrative policy.

routing metric
Any value that is used by routing protocols and algorithms to determine whether one route is better than another. Metrics can include bandwidth, delay, hop count, path cost, load, maximum transmission unit (MTU), reliability, and communication cost.

routing policy
In BGP, the process of restricting the routing information learned or advertised by filtering updates between certain BGP peers.

routing protocol
A set of standard procedures that defines algorithms used for updating routing tables and exchanging information between network devices.

routing table
A database stored in a router or other internetworking device that maintains a record of only the best possible routes to certain network destinations and the associated metrics or costs for those routes.

RTO (Retransmission Timeout)
The length of time in milliseconds that the routing software will delay before retransmitting a packet to an EIGRP neighbor.

seed metric
The initial metric used when a router is advertising to a directly connected link, usually derived from the characteristics of the interface and passed to other routers.

shortest path first algorithm
A link-state algorithm used to calculate the shortest path to each node, based on the topography of an internetwork that is constructed by each node.

SIA (stuck in active)
In EIGRP, the state that a router enters if it does not receive a reply to all its unresolved queries within a three-minute time interval.

split horizon
A mechanism for preventing routing loops implemented by distance vector protocols, where routing information is prevented from exiting the router interface by which that same information was received.

SRTT (smooth round trip time)
In EIGRP, the amount of time it takes in milliseconds for an EIGRP packet to be sent to a peer and for the local router to receive a subsequent acknowledgement.

standard IP access list
An IP access list that uses only the source IP address of a host or network for the purposes of filtering.

static route
The process of purposefully injecting into a routing table a route that takes priority over those selected by a dynamic routing protocol.

stub area
An OSPF area that carries a default route, intra-area routes, and inter-area routes, but no external routes.

stub AS
An area that accepts only default routes.

stub network
A network that has only one link to a router.

subinterface
One of many potential virtual interfaces available on a single physical interface of a networking device.

subnet address
The part of an IP address that is exclusively identified by the subnet mask as the subnetwork.

subnet mask
A 32-bit address mask used in IP to designate the bits of an IP address that are used for the subnet portion of the address.

subnetwork
Any network, also known as a subnet, that is part of a larger IP network and is identified by the subnet address. In OSI networks, the term refers to a collection of ESSs and ISSs, controlled by only one administrative domain, and that uses a single network connection protocol.

successor
In EIGRP, the best route to a destination, chosen from the topology table and injected into the routing table.

supernetting
Also called CIDR, an IP addressing scheme that uses a single IP address to designate many unique IP addresses. A supernetted IP address looks like a typical IP address, except that it ends with a slash followed by a number, called the IP prefix.

switching
The process of forwarding packets to the appropriate port, based on the packet's address.

synchronization
The rule enforced in BGP in which a BGP router should not advertise to or use an IBGP-learned route to an external neighbor unless the route is local or learned from the IGP being currently deployed.

TCP (Transmission Control Protocol)
A connection-oriented protocol offering reliable delivery of data. TCP is defined at the Transport layer (Layer 4) of the OSI reference model.

TCP/IP (Transmission Control Protocol/Internet Protocol)
The suite of protocols supporting the Internet and other internetworks. TCP and IP are the most widely known protocols in the group.

topology table
A database of all learned routes maintained by an EIGRP router for each configured routed protocol.

totally stubby area
An OSPF area that does not accept external AS routes or summary routes from other areas within the AS.

transit AS
In BGP, an AS through which data from one AS must traverse to get to another AS.

Transport layer
The fourth layer of the OSI reference model, used for reliable communication between end nodes over a network. It supplies mechanisms for establishing, maintaining, and terminating virtual circuits, for fault detection and recovery, and for flow control.

UDP (User Datagram Protocol)
A connectionless Transport layer (Layer 4) protocol in the TCP/IP protocol suite that allows datagrams to be exchanged without acknowledgement or guarantee of delivery.

unicast
A process used for direct host-to-host communication that originates from only one source and is directed at only one destination.

uptime
The amount of elapsed time that has passed since a local EIGRP router has heard from a particular neighbor in the routing table.

virtual link

An OSPF connection that provides a logical path between the backbone and a disconnected or discontiguous area.

VLSM (variable-length subnet mask)

Used to subnet a subnet by optimizing available address space and designating a different subnet mask for the same network number on various subnets.

WAN (wide area network)

LANs linked together over a DCE (data communications equipment) network. It is usually a leased line or dial-up connection across a PSTN network. Examples of WAN protocols include frame relay, Point-to-Point Protocol (PPP), Integrated Services Digital Network (ISDN), and High-Level Data Link Control (HDLC).

X.25

An ITU-T packet-relay standard that defines communication between data terminal equipment (DTE) and data communications equipment (DCE) network devices. X.25 has been made almost completely obsolete in North America by frame relay technology. X.25 uses a reliable Data Link layer protocol called HDLC Link Access Procedure Balanced (LAPB).

Index

B

backbones, 75, 105
  areas, 105, 109
  paths, 138
  routers. See BBRs
backup designated routers. See BDRs
bandwidth
  512 command, 186
  56 command, 186
  EIGRP, 180-181
  routers, 20
  value, 174
Bandwidth command, 366
bandwidth kilobits command, 180
Banyan VINES, 13
BBRs (backbone routers), 72, 105
BDRs (backup designated routers), 75, 81-82
BGP (Border Gateway Protocol), 24, 105, 134, 200
  advertisement control mechanisms, 236-239
    distribute lists, 235
    prefix lists, 236-239
  AS types, 204
  attributes, 200
    Aggregator, 211
    AS-path, 208
    Atomic aggregate, 211
    Community, 211-212
    Local preference, 210, 241-242
    MED, 212-213
    Next-hop, 209
    Origin, 209
    route selection process, 214-215
    Weight, 213, 241-242

BGP-4, 200, 203
  communities, 216-217
  confederations, 235
  configuration, 217-219
    clear ip bgp command, 219
    maximum-paths command, 219
    neighbor next-hop-self command, 218
    no synchronization command, 218
    set community command, 218
  connecting to other autonomous systems, 201-207
  implementation, 204
  keepalive messages, 201-202
  limitations, 205
  modes, 202
  multihoming default routes, 239-241
  notification messages, 201-202
  open messages, 202
  peer groups, 216
  peers, 201
  policy-based routing, 201, 207-215
  route reflectors, 230-235
    clients, 231
    cluster IDs, 234
    clusters, 231
    non-clients, 233
    originator-IDs, 233
  routing redistribution between BGP and IGPs, 242-246
    dynamic IGP routes, 244-246
    network command, 242-243
    static routes and Null 0, 244
  scalability, 228-230

How can we make this index more useful? Email us at indexes@quepublishing.com.

C

How can we make this index more useful? Email us at indexes@quepublishing.com.

How can we make this index more useful? Email us at indexes@quepublishing.com.

J-K

L

L1 routers, data packets, 142

L1L2 IS, 135-137

L2 routers, data packets, 142

LAN adjacencies, IS-IS, 143-144

large networks, EIGRP, 183

hybrid multipoint scenarios, 185-186

pure multipoint scenarios, 184

SIA (Stuck-in-Active) mode, 187

layout, Cisco certification exams, 4-6

learning environment, *PrepLogic Practice Tests, Preview Edition*, 382

Level 0 routing, 133

Level 1 IS (intermediate system), 133

Level 1 routing, 133

Level 2 IS (intermediate system), 133

Level 2 routing, 133

Level 3 routing, 133

license agreement, *PrepLogic Practice Tests, Preview Edition*, 387

limitations, BGP, 205

link-local addresses, IPv6, 53

link-state, 74

algorithms, 26-29

areas, OSPF multi-area networks, 108-109

database, 146

link-state acknowledgement. *See* LSAck

link-state advertisement. *See* LSA

link-state PDU. *See* LSP

link-state request packets. *See* LSR packets

link-state updates. *See* LSUs

metrics, configuring routers for IS operation, 152

links, 74

listings

debug eigrp packets ? command, 190

EIGRP frame relay interface configuration, 185

EIGRP serial interface configuration, 180

EIGRP summarization configuration, 62-63

IGRP routes, 18

ip helper settings, 63

IP routing table with OSPF, 36

IP routing table with RIPv2, 35-36

manual EIGRP summarization, 179

passive-interface command, 190

RIP routes, 19

show ip eigrp neighbors command, 188

show ip eigrp neighbors command holdtime values, 169

show ip eigrp topology command, 188-189

show ip eigrp topology output sample, 171

topology database table, 177

VLSM router configuration, 60

Load value (EIGRP metric), 175

loading state (OSPF operational state), 80, 83

Local preference attribute, 210, 241-242

How can we make this index more useful? Email us at indexes@quepublishing.com.

How can we make this index more useful? Email us at indexes@quepublishing.com.

How can we make this index more useful? Email us at indexes@quepublishing.com.

W

X-Z